Franny Mo

Franny Moyle has a degree in English and History of Art from St John's College, Cambridge. She enjoyed a career in arts programming at the BBC that culminated in her becoming the corporation's first Commissioner for Arts and Culture. She is now a freelance executive producer and writer as well as a director of the Hackney Empire, which is near her home in East London. She is married with three children.

DISCARD

Praise for *Desperate Romantics*:

'The jauntiness of her approach is a refreshing antidote to the incestuous, dreamlike claustrophobia of these interlocking lives. Her book is powerful, absorbing and, well, rather jolly' *Sunday Times*

'The age of the Romantics is alive and well in this fascinating book' *Tatler*

'Moyle's book captures all the sex, madness and addiction, making modern-day sagas seem downright dull!' *Glamour*

'Solidly researched book . . . *Desperate Romantics* is a cleanly written and evocative work that concentrates not only on the PRB as a group, but as individual geniuses' *Sunday Herald*

'Riveting . . . Moyle captures vividly the texture and colour of this vital world' *Independent on Sunday*

Desperate Romantics

The Private Lives of the Pre-Raphaelites

FRANNY MOYLE

JOHN MURRAY

First published in Great Britain in 2009 by John Murray (Publishers)
An Hachette UK Company

First published in paperback in 2009

11

A CIP catalogue record for this title is available from the British Library

ISBN 978-1-84854-050-7

Typeset in Monotype Bembo by Servis Filmsetting Ltd, Stockport, Cheshire

Printed and bound by Clays Ltd, St Ives plc

John Murray policy is to use papers that are natural, renewable and recyclable products
and made from wood grown in sustainable forests. The logging and manufacturing
processes are expected to conform to the environmental regulations of the
country of origin.

John Murray (Publishers)
338 Euston Road
London NW1 3BH

www.johnmurray.co.uk

To Richard Curson Smith, the cleverest and most complicated man I know

Contents

CONTENTS

Illustrations

Illustrations within the text

ILLUSTRATIONS

Acknowledgements

I AM HUGELY indebted to the scholarship of Jan Marsh, whose books on Rossetti and the Pre-Raphaelite circle have been a terrific source of information and inspiration. Virginia Surtees's research into her own relative Ruth Herbert and her editions of the diaries of both George Price Boyce and Ford Madox Brown have also been an important resource. Mary Lutyens's detailed scholarship on Ruskin and Effie has been a significant point of reference for me. Rossetti's collected letters and those of William Morris, edited by William E. Fredeman and Norman Kelvin respectively, have been at my bedside, on my kitchen table and in my handbag for the last four years and have proved invaluable.

Diana Holman Hunt's wonderful investigations into her own grandfather, Fiona MacCarthy's biography of William Morris and Tim Hilton's account of Ruskin have also been at my side. The library staff at Princeton University could not have been more accommodating in allowing me access to the Janet Troxell Collection. And the staff at the Pierpont Morgan Library in New York have proved enormously supportive of my research into the Bowerswell papers. I'd like to thank the Bodleian Library in Oxford and the British Library. Also Ayesha Williams, who helped me wade through reams of nineteenth-century newspapers and journals in order to bring the Pre-Raphaelites to life for a new public. Peter Bowker, Sally Woodward Gentle, Kate Harwood and Ben Evans have also buoyed me with their enthusiasm for the subject. And finally thanks to Anita Land and Georgina Capel for their brilliant support.

Prologue

The depictions of the details of this day are conjecture, but based on actual events and facts.

THIS PARTICULAR STORY began on the morning of Monday 10 April 1848. It was an unusually pleasant day by British standards, with a clear sky and hot sunshine warming the grey slate-tiled roofs of industrial London. But the capital's streets, factories and wharfs, which would normally have been teeming and busy even in the early hours, were oddly silent. White-collar workers were keeping to their offices. The retailers too were in cautious mood: some shops were closed for the day, with their shutters firmly bolted; others were open, but doors normally flung wide for prospective customers were on the latch. As for the heaving docks and clanking workshops – much of their work-force had not shown up at all.

Eighteen-year-old Lizzie Siddall walked every morning from her home just off the Old Kent Road to her place of work, Mrs Tozer's hat shop in Cranbourne Alley, near Leicester Square. Her journey habitually took her across Blackfriars Bridge. But on this Monday morning she discovered the complexion of her crossing point quite transformed.

Alongside the usual bustle of horse-drawn traffic and the downcast faces of work-bound pedestrians, she encountered twenty stern-looking mounted police, armed with cutlasses and pistols, on the Surrey side of the bridge. Barricades and sandbags were stacked on the footways. And as she walked towards the City, the red jackets of a battalion of Chelsea pensioners stationed on a floating pier caught her eye.

Lizzie failed to notice Annie Miller standing on the bridge at its northern end. A wild, raggedy, barefoot child of thirteen, she was indistinguishable from the mudlarks who often gathered at that time in the morning around the shores of the Thames. Skeletally thin, her long blond hair knotted and lice-ridden, Annie was off her patch. Her normal haunts were the doorways and alleys of Chelsea, where she could supplement her work at the Cross Keys public house with some coppers from a quick turn. Today, however, she had made her way along the river to watch her Dad.

For the first ten years of her pitiful and motherless life Annie had seen her father earn his crust by driving a builder's cart along the King's Road. When his health had failed, as a former soldier, he had fallen on the charity of the Chelsea Pensioners. Today she proudly observed him in his finery. His head held high again, he was on duty, armed and ready for action. Standing with his fellow pensioners on the floating pier, he was ready for a fight if the day's events should come to it.

Although London was on its guard and ready for action that morning, such preparedness and anticipation did not extend to all Londoners. Tucked up in a tiny top-floor room in his parents' small house, number 38 in the rather dingy Charlotte Street, Dante Gabriel Rossetti was still in bed. Lying in was not particularly unusual for this young man, who was just a month away from his twentieth birthday. Rossetti's timekeeping had been somewhat irregular for a while now, and though his room-mate – his younger brother William Michael – always rose early to head off for the Excise Department, where he worked, Rossetti would invariably slumber on until either hunger or his mother dragged him to his feet. And then he would drift and dabble the day away: working on a sketch here before casting it off and picking up a poem there. Rossetti was still trying to determine his *métier* and, until he did, the fate of the family income was in William's lap.

The student artist and aspiring poet – one day he professed one ambition, the next day the other – did at least have some justification for a lie-in this particular morning. Rossetti was suffering from an outbreak of boils.[1] With his neck and shoulders covered in painful, pus-filled bumps, a mixture of vanity and discomfort now kept this otherwise outstandingly beautiful young man locked away until the swellings had reduced.

But although uncomfortable, Rossetti was not despondent. He could, after all, now delay enrolling at the life-drawing class run by the portrait painter Lowes Dickinson and his brother Robert on Maddox Street for another day, which meant he had another precious twenty-four hours free to read and write. By his bed was a letter to the poet and writer Leigh Hunt, with which he intended to enclose a few of his own verses. He might even pen something about the day's purported momentous events – if they came to anything.

Not far away two other art students, John Everett Millais and his friend William Holman Hunt, were by contrast up and about, despite the few hours' sleep they had shared between them. Standing in the doorway of Millais's family home, 83 Gower Street, they were enjoying the transformation of the normally quiet, respectable residential road. Usually the traffic-free home of lawyers, surgeons and architects,[2] this morning Gower Street was alive with the chatter of men, their accents forged in workshops and their rough hands buried in their pockets, walking purposefully in twos and threes along the footways.

'Johnnie' Millais and 'Mad' or 'The Maniac' Hunt had slept in the paint-spattered clothes that they had been working in for a week. Toiling away in the basement backroom that Millais used as a studio, they had been burning the midnight oil together in order to get their paintings finished by 9 April 1848, the closing date for submissions for the annual summer show of the Royal Academy of Arts. This hugely popular public exhibition was the high point of every professional artist's year. It could make or break a career.

They had finished at the eleventh hour, sending their canvases off in the dead of night. No wonder, then, that this following morning, light-headed with relief and elation, it seemed as though they had fallen asleep in an old world and woken up in a new one.

Eighteen forty-eight was, after all, the year of revolution. All over Europe the pupal wrigglings of a modern world were beginning to crack the cocoon of old social and political structures. Europe's economies and monarchies were brittle. In January there had been an outbreak of civil disobedience in Paris. By early February there had been a revolution in Italy, establishing the second Roman Republic. And then on 22 February, just a day after Karl Marx published his *Communist Manifesto*, the worsening economic crisis in France forced the abdication of the Bourbon monarch Louis-Philippe, who fled to England.

Louis's arrival sent shock waves through the country, nowhere more than in the capital. London's middle-class shoppers were horrified to see revolutionary sympathizers riding down their main streets chanting republican slogans. They were appalled to hear that around the metropolis stirring calls to arms were being raised in popular theatres and public houses. The 'Marseillaise' had even been sung at Sadler's Wells!

But the fact was, the capital had been in disgruntled mood for some time. Louis's arrival simply brought to a head rebellious rumblings that had been going on for a while. Life had been tough for the city's underdogs, who were only too numerous. The winter of 1847 had seen fatal diseases such as influenza, measles and scarlatina rip through the working classes. Unemployment was also exceptionally high. Meanwhile the population was exploding. A new, fast-growing work-force felt disenfranchised and frustrated.

By March, London had begun to see organized protest. The political banner under which the discontented were drawn together was Chartism – a movement for political reform that wanted, among other things, to see the right to vote extended to the working man. The increasing momentum of the Chartist cause came to a head when the movement's leader, Feargus O'Connor, proposed a march in London from Kennington to Westminster, as part of which a petition for reform bearing what he claimed were 5 million signatures would be delivered to

Parliament. Fearful of civil unrest, the police commissioners agreed that the petition could be taken to the House of Commons, but they declared an accompanying march would not be allowed. Undeterred, O'Connor and his supporters decided to march illegally on 10 April, come what may.

This is why London appeared so alien on the morning in question. Queen Victoria had already fled Buckingham Palace for the Isle of Wight, the Bank of England had barricaded its doors and the Duke of Wellington had enrolled some 85,000 special constables to quell what the government feared might turn into a bloodbath.

Groups of protesters began gathering all over the city at nine in the morning. The assembly times had been planned and advertised well in advance. The 'West Division' was to gather in Russell Square – just a few minutes walk from Millais's door. Watching the brave and earnest sympathizers, the temptation to join in was irresistible. And so Johnnie and Mad grabbed their overcoats and followed the rebel hobnailed boots to the assembly point.

O'Connor and the main Chartist delegation left St John Street, Fitzroy Square, at about five past ten. They had arranged a magnificent display of power. The Chartist leaders were in a huge, 6 horse-power cart big enough to hold fifty people. But ahead of this, their precious petition for enfranchisement was carried in a brightly painted four-horse-drawn car, decorated with flags bearing mottos such as 'Who would be a slave who could be free?'[3]

Proceeding down Tottenham Court Road, the march, which began with just two hundred men, soon swelled as each little alleyway and thoroughfare fed in tributaries of protesters. Every time another delegation joined, cheers were raised. As the tumult turned east into High Holborn, the thundering cries and shouts of fifty thousand men reached the ears of Lizzie Siddall, bent over her work-bench, sewing ribbon on bonnets in Mrs Tozer's back room.

By the time the march reached Blackfriars, Annie Miller witnessed, as did *The Times*'s reporter, how 'the narrow thoroughfare had compressed the crowd into a vast moving mass'.[4] Somewhere in that seething press Johnnie and Mad were going with the flow, allowing themselves to be carried on to Kennington Common. Here the Chartist leaders were to make their speeches before progressing on to Westminster. Once at Kennington, what was later known as the 'Monster Rally' got under way.

'We did not venture onto the grass with the agitators, but standing on the cross rails outside the enclosure we could see the gesticulations of the orators', Hunt recalled. They watched as Feargus O'Connor was taken aside by a policeman before returning, now warned that 'the roofs of neighbouring houses were manned with riflemen and that concealed measures had been taken to quell any outbreak'.[5]

Number 163 Denmark Hill was well away from the alarming events unfolding in central London. In an era when the capital was defined as stretching east to west from Bow to Kew Bridge and north to south from Holloway to Stockwell, this large villa stood in semi-rural seclusion, well outside the extremities of the metropolis.[6]

In the well-furbished study, its walls adorned with landscapes by Turner, John James Ruskin, a wealthy businessman who had co-founded the Domecq sherry-importing business, paced nervously up and down his study. It was not the march that provoked his anxiety. Indeed, in their ample home, with its views across fields specked with peach and almond blossom, he and his wife, Margaret, were nicely unaffected by the Chartists' hullabaloo. But this middle-aged couple had other concerns for this particular day.

In fact, 10 April was a date of gargantuan importance for them, as well as one representing huge political concerns. Their only son, John, who was at this moment far from the bosom of his adoring parents, was about to go through an initiation that would change his life.

At the age of twenty-nine he was, much to the pride of his parents, already an established and celebrated name within the nation's cultural milieu. But now he was finally to embrace a status that had not only so far eluded him, but the pursuit of which had proved at times traumatic for this sensitive young man. He was about to marry.

The lucky girl was nineteen-year-old Euphemia Gray. While the workers were revolting in London, she and her mother were putting the finishing touches to the drawing-room at their family home, Bowerswell House, near Perth, in Scotland. Here friends and family would soon be gathered to witness the union of the devastatingly pretty and socially brilliant Effie with the celebrated young writer and critic. The match was a coup for Effie and a testimony to Ruskin's excellent taste.

But neither prospective bride nor groom was as they should have been on that morning. Effie looked pale and tense. Ruskin too, sitting alone in his room, awaiting the arrival of his future father-in-law to accompany him to the ceremony, was betraying signs of anxiety far beyond those normally associated with nuptials.

How he must have wished his parents could have been with him. They had decided against making the journey: they had their own personal reasons, and it was a long and arduous journey involving a steamer up the coast and then a lengthy carriage journey. The railway had not yet reached Perth, although the industrial revolution was now in full swing.

Oddly enough, it was thanks to the progress of the railway system that on this April Monday the fourteen-year-old William Morris found himself at boarding-school just outside Swindon. Five years earlier Marlborough College had been established in the knowledge that Swindon would be the great heart of the new railway system, housing the largest junction of the main lines from all over the country.

Morris's father, who had built his considerable wealth on the back of the industrial revolution, did not see his son arrive at Marlborough in February 1848. He had died just a few months earlier, although his speculation in mining interests would see the fees easily taken care of.

Less well taken care of was William. A boy of deep intellect, an avaricious reader who had, extraordinarily, been reading Sir Walter Scott's popular novel *Waverley* when he was just four years old, he found himself a shy outsider to the bumptious rough and tumble of public boarding-school. On 10 April he was, as usual, avoiding the break-time brawls and fracas of his fellow pupils by losing himself in his own peculiar labours. He had attached a long piece of twine to his desk and was now obsessively weaving a little fishing net that perhaps he might be able to employ later on, free time permitting.

Although Morris had few friends at Marlborough, he was not exactly unpopular. He was eccentric: he had a mass of curly, uncontrollable hair, he walked with a strange bounce, he had a bad temper, and his pursuits and enthusiasms were unlikely. But when his schoolmates berated him for his oddities, he would run at them roaring and make them laugh. He was a willing school joke and thus escaped the harsher torments visited on some of his peers.

Although not at Marlborough, and not yet known to him, there was a best friend and future collaborator waiting for Morris. Edward ('Ned') Burne-Jones was ensconced in a noisy classroom at King Edward's School in Birmingham that April. Precocious Ned, from an unpretentious middle-class background, could not yet see where his destiny lay. With at best a career as a cleric apparently ahead of him, he had no sense that the paintbrush would bring him friendship and fame.

There was a woman, too, who would one day embrace the stocky oddball Morris as his wife. Although few could have predicted it, Jane Burden, living in an Oxford hovel and on the bottom rung of the social ladder, would one day make the social leap that many slum girls must have dreamed of and walk down the aisle with a gentleman.

But then few could have foreseen the story that would embrace this collection of young people, drawn from all walks of life and different social backgrounds. Yet each of them would rise above the seething masses of their time to achieve iconic status. The men would raise British art to new, unimagined heights. The women would redefine beauty and become the supermodels of their day. As a group they would become among the first celebrities of the nascent modern world, their fame and reputation spread by a press of previously unforeseen vigour and influence among an exploding population.

Entwined in one another's personal lives, this group would be at the centre of scandals that would shake the foundations of their society. Some would pay the price of their infamy with their sanity. Others would see their fate meted out in different, quieter, personal tragedies.

I

The dark secret

IN 1843, WHEN he was barely out of Oxford University, John Ruskin had done something particularly audacious. He had published a book on contemporary art, *Modern Painters*. At the heart of this book was Ruskin's passion for Joseph Mallord William Turner, a painter who even in his own day Ruskin felt was misunderstood. But Ruskin could see how the artist's work was born from an extraordinary immersion in the natural world. And in his ability to convey nature in its true power and beauty Ruskin believed that Turner outshone his forebears.

Ruskin had been smitten by Turner's work when, as a boy, he was given a copy of *Rogers's Italy*, which the great artist had illustrated. As he matured into a young man, collecting Turner's work, or rather persuading his rich father to collect it for him, became an enduring, zealous delight. His first venture as an author was a homage to his icon. *Modern Painters* was instantly recognized by Britain's élite as the work of an extraordinary mind. By the time a second volume had been published in 1846, young Ruskin had been propelled to celebrity status.

Five foot eleven inches tall, very thin, with reddish hair and a fair complexion, this new star was an idiosyncratic addition to Britain's cultural firmament. He had his own approach to the world around him, which took little heed of the strict social conventions and niceties of Victorian England. This was born not out of some self-conscious bohemianism but out of a level of self-obsession and personal confidence, some might say arrogance, that frankly meant he really didn't much care what other people thought.

Ruskin's innate poise shone through his lean, angular face, with its long, thin nose and watery blue eyes. He was not a conventionally attractive man. He had a slightly deformed mouth, thanks to an over-enthusiastic black Newfoundland dog called Lion, which took a chunk out of the left-hand side of his lip when he was five. But he was vivacious and captivating, with a slightly delicate or feminine air. What would be interpreted today as this slightly camp manner was matched by a rather dandyish style. He was never seen without his signature bright blue neckcloth, which set off his eyes, and he would never go out without a slim greatcoat with a brown velvet collar.

Although bold and independent in intellectual terms, Ruskin was hardly on the front foot in his personal life. In terms of his domestic existence, he was still willingly cast as a dependent and submissive child, worried over and cosseted by his overbearing parents. As a result, the Ruskins cut a swath as a rather bizarre family. Notably self-contained, with anti-social tendencies, they sustained one another within something approaching a familial love affair.

Central to this close-knit threesome was Margaret Ruskin. She was a staunch Christian from an unspectacular background, who had grown up in her parents' Croydon pub before being dispatched north to Perth as a companion to her socially more advantaged aunt Mary and uncle John Thomas Ruskin. Here, living in their comfortable villa in Bowerswell on the banks of the River Tay, she encountered her future husband, their son and her cousin John James.

At nearly thirty-seven when they married, Margaret Ruskin had been four years older than her cousin. In Victorian terms Margaret was an almost geriatric bride, and perhaps this informed her adoration of the child, who was conceived slightly against the biological odds.

Margaret Ruskin had ambitions for her son, but her determination to realize these were nothing compared to her daily concern for his health and well-being. A luminary he might well be – but only if he managed to stay alive. From the very beginning

John Ruskin was wrapped in the cotton wool of his mother's almost obsessive concern for his physical condition.

Although this motherly anxiety is partly understandable, given the high infant mortality rates in the nineteenth century, there were other, darker reasons lurking behind Margaret's concern for her boy. The Ruskin family had been cursed with madness.

Margaret had witnessed this family affliction first-hand as she tended her aged uncle in his home at Bowerswell. After the death of her aunt Mary, she watched her uncle John Thomas Ruskin decline into a dotage defined by depression and drinking. Margaret witnessed the old man's final lunatic gesture. He attempted to cut his own throat. Frantically holding the sliced flesh together in her own hands while a local surgeon fought to stitch the wound, Margaret saved his life, but only for a matter of days.

After this terrible event John James and a traumatized Margaret packed their bags for London. When Margaret's son was born, he was kept by his mother's side. Margaret taught John at home rather than send him to school. And this solitary but nevertheless indulged youth no doubt formed Ruskin's impenetrable ego. As Ruskin himself observed in his own dotage, 'whenever I did anything wrong, stupid or hardhearted – (and I have done many things that were all three) – [my mother] always said "It is because you were too much indulged".'[1]

But if Margaret realized the folly of her over-indulgence later on, it was not before John's college days. When Ruskin went to Oxford University, his mother packed up and went with him. Ruskin's father, John James, not to be left out, would join the pair at the weekends once he had dispatched his weekly duties to the wine trade.

'I count it as just a little to my credit that I was not ashamed, but pleased, that my mother came to Oxford with me to take care of me such as she could', Ruskin later remembered.

Through all three years of residence, during term time, she had lodging in the High Street . . . On the Saturday [my father] came down to us, and I went with him and my mother, in the old domestic way, to St Peter's, for the Sunday morning service: otherwise, they never appeared with me in public, lest my companions should laugh at me . . . my mother did not come to Oxford because she could not part with me . . . she simply came that she might be at hand in case of accident or sudden illness . . . on several occasions her timely watchfulness had saved me from the most serious danger.[2]

The other thing that made the Ruskins stand out as a family was their insatiable passion for travel. This gypsy-like love of the open road had begun when John was a very young child and he and his mother had accompanied John James on extended wine sales trips around the country. But soon these British seasonal trips, even though they included the most far-flung parts of Scotland or Wales, could not contain the Ruskins' appetite for touring. A genuine love of adventure combined with a general belief in the remedial qualities of continental air encouraged them to cast their net further afield. And so the continent became their playground and passion.

Each year the Ruskins would go to Mr Hopkinson's in Covent Garden's Long Acre to hire the travelling carriage that would become their home for the five- or six-month trips they took to Europe. Sitting in padded comfort, Ruskin would look out of the carriage windows and draw the new world flying past him.

It was as though he was transposed into a new kind of man when he was in the continental landscape. The architecture gripped him, the people fascinated him, but above all the landscape enraptured him. The otherwise delicate Ruskin would suddenly tramp and scramble up and down mountains and hills as though nothing else mattered in life. His writing about the landscape – and particularly the mountains of the Alps – reveal a man so transfixed and infatuated by the beauty of nature, so utterly enthralled by the experience of being in direct contact with what he considered these sublime forces, that he was often in an almost trance-like state of ecstasy.

In strong contrast to the Ruskins, the Grays were quite a sociable lot. In the early nineteenth century Perth was a booming city. With a population of around 20,000, it was an ancient centre of commerce that laid claim to being the historic capital of Scotland. It had a busy port and was a hub of export and trade for many of the Scottish industries: great crates of whisky, leather and linen were hauled out of the trading ships in its docks on a daily basis. It was well positioned for the new railway system, and got its main-line connection in 1848, just after John and Effie's wedding. As a result, the town had all the services and trappings of modernization: it had its own academy and infirmary, piped water and gas, and its high street looked grand with its tall classical buildings and gas lighting.

George Gray was a lawyer with an established business in the city, a strong sense of his own status and apparently the ambition to enhance it. A man about town and secretary of the Royal Perth Golfing Society, he had married Sophia Jameson, daughter of the Sheriff Substitute of Fife. Together they had fifteen children, eight of whom survived the ravages of infant ailments. The boys were sent to public school and the girls to ladies' seminaries.

One expression of George's ambition and success was his decision to rebuild the family home that he and Sophia had acquired in 1827, a project that was completed just before the fateful marriage between their eldest child and John Ruskin. Local architects Andrew Heiton & Son confected a large Italianate villa out of the local golden-coloured stone. The house today is a little diminished by its municipal function as a home for the elderly, but it is still easy to see how the grand three-storeyed entrance tower, with its balcony and balustrade rising over an arched double front door, would have impressed the great and the good of Perth society when it was a private home.

The smaller house that the Grays demolished to rebuild in grander aspect was a pretty villa constructed at the turn of the century in Bowerswell, just outside Perth, the house in which Margaret Ruskin had witnessed the mental decline of her uncle

John Thomas. And so the links between the Grays and the Ruskins ran deep. George Gray had bought Bowerswell Villa from John James Ruskin after John Thomas's suicide. George and Sophia's first child, Euphemia, who became known as Effie, born on 7 May 1828, was probably brought into the world in the very room in which the old man's use of a so-called cut-throat razor had been only too literally applied.

Since this transaction the Grays and the Ruskins had continued to see each other from time to time. George Gray was associated with John James in a legal capacity too, administering a Ruskin family trust of which the latter was a trustee. When the Grays travelled to London, they would call or stay with the Ruskins, and every now and then they prevailed on Margaret and John James to take Effie during the school holidays: she was at boarding-school in Stratford-upon-Avon.

Effie was always welcomed. She was a pretty, well-behaved little girl, and John James liked her enough to take her sightseeing around London, to the zoological gardens and Westminster Abbey. And when John was a 22-year-old undergraduate, he was sufficiently enchanted by the thirteen-year-old house guest to write her a fairy story, 'The King of the Golden River'.

This kind gesture could not have been more timely. Effie's two younger sisters in Perth had succumbed to an epidemic of scarlet fever. And perhaps it was the timing of this gesture that planted some special feeling for John in Effie's juvenile heart. Amid all the distress at home she could find some solace and escape in a story written specially for her by this young man, who should perhaps have had better things to do.

As a very young man, John Ruskin had been less than success-ful in affairs of the heart, something he later blamed on his solitary childhood.

> I had no companions to quarrel with, either; nobody to assist, and nobody to thank. Not a servant was ever allowed to do anything for me, but what it was their duty to do ... the evil consequence

of all this was not, however, what might perhaps have been expected, that I grew up selfish or unaffectionate; but that, when affection did come, it came with a violence utterly rampant and unmanageable.[3]

Over-sensitized by the combination of his mother's indulgence and a lack of other company, Ruskin not only formed violent attachments to the few young women he encountered, but also could not cope when his affections were unrequited. This lesson was first learned at the hands of Adele Domecq. This 'graceful oval-faced blonde'[4] was the daughter of John James's Spanish business partner Pedro Domecq. One of four sophisticated girls, living in fashionable Paris, she spoke Spanish and French as well as English with 'broken precision'. She and her sisters would stay with the Ruskins, and when he was seventeen, John began an infatuation with Adele that would torture him for the next few years.

Despite being two years his junior, Adele saw nothing but immaturity and inexperience in her suitor. Ruskin's attempts at conversation were met with the kind of cruel, condescending taunts in which adolescent girls can excel when faced with the affections of awkward, inexperienced boys. Ruskin's letters to Adele in Paris were ridiculed for their poor French.

Adele's rejection did nothing to quell John's ardour. He indulged himself in his feelings for her, storing up his infatuation and wallowing in the pain of rejection. Depression inevitably followed. His parents were all too aware of the situation but poorly equipped to deal with the highly emotional young man they had created. When they learned of plans for an arranged society marriage between Adele and the Baron Duquesne, they kept this intelligence from their son, fearful of his reaction.

Ruskin's parents' concerns were well founded. When news of Adele's marriage finally reached Ruskin in his rooms at Oxford, the effects were immediate and devastating. After years of quiet, unrequited adoration, his disappointment triggered a mental breakdown. All the bitterness that had been internalized now came out.

The initial expulsion of Adele from his system came in the form of a cough and the taste of blood in his mouth. Ruskin walked round to his mother's lodgings in Oxford's High Street and told her about his symptoms. This was just the kind of ailment his mother was waiting to pounce on. The very next day he was pulled from his studies and began seeing doctors. It was early 1840. He spent the next year recuperating and travelling and did not return to university to take his degree until 1843. Adele had seemingly knocked the stuffing out of him.

Three years later, in April 1846, the second volume of *Modern Painters* was published while Ruskin and his parents were enjoying their annual jolly to the continent. The success of this book sealed Ruskin's reputation as the foremost critic of his generation and seemed to boost his parents' ambitions for him – not least when it came to marriage. It was time for John to put Adele behind him and venture once again into the world of romance.

On his return from the continent John attended a party at the socialite Lady Davy's, and here he re-encountered a girl whom he had met when she was a child: Charlotte Lockhart, the grand-daughter of Sir Walter Scott and the daughter of the Scottish aristocrat, writer and biographer of Scott, John Gibson Lockhart. Charlotte had considerable cultural heritage.

As a child Ruskin had been passionate about Scott's novels. But it was more than just a passion. In the opening paragraph of his autobiography, *Praeterita*, Ruskin claimed that Scott had been a founding influence on his outlook on life.[5] What kind of *frisson*, therefore, must have shot through Ruskin at the thought that he might align himself so personally with the great man? The notion obviously captivated him and his parents alike, and it was the notion of marrying Charlotte that now became a sudden ambition.

Ruskin began a campaign to woo her, but his attempts were now informed by caution and insecurity. His approaches were clumsy and the nature of his interest unclear. He began to write to her while working on a critical essay commissioned and edited by her father. But it is unclear whether Charlotte or her father even recognized Ruskin's advances as being particularly amorous.

In spite of apparent lack of progress, the Ruskins seemed to have set their sights on a Lockhart union, and everyone was on tenter-hooks awaiting some form of news to this end when, in April 1847, Effie returned to the Ruskin household. She was not quite nine-teen. The little girl had transformed into a precocious, attractive and confident young woman. Sketches of her show a slender frame with a tiny waist, a flat broad face with a delicate nose and cupid lips, and soft almond-shaped eyes framed by dark hair.

Highly sociable, intelligent, accomplished and flirtatious, Effie was at her best at social occasions, loving company and entertain-ment. Little surprise, then, that she had a strong band of male fol-lowers among the eligible bachelors in Perth. One of these was a young officer and regular dancing partner called William Kelty MacLeod. He was the son of Lientenant-Colonel Alexander MacLeod, a neighbour and friend who lived at Greenbank on the Hill of Kinnoull.

When Effie arrived at the Ruskins' splendid home in Denmark Hill, she was not looking for love. In fact, Effie had already had a proposal of marriage from William MacLeod. Although their engagement was 'unofficial', and thus unannounced, the two had been confirmed sweethearts for over a year.[6] William was following in his father's footsteps and pursuing a military career. As a subaltern in the 74th Highlanders he had been called away to join his regi-ment in India, with the intention of marrying Effie on his return.

Despite her attachments at home, Effie loved being in London. She was impressed by the Ruskins' wealth and enjoyed the comforts of their home and lifestyle. She bathed in the social op-portunities that the capital offered, and even if they were not opportunities that she could always take up, she lived vicariously through the son of the household, John.

The admiration she already had harboured for John ever since he wrote his fairy-tale for her now grew as she recognized his growing celebrity. Her excited letters home reveal the little Scottish girl from Perth was more than a little star-struck, and tantalized by her new-found proximity to high society. Poor Willie MacLeod must have suddenly seemed rather dull by comparison.

> He [John] seems I think to be getting very celebrated in the literary world and to be much taken notice of; on Saturday he was at a grand reunion of Sir R Peel's where everyone was, the Duke of Cambridge was there boring everybody with his noise, Sir Robert and Lady Peel were there the whole time and extremely affable. On Friday John is going to a private view of the Royal Academy, the ticket is sent to him by 'Turner' who is one of the 30 Academicians who have a ticket at their disposal so that it is the highest compliment paid to any man in London. They have got home a very fine picture by the above artist yesterday of Venice which is the largest they have and which must have cost *something*.[7]

But on the same day that Effie put pen to paper to wax lyrical about John's successes John James was putting pen to paper in different vein. He was writing to Effie's father.

London 28 April 1847

My dear Sir,

We have been friends for so many years standing that I hope our communication with each other may assume a more frank and easy and confidential form than those betwixt ordinary acquaintances usually do — we have had the very great pleasure of your Daughter's company for these few days past and what we think of her will best appear from the subject of this letter. — You know that my Son is at home — I cannot arrive at the purpose of this letter better than by giving you a short sketch of his past life — In 1836 when he was 17 I happened to have my partner the late Mr Domecq residing with his Daughters for three months in my house — I believe I have already told you that most unexpectedly to us my son became strongly attached to the eldest Daughter of Mr Domecq ... The passion however was powerful and almost threatened my son's life – various journies abroad have scarcely dissipated his chagrin nor repaired his health –

The only young lady we have had about us since from whom any thing was to be feared I will admit is your own Daughter and because both Mrs Ruskin and myself were persuaded that no young man of taste and feeling could long look upon her with indifference we felt called upon immediately to consider all consequences. For myself I am of course most deeply anxious for my son's happiness but whether it was derived from Paris or Perth, from small fortune or from great, I was disposed to let matters take their course trusting that my son would not commit any very fatal mistake if left to his own guidance in such an affair – I ascertained however that ... To Scotland and most especially to Perth Mrs Ruskin has an insuperable dislike – she has had so much misery herself in Perth that she has quite a superstitious dread of her son connecting himself in the most remote degree with the place – With knowledge of these objections in his Mother's mind and of the power of the presence of such a young creature as Miss Gray my son has been abroad and since his return he has in the society he has fallen into found a young Lady who has engaged his affections and to whom he has made proposals the result of which is not yet known.... I would not presume to say that Miss Gray cannot be daily with my son without the smallest danger to herself but I deem it more than possible from what I already see that both may fall into some danger and that very great embarrassment might arise to all of us should the favourable impression which each may be already making on the other proceed to take more definite form.... He may follow his own inclinations but as he has committed himself for the present and as his Mother if he had not seems so averse to Scottish alliances I cannot help giving expressions to my apprehensions that both you and I are placing our young people in danger and that we should at least adopt every measure of caution and safety in our power.[8]

Few people could fail to be insulted by such a letter. It takes little reading between the lines to see that in one fell swoop John James implies that Effie is flirting inappropriately, that John has found someone more suitable in terms of social circle, and that anyway anyone from Perth is instantly cursed. Hardly surprising, then, that George Gray, barely concealing his fury beneath a courteous but curt response, informed the Ruskins by return that arrangements were already in hand for a family friend, Mr Gadesden, to come and pick Effie up as swiftly as possible.

But before this emergency procedure could be activated, John discovered his parents' intentions and rebelled. He liked Effie and wanted her to stay. In the midst of a family row the Ruskins senior were forced to backtrack. Mr Ruskin hastily wrote again, attempting to shut the door despite the fact that the horse had bolted. Expressing his regret that Mr Gadesden had been contacted, Mr Ruskin now confirmed that Effie could stay after all and pointed out that Mrs Ruskin didn't want the Grays to take her views on people from Perth personally.

And so stay Effie did, until early June. She continued to write home in a jolly tone, listing her social visits, outings to galleries and pleasant walks, and avidly describing the London fashions.[9] She continued to relate in some detail John's regular encounters with the rich and famous: breakfast with the poet Samuel Rogers; dinner with the painter Edwin Landseer; the opera to see Jenny Lind with Thomas Richmond the painter; visits to an exhibition with the Duke and Duchess of Manchester. And perhaps to conceal her embarrassment over the earlier episode, her letters begin to reveal a rather playful attitude to the Lockhart affair.

I have not yet had the courage to ask John who his Lady-Love is, of the last syllable I suspect there is little, it is an extraordinary affair and I could astonish you were I at home to tell you about them. I suspect from what is said that the Lady has a fortune and that love must come after the marriage. Mr and Mrs R are always talking about marrying from reason, rather odd, isn't it. I much doubt if John will ever marry her as he has not yet asked her. I cannot understand the affair, nor I suppose can you, but at any rate if I tell you anything about them I trust you will keep it entirely to yourselves as Mr Ruskin never told me he had written to Papa about it, in fact Mrs Ruskin tells me that nobody knows and she only told me in case, as she says, that John and I *should love each other*. Wasn't it good, I could not help laughing but thanked her for her caution which however I *did* not *require* as I consider him the same as married and should never think of such a thing.[10]

Despite her protestations to the contrary, Effie was undoubtedly having some effect on John. A letter to her parents reveals that they too may have been encouraging her, by suggesting the Ruskins' commitment to Charlotte Lockhart was ill founded.

What you say about J's affaire [*sic*] is very true, if he marry the Lady it is from prudence and a false notion of duty, he has only seen the young Lady six times at parties in his whole life and does not love her a bit, but believes they have each qualities to make the other happy were they married. Did you ever hear such philosophy?[11]

If Effie was in fact waging her own subversive campaign to capture John's heart, then she may have been motivated by a turn of events at home. Her father had speculated in the great emblem of progress, the new railways, and at some point in 1847, like many others, this speculation had proved unwise. He was facing financial ruin.

Unmarried women were a burden on their families. Only working-class women worked from need, and for middle-class girls such as Effie the expectation was to be supported initially by one's parents and then by one's husband. But of course, much of a middle-class girl's attractiveness to prospective husbands would have been the dowry that their father would have settled at their marriage. With her family suddenly facing financial ruin the once extremely marriageable Effie was quickly becoming less of an interesting proposition in Perth. Should things worsen, she risked a range of unpalatable alternatives. She might have to marry speedily and pragmatically or, worse, find a means of supporting herself.

If a marriage of convenience was on the cards, she may have considered the comfortable life she was enjoying with the Ruskins preferable to a lifelong pact with one of her Perth admirers.[12] And perhaps she feared that Willie MacLeod's affections would be dimmed by her change of circumstance.

But whether Effie was attempting to draw John away from Charlotte or not, Fate played its own hand. In June Effie finally left the Ruskin household and, after a short stay in town with other family friends, took the steamer home. Once she was gone, John found himself once again in Miss Lockhart's company at Lady Davy's, where at dinner it became clear that Charlotte was not interested in becoming Mrs Ruskin: 'she didn't care for a word I said; and Mr Gladstone was on the other side of her – and the precious moments were all thrown away in quarrelling across her, with him, about Neapolitan prisons.'[13]

The Lockhart episode had exhausted John, and once again he fell ill. In July his parents sent him to Dr Jephson in Leamington, who had 'treated' Ruskin in the past. Here he pottered the Warwickshire lanes, resting, walking, drawing and, according to his diaries, thinking much about Effie, who he now realized should have been the object of his affection all along.

In August he headed for Scotland for a holiday with a university chum called William Macdonald. On the 25th his trip took him through Perth, but despite what would have been the minimum of social convention, he did not visit the Grays. Effie had already predicted this in an earlier letter to her parents in June, when she warned that 'John Ruskin will certainly be in Scotland to stay with Mr Macdonald but you need not expect to see him at Bowerswell. He cannot come for various reasons and as you know Mrs Ruskin would be miserable every moment he was in Perth or under our roof which was much worse.'[14]

The hysterical superstition of his mother, based on her memory of the dreadful throat-cutting incident at Bowerswell, was too powerful for even this brilliant man to challenge. The infantilized Ruskin's entry in his diary on the day he failed to see Effie marks his feelings of utter misery and guilt, heightened all the more by the fact that Effie had no idea of his changed feelings towards her:

I passed through Perth today, nineteen years since I was there, and I am very sad tonight. It came on dark at 10 and remained grey all day, a shower coming on just as we entered by the South Inch. All looked hopeless and cheerless; the town smoky and ugly in outer suburbs; the Bowerswell houses crowded and the ground behind ragged. . . . And I have had the saddest walk this afternoon I ever had in my life. Partly from my own pain in not seeing EG and in far greater degree, as I found by examining it thoroughly, from thinking that my own pain was perhaps much less than hers, not knowing what I know. And all this with a strange deadly shadow over everything, such as I hardly could comprehend; I expected to be touched by it, which I was not, but then came a horror of great darkness – not distress, but cold, fear and gloom.[15]

He then wrote a pathetic letter of apology to Mrs Gray, using his family's troubled history in Perth as a reason for not coming to visit. Despite Effie's prediction that this would be so, it must have seemed a weak and hurtful explanation.

But if the elder Ruskins were steering their son away from what they considered an inappropriate marriage, this diary entry reveals how, in doing so, they were plunging him into a deep depression. It was not long before Margaret began to note the signs of mental instability of which she was so constantly fearful. And so gradually over the course of August and September the correspondence between Ruskins senior and junior changed its tone, and eventually the parents began to encourage John to visit Effie after all. Once again the Ruskin family were clumsily changing their former staunch position to pander to their son's apparent wishes.

So in October, before returning back south, John stepped inside Bowerswell House. But he found no warm welcome or gratitude from Effie. Instead, for the entire week Effie was cool in the extreme and flirted conspicuously with other young men. Was this the final tease in a carefully wrought manipulation of a young man desperate not to have his affections dashed for a third time? Or was this the behaviour of a young woman who had been genuinely offended by the Ruskins' attitude to her and her family?

Whatever the intention, its effect was decisive. Ruskin was spurred to action – at least, of sorts. From Bowerswell he wrote to William Macdonald:

> I love Miss Gray very much and therefore cannot tell what to think of her – only this I know that in many respects she is unfitted to be my wife unless she also loved me exceedingly. She is surrounded by people who pay her attentions, and though I believe most of them inferior in some points to myself, far more calculated to catch a girl's fancy. Still Miss Gray and I are old friends. I have every reason to think if I were to try I could soon make her more than a friend and if, after I leave her this time, she holds out six months more, I believe I shall ask her to come to Switzerland with me next year.[16]

John's rather modern solution of a holiday together was typical of a man who cared little for social convention. Unfortunately neither the Ruskins senior nor the Grays were as socially impervious. Such an arrangement would have been totally improper, which may explain why, only a month later, Ruskin's feelings towards Effie had been converted into an offer of marriage – made by post. Effie, despite her icy demeanour at their last meeting, accepted at once.

Ruskin immediately fizzed with euphoric declarations of his love. By November he seemed a changed man, writing to his fiancée: 'My own Effie – my kind Effie – my mistress – my friend – my queen – my darling – my only love.'[17] A couple of days later Ruskin wrote again, almost hysterical with anticipation, revealing a mixture of breathless anxiety and excitement about his forthcoming marriage:

> When we are *alone* - You and I – together – Mais – c'est inconceivable – I was just trying – this evening after dinner – to imagine our sitting after dinner at Keswick – vous et moi – I couldn't do it – it seemed impossible that I should ever get you all

to myself – and then I said to myself 'If she should be dull – if she should not be able to think but of her sweet sisters – her deserted home – her parents – giving up their chief joy – if she should be sad – what shall I do – either – how shall I ever tell tell her my gladness – Oh – my own Love – what shall I do indeed – I shall not be able to speak a word – I shall be running round you – and kneeling to you . . . I shall be clumsy and mute – at once perfectly oppressed with delight – if you speak to me I shall not know what to say.[18]

Throughout these very early love letters Ruskin, all too aware of Effie's popularity with the young men of Perth, enjoys the fact he has trounced so many competitors. He shows an almost pruri-ent hunger for details from his fiancée of how she has let down his disappointed rivals. But over the next five months the tone of his letters gradually changes. The enthralled, excited young man who began by worshipping his magnificent catch, all the more precious because of the many others who had also tried to snare her, dis-appears. And in his place a demanding and dogmatic egocentric emerges, one who has a rather inflexible view of what role his wife should be prepared to play.

In one letter Effie apologizes that her handwriting isn't all it could be; by return John agrees it could be better, particularly since he expects her to be assisting him with his manuscripts. Effie checks that she will still be able to socialize with friends; John says of course, but warns her against the multitude of fair-weather folk who seek to know him because of his fame. John grumbles that Effie seems to be over-excited and has been doing too much ahead of the big day – surely she would have been better to study ahead of her new career as his wife.

Not surprisingly as these new facets of John's character emerge, Effie's tone begins to change too. Her correspondence becomes coloured by a sense of unhappiness. Rather than trying to soothe her, however, Ruskin is irritated by this: she should be the happiest woman alive at the prospect of marrying him.

Effie's despondency was now being informed by events at

home too. Her father's financial position had not improved. A month before the wedding day George Gray – the man who twenty years earlier had built a huge villa as a monument to his ambition – confirmed that he was unable to offer any income whatsoever to his daughter. She would become a total dependant of the Ruskins. They settled £10,000 on her, but Ruskin senior was not without his suspicions that the entire marriage had been orchestrated to this end.

As the wedding day drew nearer, the Ruskins announced they would not attend the wedding. Mrs Ruskin's terrible superstition and horrid memories of Bowerswell made it totally impossible for her to see her son wed, and her husband made some rather weak excuse about business.

A fortnight before the wedding Ruskin went to Edinburgh and met the Grays at Effie's uncle's home in the city. Here a gloomy Effie and her anxious father did little to conceal the fact that the Gray family's days at Bowerswell were now numbered. His nerves shot to pieces, George Gray told his future son-in-law that he would have to sell his house. They were all now relying on him, John Ruskin, to help hold the family together.

So there the susceptible John Ruskin found himself, alone on his big day. The 10th of April was now a far cry from the happy, hopeful occasion that it could have been. A young man who had never had the slightest responsibility to face was now looked to for support and encouragement. He stood in that Bowerswell drawing-room feeling sick, only to find Effie also showing signs of tremendous strain.

The ceremony went smoothly in spite of the unfolding domestic turmoil. Mrs Gray wrote to Mrs Ruskin, sending some cake and telling how John and Effie 'bore up with the greatest firmness throughout the trying ceremony and both looked *remarkably well*. They had a delightful afternoon for their journey to Blair Athol [*sic*].'[19]

But their honeymoon night did not go well. Ruskin had once waxed lyrical about being alone with Effie. But now the only part of his former reverie on their being alone together that proved true was Ruskin's utter ignorance of what to do.

When Effie stood naked before her new husband, he told her that he did not want to have sex with her. And so, humiliated and rejected, Effie put her nightclothes back on. The dark secret that would be held at the centre of the Ruskin marriage was born.

2

Long live the revolution

WHEN JOHN EVERETT Millais and William Holman Hunt returned from marching with the Chartist sympathizers, they were in high spirits, excited and inspired by the show of strength and solidarity in the name of a new cause. The events in the wider world could not have been more appropriate. For although Hunt and Millais were not 'political' as such, they were nevertheless cooking up their own rebellion. The target of their campaign was not the government but the art world.

Both Millais and Hunt had been trained at the Royal Academy of Arts. Founded eighty years earlier with the great British painter Sir Joshua Reynolds as its first President, the RA was *the* place to train as a painter and had become an institution that saw itself as the sole arbiter of Britain's standards in fine art.

The RA promoted painting in the 'grand manner', a stylistic tradition enshrined in Reynolds's own work. Drawing both its inspiration and its aesthetic from classical art and the classicized art of the High Renaissance such as that of Raphael, this kind of painting dealt in idealization. Idealization and generalization were corner-stones of the RA dogma. Nature should be improved on rather than copied.

Millais had been first to enter the hallowed walls of this august institution in Trafalgar Square – now the National Gallery – and he did so under the extraordinary privilege of being a child prodigy. Entering on the turn of his eleventh birthday, he was the youngest ever member of the Academy. All the more extraordinary given his juvenile status was the fact that he instantly excelled as a stellar pupil, who became a serial prizewinner.

Millais's exceptional ability as a draughtsman had marked him out from a very early age. Growing up in Jersey as part of a military family, his obvious aptitude for and obsession with drawing had kept him from traditional school. He was allowed to pursue his natural talent while, like Ruskin, his indulgent mother took it upon herself to tutor her gifted child. But when the level of his talent started to create something of a stir both on the island and in the other garrison towns where his father was stationed,[1] the Millais family committed themselves to a totally selfless act. After seeking the counsel of, among others, the Governor of Jersey, the family packed their bags and moved lock, stock and barrel to London.

In 1838, 83 Gower Street became their new home. This plain brick terraced house was in what had once been a particularly fashionable spot. But as the century moved on, Bloomsbury's predominantly Georgian character made it susceptible to changing taste and the Victorian appetite for more highly ornamented white stucco. It was nevertheless always a very respectable part of town, right by the British Museum, where any young artist of ambition was bound to spend many a day sketching the Classical treasures. And even towards the end of the century it was noted as a particularly quiet part of London.

Here the Millais family rallied around Johnnie's talent. The back parlour was converted into a studio, and since the terrace lacked decent gardens, the quiet street outside became a cricket pitch for Johnnie and his brother William. The former was duly enrolled into the best preparatory school of art that there was: Sass's.

Millais was a pretty child, and the early attentions his obvious talent had brought had made him just a touch spoilt. This small boy with curly hair, lace collars and a short jacket was easy prey for the older students. He was known to his contemporaries as 'the child', a name that stuck throughout adulthood, and he was often subjected to quite brutal expressions of jealousy from his fellow pupils. Once, after winning a prestigious silver medal from the Society of Arts, fellow pupils at Sass's hung Millais head downwards out of a window and left him there, suspended over the pavement below, held only by the scarves and pieces of string that his peers had selected to attach him to the iron window guards until his precarious situation was noticed by passers-by.

By the time Hunt knew him, the small boy had grown into a razor-thin 'tall youth; his bronze-coloured locks stood up, twisting and curling so thickly that the parting itself was lost'. He seems to have avoided many of the personality traits so often attached to child stardom. He was jolly and good-natured. He retained an absolute obsession with his craft and a rigorous work ethic. He even 'dressed with exact conventionality so as to avoid in any degree courting attentions as a genius'.[2] The only remnants of over-indulgence that tempered an otherwise seemingly balanced personality were a tendency to vanity (he was particularly proud of his nose) and the apparent attitude that he often expected people to carry things for him.[3]

One other thing is also clear about Johnnie Millais: he adored 'Mad' Hunt. Where Millais's features were fine and delicate, Hunt's were bold. He had straight, floppy, reddish blond hair, and in later life a long, wavy, golden-red beard. His face was broad and flattish, with wide cheekbones and a furrowed forehead. His nose was quite wide along its bridge, with a slightly *retroussé* tip. He was a keen boxer, which may have contributed to a somewhat pugnacious physiognomy.

Hunt's story was decidedly different from Millais's. Whereas Millais's parents were comfortably off and his father described as a 'country gentleman',[4] Hunt's were not. Hunt was born in London's Cheapside, a busy commercial street in the heart of the City. His father was a warehouseman employed by a City firm to manage a mercers', and drapers', depot. And Hunt was apprenticed in the City as a teenager.

Whereas Millais's passion and aptitude for drawing were encouraged and indulged, Hunt would sketch the City characters around him in his lunch breaks. His work was sufficiently praised by his colleagues for him to decide, at the age of sixteen, with characteristic determination and bravery, to set up a commercial studio.

'My release seemed very long in coming', Hunt remembered of his escape from City servitude, 'but at last I bade my sympathetic master, whose portrait I first painted, farewell. My father gave me a letter to Mr E. Hawkins of the Sculpture Department of the British Museum, asking permission for me to draw there. In accordance with my declaration of self-reliance, a suitable room in the City was found to paint the portraits impulsively ordered from me . . . Alas! the commissions nearly all proved to be empty words.'[5]

Hunt's family could not afford to indulge his ambitions to become a painter without real promise of success. Desperately trying to keep his head above water, he began doing repainting and repair jobs, small commissions, and finally, unable to meet the expenses of the studio, abandoned it. But Hunt's moniker was not without significance. 'Mad' Hunt was so called because of his steely determination and almost insane work ethic. He continued to visit the British Museum and National Gallery two or three times a week, sketching furiously.

Now Hunt began submitting drawings to the RA to gain admission as a probationer. If he was going to be a success, he realized he needed the approving initials of the establishment after his name. Hunt's first two attempts at securing a place at the Academy failed. But just as his father insisted that he would have to return to his City apprenticeship, some hope dawned. One day, while sketching in the British Museum, the seventeen-year-old Hunt noticed a younger boy leaning over his shoulder. He knew this was the famous 'child' of the Academy. Millais was impressed by Hunt's work and encouraged him that it met Academy standards. And indeed at his next attempt Hunt was in.

Johnnie and Mad soon became close friends, and the warm, welcoming household in Gower Street became a natural place for the two colleagues often to paint together. Here, in a makeshift studio crammed with swords, costumes and casts of animals, wrapped in their own world, they began to have uninhibited, idealistic conversations. And the older generation became the target of their scorn.

Hunt undoubtedly had the spark that ignited his younger friend's enthusiasm for revolutionary thoughts. He had already read Ruskin's *Modern Painters* and was keen to engage with bold analytical thinking about the role of art. He may well have also heard about the Nazarenes, a group of German artists working in Rome and living together as a 'brotherhood' in an abandoned monastery. They had already thrown down the gauntlet and challenged the supremacy of the Neo-classical tradition. Although disbanded by 1830, they had sought to imitate the work of early Renaissance and medieval painters as part of their search for a new spirituality in art.[6]

Hunt felt that British art had become fossilized by the Academy, now under the presidency of Sir Charles Eastlake. He wanted to do away with its specific aesthetic rules: that the human form should be idealized, draperies gracefully arranged and landscapes generalized. Hunt wanted to make his subjects more accessible and real. He wanted to draw from what he saw around him.

For Hunt the need to carve out a path for art came from an intellectual, intense analysis of the limitations of his predecessors and peers. Intellectualized, worried over, wrought, his words reflect this intense and earnest character. Millais, on the other hand, sympathized with Hunt because, instinctively, he wanted to capture the world in a fresh new light, born from real observation. This, after all, was 'the child' who had simply wanted to draw what he saw around him. He needed no theory to know that art had become dull.

The canvases that Johnnie and Mad sent off on the night of 9 April for the RA show were *Cymon and Iphigenia* and *The Eve of St Agnes* respectively. Compared to the Academy art that the two found such fault with, the canvases barely translated any nascent

William Holman Hunt and John Everett Millais, by Dante Gabriel
Rossetti, *c.* 1851. Sir Joshua Reynolds, founder of the Royal Academy,
is referred to as 'Sir Sloshua' because of his 'sloshy', vague backgrounds

revolutionary or avant-garde thoughts. Millais's picture still
suffered from the idealized drapery and setting that the two had
apparently railed against. Hunt's perhaps hinted more at the new
kind of work that within a year they would be producing. His
protagonists were more realistic and, rather than base his work on
a traditional Classical subject, he had drawn on a poem by Keats.

Hunt and Millais had to wait about three weeks to see if these
canvases were accepted into the RA show. The Academy had an
overt way of making its own judgement known to the visiting
public and critics. The first judgement was acceptance or rejection; the second was how the picture was hung. Unlike today,

when pictures are hung in sequence, all at eye-level, the entire walls of the Academy were at that time covered, from floor to ceiling. With up to 1,200 paintings in the summer show, only those pictures that the establishment's hanging committee deemed to be excellent were hung in the optimum position for public view – at eye-level. The further away from this critical 'line' a picture was hung, the poorer it was considered by the powers that be.

The enormous popularity of the summer show was reflected in its receipts. Entry to the show was a shilling, and for a catalogue a further shilling had to be shelled out. After the six-week run, the Academy had usually taken £6,000, with around 100,000 visitors passing through its doors.[7] Given the population of London was only around 2 million at this period, the influence of the exhibition is clear.

Imagine, then, Millais's dismay when he learned that *Cymon and Iphigenia* had not even made it into the show, a disappointment about which Hunt claimed he was 'exceedingly brave'.[8] But Hunt's *Eve of St Agnes* had made it through, and this piece of good fortune, or just desert, had a significant consequence.

Hunt's *Eve of St Agnes* is a story of love overcoming social barriers. In accordance with the tradition that, on the eve of St Agnes, virgins could go to sleep and see in their dreams the man they would marry, the picture's heroine, Madeline, believes she is dreaming of the man she loves, Porphyro. But in fact her lover is really there, having crept into her bedroom, despite the fact he risks his life at the hands of Madeline's hostile family. While Madeline's people sleep after a huge celebration ball, the lovers elope.

Among the thousands of folk who tramped through the RA to look at its latest crop, another young artist found himself so drawn to Hunt's romantic picture that he decided to track Hunt down and congratulate him in person. This young man was already attracting some attention from his peers: Dante Gabriel Rossetti.

Within days of seeing Hunt's *Eve of St Agnes* Rossetti was sitting in Hunt's studio, a grim space at 7 Cleveland Street, in the heart of Fitzrovia – close to Gower Street in terms of distance but with none of its calm or propriety. Originally a residential street, by the mid-1840s most of Cleveland Street had been converted into cheap shops and low-rent businesses. A hive of activity, it was also a place of some considerable sleaze, where prostitutes, both male and female, were active. Hunt's studio was a stone's throw from the local workhouse, but for an impecunious young artist the location served its purpose.

Up to this point Rossetti and Hunt had been on nothing more than nodding terms. Rossetti had entered the Royal Academy around the same time as Hunt, but although his attendance was irregular at best, he had gained a reputation among his peers.

Rossetti was irresistible. Looking at the few surviving photos of him as a slightly portly middle-aged man with dark rings around his eyes, it is hard to imagine the often cited powerful magnetism of his personality. Yet as a young man this was heightened by the fact he was unquestionably beautiful and immediately noticeable. Even as a student, his celebrity had been instant. His

> thick, beautiful, and closely curled masses of rich brown much-neglected hair fell about an ample brow, and almost to the wearer's shoulders; strong eyebrows marked with their dark shadows a pair of rather sunken eyes, in which a sort of fire, instinct of what may be called proud cynicism, burned with a furtive kind of energy and was distinctly, if somewhat luridly, glowing. His rather high cheek bones were the more observable because his cheeks were roseless and hollow enough to indicate the waste of life and mid-night oil to which the youth was addicted; close shaving left bare his very full, not to say sensuous lips and square cut masculine jaw. Rather below the middle height ... Rossetti ... tossed the falling hair back from his face, and having both hands in his pockets, faced the student world with an insouciant air which savoured of defiance, mental pride and thorough self reliance.[9]

In addition to his stunning looks, Rossetti, his fellow pupils had heard, was already a published poet. That his juvenilia had simply been printed by a doting grandfather did not matter. The fact that he was a 'poet' gave him a romantic allure that, combined with his Italian background and his inventive sketches, sometimes chivalric, sometimes satirical, made him a talking point.

The seedy surroundings of Cleveland Street would have hardly bothered Rossetti. He had been brought up in a nearby street that only barely boasted better associations. A lack of 'tin', as Rossetti called ready cash, was his status quo. Born in May 1828, Rossetti was a first-generation English Italian. The moniker Dante was included at his christening in All Souls Church, Langham Place, in homage to the Italian poet, to whom his father had dedicated years of study.

Gabriele Rossetti had arrived in London in April 1824, exiled from his native Naples. He was a writer, poet and intellectual of considerable renown in Naples, who for a while survived the turbulent political upheavals of his era by pragmatically changing his allegiances with the tide. He had shifted from supporting the *ancien régime* to becoming the bard of French liberty in the Napoleonic era. When this ended in favour of an Italian monarchy, he had once again refocused his pen and welcomed the return of the exiled King of Naples, Ferdinand IV. But one can only turn with so many tides.

Five years after Ferdinand's return there was a bloodless revolution in Naples, as a result of which the King was forced to introduce a freedom of speech bill and allow legal membership of what had been up to that point the secret revolutionary Carbonari society. The latter – literally 'the charcoal burners' – was a society of clandestine radical cells, organized a little like the freemasons, instrumental in the bloodless uprising in the city. Gabriele immediately aligned himself with the rebels, joined the Carbonari and styled himself as the poet of the revolution. But when the revolutionary constitution was abolished just a year later, by a Ferdinand now bolstered with the Austrian army at his side, the chameleon Gabriele's luck ran out.

He was forced into hiding and eventually escaped with the British fleet, which had been moored in the Bay of Naples. This stroke of luck was secured by the fact that the wife of the admiral of the fleet – Lady Graham Moore – had fallen in love with Rossetti's work and perhaps just a little with Rossetti himself.

And so Rossetti junior found himself born not under the shadow of Mount Vesuvius but at 38 Charlotte Street in London's West End. It was an unrespectable street, lined with pubs and working men's clubs, the haunt of Chartists and prostitutes, where Rossetti lived with his father, his Anglo-Italian mother (whom Gabriele had met in England) and three siblings: Maria, Christina and William Michael.

Gabriele had slunk from fame to infamy and finally into the anonymity of a refugee. He continued writing, began a critical study of the great poet Dante and eventually secured a position as Professor of Italian at King's College, London. But times were hard.

From early on Gabriel had a well-developed ego and a strong sense of both his father's heritage and his own artistic destiny. Although christened Gabriel Charles Dante Rossetti, at some early stage the aspiring youngster decided to reorder his name as Dante Gabriel Rossetti, embellishing his persona with the romantic associations of the poet.

And Gabriel was a poet. From his childhood onwards his creative outpourings were constantly torn between his desire to write and his equally strong ambition to become a painter, both desires born out of a personality that was at once intense and sensitive, and that indulged in idealism and mysticism.

At the point at which Gabriel commended Hunt for the *Eve of St Agnes*, the latter was well aware of Gabriel's sketches of knights rescuing ladies and lovers in medieval dress. Already his particular fascination with fallen women and tragic love was established, embodied in the distant heroines of legend such as Guinevere and stories from his namesake Dante about his doomed love for Beatrice.

His poetry circled around the same themes, although not always dressed up in medieval guise. The poor whores he had seen in his neighbourhood had also already made an impression on him. Although it is unlikely he had enough 'tin' or courage to use a prostitute at this stage in his young life, he had already written 'Jenny', a vivid description of a young prostitute, fallen asleep with her head in the lap of her latest client. Told from the point of view of the client, it examines his genuine attraction to the girl, and combines this with his pity for her situation and somewhat detached observations about the kind of society (of which he is absolutely a part) that conspires to create such a creature.

But Gabriel's youthful enthusiasm refused to limit the scope of his subject-matter quite so neatly. He was alive with invention and ambition, and there were many things that caught the attention of his pen or pencil. And he did, in spite of his boils, write about the events of 10 April in a playful revolutionary ballad.

> Ho ye that have nothing to lose ! Ho rouse ye, one and all!
> Come from the sinks of the New Cut, the purlieus of Vauxhall!
> Did ye not hear the mighty sound boom by ye as it went –
> The Seven Dials strike the hour of man's enfranchisement?[10]

But while Rossetti was already something of an accomplished wordsmith, and one who wrote with visual immediacy, at this point he lacked the technical expertise to allow him to realize his other ambition: to paint. He was far from being able to articulate these kinds of visions on canvas in the way he desired. 'Every time I attempt to express my ideas in colour, I find myself baffled, not by want of ability – I feel this, and why should I not say it? – but by ignorance of certain apparently insignificant technicalities', he wrote to his aunt Charlotte.[11]

By the summer of 1848 the twenty-year-old Rossetti had only just completed the Antique School at the Royal Academy. This was the first of three 'schools', or courses, that saw a student laboriously graduate from drawing to eventually painting. Hunt, by contrast, had already had a proper oil painting accepted in the summer show, and Millais had had one accepted two years earlier.

At the Antique School the students learned the corner-stones of their profession. They mastered perspective, made drawings of plaster casts and statues and had to attend a year's worth of compulsory lectures. Only then could they move on to the School of the Living Model – where they could draw from real models – and only after they mastered this skill could they enter the School of Painting.

Whereas Millais and Hunt had trudged through this process, Rossetti was from the outset frustrated with the constraints imposed by the RA committee men he held in such contempt. Early in his course he even went to the head of the Academy, Sir Charles Eastlake, and showed him his work – in the hope that he might be encouraged to move him on to painting – but Eastlake simply urged him just to keep drawing for the time being.

The fact was, Rossetti wanted to run before he could walk. His ambitions were lofty, he had already cast himself as an artist, but he was deeply aggravated by a lack of progress. This irritation had two direct effects, which managed only to exacerbate his situation. First he became disillusioned, suffering from a kind of paralysis born out of depression, and stopped turning up to school. And second, he began to shift focus away from painting and started pursuing other career options – such as poetry.

At around this time, fed up with the endless drawing lessons, Rossetti began to write to famous contemporary poets. He trotted off notes to Robert Browning, to the poet and artist William Bell Scott and to the poet, writer and critic Leigh Hunt. But although these approaches did secure Rossetti important new friendships that cast him within the circle of London's literary élite, they did nothing to further his progress at the Academy. If anything, his lack of focus simply prolonged his studies, which in turn fed his innate despondency.

This mix of confidence and insecurity – bursts of energy followed by bouts of paralysis, impatience yet reluctance – and his endless shifting between poetry and paint defined Rossetti's contrary, complicated personality. In early 1848 he decided to leave the RA and learn how to paint under the tutelage of a working artist. One artist he admired was Ford Madox Brown.

Brown was in many senses an independent artist. Born in Calais, the son of a ship's purser, he had trained not under the British system but at Antwerp's Academy. Nearly ten years older than Rossetti and his peers, Brown had met the Nazarenes and sympathized with their work. On his return to Britain in 1844 he produced paintings depicting historical subjects with an unusual attention to detail and sense of realism. Rossetti convinced Brown to take him on as a pupil and teach him the painting techniques that the Academy was keen to withhold from him.

Brown would prove a lifelong friend to Rossetti, arguably his closest ally amid the troubles to come. But as a teacher he immediately under-performed as far as the angry, impatient and often depressed student was concerned. Because although Brown did let him put brush to canvas, to Gabriel's horror it was to paint still-lifes of pickle jars and other similar staple exercises. The poetically motivated Gabriel quickly fell out of love with this mundane subject-matter, and his moody depressions deepened.

When Gabriel saw Hunt's *Eve of St Agnes*, he saw a picture based on a poem by one of his favourite poets, Keats. The combination of poetic sensibility and artistic virtuosity, the painting's loaded sensuality, represented everything Rossetti wanted to be able to achieve. Hunt was everything he was striving to become.

Once in Hunt's studio, the two discovered their mutual disillusionment with the establishment, and an instant friendship was forged. Hunt's dogmatic, earnest commitment to a new cause formed a solid bedrock for Rossetti's own more flighty ambitions. And their personalities were instantly complementary. The tough, gritty Hunt and the more dramatic, indulgent Rossetti were a perfect couple. They formed a profound attachment to one another, which instantly rivalled that forged between Mad and his other great friend, Millais.

Hunt was already beginning work on a canvas that would

practise what he had decided to preach. Again, it was based on a literary topic. This time Hunt had turned to the work of the now much forgotten novelist Edward Bulwer-Lytton. The author of *The Last Days of Pompeii* was a successful Victorian writer. Hunt had chosen Bulwer-Lytton's account of a revolutionary thirteenth-century figure, Cola di Rienzi. Despite a humble background, Rienzi led a campaign to bring stability and unity to a factionalized Rome. Hunt's picture intended to capture the catalytic moment when the pointless slaughter of Rienzi's brother in a skirmish between rival baronies prompts him to rebellion.

The painting's revolutionary spirit, no doubt informed by the march of 10 April, would not have been lost on Rossetti. Neither would Hunt's overt desire to paint the picture with a new realism and accessibility.

Part of Hunt's determination to be different was the inclusion of realistic detail such as dandelion puffs and a bumble bee in the foreground rather than what he described as the Academy-prescribed 'whitey-brown which usually served for the near ground'.[12] He also gave the characters real, believable faces. Who could be better as a model for the angry young Italian revolutionary than another angry young Italian revolutionary – of sorts? And so to see a likeness of Rossetti in 1848 one need look no further than Hunt's image of Rienzi, fist raised in defiance. To Rossetti's right is the kneeling figure of a knight, and this is Millais.

As Hunt and Rossetti's friendship knit closer, the latter asked if he could study with Hunt. Hunt already had a pupil, called Fred Stephens, and so initially declined, but Rossetti was not one to be put off, and by August he had done even better than securing the odd lesson from Hunt: he had secured his constant attention. The two were installed in the Cleveland Street studio together.

In fact, Hunt went to considerable lengths to accommodate his compelling new friend. He had recently taken the decision to quit his father's house in Holborn to live and work in his studio. When Rossetti persuaded him to share the space, Hunt had to rent an extra single bedroom at the top of the house.

And so in a grotty room with smoke-stained walls Rossetti set about his first painting under Hunt's guidance, but even so he struggled. He had no idea how to deal with the complex process of oil painting, and so he began by treating the process as though it was a medium he knew: watercolour. He applied the oils very thinly, using slender brushes, and he primed his canvas with white until it was as smooth as paper. As a result the oils took on a transparent aspect. In this way, almost by accident, he found himself painting in a totally fresh, new way.

At some point in the late summer of 1848 Hunt brought Millais and Rossetti together. One evening they all piled into the studio in Gower Street, and together the three looked through a book of engravings from Pisa's Campo Santo. It was the spark for a discussion that would bond them as founder-members of their own secret society. As they looked on at the simple yet highly energetic, immediate and poetic work of Pisa's medieval artists, they determined to form their own 'League of Sincerity'. The League would look to nature and the real world and, casting off the mannerism that had drowned art, seek a new kind of truth.

At this moment one of the most influential movements in British art was born, but not yet christened. The League of Sincerity was quickly renamed. Hunt, in his usual dogmatic manner, wanted better definition. He suggested that the three of them should position themselves as admirers of the 'Pre-Raphaelite' painters: those medieval artists who approached their subject with uncomplicated honesty and with the desire to convey direct spiritual meaning to the onlooker. Rossetti, fired by his romantic imagination and sense of mysticism, insisted they should define themselves as a brotherhood. This, after all, had suggestions of the Round Table, of a secret revolutionary sect, reminiscent of his father's own brush with the Carbonari and of the Nazarenes on the continent.

And so the Pre-Raphaelite Brotherhood was born. All it needed was some more members. In a bid to give their mission some weight, Rossetti and Hunt quickly expanded the group, drawing on friends and family.

Hunt's other pupil, Fred Stephens, was enlisted. So too were the young sculptor Thomas Woolner and the painter James Collinson. Finally Rossetti's brother William Michael was brought on board, as the group's secretary. Although an office worker rather than an artist, he was no mean poet and writer, and he could keep the group's journal. With membership totalling seven – a mystical number – the group closed its doors to further newcomers.

With no portfolio of work as such, Gabriel cast himself at once as the group's proselytizer, his vivacious personality whipping up the enthusiasm of the others. Millais had profile, and Hunt intellectual rigour. The others were, it seems, just glad to be included. In their conversations the PRB's ambitions had few bounds: Hunt remembers how he and Rossetti discussed reinventing furniture, fabrics, buildings and even ladies' and gents' fashions. Their discussions were full of boyish ambition and humour. They considered how they might consolidate their brotherhood: perhaps they would live together in a house where 'PRB' next to the front door would stand for 'Pre-Raphaelite Brotherhood' to the initiated and 'Please Ring the Bell' to the uninitiated. After their meetings they would spill onto the street, where 'political consistency did not prevent us from joining in the chorus of the "Marseillaise" . . . sung primarily by Gabriel as leader'.[13] The revolution had begun.

3

Muse and amusement

QUITE WHY JOHN RUSKIN refused to have sex with his wife has been the subject of much conjecture. On the wedding day itself both he and Effie were exhausted and worried. Both sexually inexperienced, there was probably a mixture of fear, embarrassment and clumsiness that held him back. But, on the point of bankruptcy, the overall tenor of anxiety exuding from the Gray camp in general had also swerved to dampen his ardour, as Ruskin himself later confessed.

'Miss Gray appeared in a most weak and nervous state in consequence of their distress and I was at first afraid of subjecting her ... to any new trials – My own passion was also much subdued by anxiety; and I had no difficulty in refraining from consummation on the first night.'[1]

That Ruskin promised he would perform his matrimonial duty one day is suggested by a letter he wrote to Effie a year later. 'I have your precious letter: with the account so long and kind – of all your trial at Blair Athol', he wrote; '– indeed it must have been cruel my dearest: I think it will be much nicer next time – we will neither of us be frightened.'[2]

But it seems that this promise was one that Ruskin had decided would not be fulfilled for some time. He suggested consummating their marriage when Effie turned twenty-five. Since Effie was nineteen on her wedding day, she was facing a six-year wait before she would experience full relations with her husband.

There are two main theories why Ruskin declined to perform his conjugal duties. One, offered by Effie herself later, was that he

found his wife unattractive in the flesh. 'He told me that he imagined that women were quite different to what he saw ... he was
disgusted by my person on that first evening', she recalled later in
a letter to her father.[3]

Some people have speculated that at the heart of his apparent
repulsion was the sight of Effie's pubic hair, and wondered whether
the fact that women had such an aspect may have even have come
as a revelation to Ruskin. The nude studies of the time that a student of art would have seen portrayed idealized visions of totally
hairless women, and even mid-century 'respectable' photographic
nude studies have the woman's hair touched out. But there was
plenty of pornography available in the nineteenth century that
showed what a woman's body was really like, as well as 'scientific'
photographs and diagrams of tribal women in the name of anthro-
pology that were more factually accurate. Notorious pornographic
publications such as *The Cremorne* or *The Boudoir* were very explicit
and readily available to any gentleman prepared to saunter into the
retail mecca for such sleaze, Holywell Street, just off the Strand.

The other excuse, also cited by Effie and offered by Ruskin
himself, was his fear of pregnancy. Ruskin did not want babies, or
at least not yet. He was desperate to get on with his writing, and
above all European travel was essential for this. Already he was
thinking about a book on architecture for which he wanted to
examine Gothic buildings on the continent. A pregnant wife
could greatly hinder this ambition. 'I was particularly anxious that
my wife should be well and strong in order that she might be able
to climb Swiss hills that year', Ruskin later offered. 'We tried thus
living separate lives for some little time and then agreed that we
would continue to do so till my wife should be five and twenty as
we wished to travel a great deal.'[4] Whatever the reasons, a barrier
came down most firmly.

If Effie was terribly put out by her continuing virginal state, her
letters from her honeymoon in Scotland did well to conceal it.
Nevertheless the first signs of what would fast turn into a rotten
marriage were already emerging. A few days into the honeymoon

John, rather extraordinarily, invited his father, who was on business in the north, to join them. Even the peculiar Mr Ruskin declined this. Then John decided to cut short his honeymoon and return to Denmark Hill because he wanted to get on with his writing.

In July, after a brief flurry of social activity in London and Oxford, the newly-weds joined the elder Ruskins for a stay in Salisbury, and the true horror of the willing infantilism of her husband in the presence of the overbearing Mrs Ruskin began to dawn on Effie.

In the White Hart Inn in Salisbury, with his parents in attendance, John Ruskin got a cold. 'John's cold is not away yet', Effie wrote home to Bowerswell,

> but it is not as bad as he had with us and I think it would go away
> with care if Mr and Mrs Ruskin would only let him alone. They
> are telling him 20 times a day that it is very slight and only nervous
> which I think it is, at the same time they talk constantly to him
> about what he ought to do, and in the morning Mrs Ruskin
> begins with 'don't sit near the towels John they're damp' ... and in
> the forenoon 'John you musn't read these papers till they are dried'
> ... and whenever they ask him how he is he begins to cough ...
> and when I never speak of it I never hear him cough once; his
> pulse and general health are perfectly good.[5]

With terrible irony Mr Ruskin began to wonder whether John's condition was caused by recent marital exertions, and the elder Ruskins insisted that Effie and John move into separate rooms for a while. If Effie was smarting at John's refusal to have full sex with her, then his parents' perception of their son as exhausted by his manly duty must have felt embarrassing and painful. Perhaps this is why she eventually snapped, barking one evening at the fusspot Mrs Ruskin for insisting that John must take a pill for his persistent cold.

This sounds like a tiny incident, and yet it is one that grew out of proportion. To Effie's horror John, rather than siding with his wife, instantly rebuked her for her lack of respect for his mother. She had been put firmly in her place.

Next, an eleven-week tour of Normandy could have done little to reassure Effie that the marriage to which she was now committed would be a happy one. Ruskin's father went as far as Boulogne with the newly-weds, before leaving them to it. Effie made the most of the new experience of continental travel. She even glossed over being sick on the cross-channel steamer with the excitement of someone on their first foreign adventure, although it was the stewards rather than her husband or father-in-law who attended to her.

Once abroad, the excitement dwindled as Effie was simply deserted. John, in a frenzy of desire to crack on with his analysis of architecture, was out almost at first light and did not return till late. The cosseted Ruskin could transform into a different being when it came to indulging and forwarding his own specific intellectual projects. The man who had allowed his mother to move him from damp towels and had resisted reading moist newspapers, would now not think twice about working long hours and drawing in unhealthy environments in his quest to 'know more about [French architecture] than any English architect, and than most French'.[6]

Effie's letters catalogue the hours of solitude, where she improves her French by reading Alexandre Dumas's *Count of Monte Cristo* or when she sits 'in the sun in the forenoon when John is sketching and draw and work by myself'. She professes happiness despite the fact that John is 'obliged to leave me for as he says such long dull hours and also after dinner'.[7]

Eventually the eccentric and self-occupied behaviour of her husband began to wear on this naturally sociable young woman, and an enforced solitude far from home was made worse by a lack of tenderness from her husband. At one point during the trip Effie learned that an aunt of hers was very ill. The news upset her. Ruskin's candour about his response to the incident, mentioned in a letter to his father, is quite chilling: 'Even when poor Effie was crying last night I felt by no means as a husband should – but rather a bore – however I comforted her in a dutiful way – but it may be as well – perhaps on the other hand, that I am not easily worked on by these things.'[8]

Why did Ruskin marry? Later he said he had been looking 'for a companion'.[9] But it seems that in his mind this companion would do exactly as he wished, would follow him unquestioningly wherever he went, would have habits and expectations that mirrored his owned. Ruskin, the only child, wanted a friend, but one that would always play his game exactly the way he wanted. In these respects Effie failed to make the grade. His early infatuation with her must have been informed by his own projections of what she might become for him. But try as she might, she could not match his expectations. Despite her attempts to be an appropriate companion in France, the experience of being with Effie did not live up to the exhilarating trips he had previously shared on the continent with his parents.

Ruskin became depressed. A man who should be living the best moments of his life began to write morose and morbid letters home. After just a few months marriage had already made him feel old. At least Effie had something to look forward to on the return from France: a brand new house. John James has secured a lease on a smart new home in one of the most fashionable parts of London, Mayfair's Park Street. Effie was only too aware of the status of the property, selected by John James quite consciously as a reflection of his son's growing social eminence. Her new neighbours were the socialite Lady Davy and the Marquess of Westminster, among others.

Effie threw herself into a round of social introductions and dinner parties. This was a side of life as Mrs Ruskin that had always appealed to her, and her letters are full of wonder at the high society she could now entertain. She was also proving to be something of a social success. The highly influential Lady Eastlake, wife of the RA's esteemed President, fast became a friend. But John did not warm to society life. He missed his life with his parents in the suburbs. He continued to spend as much time as he could in his childhood home and did not even move all his possessions from his parents' house in Denmark Hill. He could not quite sever the umbilical cord that keeping a study at his parents' house represented.

The couple's first Christmas was spent together at Denmark Hill. After their own round of parties in town came those organized by the Ruskins. Effie became ill and exhausted, but whereas the Ruskins were quick to accommodate any sign of illness in their son, the same level of concern was not extended to their daughter-in-law. When she was discovered tearful one evening, and slow in dressing for dinner, rather than being offered sympathy she was scolded. 'I asked leave to remain in my room today which John and I thought the best thing, but I was not allowed, and again today, as almost every day this week, company, six o'clock dinner and not in bed till between twelve and one', she complained wearily to her mother.[10]

Effie was now falling short of not just her husband's expectations, but also those of the elder Ruskins. At the core of their disappointment in her was her apparent unhappiness. They saw a little girl from Perth living in one of the most prestigious streets in the world, enjoying every comfort money could buy and having every society door open to her. The one human being they held above all others – their son – had offered her his hand in marriage. They were confounded by her despondency and mistook her unhappiness for spoilt ingratitude. But, of course, they did not know the whole story.

In January 1849 Effie's mother came to London, and Effie, still unwell, returned to Perth with her for what was anticipated would be a brief visit. But her stay was not a short one. Effie had been married for just nine months. Miserable and ill, she now spent the same amount of time away from her new husband. The lengthy duration of this separation would soon begin to raise eyebrows within the elevated social circles Effie had just entered.

Queen Victoria, wed in 1840 at the age of twenty, had been embodying marriage as the respectable state of womanhood for nearly a decade. And her example was well heeded. In 1851 only 29 per cent of women over twenty were unmarried.[11]

In this era when opportunities for women were so limited by the confines of rigid social expectations, girls such as Effie navigated a precarious course. Marriage was a step that determined the rest of a woman's life. Often it represented huge opportunities: it could raise a woman socially, and it could also save her from ruin. Effie, with her father now precariously poised on the brink of financial disaster, certainly enjoyed both these benefits from her marriage.

But as Effie took the long trip to Perth, she may well have wondered whether in her haste to do the right thing, secure financial stability and improve her social status she had sacrificed her future happiness. She may well have also wondered what would have become of her if she had not made the choices she had. Once in a marriage, a woman's fate was cast and her own legal identity immediately diminished. At the time of Effie's marriage, once the register was signed, all her worldly assets and possessions belonged to her husband. And if the marriage was an unhappy one for her, divorce was not an option. Until 1857 each divorce took an individual act of Parliament to effect. And even if one was prepared to pursue this difficult route, the grounds for divorce were stringent. Men could divorce their wives for adultery. Women had to prove desertion, incest, rape, sodomy or bestiality in addition to adultery. Even if a woman succeeded in divorcing her husband on one of the above grounds – unlikely in Effie's case, given the apparently celibate and potentially impotent Ruskin – she then faced being cast out from society, regardless of her innocence. Divorcees were social lepers.

While the new Mrs Ruskin was learning the lot of marriage to John, the nineteen-year-old Elizabeth Siddall was trudging from her home in the Old Kent Road to sew ribbons and lace to ladies' hats in the back room of Mrs Tozer's bonnet shop in Cranbourne Alley. Lizzie's working life, although not hard compared to some Victorian employment, nevertheless involved long hours and steady discipline. She would be up very early every morning to cross the river and reach the centre of town in time to help her employer open the shop. She would then sew all day in the back room before helping to pack the hats away again in the evening. All the stands had to come out of the window after retail hours, and all the bonnets had to be put back into cardboard boxes, which were then stacked on high shelves that ran all round the walls of the workroom. It would be eight o'clock before she stepped out into the London air again to face her long walk home.

There was something of a tradition among London's bachelors wanting to catch a glimpse of a pretty girl and perhaps walk her home: at about half-past seven Cranbourne Alley would begin to fill with young men who would linger and loiter and sometimes offer to help the ladies as they struggled with their stands and boxes. Then, as the attractive millinery girls spilled out from the closing shops, there was the opportunity for some flirting and social interaction with those admirers who knew that this particular parade of shops never failed to provide the best-looking girls in town.

Lizzie was no exception. Tall, slender and with a long neck, she had a mass of deep red hair. Her fair complexion had a pale rose tint to it, and her eyes were agate-coloured. Although the daughter of a Sheffield-born cutler, Lizzie was from a family with ambition. Despite being tradespeople, the family sensibility was that their current lot in life was the result of a misfortunate fall from grace. The Siddalls were descended, in fact, from a more aristocratic Yorkshire family who had once enjoyed a seat at Hope Hall.

There was every sense in the family that, genetically destined for better things, they gracefully suffered their current situation while waiting for the opportunity to right the boat. As such, Mrs Siddall had done what she could to groom her daughters for a respectable life and, more pertinently, a respectable marriage. They could read and write, had good manners and carried themselves with self-respect.

Lizzie was one of four girls. The eldest, Annie, was already married and away; Lydia worked in her aunt's chandler's shop in Pentonville; and the youngest, Clara, was still at home. At nineteen, Lizzie's future must have been keenly on the family's mind and agenda.

One day in 1849 an extremely handsome young man, passing time by being nosy while his mother bought a bonnet, wandered to the back of one of these shops and peeped over the blind of the glass door that led to the workshop. Here he spotted Lizzie, and in that instant he was smitten. The name of this young man was Walter Deverell.

The son of the secretary of the government's School of Design based in Somerset House, Deverell had been at the Royal Academy with the Pre-Raphaelite Brotherhood – as Millais, Hunt and Rossetti now unerringly referred to themselves. He deeply admired their love of poetry and their bold thinking on art. He himself was something of a polymath. He was a successful actor who had secured leading roles on the suburban theatre circuit, and he was also a keen amateur poet, but his primary ambition was to become a recognized painter, and as such he was eager to ingratiate himself further with the trio. He was hopeful that he too might be formally accepted into their cabal and be able to paint the mysterious initials PRB after his name, as they now did.

For the year since the Pre-Raphaelite Brotherhood defined themselves in Millais's studio they had been on a frenzied mission to create works of art that would break through in a totally new way. A few others painters such as Deverell were keen to 'join' them, but although extending formal membership was discussed at regular PRB meetings, it was resisted. Deverell attached himself to them nevertheless and was in every way, except on paper, part of the team. 'One evening Deverell broke in upon our peaceful labours', Hunt later remembered.

He had not been seated many minutes, talking in a somewhat absent manner, when he bounded up, marching to and fro about the room, and stopping, he whispered emphatically 'you fellows can't tell what a stupendously beautiful creature I have found. By Jove! She's like a queen . . . she's quite a wonder; for while her friends, of course, are quite humble, she behaves like a real lady, by clear common sense, and without any affectation, knowing perfectly, too, how to keep people at a respectful distance.'[12]

The PRBs were very fond of Deverell and saw him regularly. And it seems he had a profound influence on them. Deverell was obsessed with the lot of the unfortunate. 'He . . . had contracted the prevailing taste among the young of that day which Carlyle had inaugurated and Charles Kingsley accentuated, of dwelling on the miseries of the poor, the friendless, and the fallen', Hunt recalled.[13]

For Deverell the spectre of the beautiful, self-contained, modest Lizzie Siddall, spied working in a back-room sweatshop, crystallized the nobility of the unfortunate. In her he saw the idealized image of the humble woman, whose innate beauty shone through circumstance. And the role of women was something that seemed increasingly to fascinate Deverell and the PRBs.

While trying to find narrative subjects that would allow them to express spiritual and moral messages in their work, the PRBs also resolved to give their pictures a new kind of realistic immediacy. Their paintings were to be populated by figures that could jump off the canvas for the viewer, heroes and heroines with real faces, real body shapes and genuinely observed expressions. To this end they had begun painting themselves and their families. Still generally short of the 'tin' required to hire many professional models, Rossetti had been using his sister Christina as the model for this work, Hunt had used Rossetti and his brother William, and Millais had used the entire PRB circle as sitters for his canvas *Lorenzo and Isabella*.

In this extraordinary picture Millais truly espoused the new PRB principles of bold realism and unconventional composition. On the right of the canvas the lover Lorenzo, offering Isabella fruit, is played by William Michael Rossetti; Gabriel's profile is in the far background, drinking from a glass; and Millais's father is seen wiping his mouth with a napkin. On the left, Fred Stephens's head can be spied between a glass and the man who is holding it and staring, his fingers resting on his mouth. This is Walter Deverell.

Like Hunt's *Eve of St Agnes,* Millais's *Lorenzo and Isabella* deals with the frictions between true love and social status. Based on Keats's poem 'Isabella or The Pot of Basil', it draws on the story of Lorenzo, a humble apprentice, who falls for the boss's daughter Isabella. Her brothers disapprove of Lorenzo and murder him. On discovering this, Isabella exhumes Lorenzo's body and, after decapitating the corpse, keeps his head in a pot of basil as a memory of their love.

In the painting Isabella's brothers are seen eyeing the lovers from the left of the canvas; the one in the immediate foreground kicks out at the dog with a rapier-like leg that violently slices across the canvas. This brutal, jabbing leg gives a sense of the violence that will be visited on the lovers. And Millais, in an era before the great psychoanalyst, also makes a very Freudian suggestion in the picture. The brother in the foreground is holding up a nutcracker in his right hand. While the cracking of a nut could well indicate his desire to emasculate poor Lorenzo, the shadow he himself casts is of a brooding sexuality directed at his own sister. The shadow of his forearm on the table looks like an erect penis, a mound of white ejaculate indicated by salt spilt on the cloth.[14] The brother's foot points inappropriately and intrusively at his sister's lap. Although just nineteen, the 'child' Millais was already dealing with very adult themes and was deeply immersed in the language of sexual relationships and psychology.

In Lizzie, Deverell must have seen a new opportunity for the group. He thought Lizzie had a particularly natural and pure quality that lent itself to the PRB's ambitions. Given their interest in narratives about women and the plight of love, he could see her potential uses. As later drawings of her revealed, she has a tendency to avert her eyes and look down that gave an impression of humility and innocence.

Lizzie also had the advantage of unconventional good looks. Being tall – she was about five foot seven – was not necessarily fashionable, and of all the hair colours one might be born with, red was the least favoured. It was considered unlucky. For a group who wanted to flout the norm, how fortunate was it to find a model who could rewrite the rules on beauty?

Working in a hat shop was respectable. Modelling for artists, however, was not. In a workroom one's companions were women, and an older lady would supervise the room. The artist's studio, by contrast, was a male domain. And part of the modelling contract might be to undress. In fact, being a model was just one step from being a prostitute, and because of the reluctance of many women to suffer the potential stigma modelling threatened, artists tended to avoid respectable women and often just hired prostitutes straight off.

But millinery was a seasonal trade. Although reasonably well paid, it did not secure year-round work. The demand for new hats changed with the weather, and the work attached to them ebbed and flowed. This is perhaps one of the reasons why, when Walter Deverell approached her and asked her to model for him, with all issues of propriety thought out, Lizzie was tempted.

Propriety was dealt with by Mrs Deverell. Walter enlisted his mother, who went to the Siddall household to give the appropriate assurances about her son's intentions. Charles Siddall ran his cutlery business from a rented house just off the Old Kent Road, a thoroughfare that had long been a major route into London. The road had a mixed repute. As it cut into the heart of London the road narrowed and became hemmed in by businesses and factories. But the further away from the city centre, the wider the road became, and where the Siddalls lived it was much greener, with residential houses alternating with shops, behind which were tanneries, rope walks and market gardens stretching to the river.

The Siddalls were at 34 Kent Place, and here Lizzie and her family lived above the shop. Mrs Deverell's job was made easier than perhaps she might have anticipated thanks to a peculiar twist of fate. Of all the working-class families in the huge metropolis it seems that Mrs Siddall's was particularly blessed in its ability to provide girls that appealed to the artistic profession. In fact, Mrs Siddall's relations the Hills had a daughter who was already modelling for an artist: none other than Rossetti's tutor Ford Madox Brown. What is more, she was engaged to marry him. The Siddalls could see the possibilities Mrs Deverell's proposition might offer their own daughter. And so once Mrs Deverell had made the appropriate noises about Walter, Mr and Mrs Siddall agreed that Lizzie could sit to him.

Walter wanted a model for the picture he intended to show during the 1850 exhibition season. Although inspired by and utterly in tune with the PRB's ambitions, Walter lacked their brilliance. Rossetti, Hunt and Millais had all decided to tackle religious subjects, but in bold moves designed to defy tradition they were approaching their holy subjects in audacious spirit. Deverell, by contrast, had chosen to paint a genre picture, taking a scene from Shakespeare that would allow him to tackle the subject of love, just as Millais and Hunt had done.

His subject was a scene from *Twelfth Night*. He wanted Lizzie to model for the cross-dressing Viola in the scene where, disguised as a boy after a shipwreck, she hears the eligible Count Orsino profess his unrequited love for another lady, Olivia. Orsino, unaware that the young page he is speaking to is in truth a women who has fallen in love with him, is depicted in a reverie over Olivia while Viola sits in agony unable to reveal her feelings.

By the time Deverell revealed his find to his friends, he had already begun painting Lizzie in this role and was complaining that he was having problems with capturing her head. Hunt was engrossed with his own work: it took a lot to distract Mad from his work when he had got going. But Rossetti, struggling as usual with his, was happy to be led astray. And anyway he had already helped Deverell with the picture in question, sitting for the 'fool' who would appear alongside Orsino, whom Deverell based on himself.

Deverell was devilishly handsome. In fact, William Rossetti describes him as 'one of the handsomest young men I have known; belonging to a type not properly to be termed feminine, but which might be terms "troubadourish" '.[15] And, perhaps not surprisingly, he was a regular favourite with young women who recognised him from his stage career. It was only a matter of time before he and Lizzie became attracted to one another.

And Lizzie was prepared to throw at least a degree of modesty to the wind for her new beau and her new cause. Deverell had her in a costume that under any other circumstances would have been considered totally improper: a short tunic, barely covering her bottom and revealing her legs above the knee. As one critic of the day noted when the picture was finally shown: 'The costume of this figure is too flimsily theatrical; and we think the impolicy as well as immodesty of her very short dress must have been overlooked by the painter.'[16]

But even if Deverell managed to overlook the unconventional immodesty of the costume he had Lizzie don, the wider social constraints of the day soon weighed heavily on both of them. There was undoubtedly reluctance or caution on the part of the middle-class painter to become involved with a girl from a socially inferior background and probably, given his obvious respect for her, a reluctance to compromise her. Breaking the taboo of inappropriate social mixing would soon become a hallmark of PRB behaviour, as would extramarital sex. But it would not be Deverell who would break through the old ways and enter into a more modern approach to relationships.

It does not take much reading between the lines of accounts of the Brotherhood in this first year to see how highly sexually charged they were as a group. They were, after all, barely out of their adolescence. That Deverell's sexuality was all too apparent is perhaps supported by the anecdote that one of his friends once joked that for him 'PRB' stood for 'Penis Rather Better'.[17] But it was not just the animated, intense Deverell who would have been exuding sexual appetite.

The huge passion these young men felt, their energy, cama-raderie and relative poverty, bound them together in a social intimacy that if not directly homosexual was certainly very intense, sensual and often physically demonstrative. Diana Holman Hunt, Hunt's granddaughter, noted that later in life Woolner suggested that Hunt and Millais had had a homosexual affair.[18] And years later Georgiana Burne-Jones, the wife of the painter Edward Burne-Jones, remembered that the first time she met Hunt at Rossetti's studio she witnessed the intimate physical nature of Rossetti and Hunt's relationship:

> There entered the greatest genius that is alive on earth, William Holman Hunt — such a grand-looking fellow, such a splendour of a man, with a great wiry golden beard, and faithful violet eyes — oh, such a man. And Rossetti sat by him and played with his golden beard passing his paint-brush through the hair of it. And all evening Rossetti talked most gloriously, such talk as I do not believe any man could talk beside him.[19]

The members of the Brotherhood harboured mutual infatu-ations that were willingly and openly expressed in the most romantic terms, and they explored their friendships and obses-sions with one another during lovers' hours. Rossetti was the group's marsupial, encouraging conversations and meals that extended late into the night. The group did not drink, but a few smoked and there are accounts of PRB members lounging on the floor of Hunt and Rossetti's Cleveland Street studio smoking pipes and talking until the early hours. Often these sessions were rounded off with late-night walks that exploited the romantic potential of the twilight hours. It was only a matter of time before this pervading sexual tension growing within the group would find a release. Lizzie suddenly found herself in this remedial role. A relationship with her could unleash those pent-up feelings.

Although Hunt did not, like Rossetti, rush to see Lizzie in Deverell's makeshift studio in his parents' garden in Kew, he wrote to Lizzie to ask if she might sit for one of the women featured in his latest work. At a shilling an hour, the offer was tempting. Lizzie took it and, sitting in his shabby studio, posed for a central figure in Hunt's *A Converted British Family Rescuing a Missionary from the Persecution of the Druids*. This earnest work was to be Hunt's next offering for the Academy show of 1850.

To Victorian eyes the hard, uncompromising realism of this picture, portraying a priest seeking sanctuary with a simple early Christian family, was shocking – all the more so because it was dealing with a Christian subject. If Millais, Hunt and Rossetti had railed against Academy-approved, idealized backgrounds and foregrounds, none was offered here. The brutal persecution is caught with almost random selection in the background. In the foreground the dirt floor of a simple hovel is lovingly offered to the viewer. Bold horizontal and vertical lines frame a brightly lit priest, his bloodied hands and feet alluding to Christ and his pose reminiscent of many a *pietà*. To the right Lizzie Siddall, the hat shop girl, looks down on him with those doe eyes, her unfashionable red hair picking up the red of his robes. Serene and oblivious to the massacre and chaos around her, she prepares to tend to the priest's wounds. She is an angel, a saving grace.

Lizzie spent a lot of time with Hunt. It seems that the intimacy she shared with Deverell transferred to Mad. It also seems that Hunt may have been more relaxed with this shop girl. After all Hunt, himself from a trade background, was nowhere near as squeamish about the working class as his friends seemed to be. His parents lived in rooms over Wilson's upholstery store in Holborn, much as the Siddalls lived over the shop near the Old Kent Road. And his sister would marry one of the said Wilsons.

As for sex, it was only really the middle and upper classes who were so very prudish about it. For the rest of the urban populace, sex in Victorian London was easy. Recent studies of parish registers have revealed that up to one half of nineteenth-century brides were pregnant when they reached the altar.[20] Plenty of people didn't even bother to get to the altar. In 1849 the journalist and social observer Henry Mayhew began to collect accounts for his social survey *London Labour and the London Poor* and concluded that among the poorer classes 'marriage, and indeed much formal morality, was irrelevant'. Mayhew discovered 'it is not at all uncommon for a lad of fifteen to be living with a girl of the same age, as man and wife. It creates no disgust among his class.'[21]

Lizzie was not from the lowest echelons of the working class described by Mayhew, but her background would arguably have exposed her to more direct sexual activity than the closely guarded and chaperoned ladies of the middle and upper classes. And of course both Lizzie and Hunt would have known that Lizzie's relation Emma Hill and Rossetti's friend and mentor Brown had enjoyed plenty of extramarital sex.

Emma had begun sitting for Brown in 1849. She is first mentioned in his rather perfunctory diaries in July; by the 12th of that month he notes he met her in the fields by Highgate; on the 22nd he 'walked about all day with Emma'; and he went to Ramsgate with her for a week in September. The following year Emma gave birth to Brown's illegitimate daughter Catherine.

Emma and Brown's story and their matter-of-fact approach to their domestic situation would suggest that the notion of having extramarital sex with Lizzie would evidently not have been totally out of the question for Hunt. What may, however, have been an issue was the outcome of sexual activity, and longer-term intentions. Once Emma Hill was pregnant, Brown became engaged to her and supported her financially.

Whether any kind of sexual contact happened between Hunt and Lizzie is likely never to be known. A few years later a note in Ford Madox Brown's diary indicates that Millais thought Hunt was a virgin. But to have guarded one's virginity does not preclude having had a sexual encounter. And what is clear is that Lizzie's regular unchaperoned visits to Hunt's studio created an intimacy and ease with him that soon also extended to his friends.

As she became familiar with the other PRBs and their associates, Lizzie's modelling commitments expanded within the group. Rossetti also enlisted his mother to approach Lizzie, and from her he painted a lady in a red dress, or *Rossovestita*. Ford Madox Brown also used her.

As she became drawn into the group, Miss Siddall became commonly referred to as 'The Sid', a nickname that reflected the affection that the Brotherhood shared for this woman. As she became their communal muse, Lizzie became something like the PRB mascot, reinforcing their sense of union. Within a few months of her discovery by Walter her dull life in a shop had been transformed. Rossetti even insisted that she should drop the double 'l' in her surname for what he considered the more elegant and genteel 'Siddal'.

While Lizzie was creating a storm in her own small way within the PRB circle, the winter of 1849 saw Effie Ruskin create her own stir.

After she had left her mother and returned to Perth, Effie's life had become more miserable. Her younger brother died of whooping cough just a few weeks after she arrived back in Scotland, and the whole family was thrown into grief. The round of bad luck that began with her father's financial speculation failing seemed never-ending.

Effie herself now slumped further into some form of illness, which would almost certainly be regarded now as some form of depression. John wanted to go abroad to start his third volume of *Modern Painters* – having finished his architectural labour, published under the title *The Seven Lamps of Architecture*. It was decided that Effie's illness should not hamper his ambitions, and so, instead of returning to the care of her husband, Effie stayed in Perth to be nursed by her family while John and his parents headed off on one of their extended continental excursions.

Perhaps it was guilt that prompted John to write uncharacteristically romantic letters to Effie as he headed out. Two particularly unusual epistles seemed openly to recognize that the source of his wife's unhappiness lay in the lack of sexual affection shown by her husband. On his outbound journey John wrote passionately: 'Do you know, pet, it seems almost a dream to me that we have been married: I look forward to meeting you: and to our next bridal night: and to the time when I shall again draw your dress from your snowy shoulders: and lean my cheek upon them, as you were my betrothed only: and I had never held you in my arms.'[22] The correspondence soon included a discussion regarding the children that Effie now wanted. 'You would like a little Alice of your own – so should I: a little Effie at least.'[23]

But then the correspondence began to sour, and distance, instead of encouraging Effie and Ruskin's hearts to grow fonder, simply drove a wedge of reproachful accusations between them. It was not long before society began to notice that John was with his parents rather than with his wife. Gossip began to circulate in both Perth and London, and some concern over this tittle-tattle began to inform the letters between the Grays and the Ruskins. Defensively, Ruskin blamed Effie. She had left him and retreated to Perth, he said. He 'couldn't be fastened to his wife's waist with her pincushion'.[24]

Then the Ruskins began to get impatient with Effie's 'illness', which they saw as being the root of this separation. Their combined fury at this woman who was disrupting the family status quo and creating social ripples burst out in one particularly cutting letter from John to Mr Gray. Here Ruskin conceded Effie's unhappiness and illness but deferred any responsibility for it by stating: 'The state of her feelings I ascribe now, simply to bodily weakness: that is to say – and this is a serious and distressing admission – to a nervous disease affecting the brain . . . an illness bordering in many of its features on incipient insanity'.[25]

The Ruskins' cards were on the table. Effie and her family must now have seen how precarious her position was. As the summer wore on, the time when the couple would meet again came nearer; and as gossip about the state of the marriage escalated, the couple began to squabble about how best to orchestrate this reunion. Effie was desperate that John should come and collect her in Perth and put paid to the rumours that he no longer cared for her. But like a petulant child, John was outraged that he would have to take such a long journey to do no more than quell gossip; surely if his wife loved him as she should, she would be so keen to see him she would fly down to London. He accused her of putting pride before genuine feelings. What Ruskin could not see is that Effie may well have felt pride was all she had left.

Neverthless Ruskin took the journey to Perth, recently improved by a new railway connection, and in September he found himself back in the house in which the whole unhappy saga had begun: Bowerswell. Once there, however, he offered Effie little comfort, indicating that her life in London would be nothing but dull.

Effie had shown perspicacity before, and she now pulled a brilliant suggestion out of the bag, a suggestion that would at once return John to his beloved continent, support his intellectual needs, place the couple in a romantic setting and remove the obviously hostile influence of John's parents. Effie was nothing if not bold and was clearly prepared to fight for her marriage as best she could.

Her suggestion was strategically brilliant. In his recent letters to her, knowing she had been reading Sismondi's *Histoire des républiques italiennes du moyen âge*, John had begun to ask her to make notes on the Swiss historian's observations about Venice. This great city, its heritage and architecture, was occupying Ruskin's thoughts. And so Effie quite simply proposed that they should go to Venice for the winter.

John was delighted by this unexpected suggestion. It corresponded with his own desire to begin his formal studies of Venetian architecture for what would become his book *The Stones of Venice*. Without further ado, and knowing she faced time alone while John worked, Effie arranged for a companion to travel with them, her friend from Perth Charlotte Ker. They set off in October, and by November they were installed in the Hotel Danieli on Venice's Riva degli Schiavoni.

In 1845 Venice's population of some 122,000 was nearly

matched by the 112,000 visitors who flocked to appreciate its culture, society and bathing. The Riva degli Schiavoni was the fashionable centre for the cosmopolitan set, with newly built hotels and cafés.

By going to Venice, Effie embarked on a bold adventure. Venice was an exotic location. Its social rules were rather different from England. The city of carnival had a history of moral laxity. It was, after all, the city of Casanova. It was at once exciting and just a tad dangerous or dark. And Effie and John would be there when the city was at its most unhinged. The season of masks would begin on St Stephen's Day, 26 December, and last through to Shrove Tuesday. During this period of balls and festivities the citizens of Venice, in disguise, would interact with one another regardless of status. The whole social world became disorientated, and liberties could be taken.

Effie was immediately excited by Venetian custom. There is a sense of liberation and mild rebellion in the letters to her mother that describe how she strolled around Venetian squares and piazzas with John, but without her bonnet. Although the Grays' response to Effie is unrecorded, the news that their daughter-in-law was going native in terms of headdress – or lack of it – caused an uproar in Denmark Hill. Mr Ruskin wrote to her as soon as he heard the news that bonnets were off, expressing his disapproval.

But the interfering Ruskins senior were now thousands of miles away, and their ability to influence the couple certainly seemed to weaken. This was surely what Effie had been banking on. Effie was hoping that without her parents-in-law around she might just be able to recapture the affections and loyalty of her husband.

At first it seemed as though things were going to plan. Effie's initial letters from Venice are happy and talk of the fun the couple were having. They walked together, drank coffee in the squares and took trips on gondolas. Then something very strange happened. One morning an unexpected piece of mail arrived at Denmark Hill. It was a card, and pasted onto it, using letters and words cut from books, was a sinister message:

There was no need for pretending bad health
Miss Ker laid plans with flattering lips.
You see we shall keep him from the advice
Of his Mother and all shall be well.
What a separation.
Father let me warn you, be separated no
More from you only son, your affectionate
Son – he dearly loved his Father and Mother
I beseech you look after his health.[26]

Effie's plot, forged, according to this anonymous note, with her friend Charlotte, had been rumbled by some busybody keen to stir up more trouble within this peculiar family. The Ruskin shenanigans were now much discussed in social circles, in Perth, Edinburgh and London, and at least one observer could obviously see that the trip to Venice removed John from his parents' influence – to Effie's benefit.

The Ruskins became horribly put out by the note, which absolutely hit the desired nerve. Their hysteria about Effie grew. Mr Ruskin wrote to Mr Gray pointing out that he had only once before received an anonymous note, and that was merely from a passer-by whose brolly had got tangled in his hedge and who was therefore requesting it to be cut!

If the Ruskins were worrying that their son was suddenly beyond their influence, the Grays also began to have similar fears for Effie. After eighteen months of misery Venice was proving just the pick-me-up their daughter needed, but soon they grew concerned that she might be having a bit too much fun, not least because John had once again resorted to type and begun to lock himself away with his work.

Effie attracted attention. Unlike stiff, buttoned-up British society, the Venetians were free with their *piccolo complimento,* and Effie delighted in telling her mother how many comments on her beauty she was receiving. As soon as they had had the necessary introductions to society the attentions accelerated. By Christmas Effie was positively drowning in Italian flattery:

We get plenty of admiration and attention, and the number of our admirers increases daily and they are extremely polite and don't make love to us which is a comfort. For instance I had real mince pies sent to me today for my Christmas dinner ... Another person sent me the books of the Opera & Ballet for the Fenice tomorrow and things of that sort. Men are really great fools! And if you suppose that I ever forget my duty for an instant to my husband, you are not at all wrong in your remarks as to decorum! I have inherited a little of my Father's sense and your discretion to some purpose. In fact John would require a wife who could take [care] of her own character, for you know he is intensely occupied and never with us but at meal times, so that we can do anything we like and he does not care how much people are with us or what attention they pay us.[27]

It was not just the Venetians who were noticing Effie. It was the Austrians too. In 1814 Venice had become part of the Austrian-held kingdom of Lombardy-Venetia. In the year of revolutions, 1848, a revolt had briefly restablished a Venetian republic, but by the end of August 1849, just a few months before Effie and John's sojourn there, the Austrians had laid siege to Venice, cutting off its supplies and bombarding the lagoon, and had taken it again. Now the city was teeming with the officers of the victorious army – and they were in high spirits. The attention paid to Effie by the Austrians is testified by a collection of their calling cards, held with her letters in the archive at the Pierpont Morgan Library in New York. From this it is clear that the Baronne de Wertzlar, Colonel Prince Troubetzkoi, Marshal Duc de Raguse and Lieutenant Wilhelm Holxammer, among others, offered Mrs Ruskin their services.[28]

But there was one officer in particular with whom Effie developed a strong friendship: Captain Charles Paulizza, first lieutenant in the Austrian artillery and the man who had largely orchestrated the bombardment of the lagoon. Handsome, with a huge curly moustache, he combined obvious military brilliance with wide cultural interests.

Paulizza soon became a regular figure in Effie's letters home. She mentions in a letter to her brother George that her German is improving, not least because she is seeing Paulizza so often. The season of balls was fast approaching, and it was with the Austrian rather than her husband that Effie began practising her dance steps:

> He spent last evening with me. John always spends the evenings in his own room and Charlotte learns French at the fire and Paulizza and I play at chess and chatter German, but last night we were polkaing and waltzing, first Charlotte and then me, for we thought it necessary to practise a little as we are going to be quite gay in the end of the week.[29]

John did attend some social events with his wife, but his custom was to make an initial appearance and then leave Effie and Charlotte to continue the evening together. At the first ball of the season John made it to eleven o' clock before retiring. Effie and Charlotte danced on until between one and two in the morning.

Paulizza was not merely accompanying Effie to social events. She recounts how they spent an afternoon at the Lido and he caught little crabs and then raced them on the sand. Although Effie failed to regard Paulizza's attentions to her in terms of a love affair – even an unconsummated one – the rest of society were more prepared to make this interpretation. Effie's behaviour became a point of comment, as did her husband's apparent willingness to allow such a relationship to develop.

Friends who cared for Effie's reputation began to have words with her. One English expatriate living in Venice, Rawdon Brown, was very shocked when after one ball John returned home at midnight and it was Paulizza who took Effie and Charlotte home at three in the morning. With Effie's best interests in mind he pointed out that even within the more liberal Venetian society it was not done to leave with a man who was not your husband.

Brown's concern may well have been informed by his own ambitions regarding Effie, however: it's quite clear from Effie's letters home that his interest in her was just as persistent as that of Paulizza. He would write her flattering notes most mornings and would regularly send her little gifts. And somehow the gossip got back to Scotland. Effie's uncle Sheriff Andrew Jameson wrote from Edinburgh warning 'to keep the Austrian officers at a distance', pointing out 'they are a bad set'. He also noted that he had had 'some trouble in defending Mr Ruskin from the attacks that are made on him on account of his strange behaviour'.[30] But more than anyone else it was Effie's brother George whose concern took on a deeply worrying hue. He could not fathom why Ruskin was allowing his wife to make a fool of herself, although he had ugly suspicions.

'Tell George that John is perfectly satisfied with my conduct in every particular and is kinder to me and fonder of me every day,' Effie wrote to reassure her sibling, 'and when I find a good husband I hope I know his value properly and appreciate him enough. John is particularly flattered with the attention they pay me.'[31]

George was beginning to suspect that Ruskin's leniency was more than an idiosyncratic lack of care for society's good opinion. He was beginning to wonder whether Ruskin was encouraging Effie to commit adultery. After all, that would be grounds for divorce.

4

Town talk and table talk

IF YOU WERE an art lover and happened to purchase a copy of *The Times* on 4 May 1850, you would have found an article on page 4 of some interest. Squeezed between an account of the Queen's health after the recent birth of the young Prince Arthur William Patrick and the reports 'Express from Paris by Electric Telegraph', the item in question was headlined 'The Royal Academy Private View'. The piece noted in jubilant tones that the RA's Council had 'this year resolved for the first time to include in their invitations to the private view of their annual exhibition the leading representatives of the metropolitan press'.

Pictures were playing an increasingly large role in British, and particularly English, society in the mid-nineteenth century. For those outcasts in the provinces and beyond, local papers made sure that their readers were kept up to date with all the latest art news, aware that the galleries in other major cities would in time secure exhibitions of some of the works first unveiled in the capital. If, for example, you had been in Edinburgh, *Chambers's Edinburgh Journal* would have reminded you that down south the 'silent reign of the picture exhibitions' was getting under way and that the latest offerings from 'thousands of studios' were now hanging on London's gallery walls.

Hundreds of thousands of people would throng not only to the Royal Academy in Trafalgar Square but also to a range of exhibitions that began in March and ran throughout the summer. The British Institution, at the west end of Pall Mall, kicked the season off in March. Here established artists would show their less important pictures and sketches, and less experienced artists would try out the public.

In April three more galleries flung open their doors on the same morning: the Old Watercolour in Pall Mall East, the New Watercolour in Pall Mall West and the National Institution near Langham Place. Again they offered the juvenile artist, as well as those more experienced artists who had fallen foul of the RA, a chance to show.

The galleries also offered opportunities for social gathering. As *Chambers* reminded its readership, the cool rooms were 'places where everybody meets everybody, and where lazy hours can be conveniently lounged away, the exhibitions in some sort supply[ing] in the afternoon what the Opera and Parties do in the evenings'. The Royal Academy show, as the epicentre of the season, was attended by pomp, ceremony and something of a 'scrum':

> The first Saturday of May arrives and with it many a rumour true and false of the state of matters within the Royal Academy – of the academicians who exhibit, and of what are to be 'the' pictures. From early morning St Martin's bells have been ringing and a festival flag flies at the steeple . . . About noon the Queen's party arrives and Her Majesty is conducted about the rooms by the leading members of the Academy. Between one and two she departs; and immediately after the crowd of ticket holders for the private view cluster before the closed gratings. Punctually as the last stroke of the hour strikes, the portals are flung open and a cataract of eager amateurs rush up the staircases and make their way straight to the inner room of honour, all in quest of the picture . . . hung upon the line in the centre of the eastern wall of the apartment.[1]

That Millais and Hunt were among the few singled out for a mention in *The Times* article on 4 May would have made them the talk of the town. It was something of a disaster for them, then, that the mention was particularly negative. Millais, the article alleged, had 'sunk into extravagance bordering in one instance on irreverence, and again he is followed by Mr Hunt . . . till nothing remains of chiaroscuro, perspective, nature or truth'. The article went on to 'protest against the introduction of such a style to English Art'.[2]

The style in question, of course, was characterized by the rejection of those Academy tropes that Johnnie, Mad and Rossetti had pledged nearly two years earlier to flout. Now their stance as men 'of stubborn instincts and positive self trust' painting 'in a temper of resistance'[3] had been recognized. What Rossetti later recalled as their 'phenomenal antipathy to the Academy, and ... sheer love of being outlawed'[4] had finally been spotted. But alas this initial recognition could hardly have been less laudatory.

The pictures that so disappointed *The Times* were Hunt's *A Converted British Family Rescuing a Missionary from the Persecution of the Druids*, featuring Lizzie Siddall, and Millais's *Christ in the House of His Parents*, which became known as *Christ in the Carpenter's Shop*. Here Millais had gone to town. He had spent hours in a real carpenter's workshop in Oxford Street studying wood shavings. The figure of Joseph was modelled on a grocer from Holborn, and the heads of the sheep in the background had been supplied by a local butcher and sat stinking in his own studio while he copied them meticulously. Jesus was no classical cherub with rounded limbs or graceful posture, but a skinny child with rather large feet.

On the very same day that the journalist from *The Times* sat down to convey disapproval of these pictures and their newfangled realism, another journalist, Angus Reach, sat down to write his regular gossip column 'Town Talk and Table Talk' in one of London's most successful papers, the *Illustrated London News*. Reach, already a very successful investigative journalist, had developed this humorous column as something of a sideline. And on this particular day he had a scoop.

Reach was a friend of the sculptor Alexander Munro, who in turn was a friend of Rossetti. Of course, the over-enthusiastic Rossetti had revealed the Brotherhood's existence to his chum Munro, and had also explained the meaning of those mysterious letters – PRB – that they were all now signing after their names in their correspondence. And Munro had passed on the revelation to Reach.

Although the meaning of the insignia of the Brotherhood was supposed to be kept secret, the boys had been bold in using the initials in the previous year: Rossetti signed his pictures 'PRB', and Millais had woven the initials into the fabric of his *Lorenzo and Isabella*, for example. Now, a year on, they were being a little more cautious and were refraining from using the moniker on their pictures. Nevertheless, Rossetti's indiscretion with Munro meant that Reach now had wind of the Brotherhood and all its members.

Critics may not have cared about Rossetti signing himself PRB in 1849, but in 1850 they did care that upcoming stars such as Millais and Hunt were part of a secret rebellious movement. Reach did not pull his punches: as soon as he had the key to unlock the meaning of the hieroglyphs, he exploited the comic potential of the PRB manifesto.

'Has any casual reader of art-criticisms ever been puzzled by the occurrence of three mysterious letters as denoting a new-fashioned school or style in painting lately come into vogue', Reach wondered in his column.

> The hieroglyphics in question are 'P.R.B.', and they are the initials of the words 'Præ-Raffaelite Brotherhood'. To this league belong the ingenious gentlemen who profess themselves practitioners of 'Early Christian Art', and who – setting aside the Mediæval schools of Italy, the Raffaeles, Guidos, and Titians, and all such small-beer daubers – devote their energies to the reproduction of saints squeezed out perfectly flat ... their appearance being further improved by their limbs being stuck akimbo, so as to produce a most interesting series of angles and finely-developed elbows.[5]

To the modern eye Hunt's and Millais's pictures are far from flat. But Reach was not really reviewing the work: he was simply having a bit of fun. The damage, however, was done. This humorous but essentially non-malicious article triggered an extensive backlash that was less a real evaluation of the PRB's work than an expression of outrage at the arrogance of a group of youths who dared challenge the Academy dogma. And while Rossetti took a fair amount of bad press, it was Hunt and primarily Millais, the former child star, who got it in heaps.

The barrage was unrelenting. At first it was the art critics and those more specialized magazines and journals that catered for the intellectual élite that had their go. A pamphlet offered as a guide to the event noted:

> Especially noticeable is this unmeaning elaboration of whatever comes in his way; prepense choice of the worst instead of the best models, of pure ugliness for its own sake, is Mr Millais's interpretation of his passage from Zecharaiah, with its attenuated, distorted forms, enlarged knee-joints, the mean red-haired impersonation of the child-Christ, the serpentine leg and shoe-pinched ostentation of woe-begoneness throughout, the grimace and caricature of expression and sentiment, the exaggeration, puerility, essential aimlessness, but would be typicalness of the whole thing.[6]

But the abuse reached its nadir when Charles Dickens waded in. The lead article on the front page of the 15 June edition of Dickens's weekly journal *Household Words* was dedicated to savaging Millais and his brothers. The article begins, tongue in cheek and sodden with irony, by pointing out that in the fifteenth century a feeble artist called Raphael 'was fed with a preposterous idea of Beauty . . . in this very poor delusion, Artists have continued until this present nineteenth century, when it was reserved for some bold aspirants to "put it down" '. And then Dickens got down to the nitty-gritty of ripping Millais's work to shreds, with an attention to detail that matches the painter's own.

> You behold the interior of a carpenter's shop. In the foreground of that carpenter's shop is a hideous, wry-necked, blubbering, red-headed boy, in a bed-gown, who appears to have received a poke in the hand, from the stick of another boy with whom he has been playing in an adjacent gutter, and to be holding it up for the contemplation of a kneeling woman, so horrible in her ugliness, that

(supposing it were possible for any human creature to exist for a moment with that dislocated throat) she would stand out from the rest of the company as a Monster, in the vilest cabaret in France, or the lowest ginshop in England. Two almost naked carpenters, master and journeyman, worthy companions of this agreeable female, are working at their trade; a boy, with some small flavour of humanity in him, is entering with a vessel of water; and nobody is paying any attention to a snuffy old woman who seems to have mistaken that shop for the tobacconist's next door, and to be hope-lessly waiting at the counter to be served with half an ounce of her favourite mixture. Wherever it is possible to express ugliness of feature, limb, or attitude, you have it expressed.[7]

Even such anodyne publications as *The Ladies' Companion*, which normally dealt with botanical hints, tips on fashion and opinions about ladies' education, had a go: 'We have purposely refrained from giving any detailed account of the works of the Pre Raphaelite Brethren. As individuals we have great regard for some of them, and we grieve to see them bent on debasing the noble gift of genius which God has bestowed upon them.'[8]

It was only the *Illustrated London News*, ironically the very paper whose 'Table Talk' columnist had ignited the wholesale critical incineration of the PRBs, which stood up for the child prodigy that had graced its papers and enchanted its readers for so long. It reproduced Millais's *Carpenter's Shop* in its edition of 11 May and declared its 'pre-Raphaelism' its 'leading excellence'. But the *Illustrated London*'s support was not enough to salvage the boys from the cruelty of public humiliation when the tide was so against them. When Hunt and Millais visited the RA together, they encountered a group of students coming in specifically to laugh at Millais's picture. In addition, the Academicians were now cool to these men who had once been marked as protégés.

And then, of course, there were the commercial implications. Although Millais had secured a pre-sale on his *Christ in the House of his Parents*, the others had not been so lucky. Now the buyers went cold.

Rossetti, perhaps nervous of the Academy glare or arguably rather keen in somewhat unbrotherly spirit to present his offering before that of his colleagues, had not exhibited at the RA but had opted for the show at the National Institution, which opened earlier. Here he displayed his *Annunciation*. This depiction of the Virgin Mary, modelled on his sister Christina, as a thin, nervous adolescent in a scanty nightgown, terrified and dazed by the apparition before her, was a painting of huge power every bit as extraordinary as Hunt's and Millais's work.

Rossetti had offered it for sale for 50 guineas, having achieved 80 the previous year for his *The Girlhood of Mary Virgin*. But no one bit. Meanwhile, Hunt's *Druid* picture was returned from the Academy unsold, and a client who had commissioned some sketches from Hunt as preparatory steps towards an oil painting mysteriously forgot the commission.

The PRBs were now in dire straits. Rossetti, subsisting on thin air and looking like a ragman, wearing borrowed trousers from his brother and a brown overcoat from Ford Madox Brown, was now back living and working at home, having reneged on the rent for a share of Hunt's studio. Hunt, left high and dry with the Cleveland Street landlord thanks to Rossetti, had been turned out of his digs at least once and was now desperate for income. He found new digs near the river in Chelsea, in Prospect Place, just off Cheyne Walk. The family he lodged with turned the gaslights off at 10.30 p.m., much to the disgruntlement of the nocturnal workaholic Hunt.

With the exception of Millais, who was getting by, everyone was beginning to consider alternative jobs. There was talk of Hunt going back to the city or, even more unlikely, taking a job on a relation's farm. Rossetti, who had once explored but happily rejected the possibility of becoming a railway telegraphist, must have wondered if this fate now lay ahead of him once more.

The Millais family knew who was to blame for this disastrous reverse of fortunes. The label of sneak was firmly pinned to Rossetti's shabby lapels. The normally jolly and benign Mr and

Mrs Millais turned against 'the Italian'. The downturn was too much for Collinson and Woolner. The former abruptly resigned from the Brotherhood; the latter broke up a huge sculpture called *Generations*, which he had been working at on spec for months. Now that his membership of the Brotherhood had dissolved the possibility of securing a buyer for the work, he decided to join the gold rush and emigrate to Australia.

Nor did Lizzie escape unscathed. *The Athenaeum's* 'Fine Art Gossip' column suggested that each PRB 'sits down before some model in the selection of which he has taken no further account than as it may answer his desire to imitate the ugliness of some early master'[9] and *Blackwood's Magazine* also ridiculed the PRBs for their poor taste in mannequins, adding cruelly that they 'apparently select bad models, and then exaggerate their badness till it is out of all nature'.[10] And so Lizzie, who had staked her reputation in exchange for better prospects and perhaps a little fame, found she had been rewarded with no more than notoriety and saw her patrons in chaos. It looked as though her modelling career might already be over.

Effie and Ruskin left Venice at the end of March and were back in Park Street by the early summer in time for the exhibition season. Their last few days in Venice had been fraught and intense. Paulizza had lingered with them on the night before their departure until the last possible moment before breaking down in tears. Ruskin had embraced Paulizza's grief, hugging him and wishing him well. If the source of his pain was his feelings for Effie, then John did not appear affronted by this or even uneasy with it. The next day, as they were leaving and despite having said his goodbyes, Paulizza returned again with a final romantic gesture, a bouquet of camelias for Effie.

Back in London, the routine established in Venice was adapted. John would leave Effie in the morning and commute out of town to Denmark Hill, where he would enjoy the comfort of his childhood home and his old study. 'He says he will sometimes go out with me in the evening', Effie wrote to Rawdon Brown in Venice. 'I endeavoured to point out to him that he might shut himself up in his study here and then I might see him some time during the day, but he says he has no light in town nor his Turners and that I will soon find acquaintances and can take care of myself (which I think you rather doubt).'[11]

Ruskin did, however, attend the exhibitions. He went to the RA with the Scottish painter William Dyce, but his mind was elsewhere: his thoughts were all for the heritage of Venice, and he was not particularly interested in engaging with the current storm over the PRB. That he had read all the critics would have gone without saying, and perhaps this is why he chose to move disdainfully past Millais's picture without giving it much thought. But Dyce grabbed Ruskin's elbow and steered him back to the painting to argue its case. This was food for thought, but Ruskin would not enter into the fray quite yet.

Pretty, fashionable and chatty, Effie set about amusing herself and continued the social success she had enjoyed in Venice. Her letters are full of delight at meeting high society. She was presented at court, breakfasted with Lady Westminster and grew increasingly close to Lady Eastlake. But home alone she once again drew attention from dashing young men, just as she had in Venice. And although Effie was confident she could navigate her unusual circumstances and avoid unwanted speculation, the gossip began again. This time it involved another military man: Clare Ford.

Effie met Ford, a guardsman, at a dinner party in January 1851. He instantly latched onto her. Effie's defence in her relationship first with Paulizza and now with Ford was her propriety. She did socialize with these men, but nothing more. She was not technically adulterous. But that she invited their attentions and toyed with their attraction to her is undoubted. She was an arch-tease.

Rebutting Ford's improper approaches, she cast herself in the role of his saviour. He was a moral reprobate and, as such, needed taking in hand.

> The fact is that every woman he has been with has spoilt him and he has run into every sort of vice . . . he is particularly obliged to me for saying every thing disagreeable to him, keeping him from spending his money, drinking brandy with his coffee and smoking till three in the morning . . . I have nearly persuaded him to go and live by himself in Switzerland with a servant and get into regular hours and a healthy tone of mind. John helped me write a long letter to him.[12]

The inclusion of John in her liaison with Ford is another example of Effie's strategic thinking. Again her propriety is defended if her letters to this young man are written in conjunction with her husband.

But Ruskin's willingness somehow to encourage Effie's *risqué* behaviour was appearing increasingly perverse to the wider world. These little nuances did little to affect the bigger picture that was emerging about the Ruskin marriage. It was obvious that Ruskin was peculiar, and Effie was deserted and thus sought and enjoyed male company. The Ruskin 'arrangement' was also increasingly open to different interpretations. Was she deserted because of her behaviour? Or was the arrangement an even more scandalous one, designed to conceal some proclivity on John's part? Effie's brother George continued to hold a different theory: he felt sure Ruskin was trying to encourage his wife into an adulterous relationship with Ford that would enable the Ruskins to rid themselves of the troublesome addition to their family.

Although his picture did not sell at the RA show of 1850, and despite seeing other members of the Brotherhood throw in the towel, Mad determined to plough on. William Dyce, who was proving a good friend, recommended Hunt for a job restoring some wall paintings at Trinity House, home to the ancient corporation that acted as the General Lighthouse Authority. This made Hunt a guinea a day, and he even managed to get Fred Stephens on board as his assistant.

With at least some money now keeping him in bread and

butter, Hunt began his next large-scale painting. Once again he turned to a subject that had at its core love and abuse. From the start he knew who he wanted to model for the heroine of the piece, and that was Lizzie.

So Lizzie's next modelling assignment was to pose as Sylvia, from Shakespeare's *Two Gentlemen of Verona*. The scene that Hunt chose to depict is the moment that Sylvia's true love, Valentine, steps in and saves her from being raped by a less scrupulous admirer, Proteus.

That Lizzie's involvement with the PRB was compromising was not in doubt. At the end of 1850 Rossetti and Deverell took a grotty garret in Red Lion Square in Holborn for 20 shillings a week. Even here the landlord stipulated that 'models are to be kept under some gentlemanly restraint, "as some artists sacrifice the dignity of art to the baseness of passion" '.[13]

Deverell was particularly sensitive to Lizzie's predicament but dealt with it clumsily. It was he who was so often proclaiming and pitying the poor and abused, and it was he who saw Lizzie's beauty and had at one point begun to fall in love with her. Nevertheless, unable to negotiate awkward social situations, he still made Lizzie sit out on the balcony when his sisters came to visit the studio in Red Lion Square, so that the uncomfortable collision between gentlewomen and a model, with all the associations of her profession, could be avoided.

Whatever the reality of the situation, this is how Lizzie was seen by much of the wider world. Red Lion Square, Cleveland Street or, now, Prospect Place – wherever she knocked on the door, the curtain-twitchers of the neighbourhood would be wondering just how far her modelling commitments went.

Its associations with prostitution aside, modelling work was demanding. The PRBs shared the capacity to become so absorbed in their work and its detail that they easily lost sight of the demands on those sitting – or standing – before them. Fred Stephens remembered posing for Ferdinand in Millais's *Ferdinand Lured by Ariel*. For the picture, based on Shakespeare's *Tempest*, Stephens had to lean forward as though listening intently to the enticing words of the hovering sprite Ariel. To this end he stood bent forward over a stick for hours and became totally stiff by the end.

Hunt was a stickler for detail. For his Sylvia picture he himself sewed beads and sequins onto a dress for Lizzie so that he could paint the real things rather than rely on imagination. And that she would have had to hold a pose, like Stephens for Millais, was without doubt.

Although the shilling an hour was an important inducement, what began to emerge about Lizzie was that her motivation to model was rooted in something more profound. She put up with the superior looks of the respectable married women who saw her visit Hunt's studio, and she suffered the sore knees from kneeling as Sylvia for hours on end. She did all this because she loved being involved in art. Several of the PRBs described Lizzie as something more than a model: a true artist. Her artistic ability would soon come properly to light, but even early on there is a suggestion that she was instinctively unconventional in a way people with artistic sensibilities often are. Her clothes, for example, which she made herself, were self-consciously simple. And at a time when ladies' hair fashions were befuddling intricacies of plaits and ringlets, she wore her hair in loose bundles that fell softly around her face.

There was really only one other woman associated with the group that had anything like the same relationship with these young men, and similar poise, although she was undoubtedly from a different class and background. This was Rossetti's sister Christina. She too had modelled for the brothers, in spite of social convention. And she was writing poetry under a pseudonym for a literary magazine called *The Germ*, which the PRBs had ambitiously launched as part of their quest to rejuvenate English culture. If she was, by association, the established high priestess of the Pre-Raphaelite Brotherhood, Lizzie was quickly threatening to join her at the altar.

Christina had become engaged to James Collinson, although their engagement did not last much beyond his resignation from the group. Now suddenly the notion that Lizzie might become matrimonially attached to another PRB was raised – in jest at least.

John ('Jack') Tupper was a friend from the group's Academy days. His ambition was to be a sculptor, although to make ends meet he had taken up the post of anatomical draughtsman at Guy's Hospital in London. Like Deverell and Brown, he hovered around the PRBs. He also contributed to *The Germ*, which his father printed and published. (He sustained something of a loss when it collapsed after just four instalments.)

Tupper was particularly friendly with Hunt and called regularly at Prospect Place. During the painting of *Sylvia* he rarely found his friend without Lizzie Siddall at his side. One day, when he called with his father in tow, he must have made some sort of comment about the inseparability of Hunt and his model, because to his utter surprise Hunt revealed that he and Lizzie had just got married. Taken aback, Tupper asked for confirmation of this fact from Fred Stephens, who was also in the studio, and Fred confirmed that indeed Lizzie had become Mrs Hunt.

The PRBs were very boisterous and prankish at this time. Their letters are full of jokes, they talked in slang and called each other by nicknames, and they wrote limericks to one another. It is easy to imagine Hunt and Fred exploding into hysterics as the 'cadaver' (as Jack was known because of his sunken cheeks) and the 'baron' (as they called his father) left full of the news of Hunt's new status in life.

Quite how long the jest was maintained is unclear, but news of it reached Rossetti, who was uncharacteristically furious. 'Hunt and Stephens have been playing off a disgraceful hoax on poor Jack Tupper, by passing Miss Siddal upon him as Hunt's wife. The Baron was included as a victim', Rossetti wrote to his brother William on 3 September 1850. 'As soon as I heard of it however, I made the Mad write a note of apology at once to Jack.'[14]

Rossetti's fury is hard to fathom. It seems at surface to be on Tupper's behalf. However, a few lines of poetry that remained unpublished until after Rossetti's death, but which were dated by his brother to 1850, may reveal the cause of Gabriel's ire.

> Tender as dew her cheek's warm life;
> She was as simple as a wife,
> She was as white as lilies are.
> Her face was sweet and smooth and fair:
> Slender and very straight she was,
> And on her cheeks no paint might pass.
>
> Her fair hair was so long that it
> Shook, when she walked, about her feet:
> Eyes, nose and mouth, were perfect art,
> Exceeding pain is at my heart
> When I remember me of her.[15]

The lines, translated by Rossetti from the medieval French poem the *Roman de la Rose*, could have been written of Lizzie, if they had not in fact been conceived hundreds of years earlier. But their relevance to Miss Siddall is surely why Rossetti picked just these two stanzas out for translation. He was falling in love.

Hunt could see the root of Rossetti's anger. The slightly over-earnest tone of the letter of apology that Hunt wrote to Tupper was complemented by a sketch showing himself and Stephens contrite and weeping but with Rossetti and Lizzie as a couple of lovers in a boat under a crescent moon.

Lizzie must have gone along with the prank – she probably had little choice – but afterwards its implications hit home. Everyone was apologizing to Tupper for the deception, but no one was apologizing to her. Presumably the joke was particularly good because of the shocking inappropriateness of the match. A *frisson* of scandal heightened the lark. The fact that they had involved Lizzie in the practical joke in the first place presumed something about her. They would never have even dared involve a 'respect-able' woman such as Christina Rossetti or one of the Deverell girls in such a jape. Lizzie hated Hunt from this moment onwards, and her hatred for him would only deepen.

Fortunately for Lizzie, whether she had been boating with him or not, Rossetti was her true Valentine, waiting in the wings to save her from shame. And as 1851 dawned, so did new feelings for the Italian.

As a watery winter sun rose over a cold, grey London in 1851, Queen Victoria knew that it never set over her empire. Britain was at the height of its power. The rapidly expanding railways marked this advancement. Their web of connectivity was spreading daily. Between 1843 and the mid-1850s 2,000 miles of track grew to 8,000 miles. Effie and John could reach Perth by rail now, something they could not do in the years before their marriage; Brown and Emma could escape for their romantic, illegitimate, holidays at the seaside. This new phenomenon had nearly broken the finances of Mr George Gray, but it would soon indirectly contribute to the fortunes of the PRBs. It would also expand the sexual horizons of Hunt by providing an unexpected illicit encounter, and it had already captured the imagination of the great artist Turner, who had painted this new beast of progress searing through a canvas and bearing down on the onlooker in his *Rain, Steam, and Speed, The Great Western Railway*.

The Great Exhibition of the Works of Industry of All Nations was conceived in tribute to this new world of progress and power. Intended to show how industrial design could be enhanced by exposure to and marriage with art, it was the brainchild of Queen Victoria's husband, Prince Albert, the civil servant Sir Henry Cole and the great gardener, horticultural architect and entrepreneur Joseph Paxton. Together they imagined a palace of glass in Hyde Park on an unprecedented scale that would house both the industrial wonders and the artistic offerings of the empire and its international allies. This temple to man's ingenuity would occupy a staggering 19 acres. Huge trees and fountains would be encased in glass atria that at times would reach over 100 feet in height. It would have galleries and bridges, grand avenues and courts, and take over a fortnight to view.

Not surprisingly, the construction of this monster left London in a state of excited upheaval at the beginning of 1851. The effects of the energetic transformation of the capital into a modern metropolis were particularly evident in Mayfair, where Effie was living. She was in the habit of riding down Rotten Row, which cut through the park, but this was shut off because of building work. 'I wonder what Lord Clarendon would have said to such desecration', she grumbled, adding that 'Prince Albert's scheme is so unpopular that it may yet be removed to some other place and some of the most beautiful trees in the Park saved from the hatchet for a few more years'.[16]

Effie's hope for the beautiful trees was misplaced. A great number were felled to make way for this new wonder. One MP, Colonel Sibthorp, pointed out that 'The commissioners came like a thief in the night and cut down the most beautiful trees. A gentleman who lived near the Park and paid £110 ground rent for his house has told me that he was admiring the trees one evening before he went to bed, and when he got up in the morning to shave they were gone.'[17]

In tune with the great city around them, two of the three founders of the PRB were also feverishly working away on paintings for the next Royal Academy show. Hunt was now fastidiously working up the *Sylvia* with meticulous attention to detail, while Rossetti's brother William obligingly stood for Valentine.

Millais, more ambitiously, had decided to submit three pictures for the RA. One was a religious picture, *The Dove Returning to the Ark*, and the other two pictures were on topics of specific interest to women. *The Woodman's Daughter* was based on a poem by Coventry Patmore, which explored the fatal attraction between a young poor girl and a rich boy. The two were drawn together, but the relationship was doomed by the gap between their social positions. And then there was *Mariana*.

Johnnie based *Mariana* on Tennyson's poem of the same name. Just like Hunt's *Sylvia* and *The Woodman's Daughter*, the picture is about a woman whose true love is abused by society in the interests of social status or propriety. It tells the pitiful tale of a woman rejected by her fiancé when her dowry is lost in a shipwreck. Now valueless in a society where marriage must also bear financial reward as well as love and children, she waits by the window in the hope that perhaps her fortune will change and her lover appear.

Millais's picture shows the bored and depressed Mariana stretching from the weariness of her wait. The light shining through the window is autumnal, and brown leaves have blown into the room, indicating that she faces the unfulfilled life of spinsterhood. The little mouse is a detail from Tennyson's poem that Millais chose to include, but perhaps only because one such creature just happened to scurry across his studio floor while he was working on the picture. When it took refuge under his portfolio, he promptly trod on it to secure its modelling commitment. Otherwise, although the picture creates the same stagnant atmosphere as Tennyson's lines, it is not slavish to the poet's imagery.

The picture had plenty of resonance for its female contemporary audience, and testimony to this is William Rossetti's note that it became a favourite with the women visiting that summer's RA show. Millais's and Hunt's fascination with women and the woman's lot held huge appeal for the growing market of female consumers. The same *Ladies' Companion* that tut-tutted at the PRBs filled many of its pages with articles about marriage, money and the lot of the spinster, and this picture would have been quickly grasped by its readers.

Implicit in *Mariana* is the suicidal nature of the woman. And this dark aspect of the picture, reinforced by the ominous shadows that occupy the right-hand side of the canvas, may well have sent a shudder down the spines of the ladies looking at it. Women driven to suicide because of a change in circumstance were a familiar concern. One such woman had entered into the social mythology for her spectacularly public and flamboyant suicide just over a decade earlier. In 1838 Margaret Moyes had paid her sixpence and climbed the Monument in London, only to throw herself off it. This gesture had gripped the national press, which related the gruesome details of her body (its arm severed by a railing on descent) and followed the outcome of the inquest with extraordinary intensity.

Moyes, it was discovered, had been brought up by aspiring working-class parents to hope for a good marriage. But when her mother died, and her father's baking business was compromised by ill health, Margaret began to face a different future from the one she had expected. Illegality, sacrilege and social stigma were not enough to dissuade her that suicide was the best solution to her despair. Hell was, it seems, a better option than the kind of working life she might have to face. After the huge amount of attention and comment her actions invited nationwide, many high ledges in public places were roped off.

The significance of *Mariana* and its oblique reference to cases such as that of Moyes would not have been lost on Effie. She had seen a dowry disappear. Thankfully for her, when her father had revealed that he had lost all in his financial speculation, the Ruskins held firm and the marriage went ahead. For people like Lizzie Siddall, however, a dowry would never even have come into the equation. Although they may well have had a 'bottom drawer' full of linen, clothing and certainly, given the Siddall trade, household items, the idea of any income to be settled on them would have been almost certainly out of the question.

Some poor model had to stand for hours on end striking the pose of Mariana at her window while Millais lost himself in capturing her image. The discovery of Lizzie had whetted the PRBs' appetite for chance encounters with potential sitters. It had become something of a mission. Millais would nip out and scour the nearby Tottenham Court Road for 'stunners', as they were now referred to. Hunt was not beyond checking out the local gypsies for exotic-looking girls. Sometimes the PRBs would fish *en masse*, linking arms so that they filled the width of the pavement and then trawling through the unfortunate pedestrians using the footpath.

Whoever they plucked from the street found themselves at the centre of an incredibly concentrated focus. Millais was so fired up and intense when he was working on a canvas that he did not leave his studio. A combination of his nervous energy burning through calories and a reluctance to stop working even to eat meant that he had grown as thin as 'a paper-knife'.[18] When he weighed himself one day on some public scales in a railway station, even the guard was taken aback to see that despite his six feet he barely clocked nine stone.

But despite his incredibly slender frame and self-imposed solitary confinement, Millais remained driven and energetic. He was still painting in a temper. If anything, he had more energy than he could deal with. Fred Stephens remembered him stopping painting momentarily to do huge jumps in his studio when chums dropped by. The visitor in question would be asked to hold his arm out at shoulder height, and then Millais would take a run and leap over the arm – all this in a room that was just 19 feet by 20. Hunt, meanwhile, had a similar surfeit of pent-up energy, which would be released either in the boxing ring or against the punchbag.

In contrast to the zeal and activity of Millais and Hunt, who determined to swim against the tide of their detractors, Rossetti was sinking into apathy. Although it was his colleagues who bore the brunt of the press criticism, he had not been spared. His easily bruised confidence had been sorely hurt.

He could not settle. After returning to lodge at home Rossetti had found a studio on Newman Street above a dancing school, but when the dancing master defaulted on the rent, it was his subtenant, Rossetti, who had all his possessions seized. Then he moved to Red Lion Square with Deverell, the subsequent upheavals and transportations providing another excuse for not settling down to work. Demands on others for 'tin' were increased. He half-heartedly began a major work for the exhibition season but by February had abandoned it. Writing to Hunt in French, as he did occasionally for fun, he barely concealed his growing despondency. 'J'ai abandonné mon tableau et par conséquence l'idée d'exposer dans cette année. J'ai fait cela pour plusieurs raisons, la principale étant que je me sentais dégradé chaque jour en travaillant à une pareille cotise ... Ne me blèmes pas, je t'en prie.'[19]

By April everyone was getting ready for what would be the biggest and most ambitious exhibition season of the century. Onlookers walking around the site of the International Exhibition in Hyde Park were captivated by the glazing wagons being used to insert the glass panels into the Crystal Palace. As the building reached completion, Millais and Hunt used their last reserves of determination to put the finishing touches to their pictures for the RA. The former protégés of the Academy had been thoroughly slapped for their impertinent rebellion once. Within weeks now they would know whether the tide of public opinion would turn in their favour or whether they would suffer further catastrophes. The RA show of 1851 would make or break them.

But Rossetti had already given up. He felt that every one of his many talents had run dry: 'the waistcoat of poetry is quite threadbare', he confided to Jack Tupper. 'The breeches of Art have fared traditionally through "misplaced confidence" in PRB doctrines; the hat of cheerfulness has shrunk with the rain ... the shirt of self-respect has long needed the wash tub, till now I do not think it could be "got up" anyhow.'[20] He needed a new project, but he had not yet quite realized that she was already right under his nose.

The Great Exhibition opened its doors on 1 May 1851. Nearly 14,000 British and over 6,000 foreign exhibitors awaited a flocking crowd, some of whom had bivouacked in the park overnight to be at the front of the queue. The interior was richly decorated by Owen Jones in red, light blue, yellow and white. Three large elm trees were left growing in the main arched transept, along with smaller groups of trees some of which formed centrepieces in the restaurants.

Special policemen were at hand to be of service and keep the peace as visitors entered through the three main doors to witness the wonders inside. If you entered through the south door, a gigantic glass fountain lay ahead marking the centre of the building. The route to this focal point was flanked by groups of sculpture and tropical plants. From the fountain you could look east towards an American organ surmounted by a huge eagle. If one headed west from the fountain, one would pass the Indian court, as well as displays from Africa, Canada, the West Indies and the Cape of Good Hope. There was a medieval court and an English sculpture court, as well as courts representing the wares of Birmingham and Sheffield. There were avenues devoted to hardware, agricultural machines, mineral products, cotton, leather and fur. You could see silk being woven and lace being made. There were altars to paper and stationery, representations from Persia, Greece, Turkey and Egypt. In the Austrian section you could wonder at gorgeous furniture, and to get to the Russian display of huge ornamental vases one would pass through doors carved from solid malachite. And, of course, there was a section devoted to the railways, with engines whirring and steam spouting.

Within a few days of the exhibition's opening the nation was gripped by a feverish desire to see these treasures. On 26 May railways reported a 100,000 swell in ticket sales to London, on that day alone. Colonel Sibthorp was again moved to complain about the venture, noting that such was its magnetism that 'the poor of this country had been seduced to come up to this Exhibition. All that they had saved and all they could borrow has been in many cases spent in this foolish journey; and I know I speak facts when I state that not only have they borrowed money but pawned clothes to enable them to come up to this "World's Fair".'[21]

It was not just British countrymen and -women who were pouring into their capital. The city was full of foreigners, and so special polyglot policemen now roamed the street ready to assist bewildered tourists. While the exhibition itself attracted some 6 million visitors between May and October, with an average of 40,000 and a peak of nearly 110,000 people a day passing between its glass walls, all of London's tourist spots benefited from the influx. The Royal Academy was no exception, with attendance of the summer show swelling from 96,944 in the previous year to 136,820.[22] British art had never been more under the spotlight.

Ruskin bought Effie a season ticket to the Great Exhibition, which allowed her to attend the opening, although she did so unaccompanied by her husband, who had begun writing *The Stones of Venice* and had placed himself on a strict schedule. Ruskin did accompany Effie to see the new RA show, however, with exclusive tickets to the preview. This time Ruskin paid more attention to Millais's pictures. He was instantly struck by *The Dove Returning to the Ark*. While members of the press flocked around the picture with their notebooks, hungry for more material to decry to a public that had thoroughly enjoyed being outraged by the PRBs a year earlier, Ruskin remained shtum. Heedless of public opinion, he decided that the work was good. In fact, he decided to buy it.

While Ruskin began his inquiries into the price of the work, the critics put their pens to paper. At this crucial juncture the PRBs had at least one ally on their side. William Michael Rossetti was now the art critic for *The Spectator*, and he and Gabriel wrote a review that tried to make up for every brickbat thrown in the past. The *Daily News* also gave a good notice.

But *The Times* was as bad as ever, as were the majority of publications who had hurled mud at the PRBs twelve months earlier. And once again the missiles were directed at Millais above anyone else. Such was his growing infamy that the popular satirical magazine *Punch* now sought to caricature his work. Poor old Mariana was depicted like a lollipop with a balloon head. Millais was now even receiving personal threats, with one eminent Academician warning the former protégé that, should they meet in the street, he would be roundly snubbed.

Ruskin was disappointed to find that Millais had pre-sold the picture he wanted and was already £150 better off thanks to the loyal patronage of a Mr Combe from Oxford. But if the weight of his wallet could not support this young artist under fire, there was

MARIANA IN THE MOATED GRANGE

'Mariana' (*Punch*, 1851). *Punch* magazine's willingness to poke fun at
Millais's work also indicated the artist's increasing celebrity

of course another way in which Ruskin could transform the fortunes of this band of brothers. Idiosyncratic he may well have
been, and leading a personal life that was beginning to confound
society for sure, but Ruskin was perceived as a powerful, influential
man and a key opinion-former. And so when he settled himself in
his old study in Denmark Hill and began to write a letter to *The
Times* in defence of the Pre-Raphaelite Brotherhood, few would
have doubted that the brothers' fortunes were about to turn.

He had never met these young men – he had only recently
taken serious note of their work – but as far as he was concerned,
rather than being the downfall of British art, they were 'a school
of art nobler than the world has seen for three hundred years'.[23]

Ruskin wrote to *The Times* not once but twice. His praise was not unqualified: he did pick some holes in the work, not least in the choice of models, noting that 'Sylvia is not a person who Proteus or anyone else would have been likely to fall in love with'. Coming from a man whose own successes in the amorous domain were somewhat suspect, this was a comment that was probably best ignored, but it was not. Hunt noted it closely and determined to repaint elements of Sylvia. This must have hurt Lizzie, who to date had received nothing but negative notes from the press.

Nevertheless as soon as Ruskin's hand was shown, and seen to be generally offering golden praise, the boys knew that things would look up for them. The relief soon became elation. Not wanting to seem too desperate, Johnnie and Mad waited a couple of weeks before writing to Ruskin to thank him heartily for his support. They debated whose address to put on the letter and concluded that Millais's would be more appropriate, since Gower Street was far more salubrious than Hunt's misnamed Prospect Place. This seemingly innocent decision had ramifications more serious than anyone could have ever imagined.

It would have taken perhaps half an hour for a boy to take a letter from Gower Street to Park Street, but the letter no doubt sat unopened for several hours before Ruskin returned late from his daily commute to Denmark Hill. His response was, however, spontaneous. The very next day he would forgo Denmark Hill and set out to meet Millais and Hunt.

Effie, much in need of her husband's society, accompanied Ruskin on his jaunt to Gower Street. But when they knocked at the door, they found only one PRB at home. This was, of course, Millais. And as Millais and Effie came face to face they realized they had met before, some five years earlier.

Effie had been seventeen and had been staying at Ewell Castle, near Epsom in Surrey, in the care of her parents' friends the Gadesdens. Millais, a lanky sixteen-year-old, had been staying near by with the Lemprieres, family friends from Jersey. One evening the two youngsters ended up at the same dance at the Castle. Millais was instantly attracted to Effie and rather boldly asked to be introduced to her. But when the introduction was made, she haughtily rejected his advances.

Now their paths crossed again, under very different circumstances. Millais may well have still been lanky, but he was impressively tall and handsome. Unlike his colleagues, his dress was sharp and impeccable. He was at the height of a notoriety for his work that was now likely to turn to a greater fame than that he had enjoyed as a child. Ruskin was impressed by his draughtsmanship and naturalism. But perhaps Effie could see in his work that instinctive empathy with womankind that was so lacking in her own husband.

Ruskin immediately whisked Millais away for dinner with him and his wife at Park Street. For the next week it seems Millais and the Ruskins were inseparable. He went to Denmark Hill to be introduced to John's parents. He joined Ruskin for breakfast. For Millais it must have felt – from a professional perspective at least – like a dream. Quite what opportunity Ruskin saw in Millais beyond patronage is uncertain. He wondered whether Millais would be interested in accompanying the Ruskins to Switzerland at some point.

But the flurry of socializing with Millais was relatively short-lived that summer, and Switzerland would have to wait. The Ruskins were preparing to head off to Venice for the winter again, and Millais was preparing a trip of his own. In 1847 the London–Brighton line has been extended, allowing Londoners unprecedented access to the Surrey countryside. And so now, four years later, Millais and Hunt planned to head for Ewell, the very place where Millais had first met Effie.

Johnnie and Mad were beginning to feel frustrated with Rossetti. Over the last year he had displayed an utter inability to start anything, let alone finish it. He had become increasingly unreliable and moody. They were even beginning to wonder whether he still deserved to be part of the Brotherhood that he had helped found.

What is more, Rossetti was now spending more and more time

with Lizzie. While Hunt and Millais had been locked away working and then facing the barrage of the press alone, Rossetti had been doing nothing other than sketching her – although with little apparent aim in sight. He was beginning to get proprietorial over her and to encourage her to reserve her favours. Where once she had been the Brotherhood's shared mascot, she was now driving a wedge in their masculine unity.

Millais must have seen the opportunity to reprise the intimate friendship he had once shared with Hunt and reaffirm not so much the Pre-Raphaelite Brotherhood as the Pre-Rossetti Brotherhood. Although Ruskin's intervention on behalf of the cause had injected a good deal of optimism, Hunt was still looking for a buyer for *Sylvia*. Johnnie had the chance to show the true mettle of his friendship and affection for Mad. He handed over a chunk of his savings to ensure that Hunt would not have to give up at the very last hurdle. If Rossetti had once come between Johnnie and Mad, they were now undoubtedly back together again.

Thus Rossetti was left to stew in the stinking heat of a London summer. Ewell, by contrast, was blissful. Hunt wrote a meticulous description of this rural village with its babbling brook. The little stream began with a 'fount in its slab-formed cradle at the entrance of the village' and then grew, 'carolling along a pebble-strewed channel into a shallow pool crossed by a flat bridge, whence by the quiet searcher might be seen red-spotted trout poised in mid water'; eventually the river passed mills before discovering meadows where it 'revelled in freedom, ofttimes taking a double course around mounds of earth well furnished with flourishing growth'.[24]

Unable to find suitable accommodation in the village itself, the two rented a cottage in nearby Kingston. This was two miles from the spot Millais had chosen to paint and four miles from Hunt's location. So they got up at six, were working by eight and then tramped back home for supper at seven in the evening. Their rural location quickly suggested their next major subjects. Hunt would paint a rural shepherd tempted away from his flock by an alluring woman. Millais would also have a woman at the heart of his work – but rather than a temptress, he wanted to paint a woman destroyed by love who had drowned herself in a stream.

And so Millais sat under a brolly for days on end with nothing to sustain him other than a mug so he could drink Ewell water. The old days of boyish companionship were back. In the evenings he and Hunt would play cricket. They delighted in their daily tales of encounters with farmers or local girls. Millais got into trouble with a farmer for trespassing in a field and destroying the hay. Hunt was certain that fellow lodgers were eating their supply of butter. Millais was given a rat, which he put in the river to paint and noted that after four hours the poor things looked like a drowned kitten. Hunt employed a boy to hold down sheep that insisted on moving. They invited Rossetti down, but perhaps were relieved when he failed to show.

With the landscape detailed, sketched and studied over the course of that glorious summer, all they were going to need come the autumn were the right models to place in it. Hunt had found a local girl who might suit as his temptress. And Millais was wondering whether Lizzie would sit for him.

Lizzie had not received an ounce of praise for her image, which she had given so willingly to the Brotherhood. But Millais knew that he could now change this. His confidence was high, and his technical skills were more finely honed than ever before. In his mind's eye he now had a picture so exquisite and moving, so tragic and beautiful, that he felt sure it could not fail. He knew that he could find the incarnation of this woman that would unlock the qualities that Deverell, Hunt and Rossetti could see in her but had so far failed to transfer to canvas. He wanted to depict Lizzie as one of Shakespeare's most tragic heroines, who, rejected by her true love, Hamlet, sinks into a madness born from maltreatment. Millais wanted to paint *Ophelia*.

5

Ophelia

I F YOU WANTED to catch a glimpse of *Ophelia*, you had to wait.
When it went on show in the summer of 1852, the picture,
which is not large, was attended by a long, slow-moving file of
eager viewers. The queue remained constantly swollen from the
moment the Academy doors were opened in the morning until
their bolts were firmly slammed back into their holes in the
evening. There was a perpetual push and shove, with crinolines
and hoops pressing against one another as everyone wanted to
lean in towards the canvas and get as close a possible to see.

Some people were moved on by the press of the crowd, but,
still feeling the need to gaze longer at the haunting apparition,
they would rejoin the back of the line again and wait for another
precious opportunity to hold the picture in their eye.

The image of Lizzie Siddall as the Shakespearean heroine was
mesmerizing: her pale blue eyes staring into mid-distance and her
mouth half open; her dress billowing up around her and her red
hair like Medusa's snakes floating out into the cold, dark blue
waters that at any second were about to engulf her.

The detail of the picture was hypnotizing. It drew the viewers
in and held them close as the tiniest brushstrokes revealed Lizzie's
blonde, unblinking eyelashes caught in the sunlight and traced
each hair of her pale eyebrows. Her cheeks, not yet blued by the
water around her, are flushed with a pale blush. Her fingertips are
exquisitely pink, hovering above the water, votive. She is an offering to some watery god who now gently but greedily embraces
her, ready to pull her down into his river bed.

All around her are the remnants of Ophelia's sacrifice. The flowers she was gathering before succumbing to her new watery lover have been gently teased from her hands by the river's eddies and ripples and are now being drawn downstream. Some pinks and wild garlic are still just held in the cradle of her cupped palm, but poppies, irises and pansies are already drifting away with the current.

In painting *Ophelia* Millais, at just twenty-two years of age, created one of the most iconic images in British art. Ruskin's predictions had been vindicated. Everything came together in this one picture. The detail and realism for which Millais had been so criticized now seemed wholly appropriate in delivering the minutely observed natural world framing and devouring Ophelia. The bright colours and particularly lush greens that had outraged the Academy when he had submitted earlier pictures such as *Ferdinand Lured by Ariel* were now perfectly depicting the vibrancy and colour of spring.

Choosing to focus on just one figure, he managed to harness the almost translucent other-worldliness that his colleagues who had flirted with Lizzie had glimpsed in her but had failed to deliver. And yet Millais, who had never shown a personal interest in the shop girl, was the one who grasped the innate sadness and resignation in this young woman and had the skill to convey it.

William Michael Rossetti, years later, remembered what the Pre-Raphaelites had looked for in their models: 'living people who, by refinement of character and aspect, may be supposed to have some affinity with those personages [that the painter intends to portray] – and, when he has found such people . . . he ought, with substantial though not slavish fidelity, to represent them as they are.'[1] Millais could see tragedy already at the core of Lizzie's personality. All he had to do was paint around it. No subject could have been better designed for this girl, and no girl could have posed better for the subject.

Death was a subject that had pervaded Millais's exhibition work. *Lorenzo and Isabella*, *The Carpenter's Shop* and *Mariana* are all doom-laden. He had rehearsed his fascination with dead women further in other sketches and studies. The Tate owns a small oil sketch called *The Artist Attending the Mourning of a Young Girl*, which depicts Millais himself standing over the open coffin of a young woman. Another sketch called *St Agnes of Intercession* was based on a story written for the Brotherhood by Rossetti. It tells of a woman who dies while her husband paints her – the husband continues the portrait in memoriam, his wife's corpse before him. And yet another drawing, *The Disentombment of Queen Matilda*, features Calvinists desecrating the tomb of Matilda, the wife of William the Conqueror, and brutally breaking open her coffin.

The extraordinary potency of Millais's *Ophelia* enraptured the public and silenced the critics. As *The Times* had predicted a couple of years earlier, art was in the domain of the people now, and the people were its judge. The exhibition-goers expressed their adoration of this new goddess in no uncertain terms.

A few of the old guard critics still tried their hand, but in vain. With little ammunition the *Illustrated London News* called the picture absurd. 'Everybody knows that if a person falls into the water backwards, the head has a tendency to sink first', the paper's critic suggested, grasping at straws, '. . . that it would sink the faster if the heels were buoyed up by the clothes, or otherwise'.[2]

But others did the honourable thing and capitulated. Perhaps most telling is the column written in *Punch*. Where, more than anywhere, one might expect to find the author in combative and satirical spirit, his defences were laid down.

> Before two pictures of Mr. Millais I have spent the happiest hour that I have ever spent in the Royal Academy Exhibition. In those two pictures I find more loving observation of Nature, more mastery in the reproduction of her forms and colours, more insight into the sentiment of our greatest poet, a deeper feeling of human emotion, a happier choice of a point of interest, and a more truthful rendering of its appropriate expression, than in all the rest of those eight hundred squares of canvas put together . . .
>
> Talk as you like, M'Gilp, eminent painter, to your friend Mr.

Squench, eminent critic, about the needless elaboration of those water mosses, and the over making-out of the rose-leaves, and the abominable finish of those river-side weeds matted with gossamer, which the field botanist may identify leaf by leaf. I tell you, I am aware of none of these. I see only that face of poor drowning Ophelia. My eye goes to that, and rests on that, and sees nothing else, till – buffoon as I am, mocker, joker, scurril-knave, street-jester by trade and nature – the tears blind me, and I am fain to turn from the face of the mad girl to the natural loveliness that makes her dying beautiful.[3]

Finally, after all the mudslinging and abuse, the Pre-Raphaelite Brotherhood was vindicated and its model elevated to the status of a star.

Although *Ophelia* sealed Lizzie's fame amid an appreciative public, it did not seal her determination to continue modelling. If anything, it hardened her resolve to stop modelling. The whole history of the *Ophelia* painting had, after all, been fraught with problems.

A year earlier, when Hunt and Millais set off to renew their friendship in Ewell, leaving Rossetti to wallow in London, it had been with Lizzie that the once vivacious and ambitious Rossetti sought solace. In their own way they were both bruised by the other PRBs. Lizzie was becoming increasingly sensitive to her treatment by the Brotherhood, and Rossetti was quietly smarting from the new turn of events. Hunt and Millais had been noticed by Ruskin; Millais had even been befriended by him. Their determination and resolve had won through. Rossetti meanwhile had flunked. At the crucial moment when Fortune turned, he had failed to show a single picture. The movement he had thrown his entire energy into was suddenly breaking through, and he had given up on it, too soon.

The symptoms of his depression were clear. He was upset by Ruskin's piquant omission of his contribution to Pre-Raphaelitism. An observation that Ruskin was not only writing to *The Times* but was also about to publish a pamphlet on the PRBs is marked with a certain bitterness. 'Have you seen that Ruskin advertises a pamphlet on "Pre-Raphaelitism"', he wrote to his friend William Bell Scott. 'It will no doubt be of much service to us, though I fear that I may probably miss any personal mention, as I do not suppose Ruskin ever went to the Exhibition where I exposed myself.'[4]

A few days later Rossetti's sense of neglect had made him ill. He began to swing between utter indulgent despair and rather pathetic attempts to get back in the game. One day he would be writing to Deverell that he would 'cut Art as it is too much trouble',[5] the next day he would find himself writing to Hunt and Millais like the little boy left out in the playground. He had got wind of some news that Mr Combe, who had pipped Ruskin to buying Millais's *Dove Returning to the Ark*, had commissioned the duo to paint religious pictures in Palestine, and a trip to the Middle East was being plotted.

'Why did you not mention this to me on Sunday?' Gabriel asked hurt and dejected. 'I hope to God ... that you are not going to start before the next exhibition; in order that I may at least have a chance, by the sale of the picture I shall then have ready, of accompanying you on your journey ... Should this not happen at all ... I feel that it would seem as if the fellowship between us were taken from me, and my life rejected.'[6]

Rossetti was not a drinker at this point in his life, but he keenly sought some self-medication to soothe his pain. Lizzie, it seems, became his drug. Gradually the two of them became inseparable. One imagines them licking their wounds together as they used a growing infatuation with one another as a shield against the world. Even the name Gabriel began to use for Lizzie has the infantile ring of the kind of pet name a child might have for its nanny or vice versa. 'The Sid', as she had been formerly referred to by the PRBs, became Gabriel's 'Guggum'.

With Hunt and Millais away, Rossetti became obsessed and greedy about Lizzie. He did not want her to sit to anyone else now, partly for the sake of her already damaged reputation and partly for purely selfish reasons. He did, however, want her to sit for him. She began modelling for his next picture, *The Return of Tibullus to Delia*. This picture is based on the little-known Latin poet Tibullus, who wrote love poetry to his mistress Delia. Rossetti became infatuated with this icon of love, a woman who was adored but never totally accessible since she was married to another man. He sketched Lizzie, her eyes shut in reverie and her head leaning back.

They became cocooned together in a world built not on reality but on dreams and chivalric fantasy. Gabriel began to feed Lizzie's latent sense that she was owed a better lot in life. In 1851 Isaac Singer invented a sewing machine that would fast revolutionize hat shop life. But despite this, Gabriel persuaded Lizzie to give up Mrs Tozer's establishment, which she duly did. He would save her, he promised her. He would educate her, share with her everything he knew. He would be the knight who would come to her aid.

Millais's request for Lizzie to model for *Ophelia* must have seemed like an unwelcome intrusion into the intimate world into which Rossetti and Lizzie were retreating. But it was hard for Rossetti and Lizzie to refuse, and without an income from the hat shop there were obvious financial incentives to consider. It was just about the last modelling commitment Lizzie ever made to anyone other than her new lover. As the painter and PRB buddy Charles or 'Charlie' Collins discovered a little later when he approached Lizzie, further requests were declined with extreme frostiness.

From the moment she agreed to pose for *Ophelia*, a kind of curse seemed to descend on the project. First her scheduled sittings had to be delayed because of the sudden illness and death of her older brother Charles. Then when she did return, grief-stricken and in mourning, Millais dressed her in an old, dirty antique dress he had found and immersed her in a tin bath. It was wintertime. Millais did pay some heed to her 'comforts': he placed oil lamps under the bath to try and keep the water warm, but the lamps went out. Millais, absorbed in his work, failed to notice.

Like Fred Stephens before her, stuck prone for hours on end while Millais entered a state of trance-like concentration, Lizzie was left floating in her icy bath, in a house without the modern convenience of central heating, in a winter noted in Millais's letters for its extreme cold. Despite this, Lizzie, ever the proud professional model, did not complain. But unlike Fred, whose stiff back could be relaxed by wine and humour, when Lizzie was released from her bath, little could warm her. Millais's carelessness had far more serious ramifications.

After the session a hullabaloo ensued. Lizzie became seriously ill with what Millais's son later described as a 'cold' but could well in reality have been something closer to bronchitis or pneumonia. Her father attempted to sue Millais for £50 for loss of earnings and doctor's bills. Millais settled for a lesser sum, and the matter was resolved, but the incident marked a change in Lizzie's health. She was never the same again.

It was not just Lizzie's health that was transformed at this moment. A new side of her began to emerge. As if baptized by her experience, Lizzie would no longer be the suppliant victim of the Brotherhood's pranks and ambitions. She would become quietly strident. She had Gabriel now, and with him she must have realized that she could become something more than a working girl.

Writing after his brother's death, William Michael Rossetti claimed that Lizzie and Gabriel 'probably' became engaged 'before the end of 1851'.[7] It is odd that a brother, with whom Gabriel was very close, should be so vague about such a significant matter. But much of William's role after his sibling's death seems to have been to tidy up his reputation. Nevertheles, categorizing Gabriel and Lizzie's relationship within the terms overtly acceptable to the Victorian definitions of respectability was a tough call.

For Gabriel, a middle-class man from a down-at-heel, immigrant, but still recognizably professional bourgeois family, proposing to marry a low-grade working girl and model would have been considered a social scandal. It was an unconventional step that both Walter Deverell and Hunt had to date carefully avoided.

Brown would eventually take it, but only after he had somehow mitigated his choice of spouse by 'educating' Emma Hill, already the mother of his illegitimate offspring.

Enjoying a close relationship outside the bounds of respectable marriage was equally scandalous. Although Henry Mayhew revealed that at this time common-law marriage was widely practised among the poor, it was almost unheard of among the elevated classes. Those bold, unconventional people who chose to live together out of wedlock, such as Mary Anne Evans – otherwise known as the novelist George Eliot – and her philosopher and critic lover, George Henry Lewes, were simply considered social pariahs by all but a very few liberal-minded folk.

So what Rossetti did, it seems, was fudge. He was, after all, a paradoxical man who was at once ready to fly in the face of convention and yet fearful of criticism and rejection. There is no evidence that he did make a formal proposal to Lizzie. She did not even meet his mother until the mid-1850s, and Hunt in his memoirs claims that they had not become engaged by the time he returned from a trip to the Holy Land in 1856. Lizzie is not referred to overtly as Rossetti's lover in his letters for another year.

What is clear is that Rossetti somehow managed to circumnavigate a formal engagement – for the breach of which Lizzie's family could have sued him for compensation, and the public announcement of which would have caused social ripples – while also entering into a serious, close relationship. And he and Lizzie began slowly but surely to present themselves as lovers, without announcements or explanations.

Lizzie, thin and delicate after the tin bath episode, became like a spectre quietly floating around Rossetti. She would just be there whenever anyone called at his studio, quietly disappearing as the company arrived, slipping back into the shadowy detail of their intimate domestic arrangements. Rossetti, meanwhile, did what he could to keep the relationship secret, letting even his closest friends in on the situation only by degrees or simply allowing people to make their own conclusions.

Rossetti's friend the poet and painter William Bell Scott described how the arrangement worked. At one point Rossetti was using 'a painting room or study' in the garden of a friend's cottage in Hampstead. Scott recalls going to visit him in this little summer house, which was 'covered with ivy', and 'approached by outside wooden steps'.

> I found myself in the romantic dusk of the apartment face to face with Rossetti and a lady whom I did not recognize . . . He did not introduce her; she rose to go. I made a little bow which she did not acknowledge; and she left. This was Miss Siddall. Why he did not introduce her I cannot say . . . for myself, I had not yet heard of such a person as Miss Siddall.[8]

By consciously failing to be overt about their status Rossetti and Lizzie defied any conventional response from those around them. And so in a rapidly modernizing world their silence about their relationship made them a very unconventional and modern couple indeed. Lizzie was becoming a new kind of woman.

Effie and Ruskin missed all the fuss over *Ophelia*. They had wintered in Venice. This time Effie had travelled without a female companion, and the couple had rented a house in the city rather than stay in hotel rooms.

But the jolly Venice of balls and parties was no more. For a start, Paulizza had become ill and died. Yet despite the loss of her former companion, Effie soon got into swing of society again, and Ruskin resumed his reclusive work pattern. But the sojourn at Venice was less agreeable than before. Although during their previous stay they had been liberated from the prying interests of John's parents, now the interfering tentacles of the Ruskins senior managed to reach that distant location. Effie's and John's expenses suddenly became a matter of scrutiny. And with Effie now running a house rather than relying on the facilities of a hotel, Mrs Ruskin began to send unwelcome advice to her daughter-in-law in the form of meal planners and domestic and culinary instructions.

Even the friendly, liberal Venetian society that they enjoyed before seemed less accommodating now. Their friendship with Rawdon Brown became strained. The expat Brown and his circle were no longer so fond of Effie. 'I think they have got some idea about us that I can't make out', Effie noted in a letter to her mother.[9]

Effie's peculiar reception from Brown came to a head in a particularly unpleasant incident that Effie again recounted to her mother. On Tuesdays and Thursdays Effie was in the habit of going to St Mark's Square to listen to the band that played there. She had become tired of the noise in the square and the attention she received from other promenaders and so got into the habit of sitting out of sight in a quiet spot on the open gallery of the Doge's Palace. One day Brown found her there, quite by chance, and openly accused her of waiting for someone. His implication was obvious. Was she engaged in a clandestine relationship? If not, she was completely failing to grasp the impression her behaviour was giving, and this in itself was scandalous.

The fact that Effie too recounted this embarrassing and offensive exchange to her mother could be taken as a good defence of her innocence. However, during the second trip to Venice she had managed to fill the gap left by Paulizza with new playfellows. Two men secured their place as favourites in Effie's society: Franz, Count Thun, an Austrian captain, and a Mr Foster, a British man working for the Austrian military. They became regular playmates, and the affection of the two men for Mrs Ruskin was noted when Thun bought Effie a little dog, which she called Zoe.

Ruskin himself noted: 'I am pleased with the young men; they are so highbred – so light hearted – and so fond of each other, as well as desirous in every way to oblige us. Effie is a great catch for them, as they have no ladies in society here except one or two wives of the generals.'[10]

Effie and Ruskin, as always happy to endorse his wife's friendships with other men, took a trip to Verona with Thun and Foster at the end of their continental stay. Before they set off home they returned briefly to Venice to wrap up a few matters, but having given up the tenancy on their rented casa, they stayed in a hotel.

Here the story sours. Effie's jewels were stolen from her hotel room. There was no sign of forced entry, and the conclusion was that whoever had taken the jewellery had access to Effie's company and her private room. Foster became the chief suspect in the case. Effie and Ruskin shared the general consensus that Foster was the culprit, without sharing the general conclusion that only an unusually intimate relationship with Effie would have left her so exposed to the villain.

Their suspicions were investigated by the police and military, to no conclusion, and the Ruskins began to suspect the latter of a cover-up. With the whiff of scandal in the air Effie and John followed the advice of friends and left Venice before matters became more unpleasant. It was not a moment too soon. When they reached Verona, Ruskin was surprised by a visit from an Austrian officer, bearing a message from Thun. Thun wanted Ruskin to explain why he had fled Venice and to deny in writing that he suspected Mr Foster of theft. If Ruskin refused either of these matters, he must face Thun in a duel. Ruskin did neither and returned home.

When the pair arrived back in London in the summer of 1852, the gossip about the theft and the duel had preceded them. They found their reception in London society mixed. Certain parties and events that they would normally attend were suddenly over-subscribed and tickets unavailable, something to which Ruskin's parents were only too sensitive. On 2 August John James Ruskin wrote to Effie's father: 'There was a great party of 1200 at the Rooms of the Royal Academy last Wednesday – John and Effie should have been there. Sir Charles Eastlake said no tickets were left . . . I observe that Samuel Rogers where their card was left 14 days ago and who is at home – does [sic] no notice of them.'[11]

At the heart of this changing social attitude to the couple was the story circulating that Effie had been inappropriately linked with Foster, and Ruskin's accusation of him was born from jealousy as much as anything else.

The incident escalated when, on 21 July, those members of the public in the habit of digesting the popular *Morning Chronicle* at their breakfast tables were able to read about the story and its implications in full:

> An affair which happened at Venice a few weeks since is here the theme of general conversation. An English gentleman of some literary fame, who has been spending the winter at Lagune city with his lady, had accused an Austrian officer (an Englishman in the Austrian service) of having appropriated to himself some valuable jewellery, the property of his wife. The officer, after being tried by court-martial, has been declared innocent, and set at liberty. An unknown hand is said to have dropped the missing jewellery into that of the sentry or guard at the officer's door. This complicated and mysterious affair has created an immense sensation here, as the parties are well known.[12]

'In the Mg Chronicle of 21 July and in the Church and State Gazette of 23 July are paragraphs with false statements of the affair at Venice, making my son the Accuser – and not the police', a frantic Mr Ruskin explained to Mr Gray.

> I hope you have got all particulars from Effie as you will hear many remarks and it is very important to put the facts clearly before the people . . . for we have not good people's remarks to meet but all that scandal and malice can suggest, and from the way it appears in the papers – some will say – the Lady has been visiting the Barracks and merely dropped her jewels and that her Husband, angry and jealous, has accused an officer . . . Mrs Ruskin has been very unwell since their return and fears a serious effect on their Character – I feel it less because I have been always prepared for something though I got displeased about a Dog being bought, Given by Count Thun.[13]

Mr Ruskin's concerns were too late. Effie's reputation was now undoubtedly tarnished, and the Ruskins as a couple were now seen as sufficiently tacky to warrant the intrusions of the popular press.

Effie Ruskin had a reputation to lose. Some women had never had one in the first place. One such woman was Emma Watkins. Her brief but significant brush with the PRB occurred during that blissful summer of 1851, when Hunt and Millais were together in Ewell. While Hunt was sitting in these bucolic surroundings, he noticed a couple of sisters marching across a field. One had long red wavy hair – a little like Lizzie – but rather than having a serene angelic face, this girl had a broad, knowing face and ruddy complexion.

This was Emma Watkins. A girl from the very lower echelons of society, she lived in Kingston with her mother and brother. The latter scraped a living by picking groundsel and selling it on for bird food.

Hunt wanted to paint an allegorical picture showing a shepherd being tempted away from his flock by a sexually experienced and clearly sexually available field girl. A similarly ruddy-faced shepherd would lean over the field girl, reaching for an apple symbolically placed in her lap. Perhaps Hunt's interest in sexual temptation mirrored his own frustrations and the growing dialogue in his mind between his highly charged sexuality and his increasingly strong sense of propriety. This picture, *The Hireling Shepherd*, was eventually shown at the same exhibition as *Ophelia*.

Emma, with her rural frankness and lack of temerity when it came to the opposite sex, was ideal. When Hunt first approached her in the field, she could hardly have taken his proposition seriously. If she had, she would surely have jumped at the opportunity of the shilling an hour models could traditionally charge. But she did not follow up his proposal, and Hunt himself had to track her and her family down and negotiate with her mother.

As Millais was freezing poor Lizzie in his tin bath, Emma Watkins began making a daily journey from Kingston to Chelsea to sit for Hunt. She would come along with a sailor as chaperone, loosely described as her fiancé. The expense and impracticality of this significant daily haul for the pair became too much. After just two chaperoned visits, the sailor let his future wife travel solo to Hunt. And after several further solitary commutes Emma pleaded with Hunt to let her lodge close to him. She took a room in the very same house, under the watchful eye of Hunt's landlady, and was soon on his arm at various parties and get-togethers. It is not clear that Hunt did actually have an affair with Emma, but it is not such an inappropriate assumption that *The Hireling Shepherd* had a strong autobiographical subtext. He was sorely tempted.

And now, in an episode rather similar to the prank with Lizzie, Hunt's practical joking Pre-Raphaelite Brothers once again exploited the implications of the situation. With an artist and his model living under the same roof, it would only be a matter of time before someone cottoned on to the scandal. And Hunt's chums weren't going to wait. They took it upon themselves to draw attention to the 'fix' Mad had got himself in with this girl by staging what they saw as a hilarious hoax.

According to Hunt's granddaughter Diana, it was Gabriel who nicknamed Emma 'the Coptic', referring presumably to her wide forehead and large eyes as reminiscent of the icons of the early Christian Church in Egypt. In the same way that Effie would use her married status to divert suspicion from her friendships with men, Hunt tried to shake off the implications of his sudden intimacy with Emma by pointing out that his new model was engaged. But this just gave the Brothers ammunition. Now when calling on Hunt in Chelsea they would bang on the door, pretending to be the irate sailor, arrived to defend the virtue of his fiancée and punch Hunt on the nose for exploiting her vulnerability.

It took some seven years for a version of this story to reach the mainstream press. But eventually in 1858 Hunt's celebrity was such that any hint of scandal attached to him would guarantee newspaper sales. Charles Dickens himself published the tale of Hunt and his red-headed muse in the 3 April edition of *Household*

Words. The story spares Hunt direct embarrassment, and more pertinently the publisher from legal action, by referring to him under the pseudonym of Mildmay Strong. But the reference to eastern pictures, and travels abroad (which by 1858 Hunt would be known for) and one nice question in the text – 'Are you Mad, Mildmay' – make the allusion quite clear. Other characters in the satire are little 'Mack' McCorquhodale ARA, able to rough up his 'flossy hair' into an 'aggressive crest' (Millais) and a narrator called 'Charley' who one supposes might be Millais's friend the painter Charlie Collins, who visited Hunt and Millais while they were at Ewell.

The story seems to combine allusions to Lizzie and Emma in the single figure of a field girl called Audrey whom Mildmay finds on a trip to Sevenoaks. She is given the nickname 'Calmuck'. This sobriquet refers to Audrey's Mongolian-like features and, of course, is a satirical reference to the arrogant christening of Emma as 'the Coptic'. Mildmay woos Calmuck and her poor vulnerable family into allowing the girl to sit for him for a picture based on Shakespeare's *As You Like It*. Soon Mildmay and his followers become admired by the uneducated villagers who gave up their daughter to these men, and are both trusted and endowed with attributes of intelligence and depth of character.

When the picture is finished and shown, Mildmay decides to repaint the main female figure – just as Hunt did Sylvia after Ruskin's comments. So Calmuck is summoned up to town for a resit. Here she is neglected for several days by a busy Strong, who has other priorities and thinks nothing of keeping this mere field girl waiting. But when she packs her bags to leave, he grows angry and interrogates her. She explains that her husband, a sailor, is due back and, being a jealous sort, will not take kindly to hearing that she is staying with an artist in London.

And so Calmuck is dispatched back to her bleak life on the poverty line 'in a cart towards London Bridge Railway Station. And now occurs the only real wonder in this most unpretending of histories. Mildmay Strong – whom we all believed a model of courage, physical as well as moral, suddenly astounded us by appearing in the character of an arrant coward.'

At the heart of this piece of satire is a criticism of the Brotherhood's arrogance and in particular their lack of responsible behaviour towards the women whom they lured into their midst. Beneath a comic portrayal is an implicit sympathy for the woman, who is perceived by the callous young artists as having no reputation to lose simply because of the lot that she has drawn in life. It is also a comment on the collision of old world and new, town and country, modern·lifestyles and traditional perceptions. But the accusation of cowardice is levelled seriously. These young men were knowingly playing with fire but were not prepared to get burned.

The fact was that all the PRBs were now grappling with their attraction to, and increasing association with, the opposite sex. But their negotiation of the social implications of their exposure to women was proving clumsy, to say the least. Brown was already involved with his girl, and Rossetti obviously subsumed with his. It's little wonder that there was general intrigue within the group over who would be next to fall to the appeal of common womanhood.

Hunt was physically very impressive, toned by his boxing classes with a certain Mr Reid and trim from a mixture of frugal living and huge energy. His friends were quite aware of his desire to find the right female partner. Mr and Mrs Combe, those patrons of Millais and Hunt, had become friends and were sometime matchmakers, putting a farrago of suitable young women in his way.

Being set up with nice middle-class girls was one thing, but the appeal of working girls such as Emma and Lizzie, and Ford's Emma Hill, was quite another. Middle-class women were often inexperienced, naïve, cosseted and invariably chaperoned. If his brush with Emma Watkins revealed anything to Hunt of himself, it was that he found sluts far more attractive than respectable women. These girls were not shy of male contact. They had a directness and an earthiness. They went out into the world and could give as well as they got. The recognition of this penchant was confirmed by what Mad did next.

Chivalry, the tradition that saw men offer themselves up as guardians of and suitors to women, provided the opportunity to enjoy the companionship of undesirables under the guise of salvation. The Brotherhood was already scouring the chivalric tradition for suitable subjects to paint. It was only a matter of time before chivalry came to inform their real personal lives. If Hunt could now apply a higher moral gloss over his search for a sexual partner, he could at once resolve the argument in his mind between propriety and his actual feelings. He decided he would save a girl from herself, for himself.

Alas for Emma Watkins, she was not the focus of Hunt's new intentions. Once *The Hireling Shepherd* was finished, so was Hunt with the little field girl, and she was cast back into her life of poverty, as *Household Words* observed. But Hunt had another candidate for salvation in mind. This was the utterly stunning Annie Miller.

6

The awakening conscience

PROSTITUTES WERE NOT just visible on London's streets but rife. Henry Mayhew noted that in 1857 there were 8,600 prostitutes in London known to the police but that the true number might have been nearer to 80,000. You could pick up cheap ones in Strand or Leicester Square, or in one of the pleasure gardens and parks. Or you could get a costly high-class courtesan in Rotten Row.

Some of those forced onto the streets were women who had had relationships with men outside marriage and then been deserted. For such women, seen as un-marriageable and generally undesirable, prostitution was one of the few sources of income left open.

There was little in the way of a proper orchestrated attempt by government to clear the streets of whores, or indeed provide alternatives for poor women. But there were philanthropic groups and individuals who worked in their own different ways to 'save' these fallen women. Perhaps the most high-profile of these do-gooders was none other than the future prime minister William Gladstone, who in the 1840s began his personal crusade to restore prostitutes to safe and respectable lifestyles. His rescue work involved many, often late night, adventures in London. He would seek out and interview women, attempting to rehabilitate them by removing them from the streets and training them so that they could be reintroduced into society with a proper chance of employment, the prospect of a decent marriage or the option of being able to emigrate. Gladstone's women were forwarded to educational institutions set up to accommodate such training, specifically the House of Mercy near Windsor and a similar establishment in Soho's Rose Street.

Gladstone was far from unique, and neither were such places as the House of Mercy. In fact, the salvation of fallen women was almost fashionable in the mid-nineteenth century. Even Charles Dickens joined the bandwagon. In 1849 he put his mighty pen to paper to write a leaflet that would be handed to prostitutes taken into custody. Its aim was to persuade them to go to the rehabilitation home Dickens had founded with his friend Angela Burdett-Coutts: Urania Cottage in Lime Grove, near Shepherd's Bush.

Some of the women into whose hands Dickens's leaflet would have been thrust would have combined prostitution with other occupations. Most notoriously, artist's models, actresses and barmaids would also perform sexual favours for money. Annie Miller was able to tick off 'model' and 'barmaid' as regular occupations. By implication, turning tricks for the gentlemen of Chelsea was another of her professional attributes.

Quite when Annie Miller came to Hunt's attention is unclear. At one stage she lived in Chelsea in Justice Walk, close to Hunt's lodgings in Prospect Place, and it is likely that he spotted her either on the streets or in the local pub where she worked. Annie was very noticeable.

She was a child of the slums, delivered into unsanitary cramped living conditions in 1835. Her mother died giving birth to her, and Annie and her sister were brought up by their father. He was remembered as a pathetic figure trudging along the King's Road. When, as a former soldier, he managed to secure a place with the Chelsea Pensioners, the care of the girls then transferred to a local aunt and uncle, who struggled to keep their heads above water as a cobbler and washerwoman.

According to some accounts, the illiterate, unsanitary and foul-mouthed Annie was already modelling in her early teens, her beauty evident despite the grime and lice. And certainly by late 1852 or early 1853 she was modelling for Hunt.

Despite her more than obvious disadvantages, Annie must have had a terrific personality. Hunt became smitten with her fairly quickly, it seems. She had a beauty that in her pictures seems much more conventional than that of Lizzie or Effie, but none the less striking for that. Her hair was blonde and thick. She had an elegant aquiline nose and wonderful bone structure. But the thing about Annie, by all accounts, was that she was fun. Whether it was her early exposure to men in the pub, her sense of survival or just a natural gift, she knew how to laugh and joke with men. It was not long before the PRBs had embraced her vivacious, bubbly character wholeheartedly. Women were less keen. Lizzie Siddall loathed her, and Christina Rossetti would refer to her as the 'Queen of Devils'. But it was not women who were to secure Annie's future.

Whether it was Annie's obvious situation as a fallen woman that suggested the subject of Hunt's next project, or whether the general topicality of the subject encouraged him to hire her as the ideal model, with Annie came his decision to paint *The Awakening Conscience*. This would be a significant departure for Hunt, into social realism. No longer exploring the distant worlds of early Christianity or medieval stories, he would now explore a contemporary theme, set in the here and now of the metropolis. He would paint a prostitute in her night clothes amusing her fully clad client at a piano in some vulgar urban boudoir. Suddenly starting up, as if startled, the prostitute would be shown in the moment she grasps the full ramifications of this sorry situation, from which she is likely never to escape.

This girl would be just one of those women for whom Dickens's pamphlet was written. Annie Miller, also an appropriate target for Dickens's campaign, would model for her. But Annie would have no need to direct herself to Urania Cottage for her improvement. For the next year Hunt would extend his energies beyond the canvas into his own personal chivalric mission to rescue Annie from her fate and elevate her into a different kind of woman. He would arrange her education and improvement.

This Pygmalion-type behaviour had its precedents. Ford Madox Brown, with whom Hunt was increasingly friendly and whose situation with Emma Hill must have been a regular topic of conversation within the Brotherhood, was educating his future wife. In 1852 Brown wrote to Hunt and invited him to Hendon, where he had Emma and his illegitimate child holed up. Shortly after this, Emma was moved to Highgate, where there were many ladies' seminaries, and here Brown probably had her 'schooled' in preparation for a marriage that did indeed take place in April 1853.

Hunt had not had the means for such a venture with Lizzie, and perhaps Emma Watkins's appeal had been limited. Now, although by no means enjoying Millais's level of financial reward, he did have at least some money. In 1851, after Ruskin's intervention on behalf of the PRB cause, *Valentine Rescuing Sylvia from Proteus* had won the prestigious Liverpool Prize, which landed Hunt a neat £50, before being sold for £200 to an Irish buyer, Francis McCracken. In the following year he won further prizes in Liverpool and Birmingham and was altogether a more commercially viable prospect. He could just about afford such a project now.

Hunt's friend and former pupil Fred Stephens knew a woman in the vein of Angela Burdett-Coutts who could design and supervise a programme of improvement for the street girl. Her name was Mrs Bramah, and Stephens knew her through her nephew, his chum the medical student Thomas Bramah Diplock, later an eminent coroner.

So lodgings were found for Annie, and Mrs Bramah arranged for lessons that would include etiquette, deportment and elocution. When not at her lessons, Annie would go to Prospect Place and pose for *The Awakening Conscience*. She would stand before her saviour in an expensive nightgown, her hair let down.

If Hunt had had the opportunity to read the private diaries that Gladstone was writing, which confessed the sore temptation he often suffered when exposed to the very women he was on a mission to save, he would have been better forewarned and fore-armed. But then perhaps that was the point. Perhaps Hunt now felt that he could be tempted by this ravishing girl, who, if all went well, could one day be considered suitable matrimonial material.

When Effie returned from Venice to be greeted by the infamous article in the *Morning Chronicle*, she faced more that just the rumour mongers and gossips. A hot and smelly London summer lay ahead, but one that would no longer be alleviated by the 'at homes' she had enjoyed in her elegant Park Street address. While she and Ruskin had been enjoying Venetian canals and bridges, he had been in the process of disposing of the house in Mayfair in favour of a modest home in Herne Hill, a stone's throw away from his parents.

Effie had been presented with the decision to move as a *fait accompli*. 'I do not speak of Effie in this arrangement', Ruskin wrote baldly and callously to his father from Venice, '– as it is a necessary one – and therefore I can give her no choice. She will be unhappy – that is her fault – not mine – the only real regret I have, however is on her account – as I have pride in seeing her shining as she does in society – and pain in seeing her deprived, in her youth and beauty, of that which ten years hence she cannot have – the Alps will not wrinkle – so *my* pleasure is always in store – but her cheeks will: and the loss of life from 25 to 27 in a cottage in Norwood is not a pleasant thing for a woman of her temper – But this cannot be helped.'[1]

Effie's last pleasure, society, was in one gesture taken from her. She now faced imprisonment in suburbia. The family bonds she had sought to weaken through distance had proved so elastic that now they sprang back, and she faced being bound up even more closely than before with the nasty old Ruskins.

The house was a small, new-build, red-brick property in Herne Hill. Designed for London's expanding *nouveaux riches*, it was partly furnished in what even John agreed was the worst possible taste. The fashion-conscious and socially ambitious Effie, so aware of the aplomb of her former Park Street residence, was devastated.

Writing a memoir about Effie's marriage at the end of the century, her younger brother Sir Albert Gray pointed out the devastating effect this change in domestic circumstances had on her.

> Old Ruskin could not bear to be parted from his son, while John had always been tied to the apron-strings of his mother. The son was not content to leave father and mother; he had married, but clave to his parents. Mrs JJ Ruskin was not the ideal mother-in-law, who might have made the twin-house arrangement work smoothly. The Herne-Hill life, which was now practically continuous, was a record of jealous interference and almost perpetual friction.[2]

Perhaps it was Effie's utter distress at this new development in her situation that prompted her to turn, quite against the conventions of the day, to modelling. That her husband encouraged this was either further evidence of Ruskin's blinkered and idiosyncratic carelessness about social protocol or indicative of other more sinister motives.

Those in society already enjoying Effie's bad behaviour saw it as another example of her outrageousness, and this was noted by the elder Ruskins. But Effie still had some influential friends and allies who supported her. Despite the Venetian scandal, Effie's significant charm had secured Lady Eastlake's continuing support. Lady Eastlake was familiar with the artist to whom Effie would sit. She could easily vouch for his reputation: after all, he had attended the Academy, over which her husband presided. And so Effie persisted to sit for her one-time adolescent admirer and her husband's new protégé, John Millais.

Effie posed for Millais's *The Order of Release*. Quite how the audacious idea of a society lady modelling for an artist came about is unclear. But Millais had been commissioned to paint on the subject of the subjugation of Scotland after the Jacobite rebellion and its suppression at Culloden in 1746. Effie's Scottishness may have been all that suggested her to him.

Or perhaps, as had happened with Lizzie, Millais had recognized a fundamental quality in Effie that would lend itself to his intentions. Without knowing the details of her life, perhaps Millais had spotted a glimpse of suffering beneath the superficial façade she presented to society. Millais may well have seen the appropriateness of this brave face in adversity for a picture that would convey a broken and defeated Scotland still holding its head up high.

Millais wanted to depict a woman who had sacrificed much in the name of true love. He imagined a wife handing over release papers for a captured Jacobite officer. A baby in her arms, her grateful husband, released from gaol, leans wearily on her shoulders. Her face is proud and inscrutable. She is an image of cool stoicism and self-contained pride in the face of adversity.

And so began Millais's and Effie's friendship. Each day he travelled to Herne Hill and spent the day with her in uninterrupted intimacy. Ruskin could not have been more delighted to have Millais around the house. 'He found my head like everyone else who has tried it immensely difficult and he was greatly delighted last night when he said he had quite got it!' Effie relayed to her mother in March 1853. 'He paints so slowly and finely that no man working as he does can paint faster.'[3]

By the time the picture was hung at the RA summer show in 1853, Effie's celebrity was secured. Millais and Pre-Raphaelitism were now heralded rather than decried, and the popular press reproduced the image for readers hungry to devour it. Although nowhere near as great a painting as *Ophelia*, it is technically as accomplished. And once again Millais managed to tune in to the current cultural *Zeitgeist*, with a Highland reference that instantly appealed to a population in love with Walter Scott's stories of romantic Scotland. It was the first picture in the history of the Academy that required a policeman posted in front of it to prevent the canvas becoming damaged by the crush. And Effie wrote chirpily to her mother about seeing her own image 'above a row of bonnets' gazing in adoration. The *Illustrated London News* for 7 May 1853 keenly described 'a crowd intent on what they are about – a good sticking crowd, who, having once taken up their position opposite the object of their homage, are not inclined very soon to move on, but stand there gaping, and staring, and commenting upon the wondrous effects, without any regard to the pressure from behind of crowds preparing to occupy their place'.

Despite his wife's role in the celebrated picture, Ruskin was unable to secure *The Order of Release* for himself, since it had been commissioned by the lawyer Joseph Arden for £400. In fact, it's quite clear that during the many sittings that occurred at Herne Hill and afterwards in Millais's studio in Gower Street, Ruskin had been sufficiently disciplined to take hardly a peek at the emerging picture. Wrapped up in the imminent publication of *The Stones of Venice*, he did not even go to see the picture hanging in the RA show, relying instead on Hunt for reports of the picture's success.

'My dear Hunt,' he wrote shortly after the exhibition opened, 'I am sadly vexed at not being able to come to you – but the printers are keeping me close to my own work. – I must look to the exhibition. I have hardly seen even Millais' head of my wife, which I am curious enough about, as you may suppose – Please write and tell me how the audience of Tuesday afternoon like the picture – and how you are satisfied with it yourself.'[4] Despite his failure to engage with *The Order of Release,* Ruskin's desire to patronize Millais remained strong, and so he asked him to paint his portrait. Effie and Ruskin had been planning a summer trip to the Highlands for some time, and now Ruskin invited Millais and his brother William along too. The portrait could be made during the trip.

Millais was up for the trip, but he desperately wanted Hunt to go with him. Ever since Rossetti had released Hunt from the centre of his affections in favour of Lizzie, Millais continued to crave and rely on his old friend's company. Ruskin was becoming more acquainted and friendly with Hunt too, and had indeed done him some service by persuading Francis McCracken to buy

Valentine Rescuing Sylvia from Proteus in November 1851. And so it only made perfect sense that when Effie bumped into Hunt at a society party given by mutual friends the Monckton Milneses she attempted to persuade Hunt to join their vacation.

But Hunt, although he clearly loved his Academy chum and fellow PRB, did not share Millais's intense need for constant companionship. Ever headstrong and his own man, Mad was being pulled away from Millais by two different loadstones. One was the draw of Palestine, which now was becoming an obsession for him: he was desperate to make a pilgrimage and paint the landscape of the Holy Land. The other was his growing passion for Annie Miller, and his need to secure her future.

After initial promises to join the party Hunt eventually declined and left a distraught Johnnie to board the train north to Wallington without his best friend by his side. With easels and hampers, trunks and books, badminton rackets and fishing rods the party packed into their railway carriage and settled for the long journey to Northumberland, where everyone was to make an initial stay with family friends of the Ruskins, the Trevelyans.

From Northumberland the party made as much of their journey as possible by coach rather than rail, because of Ruskin's particular aversion to the newfangled machines. And perhaps it was because of this rather laborious travel that they put down roots at one of their first destinations beyond Edinburgh, the hamlet of Brig o' Turk.

They had originally planned to stay just two days at Brig o' Turk, but Millais quickly found an ideal location for his portrait of Ruskin: a swollen, rushing Highland stream full of salmon and bordered by ragged rocks in the nearby Glenfinlas forest. So at Brig o' Turk, a mere handful of thatched cottages, the party settled. Everyone initially stayed at the nearby New Trossachs Hotel. Its elegance and amenities stood in strange contrast to the simple rural hamlet close by, but it was there to cater for a seasonal market based on the English Victorians' obsession with Scotland and specifically a Scotland depicted by Walter Scott.

Brig o' Turk had benefited greatly from its association with the great writer. It is situated in the Trossachs, a wooded glen that stretches from the mountains of Ben Venue to the south and Ben A'an to the north and is bounded on the east and west by lochs Achray and Katriné respectively. Scott had set his extremely popular narrative poem 'The Lady of the Lake' there, on the banks of Loch Katrine, and since its publication the tourists had trickled to the site.

But the visiting season was short, and so the hotel was pricey. After just a week the Ruskin party realized that their intended long stay would prove very extravagant unless alternative lodgings could be found, but there was little choice in such a small village. Millais, though, now set on his location, could not move too far. And this may be why they ended up renting the local schoolmaster's cottage for a £1 a week – a significant saving on the £13 a week the Ruskins alone had been spending at the hotel.

Ruskin's sketch of the cottage shows a single-storey, thatched building with a single chimney, two entrances and just five windows on one elevation. It was tiny. While the schoolmaster and his wife, the Stewarts, remained discreetly in one section of the property, a parlour and two bedrooms were made available to the visitors.

And now a very strange and socially controversial decision was made. Many subsequent accounts of the trip have claimed that Millais and Effie took the two tiny cottage bedrooms, with Ruskin sleeping in the parlour and William Millais remaining at the hotel. Letters home from both Effie and Millais separately also indicate that certainly at the beginning of the holiday this was the case. But, bound up in a bundle of documents that Effie's brother Sir Albert Gray left to the Bodleian Library in 1938, with the explicit instructions that they could not be opened until 1968, is a fascinating revelation.

The documents were compiled at a time when Gray was desperately trying to protect the reputation of his family and was launching aggressive assaults on biographers who he felt were slandering Effie as an adulterer. As part of his own personal inquiry into the events at Brig o' Turk he had obviously interviewed William Millais. Gray's notes from the interview are quite clear. On House of Lords paper Gray's questions are written in a left-hand column and Millais's answers are recorded on the right. William Millais revealed that the arrangements for accommodation were, in fact, slightly different:

> WILLIAM MILLAIS: The accommodation was a sitting room & a bed room on either side with a recess bed in the sitting room where Crawley, Ruskin's man servant, slept.
>
> ALBERT GRAY: How were they occupied at night?
>
> WILLIAM MILLAIS: JEM one room ECG in the other, Crawley in the recess.
>
> ALBERT GRAY: Where did you and Ruskin sleep? At the New Trossachs Hotel or where?
>
> WILLIAM MILLAIS: Ruskin and I walked across the bog each night to New Trossachs Hotel & slept there & he had a room there for his work.[5]

Ruskin and Effie were certainly sleeping apart throughout the holiday. But more than that, at some point it seems that Ruskin chose to move back into the hotel, leaving his wife and a single man in conditions that were barely more than camping.

Effie was now twenty-five. On her wedding night John had promised that with her twenty-fifth birthday would come an end to their celibate, sterile marriage. But if she had hoped that her virginity might finally be lost during this Scottish sojourn, and perhaps her future life improved by the patter of tiny feet, then Ruskin's electing to sleep in an entirely different building could have done little to reassure her.

Even by today's standards the decision for a husband and wife to be separated by a 'bog' at night, leaving the wife in close confinement with a young single man and a servant squashed away in a recess, is bizarre. The arrangement certainly sends a clear message about the state of the marriage and put temptation squarely in Effie and Millais's way.

My Feet Ought to Be against the Wall, by John Everett Millais, 1853.
Millais's room was cramped, but at very close quarters to Effie's own
shoe-box bedroom

The new quarters were very intimate. Effie described how she
had to improvise hanging space in her minute cubbyhole, and
Millais pointed out that with his arms outstretched he could
touch both sides of his room.

Like Paulizza and then Count Thun, Mr Foster and Clare Ford,
Millais and his brother William were soon cast as Effie's daily
companions. Ruskin, when not posing for the proposed portrait
or engaging in the odd leisure pursuit (he became determined to
build a dam across the stream), would disappear into his own
closed world of work. While he compiled the index to *The Stones
of Venice*, Effie and the brothers would fish or walk or climb the
local hills, or read to one another.

The holiday started well, with the group energetically taking
full advantage of their romantic environment. Effie evidently felt

a new kind of freedom in this Highland setting and would walk bonnetless through the woods. She would enjoy packing up hampers for the party, who would then picnic on the rocks by the stream. And if the weather proved inclement, then the party would play shuttlecock indoors, enjoying fearsome battles of bravado between Millais, who became known as the Jersey Stunner, and Ruskin, the Herne Hill Gamecock.

But then the weather really set in. The summer became dominated by rain. Day after day of soaking, torrential downpour. And with it came a mounting unease in Millais, stemming from his inability to progress his work as fast as he would like along with a gloomy realization that Ruskin was not quite the friend and companion he had hoped for.

Three and a half weeks into the trip, on 17 July 1852, Millais wrote to Hunt:

> The last four days we have had incessant rain, swelling the streams into torrents ... the dreariness of the mountainous country in wet weather is beyond anything. I have employed myself painting little studies of Mrs Ruskin whilst poor William has given way to whisky and execration ... The greatest change which has occurred since I left Town is the increased growth of my whiskers – they are now so perceptible that Mrs Ruskin in drawing my profile positively pencilled them a-down my cheek ... having the acquaintance of Mrs Ruskin is a blessing. Her husband is a good fellow but not of our kind, his soul is always with the clouds and out of reach of ordinary mortals.[6]

Effie was sketching Millais because he had agreed to teach her to draw during the trip. Whether this was an agreement that had been born during her modelling sessions, or one forged from the boredom of being trapped in a tiny rain-drenched cottage, it became a fairly serious undertaking and an obvious source of relief for an otherwise increasingly miserable Millais.

'I wish there was a monastery I could go to', Millais moaned to Hunt, 'I am beginning to be perfectly sick of life ... like you I have much that I could tell you but cannot in a letter.'[7] The story that

Millais felt unable to relate to Hunt in his letter is easily told through his sketchbook. Here his despondency with the weather goes hand in hand with his increasing delight in Effie, whom he nicknamed 'The Countess'. In July he gently and affectionately caricatured his new pupil's ambitions as an artist, warmly depicting her painting a vast epic picture with studio assistants arriving with huge pots of paint. Later he showed her in haughty mode, her paintbrush disdainfully extended to a small canvas that is obviously beneath her talents.

Three days after the letter to Hunt in which Millais noted her company to be a blessing, we see Effie and the Millais brothers salmon-fishing together. Effie and Johnnie sit side by side in a boat while William chats away to them. A sketch from later the same day reveals a change in the weather, and the three of them bent over with their coats and cloaks buttoned and wrapped against the elements.

In another sketch, entitled *The Countess as Barber*, dated 25 July, we see Effie cutting Millais's hair. He is pathetic, sat on a chest and bent over while she appears calm and tender. In fact, Effie on this particular day had proved more than just a barber. A closer glimpse at the sketch shows Millais with his left hand heavily bandaged and his nose with a plaster across it. Earlier that day he had been bathing in a pool when he slipped and smashed his head on a rock. Then later he had crushed his thumb. Millais, always rather vain, was reeling from both the pain and humiliation of the experience and a genuine anxiety that his good looks had in one fell swoop been greatly reduced. So now Effie was his nurse too, soothing and bandaging him.

Another sketch, entitled *Highland Shelter*, shows Effie and Millais cowering against the rain under a blanket – or plaid. Another, dated 31 July and affectionately entitled *Cruel Treatment of a Master to His Pupil*, depicts Millais, again wrapped up against the sodden weather, tickling and teasing Effie with a fern. Yet another reveals Millais in chivalric mode, kneeling by the edge of a stream, offering Effie water he has scooped up for her in a little bowl. But perhaps the most telling image of all is the tender sketch Millais made of himself painting Ruskin's portrait, entitled *Two Masters and Their Pupils*. The figure of Ruskin posing for his portrait has long ago been cut out so that the viewer now has to focus on the two foreground figures of Effie and Millais. He is cross-legged on a low stool, his canvas propped on the ground. Effie sits next to him, reading to him while he works. The are practically back to back, leaning intimately on one another. Their left arms are pressing together, practically entwined. If one did not know Effie's husband was just feet away, it would be instantly recognizable as the image of two lovers, content in their intense proximity to one another.

At some stage during this holiday Effie revealed the truth about her sham of a marriage to Johnnie. The revelation threw Millais into a state of near breakdown. He was obviously deeply in love with Effie now and could hardly cope with the fact that she was trapped in such a strange state of affairs.

The intimacy of the situation also brought certain 'arrangements' very much to the forefront of Millais's attention. His correspondence from this holiday remains largely intact in the Pierpont Morgan Library. There are a handful of Millais's letters that have been quite clearly censored, with comments made to the recipient, his friend Charlie Collins, obscured by thick black swirls applied by a different pen. It is tempting to think that the obvious lack of sexual contact between Ruskin and Effie was only serving to heighten Millais's own desires for her, the frank admission of which has been effaced to conceal the burgeoning love affair from future inquiries.

On 4 August Millais wrote to Charlie, and one can barely make out beneath the censorial swirls a confession that begins 'Ruskin is having his bed made in the sitting room and the bed of his wife is too small to admit'[8] but is thereafter indecipherable. And then a fortnight later, in another letter to Collins, there is another of these tantalizing deletions. In this note, on 17 August, Millais describes how the inclement weather had once again confined

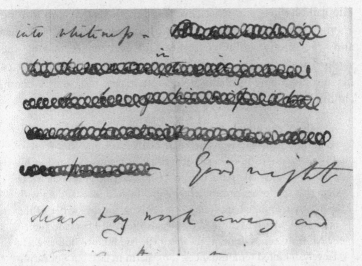

Photograph of Millais's censored letter to Charlie Collins, 4 August 1853. Underneath the heavy ink swirls of the censor one can just make out Millais's writing: 'Ruskin is having his bed made in the sitting room and the bed of his wife is too small to admit ... [?] person.'

the party to a game of shuttlecock, but again another passage has been retrospectively inked out at the end of the letter: 'It is rather late now, quite dark and threatening rain, there is a bagpiper piping away at the inn opposite and to add to my melancholy ... [DELETED]'.[9]

Ruskin began to make a note in letters of how odd Millais's behaviour was becoming. 'I wish the country agreed with Millais as it does with me ... but he does not know how to manage himself', he related home. He paints until his limbs are numb ... sometimes won't or can't eat breakfast or dinner ... sometimes eats enormously without enjoying it. Sometimes he is all excitement, sometimes depressed, sick and faint as a woman, always restless and unhappy.'[10]

The degree of Millais's frustration may well reflect a love affair with Effie that in fact pre-dated the Scottish trip. Even if the

Highland holiday was what confirmed the lovers' passion for one another, there are suggestions that it had been brewing far earlier and was already visible to those with eyes to see, during the sojourn with the Trevelyans. In the unexpurgated manuscript of his autobiography William Bell Scott makes just such a claim, although it is an assertion that never made its way into print.

> Already apparently before they reached Northumberland, the handsome hero had won the heart of the unhappy Mrs Ruskin, whose attentions from her husband had it seems consisted in his keeping a notebook of the defects in her carriage or speech. More than that the lovers had evidently come to an understanding with each other, founded apparently on loathing for the owner of the notebook. Mrs Ruskin used to escape after breakfast, and joined by Millais was not heard of till about the late hour of dinner. Lady Trevelyan hinted remonstrances, took alarm in fact, but not caring to speak confidentially to the lady who acted so strangely in her house, got Sir Walter to talk to rouse the apparently oblivious husband. Her quick eyes of course had discerned something of a telegraphic language between the lovers, and she was mystified by Ruskin's inexplicable sillyness as she inadvertently called it to me. Sir Walter was also mystified, having pretty good eyes of his own, but was less given to forming conclusions or speaking of what was passing. He agreed however to take Ruskin into his confidence. But that innocent creature pooh-poohed him. Really he didn't believe there was any harm in their pleasing themselves.[11]

On 18 August Effie went to Bowerswell for a brief trip, chaperoned by the schoolteacher's wife, Mrs Stewart. William Millais left with the party, as he was returning to London. Ruskin encouraged Johnnie to go too, but he resisted, perhaps because Effie had by this time also shared with him her brother's theory that Ruskin was trying to force her to commit adultery in order that he could effect a divorce. Perhaps this is why Millais also moved out of the cramped little cottage and back into the hotel.

But in a deeply gloomy letter to his cousin Emily Hodgkinson he reveals that his sojourn at the hotel had not lasted. 'Tell

John Ruskin, by George Richmond, *c.* 1843. Idiosyncratic and brilliant, the young Ruskin had been propelled to cultural stardom, but his relationships with women had been far from successful

Euphemia ('Effie') Gray, by George Richmond, *c.* 1851. Highly sociable, intelligent, accomplished and flirtatious, it's little surprise that Effie had a strong band of male followers

John Everett Millais, by William Holman Hunt, 1853. Millais was a child prodigy who, despite being the youngest member of the Royal Academy, was also its stellar pupil

William Holman Hunt, by John Everett Millais, 1853. 'Mad' or 'Maniac' Hunt was so called because of his steely determination and almost insane work ethic

The Eve of St Agnes, by William Holman Hunt, 1848. After the Eve of St Agnes celebrations, Madeline and Porphyro elope while the party-goers slumber

Self-Portrait, by Dante Gabriel Rossetti, *c.* 1847. The young Rossetti's attractive personality was heightened by the fact that he was physically beautiful and immediately noticeable. Even as a student, his celebrity had been instant

Ford Madox Brown, by Dante Gabriel Rossetti, 1852. Brown proved a lifelong friend to Rossetti amid the troubles to come

Cola di Rienzi Vowing to Obtain Vengeance for the Slaughter of his Brother, by William Holman Hunt, 1848–9. Who better as a model for the angry young Italian revolutionary Rienzi than another angry young Italian revolutionary, Rossetti? The kneeling figure of a knight is based on Millais

Lorenzo and Isabella, by John Everett Millais, 1848–9. Millais used the entire PRB circle as sitters for this canvas. The lover Lorenzo, offering Isabella fruit, is William Michael Rossetti; Gabriel's profile is in the far background, drinking from a glass, and Millais's father is wiping his mouth with a napkin. On the left, Fred Stephens's head can be spied between a glass and the man holding it: Walter Deverell

A Converted British Family Sheltering a Christian Priest from the Persecution of the Druids, by William Holman Hunt, 1850. The uncompromising realism of this picture shocked Victorian viewers. Lizzie Siddall modelled for the girl who is preparing to tend to the priest's wounds

Christ in the House of His Parents (*The Carpenter's Shop*), by John Everett Millais 1849–50. This picture triggered vicious criticism that was less about a real evaluation of the PRB's work than about outrage at the arrogance of a group of youths

Above: *Valentine Rescuing Sylvia from Proteus*, by William Holman Hunt, 1851. The painting is based on a scene from Shakespeare's *Two Gentlemen of Verona*. Lizzie was the original model for Sylvia, but Hunt repainted Sylvia's face after Ruskin was disparaging about it

Right; *Mariana*, by John Everett Millais, 1851. Inspired by Tennyson's poem, *Mariana* tells the pitiful tale of a woman discarded by her fiancé when her dowry is lost in a shipwreck. She waits by the window in the hope that perhaps her fortune will change and her lover return

Ophelia, by John Everett Millais, 1851–2. In painting *Ophelia* Millais, at just twenty-two years of age, created one of the most iconic images in British art and revived the fortunes of the PRB. The picture also established Lizzie Siddall as the group's greatest model

The Hireling Shepherd, by William Holman Hunt, 1851. Despite its strong moral message about the dangers of temptation, there is also an autobiographical note in this picture, reflecting Hunt's own attraction to the country girl model Emma Watkins

Above: The Awakening Conscience, by
William Holman Hunt, 1853. Annie Miller
was the obvious model for this picture,
showing a prostitute on her fancy man's lap.
When it first went on show, Annie proudly
strutted like a peacock in front of it

Right: Annie Miller, by Dante Gabriel
Rossetti, *c.* 1860. From a background of
terrible poverty, the prostitute Annie Miller
was perhaps the most conventionally
beautiful of the PRB models

The Order of Release, by John Everett Millais, 1852–3. It was very unconventional for respectable women to model, and Effie's preparedness to sit for this picture raised many an eyebrow

William I have returned to sleep here in my old emigrant [?] cot, as I did not sleep well at the hotel, for the noisy awakening of parties desiring to rise at 3 o'clock in the morning, to be in time for the coach that started at ten . . . like wise inform him . . . that the weather for painting has grown worse ever since he left and that I have only worked one day this week out of doors.'[12] Perhaps it was the noise that kept him from the hotel. Or perhaps it was Millais's utter submission to Effie's charms that, despite his better judgement, led him back to his little cupboard bedroom after just a fortnight.

By October Millais's portrait of Ruskin was nowhere near finished, thanks to the combination of dreadful weather conditions and his meticulous approach, which accomplished barely an inch of finished canvas a day. But Effie and Ruskin were preparing to leave since Ruskin had a commitment in Edinburgh – a series of lectures.

Millais, facing the loss of Effie, became hysterical. Unable to reveal the real source of his tears, he told Ruskin that it was Hunt he craved so desperately. So concerned was Ruskin that he wrote to Hunt immediately:

My dear Hunt

I can't help writing to you to night; for here is Everett lying crying upon his bed like a child – or rather with that bitterness which is only in a man's grief – and I don't know what will become of him when you are gone – I always intended to write to you to try and dissuade you from this Syrian expedition – I suppose it is much too late now – but I think it quite wrong of you to go. I had no idea how much Everett depended on you, till lately – for your sake I wanted you not to go, but had no hope of making you abandon the thought – if I had known sooner how much Everett wanted you I should have tried.[13]

Hunt never came, not least because Effie told Millais about Ruskin's letter, and Millais wrote instantly to Hunt asking him to ignore it. Then Effie and Ruskin left, and Millais stayed alone at

Brig o' Turk with the aim of ploughing on. But he lasted barely two days before packing up his easel and paint box and heading not for London but for Edinburgh, to be with the Ruskins once again.

And here it seems the game was up. If Ruskin had been genuinely blind to the infatuation that had developed between Millais and his wife during their holiday, he now saw it. Millais could hardly bear to be separated from Effie. If this utter obsession was what Ruskin had been cultivating in order to get Effie off his hands, he could now see his plan was nearing completion. And if Effie had remained totally innocent throughout her friendships with Paulizza, Thun, Foster and Ford, it seems that with Millais things were quite different. Something had happened during those long days together in the Scottish countryside and those nights in the little cottage.

Millais fled back to London. Once the Ruskins returned, he wrote to Effie. But now Ruskin and his parents had their eyes to the main chance and were, it seems, beginning to build a case against Effie. A different complexion was now cast across the exchange of correspondence between Johnnie and the Countess.

Effie and her parents quickly became fearful that things were about to turn very nasty. Sudden emergency measures were taken to prevent a scandal breaking. Effie's mother wrote to Millais urging him to stop writing to her daughter before Ruskin made a public accusation.

'Believe me I WILL DO EVERYTHING YOU CAN DESIRE OF ME, so keep your mind perfectly at rest', he replied.

I should never have written to your daughter had not Ruskin been cognisant to the correspondence, and approving of it or at least not admitting a care in the matter – If he is such a plotting and scheming fellow, as to take notes secretly to bring against his wife, such a quiet scoundrel ought to be ducked in a mill pond – His conduct is so provokingly gentle that it is folly to kick against such a man – From this time, I will never write again to his wife, as it will *be better*, and will exclude the possibility of his further complaining, although sufficient has passed to enable him to do so, at any time he may think fit. One is never safe against such a brooding selfish lot as those Ruskins – His absence in the Highlands seemed purposely to give me an opportunity of being in his wife's society – His wickedness must be without parallel, if he kept himself away, to the end that has come about, as I am sometimes inclined to think, altogether his conduct is incomprehensible, he is either crazed, or anything but a desirable acquaintance –

The worst of all is the wretchedness of her position, whenever they go to visit she will be left to herself in the company of any stranger present, for Ruskin appears to delight in selfish solitude. Why he ever had the audacity of marrying with no better intentions is a mystery to me, I must confess that it appears to me that he cares for nothing beyond his Mother and Father, which makes the insolence of his finding fault with his wife (to whom he has acted from the beginning most disgustingly) more apparent – I shall never dine at Denmark Hill again, and will not call at Herne Hill to see either, but will leave a card which will suffice – I shall be out of England next year, so that there can be no more interference from me – If I have meddled more than my place would justify it was from the flagrant nature of the affair – I am only anxious to do the best for your daughter – I consider Ruskin's treatment of her so sickening that for quietness' sake she should as much as possible prevent his travelling, or staying a summer in company with a friend, who cannot but observe his hopeless apathy, in everything regarding her happiness. ... Again I must promise you that I will never more give occasion for the Ruskins to further aggravate her on my account – Everything on my part will be as you wish – I have scarcely time to sign to save post ...

I think the Ruskins must not perceive too great a desire on your part to keep quiet, and submit to anything as they will imagine it to be fear; – she has all the right on her side and believe me the Father would see that also if he knew all.[14]

With this final terrible hint Millais must have rushed to catch the post. What Millais already knew about Effie's 'marriage' instinctively led him to believe Effie could be vindicated and released. But the road to such release would be complex and fraught with legal hurdles.

Effie was, however, beginning to realize that she had little choice but to investigate these options. She was now suffering a nervous tic above her eye because of the stress of her situation. Almost daily she felt a new injustice was being visited on her by the Ruskins, who now found nothing but fault with her. She knew that unless she acted, the Ruskins would. With few rights, no money and a reputation at total risk, a divorce would have finished her.

Effie was as low as she could be. Her back to the wall, she now made one last attempt to fight back. She put pen to paper and revealed to her father the truth about her marriage night. Writing from Herne Hill, Effie revealed to George Gray:

As I feel now so ill and in perpetual nervous distress, [I] feel that perhaps I may be adding to yours by a silence which I have kept on John Ruskin's conduct to me ever since I left your care . . . You are aware that since 1848 to this last year I have never made any formal complaint to you . . . fearing your anger against John Ruskin who has so ill treated and abused me and his Parents who have seconded him, although so far they are innocent not knowing the gravity of the offence with which I charge him and from which proceeds all the rest . . . Feeling very ill last week and in the greatest perplexity about my duty to you – I went and consulted Lady Eastlake and also partly Ld Glenelg, the two persons in London for whom I have most respect. . . . I took the advice of Lady E to permit her to make the necessary enquiries of how the English Law would treat such a case as mine . . . I enclose Lady E's most kind and noble letter, it will best show you what she is, as well as perhaps help you, although cases of this description may have come under your own knowledge in the course of your life. I have therefore simply to tell you that I do not think I am John Ruskin's wife at all – and I entreat you to get me released for the unnatural position in which I stand to him – To go back to the day of my marriage the 10th April 1848. I went as you know away to the Highlands – I had never been told the duties of married persons to each other and knew nothing or little about their relations in the closest union on earth. For days John talked about this relation to me but avowed no intention of making me his wife – he alleged various reasons, hatred to children, religious motives, a desire to preserve my beauty, and finally this last year he told me his true reasons . . . that he imagined women were quite different to what he saw I was, and the reason he did not make me his wife was because he was disgusted with my person the first evening of April 10th. . . . This last year we spoke about it, I did say what I thought in May – He then said as I professed quite a dislike to him that it would be SINFUL to enter into such a connexion as if I was not very wicked I was at least insane and the responsibility that I might have children was too great, as I was quite unfit to bring them up . . . I cannot bear his presence – Once this year I did threaten him with Law, but I really did not know myself about it, as it was in Edinburgh . . . I should not think of entering your House excepting as free as I was before I left it – All this you must consider over and find out what you can do.[15]

Quite how Mr Gray must have reacted one can only imagine. It must have been somewhere between horror and relief. At least it looked as though there was now a way to save Effie.

And Millais was there waiting in the wings to step in when the moment was right. And so as 1853 closed and 1854 dawned the members of the Brotherhood found themselves in new roles. They were all to be saviours of women: Rossetti would save Lizzie from his colleagues; Hunt would salvage Annie from street life and prostitution; and Millais would rescue Effie from her matrimonial unhappiness. These knights were about to go into battle on behalf of their ladies and themselves espouse the moral doctrines so often conveyed on their canvases.

7

Luscious fruit must fall

The two Rossettis (brothers they)
And Holman Hunt and John Millais,
With Stephens chivalrous and bland,
And Woolner in a distant land —
In these six men I awestruck see
Embodied the great PRB.
D.G. Rossetti offered two
Good pictures to the public view;
Innumbered ones the great John Millais,
And Holman more than I can say.

William Rossetti, calm and solemn,
Cuts up his brethren by the column.[1]

The PRB is in its decadence:
For Woolner in Australia cooks his chops,
And Hunt is yearning for the land of Cheops;
D.G. Rossetti shuns the vulgar optic
While William M. Rossetti merely lops
His Bs in English disesteemed as Coptic;
Calm Stephens in the twilight smokes his pipe,
But long the dawning of his public day;
And he at last the champion great Millais,
Attaining academic opulence,
Winds up his signature with A.R.A.
So rivers merge in the perpetual sea;
So luscious fruit must fall when over-ripe;
And so the consummated PRB.[2]

CHRISTINA ROSSETTI TURNED out this particularly pertinent ditty in response to a note Gabriel had penned her on 8 November 1853: 'Millais, I just hear, was last night elected Associate', he revealed miserably. 'Now the whole Round Table is dissolved!'[3]

It was all true. While Millais was in the final throes of the ghastly Scottish trip with the Ruskins, back in London behind the closed doors of the venerable establishment in Trafalgar Square, he had been elected ARA – Associate of the Royal Academy. This honour, it should be noted, was one for which Millais himself had to put his name forward. Being an ARA was the first step on the establishment rung and a necessary hurdle before being elected to the yet more prestigious title of RA, of which there were only forty-two, from whom the President was elected for life.

So just five years after the band of idealistic rebels had set out to obliterate the reputation of the hallowed Academy, their most high-profile and prolific member had been embraced by the enemy. It was at once both a sign of victory and defeat. The PRBs could claim cause to rejoice because their art, once so spat upon, was now deemed acceptable. But this in itself was cause for sorrow. For without a cause why the need for a campaign?

In fact, the Brotherhood had already begun to fall apart. William Michael Rossetti had had some trouble keeping the PRB journal. Although in the early days there would be several entries a month, he almost ground to a halt after the Academy show of 1851.

Just getting them all together in one room began to prove harder and harder. It's not that they stopped seeing one another. Indeed, from reading their letters and memoirs, it's clear that throughout the early 1850s they continued to socialize and work together with some intensity. There was an endless round of breakfasts and dinner engagements, visits to one another's studios and excursions to the theatre and exhibitions. But getting all of the PRB in the same room for a formal assembly seemed nigh on impossible.

Rossetti would often skulk in his depressive self-deprecating mode, cancelling meetings at the last minute. 'My dear Holman,' he moaned in November 1852, 'much as I desire to set eyes on you again, I shall not come tomorrow evening to the meeting at your place. What between remissnesses & disappointments in my painting, it has come to pass with me, that until I have done something decisive & got again into the field, I should feel like a pretender at any meeting connected with the artistic interests of the brotherhood.'[4] Then, of course, there were the extended trips to Ewell and Oxford that Millais and Hunt would take.

But any trip they took could not compete with that of Woolner. In July 1852 his resolution to emigrate was fulfilled when he boarded a steamer called the *Windsor* at Gravesend. Hunt, Brown and the Rossetti brothers went to see him off. Disappointed with his lack of success and even more by his inability to make a decent living, Woolner joined the huge rush of emigrants from all over the British Isles who, in 1852 in particular, were inspired by reports in the press and in Parliament to go and dig for gold in Australia. The *Windsor* finally landed in Victoria at the end of October.

The once shared interests of the PRBs were also diverging. Rossetti was still smarting from the public slapping that the PRB had got back in 1850 and had spent much time since moving from one studio to another, bothering all his friends and achieving little. 'All this while Rossetti was staying at Newman St with me', Ford Madox Brown recalled in his diary, accounting for the summer of 1851, 'keeping me up talking till 4 a.m. painting sometimes all night, making the whole place miserable and filthy, translating sonnets at breakfast working very hard and achieving nothing.'[5]

In contrast to the almost paralysed Rossetti, Millais was becoming increasingly prolific, embracing the growth in the press and media that made his work more and more available to the people at large. New periodicals and papers were springing up and established ones growing in response to the development of the steam press and the growth of the railways. Papers could be printed fast and then distributed quickly all over the land to Britain's expanding and increasingly literate public. These new ventures were seeking illustration. The market for stand-alone prints of paintings was also growing. And Millais, whether by luck or design, was espoused by the publishing industry in both these regards. *The Order of Release* was the first PRB painting to be made into a large print for popular consumption.

Even when he was on his miserable Scottish trip Millais still managed to have an eye for the mainsail and sent *Punch* a series of self-mocking caricatures featuring himself variously caught out by the wind, blown off his painting stool and wearing a sack on his head with eye-holes cut out as protection against midges. These were published for public consumption in October and November 1853.

But another major solvent of the organization was women. The Brotherhood dissolved much faster when sisters were introduced. Rossetti would often sacrifice the company of the Brotherhood for that of Lizzie. 'I have written to Hunt, as I told you I should do, to decline attending the meeting tomorrow', he scribbled to William Michael. 'In case I should not see you before then, I write to beg that you will avoid asking him (should it enter your head) to come down here on Saturday, as I have Lizzy coming, and do not of course wish for any one else.'[6]

This note is doubly pointed. Just a few days before it was written, the siblings had moved into a new apartment at 14 Chatham Place, near Blackfriars Bridge, a residence that William Michael paid for since his brother remained, as always, hopelessly short of 'tin'.

Reading the little letter written just a week into their joint tenancy of their new home, and probably sent to his office at the Inland Revenue, where Gabriel often ran off last-minute requests,[7] William Michael must have realized that in not so many words his sibling was banning not only Hunt from the apartment, but also its co-tenant. This became a regular state of affairs that the long-suffering William seemed to put up with. Although in name Chatham Place was his, in practice it belonged to Lizzie and Gabriel.

'In these years Dante Rossetti was so constantly in the company of Lizzie Siddal that this may even have conduced towards the breakup of the PRB as a society of comrades. He was continually painting or drawing from her', William Michael conceded in his memoir of the Brotherhood, before adding a rather unconvincing layer of whitewash:

> The reader will understand that this continual association of an engaged couple, while it may have gone beyond the conventional fence-line, had nothing in it suspicious or ambiguous, or conjectured by anyone to be so. They chose to be together because of mutual attachment, and because Dante was constantly drawing from Guggum . . . He was an unconventional man, and she, if not so originally, became an unconventional woman.[8]

But in addition to distracting the members of the Brotherhood, these women were also beginning to create internal conflicts that strained once impregnable fraternal bonds. Lizzie's loathing of Annie Miller and her obvious dislike of Hunt were tricky. And this was just the beginning.

As part of a new year's resolution to try to keep the Brotherhood going, William Rossetti picked up his pen in January 1853 and wrote, 'I at last resume the PRB journal', but he instantly admitted that he was 'not too sanguine of continuing it for long. Our position is greatly altered.'[9]

Eighteen fifty-four got off with a bang. A restless Europe that had seen revolution after revolution erupt since 1848 now exploded into war. Tensions had been rising between the Russian and Ottoman empires over the former's influence in the Holy Land, which was controlled by the latter. The Ottoman sultan had wrested control over the Christian interests in the Holy Land from the Russians and placed it instead in the hands of the French Catholic Church. By November 1853 the Russian armies had been mobilized and were attacking Ottoman frigates in Turkish waters. Both Britain and France mobilized their navies to maintain the security of the Ottoman empire, and by March 1854 they were at war with Russia.

And now the PRBs suffered their own bomb blast, one that would finally rip through the already emerging cracks in their union. Hunt left the country and headed for that Holy Land, which was at the centre of hostilities. He had been the magnet who had held the core members of the group together. With Hunt gone, the lack of personal sympathy between Millais and Rossetti meant the future of the Brotherhood was in peril.

Rossetti and Millais had done what they could to prevent Hunt going, but when they realized it was no use, they prepared for his departure like forlorn lovers. Millais commissioned a gold signet ring for Hunt, set with a round sardonyx in which Hunt's and Millais's intials were combined to form a monogram that, when viewed from a particular aspect, appeared to read as PB.

Rossetti, meanwhile, who had stuck to Hunt like glue for his last few days, had a daguerreotype made of *The Girlhood of Mary* to which he added the dedication:

> There's that betwixt us been, which men remember
> Till they forget themselves, till all's forgot,
> Till the deep sleep falls on them in that bed
> From which no morrow's mischief knocks them up.[10]

Finally, Hunt ran out of excuses for staying. All the arrangements for Annie were in order, and a fund to pay for her education had been established, to be managed by Fred Stephens.

Hunt left Stephens a list of painters that Annie could sit to – and by implication, therefore, also a list of those she could not. Intriguingly Rossetti was not on the list. Who knows whether this was a mere oversight or an astute assessment of Rossetti's susceptibility to beautiful women, and the appeal he could hold for them, despite his attachment to Lizzie?

Rossetti was still devilishly handsome at this period. A photo of him and his brother dating from around 1853 reveals Gabriel as still thin with a heavy intense brow, dishevelled hair and rakish manner. And he could still be the source of wild fun when he wanted. Brown was often grumbling amiably that, when he went out with Rossetti, the latter would spend all his money in a night of abandon and excess. Millais, on the other hand, was a total gentleman. He earnestly promised to use Annie for a couple of heads.[11]

When the last touches were applied to *The Awakening Conscience*, Hunt knew there was nothing further to keep him. He wasted no more time, and was gone.

The spring of 1854 did not fail to offer further surprises for the PRBs. Ruskin began to extend his influence beyond the group's shining star and cast his gaze on the group's most idiosyncratic member. Millais was still finishing the Glenfinlas portrait of him back in London, but the necessary meetings to this end had been tense and frosty, to say the least.

That Ruskin's gaze fell on Rossetti was down to the Irish businessman and collector Francis McCracken. He had encouraged at least one finished piece of work from Rossetti in this year, in the form of a commission of a watercolour. Since his last exhibited oil, *The Annunciation*, Rossetti was still struggling with the technical aspects of this medium. And so he had returned to watercolour, where he applied the vivid coloration and realistic detail that Hunt and Millais were pulling off in oil.

The watercolour in question was *Dante on the Anniversary of Beatrice's Death*, and the commission was worth £35 – much needed by the still impecunious artist. A spookily prophetic picture, it showed Rossetti's namesake grieving at a window for his dead love, Beatrice. He is surprised by a couple of visitors, and as he turns to meet them they recognize the sad contemplation in his face.

With a certain business acumen McCracken made sure his commission was sent to Ruskin for his opinion. No doubt he was hoping Ruskin would begin to 'push' the one founder of PRB who had yet to make a breakthrough, and in doing so enhance the value of his investment. The wily Irishman's scheme paid off.

On Monday 10 April 1854, fortuitously the anniversary of the Chartist March in 1848 and less happily the anniversary of his wedding, Ruskin made his first direct approach to the elusive Rossetti in the form of a silver-tongued note.

'My dear Sir', he wrote,

> When I heard of McCracken's intention to ask you to send your drawing to me, I was ashamed to allow him to do so – but permitted my shame to be conquered by the strong desire I had to be allowed to have the drawing by me for a day or two; I was quite sure that I should be able at once to write to Mr McCracken that any work of yours was quite above having opinions passed upon it; and I have only to thank you for your condescension in allowing it to be sent to me on such terms – and still more – for the very great delight I have had in keeping it by me for a day or two. I think it is thoroughly glorious work – the most perfect piece of Italy, in the accessory parts, I have ever seen in my life – not of Italy only – but of marvellous landscape painting.[12]

Four days later Rossetti dropped Brown a brief note with the news: 'MacCrac of course sent my drawing to Ruskin, who the other day wrote me an incredible letter about it remaining mine respectfully (!!) and wanting to call. I of course stroked him down in my answer and yesterday he came. His manner was more agreeable than I had always expected, but in person he is an absolute Guy – worse than Patmore. However he seems in a mood to make my fortune'.[13]

A few days later Rossetti revealed to Brown that it was not just his fortune that Ruskin could make but also Lizzie's. 'I mean to show her productions to Ruskin, who was here again this morning,' he declared, 'and who I know will worship her.'[14]

The productions that Rossetti was referring to were Lizzie's pictures . . . pictures that is, painted by her. Since her determination to stop modelling to anyone but her lover, Lizzie had been concentrating all her efforts on becoming an artist herself. The audacity of this ambition, encouraged by Rossetti, matched the boldness of her personal circumstances. All in all, Lizzie was becoming a very modern woman indeed.

Quite when Lizzie decided to become an artist is debatable. Most have bestowed on Rossetti the role of the Svengali who initiated her interest in painting and fired her ambition. That he tutored her is unquestionable, but it may well have been that beneath Lizzie's quiet, contained personality lay a steely, unconventional purpose that pre-dated the Brotherhood. It may have even been this quality in her personality and demeanour that made her so appealing to them in the first place.

The whole history of the Brotherhood is dominated by the writing of the PRBs themselves. Eloquent and prolific, their letters, diaries and later memoirs give a vivid picture of their relationships with one another. But the women are harder to hear. If they did have journals, they don't survive. Letters are few and far between. But there is the odd clue that may help unlock Lizzie's perspective on events.

There are a few moments when one perhaps hears her voice through that of another. Just a few years later the *Sheffield Telegraph* carried an obituary for Lizzie, written by William Ibbitt, a relation she befriended during her trip to the city. His version of events – a version that one assumes comes from Lizzie – is that right from the start she wanted to be an artist. And even as early as those sittings with Walter Deverell for his *Twelfth Night* she was showing her drawings to Deverell's father, who was principal of the Government School of Design.

A career as an artist was not something a Victorian woman could easily pursue, let alone a woman with few means. There was some recognition of women's role in the decorative arts, and there was a Female School associated with the Government School of Design, but to study for a career in fine art was another matter. The RA did not admit women pupils until the 1860s. Women from established artistic families sometimes followed in the slipstream of parents' or siblings' successes – Hunt's sister Emily, for example, became an artist but was much helped by her brother and his associates – or those with means studied abroad. But for someone like Lizzie, looking out from behind her hat shop window, without contacts or money, it must have seemed hard to see how she could achieve any ambition in this direction.

Perhaps, then, Lizzie was prepared to model not just because of an interest in art but because she wanted to learn to paint. She saw that these young men offered a potential way in. Although neither Deverell nor Hunt delivered in this respect, Rossetti finally did. Whether her ambition pre-dated her relationship with Rossetti, Lizzie obviously gave Ibbitt an account of herself that did not make her appear to be beholden to him. She wanted to be perceived as someone serious about her calling, independent of the influence of certain men. If it had not always been thus, this is how it became.

In the early days of their relationship Rossetti was not producing much for public consumption, but this did not mean he was not beavering away, beginning projects but finishing few. As Brown commented, he was very busy achieving nothing. Much of this time was dedicated to drawing Lizzie, which he did, it seems, almost obsessively.[15] His sketches capture the seriousness of his muse. Nearly always seated, her image has a stillness in his hands. Her eyes, often downcast, give the sense of a woman wrapped in an interior world. We rarely see her smile, we rarely get a sense of her being particularly active.

In Rossetti's hands Lizzie's idiosyncrasies are his fascination: her slightly wide-spaced eyes, the heavy lids, her very thick hair. He captures her languid elegance. He often draws her with her head leaning back in the chair, her neck extended and exposed, relaxed, sensual and heavy. Her mood is usually reflective or meditative.

In his drawings of Lizzie, Rossetti would rehearse his own personal infatuations: hair, necks, eyes, lips. Even her apparent introspection became a motif for him. Eventually these would become fascinations, fetishes even, that would extend to women beyond Lizzie. But for now they were developed in association with her, and her alone.

William Michael knew the extent to which his brother had fallen for her. In 1903 in a short article for the *Burlington* magazine he conceded that 'To fall in love with Elizabeth Siddal was a very easy performance, and Dante Gabriel transacted it at an early date'. Once in love, his obsession became complete, as William Michael also noted: 'Mrs Hueffer, the younger daughter of Ford Madox Brown, tells an amusing anecdote how, when she was a small child in 1854, she saw Rossetti at his easel in her father's house, uttering momently, in the absence of the beloved one, his pet name for her "Guggum, Guggum".'[16]

Lizzie's solemn, still introversion was sometimes interpreted as sulkiness or gloominess. She could be accused of being haughty, which her downward gaze, directed along her long thin nose, did nothing to dispel. But Lizzie must have had a lighter side. There are plenty of accounts in Brown's diary of the Rossettis living quite a vivacious social life, going out to theatres and holding supper parties where Lizzie would serve up chops or similar to welcome friends.

One sketch of Lizzie does show some animation. Dated 1853, it shows her leaning keenly forward over a drawing board; her lover is opposite her, his feet casually placed on a chair between them. The tables have turned. He is no longer drawing her, but she is sketching him.

Rossetti's colleagues always recognized that he was generous in his praise of others and never happier than when proselytizing. Now the Brotherhood had achieved a momentum of its own, Lizzie fulfilled his need for a new project to trumpet and triumph. Neither Deverell nor Hunt could have offered Lizzie this level of unbounded enthusiasm and unequivocal support. Rossetti's need for a 'cause' to champion, at once wrapped up in his other feelings for Lizzie, made for a very potent attachment – initially, at least.

Unlike the rigorous, formal and slow-moving tuition that was offered at the RA, the school of Rossetti was fast-moving. It seems that from the outset Lizzie was encouraged to attempt full compositions and to begin painting in watercolour as soon as she could. William Michael tried to imagine what it must have been like to have been taught by his brother:

> The first question which my brother would have put to an aspirant is, 'Have you an idea in your head?' This would have been followed by other questions, such as: 'Is it an idea which can be expressed in the shape of a design? Can you express it with refinement, and with a sentiment of nature, even if not with searching realism?' He must have put these queries to Miss Siddal practically, if not *viva voce*; and he found the response on her part such as to qualify her to begin, with a good prospect of her progressing. She had much facility of invention and composition, with eminent purity of feeling, dignified simplicity, and grace.[17]

Many of the ideas in Lizzie's head came from the romantic poetry that she doubtless heard read out loud by Rossetti and his friends and, of course, clearly read herself. Tennyson was a PRB favourite. There are accounts of various PRBs rushing into one another's studios when new editions of poems were released. Lizzie herself apparently first came across Tennyson not in one such scenario but in a far less cultural retail climate: she was buying butter and discovered one of the great poet's works reproduced in the newspaper wrapped around her purchase.

It is tempting to find some autobiographical clue to the enigmatic Lizzie in the particular poems and passages that she latched onto and reworked as pictures. From the beginning her art has a melancholy tone. The portrayal of women in 'situations' seemed to appeal: cursed women, deserted women, women who are not what they seem, women who sacrifice themselves to men, women who court death. Her male colleagues were also choosing to portray such situations – but in her hands these subjects acquired a different weight.

Lady Clare was one particular subject that she worked up into watercolour a little later in her career and is perhaps the most directly autobiographical. It is based on a poem by Tennyson about marriage between different social classes, set in medieval times. Lady Clare is about to marry the Knight Ronald. Before the big day Clare's maid Alice reveals that Clare is not in fact a noble lady but Alice's own humble child, swapped at birth. Alice begs Clare not to tell her fiancé and risk losing her engagement. But Clare reveals all to Ronald, who happily does the right thing and marries her anyway. In the poem Clare says:

> He does not love me for my birth,
> Nor for the lands so broad and fair,
> He loves me for my own true worth.

Lizzie's picture shows Alice begging Clare to remain silent, while Clare is calm and resolute in her determination to tell all. Clare's expression is mysterious, though. It is not one of confidence; it is something closer to resignation.

It is natural to wonder to what extent this particular picture was directed at Rossetti. Without question he loved Lizzie, despite her background and for her 'own true worth'. He had shown his cards as her protector and tutor, he was undoubtedly her lover, but he had not yet married her. Just when he might take this final step would soon become a huge issue for Lizzie, as well as for those close to the couple. Was this picture an assertion of her faith that Rossetti would one day formalize their relationship in marriage, or a challenge to his cowardice in having so far failed to do so?

If the subject of marriage was to become a burning issue with Lizzie within the next couple of years or so, it seems that in the earlier years of 1853 or 1854 the topic was kept at bay by the need to get on with projects in hand. Lizzie needed to progress her art, and for that matter so did Rossetti. He was in no financial state to marry yet. And so the couple seemed to muddle along in Chatham Place with their unconventional life of love and work.

William Michael was more than prepared to concede Lizzie's shortcomings with regard to her new chosen profession. She had 'little mastery of form, whether in the human figure or in drapery and other materials; a right intention in colouring, though neither rich nor deep. Her designs resembled those of Dante Rossetti at the same date: he had his defects, and she had the deficiencies of those defects. He guided her with the utmost attention, but I doubt whether he ever required her to study drawing with rigorous patience and apply herself to the realizing of realities.'[18]

But William Michael did concede something about Lizzie's work: 'in the present day,' he wrote in 1903, 'when vigorous brush-work and calculated "values" are more thought of than inventiveness or sentiment, her performances would secure little beyond a sneer first, a glance afterwards, and a silent passing by. But in those early "Præraphaelite" days, and in the Præraphaelite environment, which was small, and ringed round by hostile forces, things were estimated differently.'[19] The fact was that there was a simplicity and naïvety about her work that gave it a freshness and immediacy.

Rossetti knew that to get on in the world of art you had finally to work in oil. He himself, having lacked the patience to become technically trained in oils at the RA, was still struggling with the medium. Nevertheless he got Lizzie going on an oil painting: her own self-portrait. And it is in this piece of overtly autobiographical work that perhaps we first begin to get a sense that, despite apparent mutual adoration, there were some tensions building in the relationship between Lizzie and Rossetti.

Despite his apparent adoration of Lizzie, and in spite of the fact that she had reached a crucial point in her tuition, Rossetti felt a need for sudden escape and decided to take a holiday just as she began this oil picture, in the summer of 1853. He left Chatham Place without having paid the rent and, as usual, turned to the ever amenable William Michael to assist him in the matter. In his note to his brother he made clear his anxiety that, though Lizzie would be staying at Chatham Place during his absence, she should not be found living there. Lizzie was an open secret – but still obviously only up to a point. And poor William Michael, it seems, still had little access to his own official lodgings.

With Gabriel away, Lizzie was left on her own in a stinking, filthy and plague-ridden town. Cholera was beginning to get hold of London again. Since the 1830s the disease was becoming increasingly endemic in the capital, and the new outbreak would grow over the next year into the greatest epidemic the city had ever seen, wiping out some 12,000 Londoners. Then there was the beginning of the annual stench that clamped around inner London in the summers and which would have been particularly noticeable at Chatham Place. Rising population and growing industry created more and more raw sewage pouring into the Thames and coursing through an old drainage system only ever designed for rainwater. The odour reached its peak in 1858, when the Houses of Parliament were forced to drape curtains soaked in chloride of lime to protect its members from the Great Stink of the river.

Perhaps, then, painting amid these solitary, miserable conditions, it is little surprise that Lizzie's self-portrait turned out to be a dour thing. It reflects none of the beauty that her male admirers saw in her. Instead, she depicted a very thin, pinched face, lips pursed and brow slightly furrowed. The radiant copper-coloured hair that Rossetti relished painting long and flowing is tied back and not indulged by its rightful owner.

In fact, Lizzie looks at herself in her mirror with a face that gives little away other than resignation. The tightly closed lips and slightly inward gaze fall short of offering determination or optimism. There is little sense of happiness even. If anything, Lizzie paints herself as someone who must make do. This is, after all, just what she was doing, while Gabriel escaped on a jolly.

William Michael described this rather severe image as an 'excellent and graceful likeness, and truly good: it is her very self'.[20] If so, then Rossetti's brother must have understood that this solemnity Lizzie chose to portray was at the very root of her being.

8

The order of release

IT WAS ANOTHER case of boils that had driven Rossetti out of town and away from Lizzie at such a crucial time. He had begun complaining about them in May 1853. This recurrent problem could prove so painful that he could barely put his coat on, and he became so low when in the midst of their grip that he described them as turning 'all my ideas to hieroglyphic'.[1] His friends began to notice his poor health and moodiness.

A holiday seemed to be the solution, despite the inevitable lack of 'tin' to finance it. Everyone was holidaying. Millais, after all, would be heading for Scotland, and Hunt too perhaps. On 7 May Rossetti wrote to his friend the poet and painter William Bell Scott and asked him, 'Where are you going just now to the seaside? I too am going to rush off and try and lose myself somewhere.' On 13 May he wondered in a letter to his mother whether he should go to Frome. By the end of the month he wrote to Deverell that he and William would probably go to Jersey together. And then in typical Rossetti fashion he did none of these things but headed north to Newcastle, alone.

Gabriel took a train from the recently opened King's Cross station on Friday 17 June at seven in the morning. By the magic of locomotive power he was with William Bell Scott and his family at 3 Thomas Street, Newcastle, between nine and ten that night. A fortnight or so later the two chums were making excursions into the nearby countryside, through Wetheral, Carlisle and Hexham.

Hexham, a medieval town with an abbey and picturesque

timber-framed buildings, appealed to Rossetti's medieval sensibilities, and here at the White Horse inn he and Scott sat in a
window seat and chatted. Women were the dominant topic of
conversation during the holiday, perhaps born from Scott's inquiries into Rossetti's current situation with Lizzie. Scott's accounts
imply that Rossetti certainly had entered into this relationship
with Lizzie with the intention of seeing it through by marrying
her when he could and doing his duty.

But what may have begun as light banter turned into a full and
serious debate about free love or 'self culture', as Scott called it.
This subject of sex outside marriage became a topic that the two
men returned to again and again during their stay together and
continued in their correspondence afterwards.

Scott was writing a poem, 'Rosabell', on this subject. It was a
miserable morality tale that by sheer coincidence corresponded
perfectly with Hunt's *Awakening Conscience*. In fact, the picture
could have easily illustrated one particular section in the piece.
Scott was still amending and redrafting the piece during his time
with Rossetti, and Gabriel persuaded him to alter the title and the
name of the girl from Rosabell to Mary Anne. No doubt with his
own poem 'Jenny' in mind, Gabriel argued that Mary Anne was a
more believable name for a rural field girl, and indeed when the
poem was published in 1854 it bore Rossetti's proposed title.

The narrative of the poem traced a young country girl through
her short, tragic life. Scott first portrayed her as a child, the daughter of a shepherd, going to a rural village church on Sunday. Then
at sixteen she is in love with a local lad, Andrew. They are depicted
as children of nature, uninhibited, making love in the fields. But
one senses Andrew's intentions are true and meant. But by the age
of seventeen Mary Anne is experiencing the corrupting influence
of the big city, where she has secured a job as a seamstress. And
here in the workroom she falls under the influence of a good-
time girl called Joan.

A year later her mother and Andrew walk for two days to see
her, but they find her changed. He hair is up, her dress is smart and

she is cold and haughty. There is a new man in her life, Archer, who has altered her name to the more fashionable Marian.

By the age of nineteen she is installed in a suburban room as a mistress, much like the girl in Hunt's *Awakening Conscience*. But after just a year Archer is bored with her and, like the commodity she has become, she is passed on to his friend Thorn. Thorn is a lounger and ne'er-do-well. Under his dreadful influence she succumbs to vices far beyond sex. 'Wine' and 'poppy juice' help her through her now sordid existence, but even these cannot assist when Thorn finally disappears.

The men in the story are inactive. Andrew weeps at home with her mother, wondering what has become of his former love, and Archer too asks himself what has happened to her now Thorn is gone. But Andrew's concern is not converted into action, and Archer's inquiry is uninterested. He does not really care what has become of her but is simply inquisitive.

Mary Anne finally hits the streets. At the age of twenty-five she is fighting dogs for discarded bones, being turfed out of doorways by respectable householders and has succumbed to the ravages of the elements. She is almost certainly the lowest form of prostitute now. The last chapter portrays her in her shroud in a mortuary. It is no longer possible to tell her age, and no one cares.

There are strange echoes of all the PRB girls in the poem. There's a bit of Emma Watkins, the field girl. The fact that Mary Anne becomes a seamstress is reminiscent of Lizzie sewing ribbons in the bonnet shop, and the fact that Archer alters Mary Anne's name reminds us that Gabriel did just this to Lizzie's, insisting that she should amend 'Siddall' to what he considered the more elegant 'Siddal'. And Mary Anne is just what Annie Miller had become: a kept woman. Surely Rossetti must have seen these semblances and recognized a shadow of himself and his colleagues in the men?

Perhaps this is why he took such a stance against the poem and the irresponsible men that it depicts. Horrified at the mirror it held up to his own circumstances, he determined to seem better than these fictional versions of himself and Hunt. He argued that the poem should end differently. He felt the men should not be absolved of responsibility. In fact, he insisted he felt so strongly about the matter that he would base a painting on the poem. Significantly it would be his return to oil painting, a major exhibition piece, and it would portray Andrew making his way to town and saving his former lover from the dreadful street life. He would call the piece *Found*.

Once Rossetti had returned home to London, his preoccupation with the theme grew. He did some reading around the subject. He picked up a copy of St Augustine's *Confessions,* going over the story of the concubine with whom St Augustine lived for some time before deserting her. Rossetti offered indignation at Augustine's treatment of his lover, writing to Bell Scott and pointing out that 'As soon as the saint is struck by the fact that he has been wallowing and inducing others to wallow it is all horrible together, but involves no duty, except the comfortable self-appeasement of getting out of it himself. As for the women, no doubt they are nascent for hell.'[2]

And yet in spite of this outspoken chivalric stance, which recognized the plight of women and understood men's duty to them, there is also a sense that Rossetti was beginning to face his own dilemma in this regard. His protests masked his own failings in this very domain. His belief in duty was beginning to conflict with his developing feelings towards Lizzie.

This was the beginning of a debate that Rossetti would fight within himself and with Lizzie until the end of her life. From now on his sense of duty towards Lizzie, and his realization that, contrary to initial expectation, she was not perhaps the woman he wanted to share his life with, would be in constant conflict. Familiarity had, it seems, bred some contempt between Lizzie and Rossetti, and as the latter grew more experienced in life, he realized that other women also held appeal for him.

Ten months later Rossetti found himself sitting at a very pleasant and friendly late lunch 'en famille' with the Ruskins in Denmark

Hill.[3] It was 24 April 1854. The business with Ruskin was going very well indeed.

During what was obviously an afternoon of deep mutual adoration Ruskin commissioned a watercolour for which Rossetti offered a loss-leading fee of 15 guineas. Ever the evangelist, Rossetti then read some poems from his friend William Allingham's book of *Day and Night Songs*. When Ruskin professed his approval of the poetry, Rossetti gave him the book. Ruskin then reciprocated by providing Rossetti with a volume of his collected works. Rossetti, feeling that no moment could be better, told Ruskin all about his pupil, and as he wrote that night to Allingham, his pitch in Lizzie's cause was successful. 'I have told Ruskin of my pupil, and he yearneth.'[4] Perhaps Rossetti was on his way to making not just his own fortune, but several.

As well as being successful, the day turned out to be a particularly frantic one. In fact, the whole week turned out to be exceptionally momentous all round. Before lunching with the Ruskins, Gabriel had taken Lizzie to Hastings. Then his session at Denmark Hill was interrupted by urgent news that his father was gravely ill, and he rushed back into town. Gabriele Rossetti did indeed expire just two days later.

It is not entirely clear whether Effie attended the lunch with Rossetti. It is most likely, from Rossetti's comments after the event, that she was busying herself at home in Herne Hill, and the 'famille' in question was the elder Ruskins. Effie's sister Sophie had been staying and was due to leave the next day. Effie was planning to accompany her to Perth for a short sojourn there. It would not have been hard for her to excuse herself to make last-minute preparations for the trip.

But Effie's absence was more ominous than the Ruskins or Rossetti could have ever imagined. The day after the merry lunch Ruskin took Effie and Sophie to the station and saw them off as they headed for Scotland. But Effie and Sophie, far from settling into a long journey to the other end of the country, alighted just a few stops down the line at Hitchin, where their parents were waiting for them. Unbeknown to the Ruskin camp, the Grays, rather than being at home in Perth, had been staying of late in London, in rooms at 28 Bury Street, St James's. At six o'clock that day court officials arrived at Denmark Hill to serve a citation on Ruskin, alleging the nullity of his marriage.

Effie's flight had been meticulously plotted. After her confession to her father, written in March 1854, the Grays lost little time in securing legal advice as to their daughter's situation. Lady Eastlake was also quickly brought into the plans for Effie's 'release', as was Rawdon Brown, Effie's friend from Venice, who found himself in London on business.

By mid-April Effie's father was confident that he and his legal team had found a precedent which indicated that Effie would be able to annul her marriage, and the mechanisms of Effie's escape began to be constructed. Key to the Grays' plans were secrecy and surprise, presumably to prevent the Ruskins launching a pre-emptive strike. But a widening circle of conspirators made the days in the run-up to 25 April fraught with tension.

Originally, the date of Wednesday 19 April had been set for the flight. On Monday 17th Effie wrote to Brown. Aware that her plans were now becoming known to an increasing number of sympathetic parties, she reminded him of the need for secrecy: 'I am off to Scotland on Wednesday. . . . The Ruskins have not a suspicion. What a state of astonishment they will be in on Wednesday night.'[5]

On the 18th a flurry of letters between the parties indicated everyone's anticipation that the following day would see Effie leave Herne Hill and never return. Lady Eastlake had already sent a hamper to Bury Street to await Effie, and a whole coterie of friends were in on what was about to happen. Ruskin's manservant Crawley was implicated in the flight. The publisher John Murray's maid had been put on stand-by to attend Effie when she arrived in Bury Street, and was awaiting news from Crawley.

Millais also wrote to Mrs Gray on the 18th. Although clearly aware of the plans in general, he was unclear about the specific date set for Effie's escape. Not quite *au courant* with the latest development, Millais found himself watching Ruskin for signs that events might have moved on at home. For the moment, from 'JR's manner and conversation' he perceived that they had not.[6]

Then, at the eleventh hour, the proposed flight was called off. Effie wrote urgently to Brown informing him that 'lawyers had advised remaining in London another week' and asking him to pass the word and to tell anyone who knew of the plan to remain quiet. The week that ensued was full of anxiety. With everything set and ready, Effie's camp had the opportunity to consider what might await her after the event. For the first time concerns of scandal began to be expressed. On 22 April Effie received a letter from her brother George which revealed how concerned Effie's uncle was about the 'notoriety' that would inevitably ensue when everything finally became public.

The question of notoriety had not been overlooked by Lady Eastlake, who had begun an audacious pro-Effie campaign in anticipation of her flight. Lady Eastlake had already seen Lady Davy, who, she related to Effie on 18 April, was anxious to help plead Effie's cause. The support of influential friends such as Lady Westminster was already being canvassed. And so many of the great and good were already well prepared for the bombshell that was finally dropped on the unsuspecting Ruskins on 25 April.

After her escape, although her father stayed in London, Effie fled to Scotland with her mother to be spared London's direct gaze. 'JR went to the station at 9 o'clock with me', Effie revealed to Rawdon Brown a couple of days later from Bowerswell.

There he was parading up and down not uttering a word. On saying that he would expect to hear from me when I reached Perth Mr Stirling of Kew . . . came . . . I was glad of this as John might wish it to be thought by & by that he did not know of my going and as he stood talking for some minutes with Mr S I thought it fortunate . . . 20 miles out of London my father and mother were waiting. Sophie jumped out to her father & mama came in beside me. I gave Papa a parcel directed to Mrs Ruskin containing my accounts and all my keys ... If John had not parents I am convinced that at this moment he is so mad & besides has always had ... the idea of becoming a monk that he would ... become one in earnest. We shall see.[7]

In addition to the parcel for her mother-in-law, which also contained her wedding ring, Effie also left a note for Mrs Ruskin, attached to a pincushion.

My dear Mrs Ruskin

You have doubtless been wondering why I did not, as was usual with me, pay you a visit at Denmark Hill to bid you goodbye before going to Scotland, but I felt that owing to the circumstances which induce my addressing you this letter that rendered it not only impossible for me to see you now or indeed ever again – but also required that I should state to you the reasons of my sending you my Keys, House Book, wherein will be found a statement of this year's account – together with an explanation of the money received and spent by me and also you will find enclosed my marriage ring which I return by this means to your son with whom I can never hold farther intercourse or communication. You are aware that I was married by the Scottish form in my father's house on the 10th April 1848. From that day to this, your son has never made me his wife, or wished to do so, as he at first overcame my judgement which was ignorant on such points, by a variety of arguments which, even showing him the words of Scripture, did not refute or cause him to change his opinions in the least about. Whilst we were at Salisbury when you caused me to be put in another room on account of an illness, which he told me his Father supposed to arise from his recent connexion with me, he used to laugh & say his father was imagining things very different to what they were. His conduct and manner went from bad to worse until I felt I could no longer submit to his threats of personal cruelty and desires to get rid of me in any manner consistent with his own safety and comparative freedom, I always resisted the idea of a separation and would take no steps in such a matter, and threatened him with the course I have now pursued if he did not treat me in a becoming manner, he said 'Well what if I do take all the blame, you would make a great piece of work for your Father and go home and lose your position.'

I have gone through this winter and thought at last that I must either die or consult my parents to take proper steps to ascertain what relief could be got, since your son almost daily heaps one insult upon another, more especially accusing me of insanity. My father and mother came instantly they knew what I suffered to Town and are only sorry I have lived in such an unnatural position so long. I believe you have been all along in total ignorance of this behaviour of your son – The Law will let you know what I have demanded, and I put it to you and Mr Ruskin to consider what a very great temporal loss in every point of view, your son's conduct has entailed upon me for these best six years of my life. Your son said he wd marry me when I was 25 – then on arriving at that age last year – I enquired on what terms we were to live, he said I was quite mad, quite unfit to bring up children, and beside did not love or respect him sufficiently. I said that last was quite impossible after his perpetual neglect – but that I never would refuse to gratify his wishes. He then put it off again and said he should try and break my spirit to induce me to leave him and return to Perth as I bored him. I think he will be glad I have taken this step. I hear that our affairs are perfectly known in London society; and nothing more will be said, since the fact of our marriage not having being consummated was known to many and your son's personal neglect of me notoriously condemned – this has likewise been the case in Perth – My parents have entirely approved of the steps I have taken and my mother accompanies me to Scotland.

I remain yours truly
Euphemia C Gray.[8]

And with that Effie Ruskin was gone and Miss Gray reborn, in spirit if not yet legally.

Fury erupted among the senior Ruskins. Although Millais was not overtly implicated, John James immediately blamed him and apparently attempted to slash the portrait of his son that Johnnie had been working on since the previous summer. Ruskin, seemingly able to detach the portrait's origins and author from his appreciation of its aesthetic value, hurriedly removed the picture from his father's reach.

Detachment seems the best way to describe Ruskin's reaction to the situation overall. While everyone around him descended into hysterics, he wrote to a friend 'the world must for the present have its full swing. Be assured I shall neither be subdued, nor materially changed, by this matter. The worst of it for me has long been past.'9

And the world most certainly did have its full swing. London society's jaw was on the floor. Millais wrote to Hunt to bring him up to date with events. The only topics of conversation in London society were the war in the Crimea and the Ruskin marriage, he told him.

'As I expected, I hear now that my name is mixed up in the affair, and by some in a manner that makes it advisable that I do not for the present see anybody connected with you', Millais wrote to Mrs Gray on 18 May. 'Any personal communication with your family just now would certainly forward the scandal, which has reached the extreme limit of invention. There must be a large portion of vagabonds in the world to set such rumours afloat – I am so disgusted with London society I shall be right glad when I am out of it.'10

As the rumour mongers got into full swing, Millais consoled the Grays that at least the scandal would be short-lived:

I have just come from the private view where I met Lady Eastlake who spoke a few words upon the subject. I was glad to hear that she had received good news about the Countess since your return. Everybody agrees with the step she has taken and only wonder at her delaying so long . . . I did not hear what most people said at the RA as I punctually escaped when the subject was mentioned – As you say it will be nine days wonder and it will be all over. One great battle with the Russians will swamp the little talk there will be for the present, in the meantime she's out of it all, and when she sees her friends again it will be an old story.11

But Millais's optimism was misplaced. The scandal began to acquire an almost mythological status. In light of this the Eastlake campaign proved much needed, and apparently fairly successful.

'I met Thackeray who was speaking on the subject last night, most people look upon JR as partly mad', Millais related to the Grays. 'Lady Eastlake introduced me to Sir Robert Inglis who wanted me to dine with him and . . . a Mr Mills wrote me a long letter about the matter thinking I knew nothing of it. I must have met him somewhere but do not remember the name.'[12]

And Rawdon Brown, having dined at Lady Davy's, kept Effie abreast of affairs, revealing that everyone was 'with' her.

> Had [Ruskin senior] maintained that his son was a man of great gallantry over attentive to the female attendants at Denmark Hill, and the fond parent of a score of natural children, you might have dreaded some trouble in the prosecution of a suit, the justice of which however seems now to be at once tacitly admitted by the defendants; and even were there any question of temper . . . the sternest judge . . . would allow that there are circumstances which warrant some little ebullition . . . the general opinion is that this affair must seriously injure [Ruskin's] popularity; and to diminish such a mischance I trust that the elder may at once accede to making you a handsome settlement.[13]

Effie was not idle during this period. Following Lady Eastlake's lead, there is plenty of evidence that she also launched her own letterwriting campaign, no doubt attempting to enlist the sympathy of influential women who could have some sway over their husbands. While there are plenty of sympathetic responses to her in existence,[14] it is clear that Ruskin managed to retain the loyalty of some.

William Bell Scott was staying with the Trevelyans during this period, and again in the unexpurgated version of his autobiography he recalls the poignant fact that 'every other day Lady Trevelyan laid certain letters aside, these I believe from Mrs R beseeching sympathy with the painful position of a wife, who for the first time in life knew what love was, confessing that John was loathsome to her, and that at any pains and penalties of exposure and shame she must from him be separated.'[15] However, Lady Trevelyan was not of the same mind as Lady Eastlake and the London set. Effie's letters to her went unanswered.

In mid-May Ruskin left for Switzerland, putting turmoil behind him. He had all his paintings delivered to Rossetti for safe keeping. This bizarre decision to leave precious effects in the care of one of the most unreliable souls in town seems barely explicable, but perhaps it shows just how much Ruskin wanted Rossetti's friendship and was determined to seal this with some significant gesture of trust. Anyway, he had to remove Millais's portrait from Denmark Hill lest John James should have it destroyed while he was away.

In terms of the Brotherhood, such as it was, Hunt was well out of the whole affair. But Rossetti found himself caught well and truly in the middle. His letters in May are full of allusion to the goings-on, and one detects more than an ounce of sympathy for Ruskin, so recently confirmed as a new patron and friend. 'That Ruskin business seems a wretched affair', Rossetti wrote to his friend William Allingham. 'I wrote to R at some length the other day, but of course avoided that except a mere allusion.'[16]

A few days later he wrote to Brown:

The Ruskin row seems to have grown into a roar in London but I suppose it has not reached the wilds of Finchley. Mrs R will get a divorce it seems — her husband is — or is not — I know not what. There are other 'solitary habits' besides those which you indulge in — more things in heaven and earth than are dreamt of even in Turner's philosophy. It seems Mrs R's seven years of marriage have been passed like Rachel's seven marriageable years — in hope. I suppose it is more the right time to be in favour with her than with him, but hear that he has something anent me in his Lectures just published. He seems to take it very cool ... He is gone to Switzerland, and says he has ordered all his works to be sent to my crib.

Millais has written to me that Gambart[17] wants me to paint him something, so I imagine Ruskin is beginning to bear fruit —

i.e. after his kind. MacCrac has kindly asked me to accept £50 instead of 35 guineas for the watercolour.[18]

Finally Rossetti's career was beginning to look up. Even with the Effie business suddenly casting a pall over his social palatability, the hand of Ruskin still seemed effective in the business of art. But just as one aspect of Rossetti's life began to improve, another was entering difficulties. His relationship with Lizzie was becoming yet more complex. She was ill.

The first mention of illness comes in his letters in mid-April: 'Dear Lizzy is very unwell indeed, and I think on Saturday I shall probably be taking her down to Hastings for her to stay there some time at a place that Barbara Smith, who has got quite thick with her, has recommended as cheap and nice.'[19]

Barbara Leigh Smith was a minor painter who had befriended Lizzie and taken her under her wing. For someone like Barbara, Lizzie was an appropriate charitable cause. She quickly wrote to another like-minded friend, the writer Bessie Parkes, about Lizzie. Her note is revelatory. If Lizzie had been labouring under the impression that she was the future Mrs Rossetti, her contemporaries clearly could not see how this might ever be possible.

Dear B

I have got a strong interest in a young girl formerly model to Millais and Dante Rossetti, now Rossetti's love and pupil, she is a genius and will (if she lives) be a great artist her gift discovered by a strange accident such as rarely befalls woman. Alas ! Her life has been hard and full of trials, her home unhappy and her whole fate hard. Rossetti has been an honourable friend to her and I do not doubt if circumstances were favourable would marry her. She is of course under a ban having been a model (tho' only to 2 PRB's) ergo do not mention it to anyone.

Dante R told me all about her secret then, now you are to know because you are to help. She Miss Siddall is going down to Hastings on Saturday for her health will you give her tea on

Saturday and will you dear see if the room Venus had by St Clements Church is to let.[20]

To Hastings Lizzie went, and there she stayed swaddled in the concern of these middle-class women. Rossetti received worried notes from them and wrote worried notes back as well as to his friends, offering them updates on her condition. Eventually he packed his bags and joined her in May, after his father's funeral.

Concern over her condition grew over the next few weeks. The women were favouring some form of hospitalization: the Sussex Infirmary was mentioned, as was a Harley Street sanatorium, at which Barbara Leigh Smith's cousin, one Miss Florence Nightingale, was superintendent before she headed for the Crimea. Letters detailing Lizzie's symptoms were sent to different doctors, whose recommendations were eagerly awaited. Some days she was better, other days she was worse. In the end everyone agreed the public infirmary would be too grim for someone such as Lizzie, and Miss Nightingale's services were not taken up.

Rossetti toed and froed between London and Hastings until the end of June, when he and Lizzie returned. Her illness continued until at least July, when mentions of her being unwell cease in his letters. Amid all the flurry of concern, the 'symptoms' so frequently referred to are never outlined, nor a diagnosis offered. It is almost impossible to tell what was wrong with Lizzie, but there are a few clues. Some accounts of her life cite a rumour that she may have become pregnant in the 1850s and had a back-street abortion. The sudden eruption of concern over her in May 1854 and her removal from London suggest that, if these rumours were based on truth, her stay at Hastings may well have been precisely to deal with the after-effects of this horrific procedure. The sudden and intense intervention of a group of liberal-minded women is also significant in this respect.

One incident that fuels this speculation was a bizarre row that erupted between Hunt, Brown, Rossetti and the poet Algernon

Charles Swinburne in 1862. At a party Swinburne, who was particularly close to Lizzie in her later life, told Hunt that for Rossetti 'procuring abortions was an everyday amusement'.[21]

Swinburne was wild and eccentric, often drunk and a terrible gossip. But he knew both Lizzie and Gabriel very well indeed and had become something of a confidant for Lizzie. Hunt told Brown about this claim. Brown told Rossetti, who challenged Swinburne, and Swinburne had memory failure and claimed he had said no such thing.

Perhaps Rossetti had indeed procured a back-street abortion. Still hopelessly short of 'tin' and in debt to Brown, William Michael and Aunt Charlotte in particular, he would have been in no position to marry Lizzie if she was pregnant. Lizzie was in the midst of her studies and would have resisted being sent somewhere out of the way with a new baby like her cousin Emma.

If not an actual interventionist back-street abortion, itself fraught with danger and possible side-effects such as infection and blood loss, Lizzie may have taken one of the noxious potions that less than salubrious chemists would sell and certain apothecaries advertised to remove female 'obstructions'. These poisonous draughts quite frequently failed to do anything more than damage the baby, but often had long-term effects on the mother.

Or perhaps the reluctance to specify Lizzie's symptoms during this period of very vocal concern for her had less to do with the concealment of tell-tale signs of a terminated pregnancy than with a different kind of concealment. The other often proffered theory is that Lizzie was suffering from some form of nervous disorder. From this time onwards she is mentioned as someone who just seemed to lose more and more weight. Brown described her at around this time as 'looking thinner and more deathlike and more more beautiful and more ragged than ever'.[22] Was she suffering from anorexia or something akin to it? And to what extent were the physical manifestions of some form of illness a way, either consciously or subconsciously, of maintaining a hold on Rossetti? While she was ill, he was ensared by guilt and duty.

If he was beginning to wander, then how better to maintain his attentions than by the tyranny of invalidity?

There is a small clue that this latter may have been the case, that Lizzie's illness, although suddenly particularly acute in May 1854, was anything but new. 'I have known her several years,' Rossetti wrote to a worried Bessie Parkes, 'and always in a state hardly less variable than now; and I can understand that those who have not had so long a knowledge of her, would naturally be more liable to sudden alarm on her account than I am. Nevertheless I am quite aware that she is in a most delicate state.'[23]

A couple of months later the guilt that Lizzie could instil in her lover bubbled up in a moment of what seems to be a strange, lucid honesty. Rossetti wrote to Allingham that July and admitted:

> It seems hard to me when I look at her sometimes, working or too ill to work, and think how many without one tithe of her genius or greatness of spirit have granted them abundant health and opportunity to labour through the little they can do, or will do, while perhaps her soul is never to bloom nor her bright hair to fade, but hardly escaping from degradation and corruption, all she might have been must sink out again unprofitably in that dark house where she was born. How truly she may say, 'No man cared for my soul'. I do not mean to make myself an exception, for how long have I known her, and not thought of this till so late – perhaps too late. But it is no use writing more about this subject; and I fear too my writing at all about it must prevent your easily believing it to be, as it is, by far the nearest thing to my heart.[24]

Cholera raged in London in 1854. Brown described 'bodies taken from Middlesex Hospital in vans. In the pest-stricken street groups of women and children frantic for their relations taken off. Police and others with stretchers running about. Undertakers as common as other people in the street, running about with coffin like lamplighters. Hearses with coffins outside as well as in.'[25] Amid this plague-besieged city the Royal Academy show that year opened as usual. But those looking for a strong showing from the PRB were disappointed.

If Millais had at one point intended to show the portrait of Ruskin, events had overtaken this and it lay unfinished in Rossetti's studio, of all places. He had been unable to complete anything else. Rossetti, of course, would have nothing to show. Woolner was overseas, ostensibly digging for gold, although in fact he had found none and had set up a small sculpture studio in Sydney. And Fred Stephens had not submitted.

Deverell's work was missing too. He had died. The astonishingly handsome sometime actor ended his life in poverty. His father, the former principal of the design school, had died some time earlier, and so Walter had taken on the burden of supporting his family. But while his painting career foundered, his health had also deteriorated. He had a chronic kidney condition, Bright's Disease.

Everyone knew he was ill. Millais, Hunt and Rossetti had rallied around. They had bought some of his paintings anonymously. Millais busied himself arranging nurses and enlisting the Ruskins, who sent food and help to the patient. But it was all in vain. On Thursday 2 February 1854 he passed away.

Millais was even in the house at the point Deverell expired and wrote to break the news to Hunt. Everyone was shattered. William Bell Scott, who had known him well, remembered him as 'of great but impatient ability, and of so lovely yet manly a character of face, with its finely-formed nose, dark eyes and eyebrows, and young silky moustache, that it was said ladies had gone hurriedly round by side streets to catch another sight of him'.[26] It was as though Deverell's death embodied the end of everything that had once been youthful and golden.

So it was Hunt, exhibiting in absentia *The Light of the World* and *The Awakening Conscience*, who with the PRB associate and particular friend of Millais's Charlie Collins bore the Pre-Raphaelite standard. Rossetti went to the show and found himself furious with Hunt. Quite how he had managed to remain so in the dark about *The Awakening Conscience* is hard to fathom. But now its obvious proximation in terms of subject-matter to Scott's

'Rosabell', and hence his planned picture *Found*, drove him into a fury. He had not exhibited for years, and the minute he had begun an exhibition picture, Hunt pipped him to the post.

But perhaps Rossetti should not have felt so jealous of Hunt's picture too soon. The reviews were disappointing. What was worse, more was being said about *The Awakening Conscience* than was conveyed in print. Millais told Mrs Gray that 'barbarous stories' were circulating 'in connexion with my friend Hunt's works'.[27] The press found the subject-matter quite disgusting. One can only presume that what they could not print was the equally unpalatable gossip that the model for this essay on whoring was apparently the artist's own prostitute lover. The embers of scandal were fanned by Annie herself, who according to Violet Hunt turned up at the private view to peacock in front of the picture.[28]

To the horror of many, Ruskin rose to Hunt's defence. Not even a fortnight after Effie's now notorious bolt, Ruskin wrote to *The Times* first to defend and explain *The Light of the World* and then a couple of weeks later to defend *The Awakening Conscience*. The pro-Effie camp were outraged. Many of them felt Ruskin should retire from public life. The fact that he was writing publicly on subjects touching morality and the treatment of women just days after the story of his own peculiar tale had errupted into the public arena was considered totally shocking.

For Effie the wave of salacious interest in her personal life was just the beginning. She now faced the ordeal of having to prove the virginity she alleged, and she also had to wait to see whether Ruskin would challenge her application to declare the marriage null and void on the grounds on non-consummation. The case was pursued through the Commissary Court of Surrey. Two doctors, Charles Locock and Robert Lee, were appointed to examine both Ruskin and Effie, but while Effie made herself available to this ordeal, apparently on 30 May, in the rooms her parents had rented in Bury Street, Ruskin avoided the inspection by being in Lausanne. 'We saw that the actual signs of virginity are perfect and that she is naturally & perfectly formed & there are no impediments on her part to a proper consummation of the marriage', the medics testified in court.[29]

On the day in question Effie, who attended the hearing, gave brief accounts of her life with Ruskin. She noted the date they had married, the places they had visited on honeymoon and listed their various homes. She then stated that Ruskin 'used to tell me he would marry me when I was 25 – he had a good dislike to children and he saw that as one reason for his abstaining from marrying me. I was living with him occupying his same bed for near upon a year after I had attained 25 years of age but it was the same after this as before.'[30]

Ruskin's proctor, F.W. Potts, failed to offer any defence in the annulment of his marriage. However, Sir Albert Gray's papers, filed in the Bodleian, reveal that he did make some allegations against Effie to his proctor in some pre-hearing interview with him. Although Gray apparently made a copy of the document, its whereabouts remains unclear. However, according to Ford Madox Brown's recollections of a conversation with Millais, the latter revealed that after the split Ruskin had written to several friends alleging Effie was 'impure' – presumably citing either Paulizza, Ford, Foster or Millais (or all of them) in this respect. Once the examination pertaining to her annulment had revealed otherwise, Ruskin's claims of adultery would have had no purchase in court, which is presumably why they were never levelled.

On 15 July 1854 the court declared the marriage void, stating

that the said John Ruskin being then a bachelor did at the time libellate contract a pretended marriage with the said Euphemia Chalmers Gray then and still a Spinster but since falsely called Ruskin and we do also pronounce decree and declare according to the lawful proofs made in the said Cause as aforesaid that the said Marriage howsoever in fact had between the said John Ruskin and the said Euphemia Chalmers Gray falsely called Ruskin was had and celebrated whilst the said John Ruskin was incapable of consummating the same by reason of incurable impotency.

Wherefore and by reason of the premises we do pronounce decree and declare that such marriage or rather show or effigy of marriage so had and solemnized or rather profaned between the said John Ruskin and Euphemia Chalmers Gray falsely called Ruskin was and is null and void.[31]

Although Millais was carefully keeping his distance from the Ruskin débâcle, on the day the decree was released, the Grays sent him a copy. It was, after all, he who had in so many ways initiated the entire process.

For Hunt, so far from home, it must have been strange to receive accounts of the goings-on. Sitting in Cairo, remembering the early days so full of camaraderie and playfulness, ambition and purpose, he must have wondered at what was left of it all, with Deverell dead and gone and the others changed by life. The complex web of personal allegiances and animosities, compromising situations, emotional distractions and private turmoil must have seemed a sad conclusion to what had begun in 1848. The Brotherhood had become tainted, its chivalry tarred and its ideals breeched by nothing more than facts of life, love affairs and human weakness.

9

Dim phantoms of an unknown ill

O<small>N WEDNESDAY</small> 12 February 1862, at half-past one in the afternoon, a group of thirty or so people assembled at the Bridewell Hospital on New Bridge Street, near Blackfriars Bridge. It was a grim, austere place that offered none of the facilities or services associated with the term hospitalization as it is understood today.

Based around a large quadrangle, Bridewell's ominous four-storey, red-brick medieval buildings, with their small, dark, barred windows, spoke of a notorious past. It had been many things during its three centuries of life: a palace for Henry VIII, a school, a prison and for a significant proportion of its existence a house of correction for vagrants and prostitutes. Synonymous with terrible punishment and forsaken hope, the institution had been shut down in 1855 and denounced as an example of the worst failures of penal justice. Now its condemned buildings, which would be finally razed to the ground in 1863, were used for courtrooms and civic offices.

Although the worst of Bridewell's grisly history was behind it, those who found themselves there that day could not have much relished the task in hand. They had been summoned to an inquest. William Payne, the coroner, had issued warrants the previous day, and now twenty-four potential jurors and seven witnesses arrived to take part in the unpleasant hearing.

The inquest was into the sudden death of Elizabeth Eleanor Rossetti, *née* Siddall. She had died at around seven o'clock on the morning of Tuesday 11 February. The inquest had been called almost immediately to decide whether hers was a case of suicide, murder or just plain accident. The witnesses were: Mrs Sarah Birrell, a housekeeper; Catherine Birrell her daughter; Ellen McIntyre her niece; Francis Hutchinson, a doctor; Algernon Charles Swinburne, a poet; and Clara Siddall, the deceased's sister. The final witness was the deceased's husband, Dante Gabriel Rossetti, who had to walk just a few hundred yards from his apartments at 14 Chatham Place to the grim location. Rossetti's brother William Michael was at his side and sat with him throughout the proceedings for moral support.

If the witnesses' accounts, as they are preserved in the Corporation of London records, are written in the order in which the statements were given, then Mrs Birrell, the Rossettis' housekeeper at Chatham Place, went first.

Cautious of presenting Lizzie and Rossetti's relationship appropriately in such a public hearing, Mrs Birrell related that she had known Lizzie for nine years, and that Lizzie had lived at Chatham Place for the last two years. She testified that Lizzie was in bed in the afternoon of 10 February, and when she saw her at four in the afternoon she was quite cheerful. At eleven o'clock she was asleep. 'I was woken up at half past eleven by her husband. I saw her in her bed. She looked . . . blue in the face. A doctor was called for and he came directly and he tended to her.' Birrell explained that Lizzie 'used to take laudanum' to help her sleep and admitted that she saw 'a phial of it under her pillow'.[1]

Clara, Lizzie's sister, said that she had last seen Lizzie on the Saturday, when 'she seemed in tolerably good spirits'. Clara admitted that she knew of Lizzie's laudanum habit. She explained that she was called to Chatham Place at three on the Tuesday morning and there saw her sister 'alive but . . . unconscious'.

Rossetti, next to give evidence, explained that that Monday afternoon his wife had been 'fairly well' and at six or seven o'clock they went out to dinner,

but when we started she appeared drowsy and when we got half way in the cab I suggested going home again. She wished to go on and we dined at the Sabloniere in Leicester Square with a friend. She seemed somewhat between flightiness and drowsiness, a little excited. We left there at 8 and came straight home. I went out again after nine, leaving her just going to bed. She seemed as right as before. She was in the habit of taking large doses of laudanum. I know that she had taken 100 drops . . . I returned home at half past eleven and then she was a bed and snoring, I found her utterly without consciousness. I found a phial on a small table by her bedside. It was quite empty. The doctor was sent for and he attended her. She had not spoken of wanting to die. She had contemplated going out of town in a day or two and had bought a new mantle the day before.

The doctor, Francis Hutchinson, picked up the story. He explained he knew Lizzie because he had 'attended her in her confinement in April and May last. Her child was born dead and had been dead for a fortnight before it was born.' When he arrived at the house at about half-past eleven on the night in question, she was already in 'a comatose state and I tried to rouse her but without any avail. She could not swallow anything. I tried the stomach pump but it had no effect . . . I stayed with her till six in the morning . . . I believe that she died from the effects of laudanum which must have been a very large dose. The phial, found in the room, was about a 2 oz phial. It was labelled Laudanum poison.'

Swinburne confirmed that Lizzie and Rossetti had indeed dined with him on the Monday, and noted that he 'saw nothing particular in the deceased except that she appeared a little weaker than usual'.

The witnesses, brief and to the point in their accounts, had little else to say, although there was a general concern to point any finger of blame away from Rossetti himself. Clara noted that she did not suspect anyone of wanting to harm her sister; Catherine Birrell added that she knew of no hurt to Lizzie and that the Rossettis lived happily together, and her mother the housekeeper confirmed this.

Although a verdict of accidental death was duly recorded, and both Lizzie and Gabriel's reputations spared, some of those who had come to the house during that terrible night knew that key evidence had been withheld from the coroner: evidence that would have left little doubt that Lizzie had in fact had every intention of taking her own life and was well aware that the amount of laudanum that she was going to take was fatal.

Despite the testimonies to the contrary, all those who gave evidence would have also known that, far from being a happy marriage, the relationship with Rossetti was an extremely difficult one and that Lizzie, depressed and ill, might well have had several reasons to punish her husband with the ultimate gesture of despair.

On 18 February *The Times* made a brief note of the incident in its Deaths column, simply listing 'On 11th last at 14 Chatham Place, Blackfriars Bridge, Elizabeth Eleanor, wife of Dante Gabriel Rossetti, aged 29'. And with this cursory notice of her exit from the world, Lizzie, once the toast of the Brotherhood, once so full of hope and ambition, was gone. She had become a ghost of her former self: half mad, desperate and drug-addicted. Real life had imitated art as she herself had played the role of the tragic woman that had held such intrinsic fascination for her male colleagues.

To understand the source of Lizzie's unhappiness one has to go back to 1855. That year the Crimean War was still raging, although the handling of this conflict, which was now claiming the lives of thousands of men, had become a national scandal. The casualties were rising daily, but the greatest threat to Britian's soldiers was proving to be not so much the enemy as disease, poor food and inadequate hospital provision. *The Times* began to wage a campaign against the architects of this chaos. In January the outrage over the troops' conditions brought down the Prime Minister, Lord Aberdeen, and his coalition government. Aberdeen was replaced by Lord Palmerston.

The art world in London seemed fairly unperturbed by matters overseas. In Blackfriars it was Ruskin, rather than the war, that was of immediate interest to Rossetti and Lizzie. The latter's influence began to take hold of Rossetti and his pupil lover at this time, to no mean effect. Encouraged by Ruskin, Rossetti was now beginning to finish work and was producing beautiful watercolours, many of them on Arthurian themes. Of the ten or so he finished in 1855, Ruskin himself bought seven. The latter was also overtly promoting his new protégé among other members of the art-buying community.

Ruskin had also persuaded Rossetti to begin teaching at the Working Men's College in Red Lion Square. This institution, in the very square where Rossetti and Deverell had once shared rooms, was one to which Ruskin also offered his own services. It had been founded the previous year by a group of high-profile professional men with strong philanthropic and socialist leanings. The lawyer Tom Hughes, later to write *Tom Brown's Schooldays*, the academic Frederick Denison Maurice and the writer Charles Kingsley were founding members. With the Chartists' cause not far from their minds, they wanted to further the educational opportunities for the rapidly expanding working class.

It is hardly surprising that, now they were united in a common quest to share their skills with the less fortunate, the subject of Rossetti's own pupil and philanthropic cause came to the fore. And so in March Rossetti finally introduced his patron to Lizzie. Ruskin did not disappoint. 'I had a letter from Rossetti Thursday saying that Ruskin had bought all Miss Siddall's ("Guggums") drawings and said they beat Rossetti's own', Ford Madox Brown mused in his diary on 10 March 1855. 'This is like R, the incarnation of exaggeration, however he is right to admire them. She is a stunner and no mistake.'[2]

A month later Ruskin had gone yet further still. 'Ruskin the rogue had made two propositions to Miss Siddall', Brown noted in his diary on 13 April, 'not proposals although he would be capable of that – one to buy all that she does one by one – the other to give her a £150 a year for all she does . . . DGR in glee.'[3]

This was a huge break for Lizzie, and by the standards of the day an extraordinary offer. Expert seamstresses would have earned around £60 a year, and female shop assistants would rarely have managed £50.[4] And as far as artists went, the necessity for many far better-trained and established men either to give up or to emigrate, as Woolner had done, showed that this kind of subsidy only very rarely fell into male laps, let alone the lap of an un-exhibited woman. Even poor Brown, the recipient of all this news about Lizzie's change in fortune, had just a few weeks earlier resorted to writing out an advertisement regarding the one asset he had: 'Wanted £300 on mortgage of good freehold property'. He was also considering emigrating, to India.

So Lizzie and Rossetti had struck gold. But Ruskin's new-found patronage, although a blessing, raised other thorny issues. For example, there was no longer a financial barrier to their tying the knot. 'Rossetti once told me that when he first saw her he felt his destiny was defined', Brown remembered in his journal at around this time. 'Why does he not marry her?'[5]

Even Ruskin, despite his own personal allergy to matrimony, inquired: 'I should be very grateful if you thought it right to take me entirely into your confidence, and to tell me whether you have any plans or wishes, respecting Miss Siddal, which you are prevented from carrying out by want of a certain income, and if so what certain income would enable you to carry them out?'[6]

Why did he not marry her? The two had been together half a decade now, with Lizzie practically living in Chatham Place since the Rossetti brothers acquired the lease in 1852. If the couple were still worrying about their financial situation vis-à-vis matrimony, Ruskin could now ease concerns in this department. And surely Rossetti was sufficiently robust now to deal with the issue of social unsuitability.

By 30 April 1855 Ruskin was urging Rossetti to marry Lizzie in no uncertain terms: 'it would be best for you to marry, for the sake of giving Miss Siddal complete protection and care, and putting an end to the peculiar sadness, and want of you hardly know what, that there is in both of you.'[7] Yet Rossetti remained, as ever, vague and fudging. He took some steps that perhaps indicated an offer of marriage was to be forthcoming. After introducing Lizzie to Ruskin, he finally introduced her to his mother. And he wrote to his aunt Charlotte that he hoped to introduce Lizzie to her too at some stage. But for every step he took towards formalizing his relationship with Lizzie, Rossetti also seemed to take a couple back. Perhaps he now suggested that it was less money and more Lizzie's poor health that was postponing nuptial arrangements. Lizzie was seen by everyone, including herself, as having some ongoing malady. What exactly was the matter with her remained unclear, however, and seemed to be the subject of endless differing opinions, both professional and otherwise.

Eager to please his new friend, Ruskin joined in the concern for Lizzie's well-being. By May he had arranged for her to stay with his great friend and former university chum Henry Acland. Acland was famously genial and hospitable. He was Reader in Anatomy at Christ Church, Oxford, a fellow of All Souls as well as the librarian and physician to the Radcliffe Infirmary. He was a philanthropist of huge generosity whose home was nearly always fulls of guests and 'causes'. And so Ruskin quickly added Lizzie to the list.

Rossetti was soon corresponding with Acland in similar vein to the previous summer's exchanges with Barbara Leigh Smith and Bessie Parkes. His letters show all the concern of a genuine, devoted lover. He thanks Acland 'for your kind promise to tell me how 'she bears the journey' and hopes that Acland will tell him what he thinks 'as to her state of health'. This Acland did in due course. Then Gabriel relayed Acland's diagnosis to his mother in a move than can only be seen as an attempt to encourage his family to accept Lizzie. In a letter home he relayed how popular Lizzie had been:

> I went to Oxford some weeks ago when Guggum was there, and met some nice people, Dr Acland and his family, who as well as many others, were most kind to her there – too kind, for they bothered her greatly with attentions. Acland wanted her to settle at Oxford and said he would introduce her into all the best society.

All the women there are immensely fond of her . . . A great swell,
who is the warden of New College, an old cock, showed her all
the finest MSS in the Bodleian Library & paid her all manner of
attentions; winding up by an invitation to a special treat at his own
house, which consisted in showing her a black beetle painted by
Albert Durer . . . This she never went to enjoy. Acland examined
her most minutely & was constantly paying her professional visits
– all gratuitously being an intimate friend of Ruskin . . . he thinks
her lungs, if at all affected, are only slightly so & that the leading
cause of her illness lies in mental power long pent up & lately
overtaxed . . . By his advice, she is likely to leave England, probably
for the South of France, before the cold weather comes on
again.[8]

But one could never take Rossetti at face value. Although
attentive and concerned, new aspects of his life were emerging
that undermine the appearance of total devotion. While one day
he was attempting to 'sell' Lizzie as a potential wife into the
bosom of his family, on another day his interests lay elsewhere.

In June, after her stay with the Aclands, Lizzie holidayed in
Clevedon with her sister. Rossetti joined them for a couple of
days. Just before breakfasting with Lizzie on this holiday, he dashed
off a quick line to his friend Allingham: 'My rapports you ask of
with that "stunner" stopped some months ago after a long stay
away from Chatham Place, partly from a wish to narrow the circle
of flirtations in which she had begun to figure a little', he confided
to Allingham, 'but I often find myself sighing after her, now that
"roast beef, roast mutton, gooseberry tart" have faded into the
light of common day. "Oh what is gone from them I fancied
theirs?" '[9]

William Michael, forced to explain these references to the
editor of Allingham's and Rossetti's letters at the end of the
nineteenth century, conceded his brother had had an innocent
flirtation with a waitress. It is tempting to read William's explanation, coming from the pen of a man prone to whitewash and
evidently keen to preserve what was left of his sibling's reputa-

tion, as yet another attempt to gloss over a less salubrious truth.[10] Might Rossetti, the caring, considerate lover and proselytizing tutor, also have been the unfaithful partner? A pattern of betrayal and womanizing that within just a few years would define him seems as though it may have begun with this first 'extramarital' liaison.

This nameless 'stunner' served tables at one of Rossetti's regular local haunts, the Belle Savage inn on Ludgate Hill, a mere stone's throw from Chatham Place. Situated on the north side of Belle Savage Yard, its sign a bell perched on a hoop, this well-known establishment was close not only to Rossetti's apartment but also to the intriguingly titled Naked Boy Close, Fleet Street, the Old Bailey and the notorious Bridewell Hospital, where seven years later Lizzie's sad story would end.

It is not hard to imagine the raucous clientele that must have graced the Belle Savage in Rossetti's day: a mixture of high and low life, barristers and journalists, criminals and merchants. Its vivid, vulgar colour clearly appealed to Rossetti. He adored speaking in his own customized version of street slang, the language of 'stunners' and swells. This was the very world that the aspirant, quiet, delicate Lizzie wanted to move away from, but her lover could not help but be drawn to it.

The first mention of the waitress in question comes a year earlier, again in a letter to Allingham. 'I went to Belle S the other day, and was smiled on by the cordial stunner who came in on purpose in a lilac walking costume. I am quite certain she does not regret YOU at all.'[11] Is the implication that she had already slept with Allingham before moving on to Rossetti? This too is interesting, for Rossetti would quickly develop an appetite for women associated with other men.

Lizzie was aware that he was changing. A relationship that had once seemed like a dream come true was turning into a nightmare, and part of the nightmare was an 'unknown ill' descending upon her. Lizzie expressed all this in a poem written on the back of a letter to Emma Brown in 1855:

Slow days have passed that make a year,
Slow hours that make a day,
Since I could take my first dear love,
And kiss him the old way;
Yet the green leaves touch me on the cheek,
Dear Christ, this month of May.

I lie among the tall green grass
That bends above my head
And covers up my wasted face
And folds me in its bed
Tenderly and lovingly
Like the grass above the dead.

Dim phantoms of an unknown ill
Float through my tired brain;
The unformed visions of my life
Pass by in ghostly train;
Some pause to touch me on the cheek,
Some scatter tears like rain.

A shadow falls along the grass
And lingers at my feet;
A new face lies between my hands –
Dear Christ, if I could weep
Tears to shut out the summer leaves
When this new face I greet.

Still it is but the memory
Of something I have seen
In the dreamy summer weather
When the green leaves came between:
The shadow of my dear love's face –
So far and strange it seems.

The river ever running down
Between its grassy bed,
The voices of a thousand birds
That clang above my head,

Shall bring me to a sadder dream
When this sad dream is dead.

A silence falls upon my heart
And hushes all its pain.
I stretch my hands in the long grass
And fall to sleep again,
There to lie empty of all love
Like beaten corn of grain.[12]

Hand in hand with her persistent illness came a change in her behaviour. This was a period when Lizzie was much indulged and flattered by both Rossetti and Ruskin; she had been fussed over by impressive women in the form of Barbara Leigh Smith and Bessie Parkes, and had been the focus of much attention in Oxford. Although perhaps to her liberal, middle-class associates Lizzie was no more than the embodiment of several worthy causes, Lizzie herself lacked the objectivity to see herself in this light. She took this indulgence at face value.

Lizzie also had Rossetti as her primary role model. Again it is in the passages in his autobiography that he chose to edit out that we get a sense from Bell Scott of just how Lizzie's personality was transformed under Rossetti's tutelage. 'She had taken to the fastest ways, and to self taught proclivities in her assumed views of morals and religion, which he (DGR) only laughed at; and she had become a genius in art imitating her husband's inventions in water colours in a way I clearly saw to be damaging to peculiarities of his own works, though her uneducated performances were at once praised by him immoderately.'[13]

Lizzie became what Ruskin described as 'headstrong', although others might have interpreted her behaviour as prima donnaish. She left the Aclands so abruptly, for example, that Ruskin had to smooth Mrs Acland's slightly ruffled feathers: 'As far as I can make out, she is not ungrateful but sick, and sickly headstrong.'[14] She fell out with Rossetti's sister Christina at around this time, according to Brown's diaries, and the very same journal notes some kind of coolness between Gabriel and Fred Stephens over the latter's comments about Lizzie.

Lizzie and Rossetti's stay at Clevedon was followed by a strange period of indolence, in terms of work at least. On return to London their quiet, intimate world of sketching and mutual support dissolved into a round of intense socializing and late nights. Extravagant outings were made to theatres and restaurants. They went to Astley's – a hippodrome on Westminster Bridge Road that was the home of huge crowd-pulling spectacles – and to the Theatre Royal in Drury Lane. They ate out and hired sporty phaetons in which to cruise London's sights..

The formerly unostentatious couple upgraded their appearance. Quite unlike her former self, who had made her own simple grey frocks, Lizzie was discovered by Brown one day dressed like a 'queen' in an outfit that cost £3. Even Rossetti himself looked half-decent according to Brown, who, rather taken aback, noted that 'Gabriel was such a swell as I never saw before but looking really splendid. Everything about him perfect except his shoes, it will be some time before he goes that length.'[15]

Hand in hand with the late nights came late mornings. Notoriously undomesticated and messy, Gabriel and Lizzie became rather decadent. Ruskin became horrified not only by the hours they seemed to be keeping but also by the terrible mess he found Chatham Place in when he visited in the mornings. One day Ruskin turned up to find the Browns lounging in the apartment. Having talked until 3 a.m. the night before, they had stayed overnight, and when Ruskin called at a thoroughly respectable hour he was appalled to find Ford still in his shirt-sleeves. Ruskin was clearly in no mood for pleasantries with folk he saw as contributing to the general lethargy and bad behaviour of his two new protégés. Ruskin's pension seemed to be financing fun rather than work.

It was not just Lizzie and Rossetti who were making Ruskin tense. Some ten days or so before his grumpy encounter with Brown, the Effie business had resurfaced. On 7 July 1855 news of the marriage between Euphemia Chalmers Gray and John Everett Millais was published. Although readers of *The Leader* newspaper might have missed the news, which was bizarrely printed in the paper's Deaths column, readers of the *Morning Chronical* would have seen the nuptials happily announced four days earlier. 'On 3rd . . . at Bowerswell, John Everett Millais Esq. RA to Euphemia Chalmers, eldest daughter of George Gray Esq.'[16] The ceremony had taken place in the very same Bowerswell drawing-room where Effie and Ruskin had tied the knot some seven years earlier.

Millais had been careful to keep his distance from Effie, although he had written to her, until April 1855, at which point he went to Bowerswell. His stay was short but fruitful, as he explained in a letter to Hunt, who was still far away in the East:

> I was there only a few days as I was backward with my work, and had to return in haste, however I saw enough of her to arrange matters to this end. She dislikes naturally coming to London after her life in it and I much fear it will never cease to live in her memory, and will always affect her spirits, but time will shew. I have so little belief in my own ability to blot out this ruin in her first life that I am often very desponding in the matter, but I cannot see how this marriage could have been otherwise, everything seems to have happened to work out this end, and perhaps I should allow myself to go placidly with the stream, instead of worrying myself . . . Ruskin I have long since finished with . . . I hear of him of course continually, that is one thing which disturbs me, as She will never escape hearing his name mentioned . . . All London knows now of my marriage and comments upon it as the best thing I could do, the noblest, the vilest, the most impudent &c&c&c.[17]

The effect of the dash to Perth to propose showed on Millais's entry to the RA show that year. *The Rescue* was another dramatic human moment in which a firefighter is seen saving children from a burning house and delivering them into the desperate arms of their frantic mother. But the brushwork was not up to Millais's usual photographic standard. His personal life in turmoil, he had had to rush. Two days before the closing date for entries he had realized that he would have to work through the night to finish. Charlie Collins came to help and painted the fire hose.

When the RA show opened, Millais was horrified to find that the hanging committee had hung his picture above 'the line'. It had been two years since he had shown, his personal life was on everyone's lips and now his latest exhibition piece was placed so high that its viewers could not see it properly. Millais erupted.

His anger turned eventually to depression. In the letter in which he revealed his forthcoming marriage to Effie he confided to Hunt: 'I feel the want of you more than ever and Art wants you home. It is impossible to fight single handed and the RA has too great a consideration to lose sight of with all its position with the public ... I want you back again.'[18]

The old friendship was still there, but its fire had burned to embers. The strength of the allegiance that had once combined the enthusiasm of Hunt and Millais, that had harnessed the powerful pen of Ruskin and the dazzling will and spirit of Rossetti, was much weakened. It was really impossible for Millais and Ruskin to carry on as confrères. Ruskin, as always putting his love of art and intellect before personal affairs, tried to maintain the friendship. This step, as socially blinkered and idiosyncratic as ever, simply added to the increasing distaste in which he was held by Millais.

Just before Christmas 1854 Ruskin had dropped Millais a line to tell him:

> We have just got the picture [the Glenfinlas portrait] placed – in I think the very light it wants – or rather – for it cannot be said to want any light – in that which suits it best. I am far more delighted with it now that I was when I saw it in your room. As for the wonderment of the painting there can of course be no question – but I am also gradually getting reconciled to the figures in the way. On the whole the thing is right and what can one say more ... please send me your proper address, as I may often want to write to you now.[19]

'My address is Langham Chambers, Langham Place,' Millais replied, 'but I can scarely see how you conceive it possible that I can desire to continue on terms of intimacy with you. Indeed I concluded that after finishing your portrait you yourself would have seen the necessity of abstaining from further intercourse. The barrier which cannot but be between us personally does not prevent me from sympathising with all your efforts to the advancement of good taste in Art, and heartily wishing them success.'[20]

'Sir,' Ruskin responded,

I can only conclude that you either believe I had, as has been alleged by various base or ignorant persons, some unfriendly purpose when I invited you to journey with me in the Highlands, or that you have been concerned in the machinations which have for a long time been entered into against my character and fortune. In either case I have to thank you for a last lesson, though I have had to learn many and bitter ones, of the possible extent of human folly and ingratitude. I trust that you may be spared the natural consequences of the one, or the dire punishment of the other.[21]

And that should have been that, but for one final show of intellectual disinterest by Ruskin, who in May 1855 came out in favour of *The Rescue*, claiming that the fast, rushed brushwork added a sense of urgency to the painting that was entirely appropriate. It was the last time Ruskin's treatment of his former protégé would remain so unbiased. Soon his pen would turn. But so would those of other critics and observers, against Ruskin. The ripples of Ruskin's personal life would reach out and rock his professional standing, just as he would begin his own attempts to erode Millais's reputation.

The story of the Ruskin marriage had become a grotesque obsession for all those within the orbit of the protagonists. The weird pantomime of a story began to seep into people's subconscious, touching them at some profound level. Brown began having monstrous dreams about Ruskin. 'Woke up on the sofa in the parlour at 4 a.m. Dreamt I had been dining with Ruskin who boasted he had got one child out of his late spouse at least, whatever the slanderous world might say.'

In his diaries Brown jokes about Ruskin's emasculation. Playing with the Victorian slang word for testicles ('stones') and Ruskin's own *Stones of Venice*, he records that 'According to his [Ruskin's] account he is not stoneless far from it. On the contrary, during his years of marriage, "he proposed three or four times to his wife" that "they would live as man & wife" but she declined – what an impassioned husband.'[22]

A whole year after the rupture of the Ruskin marriage its ramifications still hung like a pall over the entire set of PRB relationships. 'No tangible combination now showed itself among the working and sleeping members of our Brotherhood', Hunt realized when he returned from his travels at the beginning of 1856, 'neither was there any professed tie between us and the outside adherents or our reform. For two years there had been no night excursions, no boating and no corporate life of any kind. In earlier days it seemed as though we could always trust one another, if not for collaboration, at least for good-fellowship and cordiality; it proved however that these, too, were things of the past never to be revived.'[23]

'It became obvious at once that no one could . . . be cordially intimate with both Millais and Ruskin', Hunt observed.[24] Hunt, Millais's greatest friend, nailed his colours to the mast. Brown loathed Ruskin, and so it was easy for him to jump into the Millais camp too. But Rossetti not only stuck with Ruskin, his patron, but also chose to believe his account of the relationship with Effie. Brown noted in his diary that on 1 April 1855 Rossetti had been 'abusing Mrs Ruskin and praising Mr. I the reverse.'[25]

Millais got wind of Rossetti's stance, which merely widened the schism that had already developed between them. Brown attempted to breach it, inviting Millais to visit Rossetti's studio with him, where he was working on a watercolour, *Paolo and Francesca*, based on a story from Dante.

'I found he was adverse to going to Rossetti's, he first said R had never shown him any thing for 3 years . . . then it came out that Rossetti was always speaking of Ruskin as though he was a saint of the calendar & not showing one word of sympathy for his wife', Brown noted. 'However I got him to go to Chatham Place & certainly I never witnessed a mortal more delighted than he was when he saw Francesca. . . . After he went I told Rossetti of Millais's soreness and he seemed penitent.'[26]

Rossetti's *Paolo and Francesca* is a depiction of doomed and tragic love. It is a tale of adultery, much like the Lancelot story, in which Francesca and her brother-in-law Paolo fall in love. They are murdered by Francesca's husband for their illicit affair, and together float through hell. The tale's pertinence to Millais's recent history could not have been missed. Its relevance to Rossetti's own story had yet to be played out.

In spite of Rossetti's apparent penitence and a fleeting reunion with Millais, this liaison was not repeated. Like a flower blown on the wind, which rests for a moment before being carried further away, the friendship caught fleetingly and was then gone.

After their marriage Millais and Effie enjoyed a short honeymoon in Scotland before moving to a house called Annat Lodge in Perth, close to Bowerswell. A handsome late eighteenth-century house, built in golden stone with a double storey of large, rounded bay windows overlooking a beautiful garden, it must have felt like a welcome break from the dirty, smelly, disease-ridden streets of an increasingly crowded London. And here Millais and Effie could put the London chatterboxes behind them. Within a year they would become parents.

On Thursday 29 May 1856 London enjoyed a spectacle that it would not forget in a hurry, as *The Times* reported to its readers the following morning: 'The ceremony of yesterday will long live in the memory of all who witnessed it as an occasion on which all classes of the inhabitants of this great metropolis and thousands of others who came from far and near to participate in the general rejoicing, laid aside their varied occupations of their daily lives . . .

and abandoned themselves to the celebration of a joyous epoch in the nation's history.'[27]

The cause of celebration was the return of peace in Europe. The dreadful, draining Crimean War had finally concluded with an Allied victory. The government had gone to enormous expense to win back the support of a population that had become weary of war, weary of injustice and weary of a capital that seemed always in the throes of one epidemic or another. It was, as ever, the working classes who were weariest. With the armies, which had been furnished from working homes, now returned from the East, the government provided fun in buckets. Anticipation had been building all week. As *The Times* reported two days before the day of celebration, 'upwards of four hundred ambulances and artillery wagons left Woolwich arsenal last week for London, laden with the wooden frames and fireworks to be erected in the parks. Last evening about 50 others were dispatched.'[28]

Illuminations were erected in all major London streets and around major buildings. The *Illustrated London News* dedicated two of its issues to engravings of the spectacle: Buckingham Palace was ablaze, as were Regent Street and the Strand, East India House, Waterloo Place, the Admiralty and Horse Guards. Spectators on Hampstead Heath could see London alight as never before and then in addition enjoy firework displays in Hyde Park, Green Park and on Primrose Hill.

Lizzie was not in town to witness the festivities. Rossetti had dispatched her off to Nice in the south of France the previous December, on Ruskin and Acland's recommendation. First the pair had travelled to Paris together, where by all accounts they behaved like a pair of young lovers and seemed utterly devoted to one another. Millais's *Ophelia* was on show in the French capital as part of the Exposition Universelle, and Lizzie must have enjoyed her celebrity extending to the continent.

But once Rossetti had returned home, and after weeks in the south away from her lover, Lizzie's letters from Nice reveal how anti-social she had become. Although in the elegant setting of the

Côte d'Azur, it is not the blue of the sea, the vibrant flower market or the fashionable cosmopolitan set strolling on the Promenade des Anglais that she chooses to describe. Rather, she writes home about the ordeal of securing money, how she prefers to dine alone, how she feels stared at for her thinness, and how thankful she is that English food is on the Christmas menu. She is dismissive of her foreign environment. Although her intelligence and dry wit come through, so too does her negative introspection.

Rossetti, with his indulgent romantic Italian heritage, was ready to meet someone totally unlike Lizzie that summer, and so he did. During the post-war celebrations he encountered, by chance as ever, one of his most controversial female associates, who would become intrinsically linked with Lizzie's death. She was born Sarah Cox but became known as Fanny Cornforth.

There are a few versions of the fateful meeting between Rossetti and Fanny. William Bell Scott claims that Fanny passed Rossetti in the Strand. In a gesture that seems wrought with Freudian implication, she was apparently cracking nuts provocatively between her teeth, spitting the shells out at Rossetti as he passed. In other accounts this meeting, nuts and all, takes place at Cremorne Pleasure Gardens in Chelsea. London's great pleasure gardens were places of abandon and wanton behaviour. With their bandstands and dancing platforms, regular fireworks, balloon ascents, beverage tents and promenades they were the haunts of swells on the pull. Respectable women did not grace them, but working-class girls and prostitutes after men and a good time did. That Fanny was a prostitute seems unchallenged, and placing her in either Cremorne or the Strand – a notorious haunt for London's 'gay' girls – simply reinforces her reputation.

But Fanny's own version of her first meeting with Rossetti is slightly different. She gave it some twenty-five years or so after the event to Samuel Bancroft, an eminent collector of Rossetti's art and manuscripts. According to Fanny, it was thanks to that 'infusion of the provincial element' into the capital for the Crimea celebrations that Rossetti first cast eyes on the woman who would become one of the dominant faces in this later work:

> Among others attracted to London to see the sights was a very young girl from the village of Steyning in Surrey named Sarah Cox, who came up on the invitation of an elderly cousin living in London, who took her with a party in the evening to see the fireworks in old Surrey gardens. During the evening there came in a party of . . . artists wandering about to find subjects and models consisting of Ford Madox Brown, Dante Gabriel Rossetti, Edward Burne-Jones . . . They were attracted by the great beauty of this country girl and especially her great wealth of magnificent golden hair; and one of them 'accidentally on purpose' in passing behind her, gave it a touch with his fingers so that it all fell down her back. The result was apologies and a conversation in which an agreement was made that the elderly cousin should take her the next day to Rossetti's studio at Blackfriars Bridge.[29]

Whatever the actual circumstances of the encounter, Rossetti met Fanny in carefree holiday spirits. And she did not disappoint. From the moment he met Fanny, Lizzie was one way or another doomed.

Fanny was a big girl. She had an earthiness and frankness that Rossetti found intoxicating. The name she chose to model under, taken from a maternal grandmother, summed up her frank, fun-loving personality, driven by an open sexuality that lacked self-consciousness and was unaffected by social constraints. She was free like the breeze in a cornfield, as were her favours. Fanny sat for *Found* almost instantly, and Rossetti instantly adored her.

In his compulsive drawing of Lizzie, Rossetti had explored his own personal fetishes: his love of her long red hair; his fascination with her introspective manner; her unusually long neck and petulant lips. The exploration of these fetishes once on paper or canvas became trained in pursuit of an idealized vision of womanhood. Ideal womanhood would be *his* subject: he would explore it again and again. But when Fanny entered his world, Rossetti began to see that female idols could take many forms. Rossetti saw that there were other altars at which he could worship beyond that of the pure, tragic heroine. There were profane, worldly goddesses.

Around the time of Fanny's arrival on the scene Rossetti's character exhibited a marked change. William Bell Scott put it more forcefully. Rossetti 'underwent a surprising development. His curious materialistic piety disappeared, burst like a soap bubble . . . the early views of self culture and self sacrifice . . . underwent a similar bouleversement.'[30] This 'bouleversement' was undergone not just in connection with Fanny Cornforth, or for that matter the stunner in lilac at the Belle Savage. Rossetti never did anything by halves. There was yet another woman in his own 'widening circle of flirtation' at this time, and she was none other than his friend Hunt's proposed future wife, Annie Miller.

There seemed to be a facet of Rossetti's personality that was now beginning to confuse the idealized woman and the real thing. Lizzie, with her small-time background, illness and tricky behaviour, was increasingly failing to live up to the obsessive images of her that Rossetti was so endlessly producing and investing in. Meanwhile, as fresh models entered his orbit, his new exploration of their beauty on canvas quickly became confused with his feelings for the real women in front of him. As one of Rossetti's friends would later observe, he 'was addicted to loves of the most material kind both before and after his marriage, with women, generally models, without other soul than their beauty. It was remorse at the contrast between his ideal and his real loves that preyed on him and destroyed his mind.'[31]

10

Not as she is but as she fills his dream

A T THE END of 1855 Hunt left the Holy Land, where he had been for nearly two years, and decided to see for himself the carnage of the Crimea. He was in low spirits. He had started out east just as the war was in its infancy, and he had anticipated swift victory. But now the image of a masterful British race was eroded. 'Our long-retarded and still incomplete triumph had marred our prestige, and it was easy to see that we should have to fight for it all again in the East', Hunt gloomily recounted. Earnest and political as ever, Hunt travelled to Beirut, 'which was to be my place of embarkation for the seat of War, [and where] it was natural for me to speculate on the future prospect of our arms; this national question occupied my attention in alternation with the thoughts of what the members of our fraternity had done and were doing, and how my best friends would care for the small store of work I should be able to show them. My curiosity was the greater as, having assured them by post that I was on the point of starting for home, I had received but few letters for the last few months.'[1]

There was good reason why Hunt had not had much mail. While he had the burden of the world on his shoulders and was wondering what his brethren were up to, his brethren were unburdening themselves from the cares of the world in the company of his supposed ward.

From the moment *The Awakening Conscience* was shown in the summer of 1854, Annie was marked out as a wonder, and almost as soon as Hunt had left London, his friends had pounced on her.

Although Hunt had appointed his PRB colleague and former student Fred Stephens in charge, written careful lists of respectable artists who would pose no threat to the extremely vulnerable girl and paid her lodging and tuition, Annie was apparently considered fair game. And Annie was apparently happy to be thus perceived.

Her extraordinary charms extended far and wide. Rossetti's friend the artist George Price Boyce was quick to jump to her side. So was Rossetti himself. But more surprising perhaps was that the more considered William Michael Rossetti also got involved with her. So did another artist friend of Hunt's, Mike Halliday, and even Stephens himself. It was as though she was totally irresistible.

They took her out to restaurants and danced with her at the Cremorne Gardens. Sometimes their expeditions were discreet, and other times less so. Stephens took Fanny boating and managed to tip up the boat, possibly owing to some clumsiness caused by an unspecified disability with which he was apparently afflicted.

Stephens was keen to pretend to Hunt that the latter's trust in him had not been misplaced and so confessed in a letter to Hunt that Annie had been sitting to a few artists; he also assured him that he had spoken firmly to both Annie and Rossetti (one of the artists in question). And so Hunt, far away in his desert lands, suspected no more than that Annie had at one stage modelled a little more widely than he had hoped.

But Rossetti's attachment to Annie extended way beyond modelling. There are accounts of her dominating Chatham Place and even playing hostess there, no doubt facilitated by Lizzie's increasing trips out of London on account of her health. Rossetti's drawings of Annie become reminiscent of his depictions of Lizzie in their relaxed intimacy. Annie appears with her hair let down, as does Lizzie so often. They are even drawn in what seems to be the same spoon-backed chair. But Rossetti's pictures of Annie speak for themselves. He doesn't have the intense engagement with her image that he does with Lizzie's, but Annie is clearly more conventionally beautiful. Her image is less powerful than Lizzie's, but her beauty is less imagined. What Annie also had that Lizzie feared

DESPERATE ROMANTICS

was the ability to 'have a laugh' with the boys. She loved going out with men and having raucous fun. This was not something one naturally associated with the more restrained Miss Siddall.

Annie's escapades with the lads, however, extended beyond the Pre-Raphaelite circle. During the whirlwind of socializing she was enjoying while Hunt was away she had encountered Thomas Heron Jones, Lord Ranelagh, a viscount and military gent with property and money and with a reputation for bad behaviour.

Ranelagh had taken her to Mr Bertolini's well-known restaurant on St Martin's Lane and apparently drank champagne from her slipper. So she had become his mistress too. Ranelagh must have been delighted that his latest acquisition was benefiting from the tutorials and deportment sessions provided at Hunt's expense. Annie's hair was now beautifully dressed, she was fashionably clad, her manners and speech were improving and she was beginning to read and write.

If these attachments with other men had begun as early as Hunt's departure, they were certainly still ongoing when he made his return. Hunt came back with the first wave of soldiers dismissed from the Crimea. *En route* home he met none other than Mike Halliday, who had had a relationship with Annie Miller. Halliday did not, it seems, put Hunt in the picture. They travelled back together, making their way across Europe's railway system second-class. Finally they found themselves back in London at three in the morning. Hunt made his way to Millais's studio in Langham Place, discarded since his move to Scotland, but occupied by friends. 'To my surprise my excellent friend Lowes Dickinson opened the door,' Hunt remembered, 'welcoming me with as great cordiality as any long lost wanderer.'[2]

Hunt found a house in Pimlico, settled with Halliday and was joined there by another artist, Robert Martineau. Gradually he began to catch up with people. On asking Brown about Rossetti and Lizzie, who Fred Stephens had indicated in his letters were engaged, he was surprised to discover that, according to Brown, they were not. Lizzie was merely Rossetti's pupil, Brown claimed.

Hunt's initial conversations with Rossetti were all about art. Hunt wanted to know what to do about the imminent Royal Academy show. He had only a few weeks to sort out his work and submit for the annual exhibition. After so long away he needed both a quick sale to replenish the coffers and some publicity to re-establish himself at the vanguard of British art.

Typically, Rossetti advised him one thing, then the other. First he advised him to show at the RA. Then he wrote to him and strongly advised him not to do so, but to hold a private exhibition that would show all his 'Eastern' work together. Hunt decided to show at the RA, but one assumes that this decision had little to do with Rossetti, who was as changeable as a barometer.

The picture Hunt returned with was a genuine departure, called *The Scapegoat*. The history of its making is full of tales of one poor goat being transported and tethered on the banks of the Dead Sea, of said goat expiring, of Hunt packing salt and rocks and bones from the location onto his mule train and returning to Jerusalem, where another goat was procured and also died. All the while sheikhs and bandits were encountered and dealt with, fevers and hashish-induced hallucinations were experienced and death was dodged with alarming frequency. It was hardly surprising that the resulting piece of work was extraordinary in comparison with other works that showed that season.

Painted with vivid, luminescent colour, the picture is deeply symbolic. Taken from a passage in the Talmud, it refers to the Judaic tradition of expelling a goat from the Temple on the Day of Atonement. Driven into the wilderness, the goat carries the sins of the congregation on its back. And if the scarlet braid wrapped around its horns turns white, then the congregation has been delivered from its sins and forgiven. In Hunt's hands the goat has become a symbol of Christ, depicted with the vivid realism that was his established trademark.

When Hunt had left for Palestine there had been some tension between his apparent quest to create informed religious work and his own moral behaviour. His relationship with Annie Miller aside, according to Millais he also enjoyed a risqué sexual encounter on the train to Paris on the very morning of his departure. But whatever sins Hunt had left behind him in London, he must have felt as though he paid for them during his adventure to the shores of the Dead Sea. After taking genuinely great risks in crossing the desolate and dangerous desert terrain to paint this picture on the actual shores of the sterile salt lake, and having survived hostile tribal peoples in the name of his art, the tittle-tattle of the London society to which he returned must have seemed particularly inane. His colleagues could scarce have appreciated the perils Hunt had faced as part of his personal quest, and perhaps this is why their disloyalties, when finally discovered, hurt him so deeply.

In spite of its bold unconventionality, *The Scapegoat* was hung on 'the line' and sold for 450 guineas. Hunt was back with something of a bang.

Despite the presence of Hunt once more in London and despite Lizzie's return from the Côte d'Azur, Rossetti continued to see Annie, who, ever the pragmatist, was more than prepared to keep her options open.

If the order of events as described in Brown's diary is anything to go by, it was Hunt who got wind of things first. On 6 July Brown noted that Hunt told him 'about Annie Millar's [sic] love for him and his liking for her, and perplexities, and how Gabriel like a mad man increased them taking Annie to all sorts of places of amusement which he had implied if not stated should not be . . . And having allowed her to sit to Gabriel while he was away Gabriel has let her sit to others not on the list and taken her to dine at Bertolini's and to Cremorne where she danced with Boyce, and William takes her out boating . . . They all seem mad about Annie Millar and poor Hunt has had a fever about it.'[3]

Although Hunt had obviously finally been told about the socializing with Annie, it is not clear just when the full depth of Rossetti's affair with her was rumbled. It seems that Lizzie realized the full scale of the relationship first. Ten days after a 'feverish'

Hunt had cried on Brown's shoulder, a hysterical Lizzie was crying on his wife's. 'Emma called on Miss Sid yesterday who is very ill & complaining much of Gabriel. He seems to have transferred his affections to Annie Millar and does nothing but talk of her to Miss Sid. He is mad past care.'[4]

By September, however, the ding-dong between Rossetti and Hunt over Annie was apparently resolved, according to Brown at least. He now recounted that 'Hunt and he [Rossetti] seem all right again. Gabriel has foresworn flirting with Annie Millar it seems, Guggum having rebelled against it. He & Guggum seem on best terms now, she is painting at her picture.'[5]

But Brown's version of events was hopelessly over-optimistic. Brown failed to recognize the damage to Rossetti's relationships with both Hunt and his future wife. In his diary it is Rossetti's own dismissive and evasive summary of the situation that rings true. He could always look on the bright side.

But in fact the rupture between him and Hunt would be far more serious than he imagined. Over the next few months the full scale of Annie's disloyalty to her guardian and the extent of Rossetti's deception dawned on Hunt. Rossetti had misjudged both Hunt's depth of feelings for Annie and how seriously he took the issue of loyalty when it came to women.

Although they continued as professional colleagues for a while, Hunt saw Rossetti as the root of all this trouble with Annie. He had led her astray. His resentment at Rossetti's betrayal only grew in time and finally became an insurmountable obstacle to their continuing friendship. As William Michael also conceded, as ever attempting to underplay the truth behind his summation of it: 'I understand perfectly well what it is that Mr Hunt terms "the offence" but if my reader chooses to ask the old question "who was the woman?" he will . . . chance to remain for ever unanswered . . . it behoves me to say that Mr Hunt was wholly blameless in the matter; not so my brother, who was properly, though I will not say very deeply, censurable.'[6]

Hunt, thrown by news of Annie's gallivanting, could no longer look forward to a quick marriage on his return, as he had hoped. Marriage was still his intention, but he wanted her to get a little further with her studies, despite encouragement from Millais, who, on hearing he was home, wrote: 'Man was not intended to live alone. . . . marriage is the best cure for for that wretched lingering over one's work . . . I think I must feel more settled than you all. I would immensely like to see you all married like myself and anchored.'[7]

Millais was not referring to Annie in his encouragements. He was attempting to veer Hunt towards more appropriate candidates. Hunt, however, was hooked on the little girl from the slums, and Annie, who after two years waiting for her benefactor to return was clearly expecting a proposal and a date, very grudgingly continued with her 'improvement'.

The following year Hunt moved Annie into new lodgings at 11 Bridge Road, near Pimlico, with a landlady called Mrs Stratford. A governess called Miss Prout also lodged at the address. Hunt immediately employed the latter to continue Annie's studies.

The odd thing is that Hunt continued to use Stephens as a go-between between himself and Annie. He would give Stephens funds, and Stephens would pass these on to Annie. Stephens would liaise with Mrs Stratford and deal directly with issues regarding her welfare. Although this arrangement made perfect sense when Hunt was absent, its continuation on his return reveals Hunt's desire to retain a distance from Annie until he considered her ready to marry him.

By January 1858 Hunt was still unsure about his ward. He swung from believing one day that marriage was possible to thinking the next day it was impossible. But whether it was on or off, the question of Annie undoubtedly haunted and obsessed him.

'Hunt who was all hot about Anny M has somehow quite cooled again in a few days & now says that it is never to be', Brown noted in his diary.[8] But then just a few days later George Price Boyce noted in *his* diary a visit from Hunt that indicated that all was on again.

Having in prospect to marry Annie Miller, after that her education both of mind and manners shall have been completed, he wished to destroy as far as possible all traces of her former occupation, viz, that of sitting to certain artists . . . and as mine was the only direct study of her head, as it was, he would hold it a favour if I would give it him and he in return would give me something of his doing that I might like. At first I resisted stoutly, but finding that it was a serious point with him, and that my refusing would be in some degree an obstacle in the carrying out of his wishes with regard to her (which it would be both selfish and unkind and foolish in the remotest degree to thwart) I at last reluctantly assented to give him the study, the most careful and the most interesting (to me) and which I prize the most I have ever made.[9]

Despite steps taken by Hunt to edit Annie's past, a few months later he was once more feeling negative about the situation. Writing to his friend Jack Tupper in June 1858, Hunt revealed that, although he had been back for two years now, and although he had been educating Annie for twice that time, she still fell short of his exacting standards:

She is not far enough advanced to make it certain that she could master all the things necessary for a wife of a man who must count his halfpence – read, write, think, know believe, teach control and do, and have her do the same. My object was to give her the best opportunity and then decide by her advance.

Heaven knows it goes against me to assume this high tone about a woman's love and such a woman whom I would scarcely have dared to kneel to had fate ordered her beginning with only common advantages of instruction. Her imagination is of high order as her physical beauty but it remains to be proved whether after so long a season of neglect she can be trained and harnessed to household uses.[10]

Where did Hunt's image of womanhood come from? Few of the married women in his immediate circle could have matched this ideal. Brown's wife, Emma, seemed as full of flaws as the rest of humankind – they muddled through, though from Brown's diaries there is plenty of evidence of fearsome rows and average short-comings. Perhaps it was Effie that Hunt was setting as his gold standard. She was without doubt something of a social and domestic goddess, but then her background was much more privileged. And her reputation was hardly flawless after the Ruskin scandal.

Or perhaps the role model against which Hunt measured poor Annie was in Hampstead in the form of Mrs Emily Patmore, the wife of Hunt's good friend the poet Coventry Patmore. Patmore had been a PRB collaborator since the early days. He had contributed to the ill-fated *Germ* and had encouraged Ruskin to support the group. His wife held the dubious credit of being the original muse for his best-selling poetic saga *The Angel in the House*. Written in 1854 and published in instalments between 1855 and 1860, this incredibly long piece is a poetic essay on courtship, love and marriage. At its centre is the idealized vision of a woman who would and could be all things to her man. The Victorian public took to this image of a mild, subordinate woman, who was an embodiment of purity, elegance and manners, designed to support her husband come what may and to set an example despite his shortcomings. Painted by Millais in 1851, however, Emily had none of Annie's breathtaking beauty. Her picture shows a doe-eyed girl with a face too narrow and a nose too large to be called conventionally beautiful.

Whether or not it was Emily Patmore that offered Hunt the standard against which he measured Annie, Annie herself had different views on what a woman should or should not do. She remained pragmatic. Every scrap of opportunity that was flung her way she grabbed avariciously. She was even exploiting Hunt's self-imposed distance from her. When Hunt's eyes were averted, she went astray.

She began to spend the money that Hunt provided for her rent and governess on other things. Eventually Mrs Stratford got sick of Annie's arrears and contacted the police. Annie put the police onto Fred Stephens, who in turn contacted Hunt. The police did not come round, but now Mrs Stratford was on the warpath. She let it be known that Annie, far from being a diligent student, was in the habit of putting on her glad rags and taking off with other escorts. All this was laid at Stephens's door. He in turn became worried and shared his concerns with Hunt.

Hunt, rather than going to talk to his potential future wife in person, asked Stephens to lay down the law to Annie. She must keep accounts, must stop modelling for others and, if she needed more money, must take a respectable job. Annie, no doubt furious at the way she was being handled, refused all Hunt's requests and stopped seeing him. She had had enough of being a social experiment. The relationship apparently at an end, Hunt and Annie remained quite separate for a few months.

The impression given of Hunt in the diaries and letters of his friends at the time is of a man in turmoil. Driven by his work, fuelled as before by incredible energy, he was also climbing socially. Ever since his return from the Middle East he had been in demand on the dinner party circuit. He was handsome, talented, famous and single. This heady combination made him irresistible to the capital's socialites, and he took the bait. His tailor's bill went up, his suits were sharp and his public profile clearly began to matter. Highly aware of his status as a self-made man, he could come over as pious and self-important. Boyce summed this up once when he noted in his diary that he saw Hunt 'from an omnibus top . . . with nose high in air'.[11]

But Hunt was also tortured. After his years in the wilderness he was packed with pent-up sexual energy, which his sense of his own respectability now prevented him from venting in loose extramarital relationships. Millais noticed how damaging this personal conflict was becoming to his friend. Brown recalls in his diary Millais going on about Hunt's sexual restraint as being totally unhealthy. Millais was writing about the issue to their mutual friends and patrons the Combes too. Everyone could see that celibacy was proving a genuine difficulty for someone with so much 'energy'.

This is perhaps why Hunt went back to Annie. Driven by his

barely contained lust, he turned up in Bridge Road again towards the end of 1859. His frustration found some release: he began drawing her again. She was like a drug. As Hunt's granddaughter pointed out, 'On the same principle that induced Hunt to boil a horse to produce a skeleton on which to base an accurate portrayal of its outward appearance, he invariably painted his models in the nude before adding clothes.'[12] And Annie was extraordinary when she was undressed. As Diana Holman Hunt also notes, a friend of Hunt's once called by and saw the nude studies of Annie that Hunt made for the *Lady of Shalott*.

> When I saw this canvas in April, the figure of the Lady was nude, and I could not but tell the artist that it seemed to me almost a sacrilege to drape so fair and exquisite a conception, which taught the lesson at one flash that modesty had no need of a cloak. This lovely figure bore no evidence of having been servilely copied from a stripped model, who had been distorted by the modiste's art. It did not suggest unclothedness, for the simple reason that it gave no impression that it knew the meaning of clothes at all.[13]

But soon tensions erupted, and once more it was because of Annie's continuing liaisons with other men. One evening Hunt spotted a letter on Annie's fireplace that he thought was in Boyce's handwriting. Annie threw it on the fire before he could open it. A few days later Boyce and other friends joined Hunt for supper. Under the impression that his relationship with Annie was definitely off, rather than hovering between on and off, they revealed the true extent of her deception. Now the stories about Lord Ranelagh came out:

> I learnt this creditable fact of the young lady who has caused me so many miseries that immediately before I sent her to school she was seen walking with a swell Regent St whore – and also that she was met one day dressed in the extreme of fashion walking down St James's Street, with a love Lord Somebody – a great rake – a discovery which does not astonish me now, it disgusts me however to think that the person who saw her there who had met her with

A Nightmare, by Frederick Sandys, 1857. This cartoon satirized Millais's picture *Sir Isumbras at the Ford*, and showed Rossetti, Millais and Hunt riding on the 'ass' Ruskin's back

me only a few days before and who seems to have known what my feelings were for her then did not tell me at the time.[14]

Hunt, like Millais, had had his share of public attention by 1859. His work had been the subject of praise and criticism in the major papers of the day for nearly a decade. And if satire is the measure of fame, then he could count himself as a genuine celebrity. His works were caricatured for popular consumption. One cartoonist, working under the name Buskin, produced parodies of both *The Awakening Conscience* and *The Hireling Shepherd* in 1857, in response to Hunt's work on show in the hugely popular Manchester Exhibition of Art Treasures.

This exhibition was mounted in response to the phenomenal success of the Great Exhibition six years earlier, but whereas the former had presented art and industry together, Manchester's show paid homage to the celebrity of art and the artist alone. Sixteen thousands works were brought together, and Millais's recently painted *Autumn Leaves* and Hunt's above-mentioned canvases were exhibited alongside treasures by Michelangelo and Rembrandt. If the growing attendances at the Royal Academy shows had served to make Hunt and Millais famous, this exhibition, which saw a staggering 1.3 million people pass through its doors in 142 days, raised them to superstardom.

And in the same year it was not just Hunt's work but Hunt himself who starred in a cartoon that took London by storm. The print was a spoof on one of Millais's pictures at the RA that year, *A Dream of the Past – Sir Isumbras at the Ford*, in which Millais, Hunt and Rossetti, the famous PRB three, were seen riding on Ruskin the mule.[15] And then, of course, a year later Dickens introduced Mildmay Strong to the nation in his wicked satirical piece about Calmuck.

But this new kind of stardom, which went hand-in-hand with exhibition success, progress and print, had its price. Only too sensitive to his public standing, Hunt began to imagine that details about Annie were seeping out into the fabric of his public world. Everywhere he looked, Annie's deceptions seemed to be reflected back. He wrote to Stephens, convinced that details of her infidelities were being communicated in the smalls ads of newspapers, where lovers would often leave messages for one another in their own private shorthand. Hunt became so convinced that the classified section of *The Times* was being used as a medium to discuss his private affairs, he even began to worry that he would soon be actually named there.

It is tempting to see Hunt's paranoia developing a worrying delusional aspect. His friends must have felt so too. He had experimented with drugs in Palestine, and had subjected himself to genuine hardship and peril. He had also fallen in love with a girl whom his own sense of convention meant he could never realistically marry, and with whom his dearest 'brothers' had shamelessly consorted. Fame was now magnifying his dilemmas. Hunt was having a breakdown, and his friends got him out of London to recuperate.

*

It was not just Hunt whose mental health was proving fragile. With the Annie affair revealed and now behind him, Rossetti's personality began to swing wildly. His mercurial behaviour, once confined to relatively unimportant events such as keeping rendez-vous and sticking to holiday decisions, now applied to life-changing decisions. It was as though he could no longer consider anything profoundly, pursuing life as though it were a string of whims.

On 8 October 1856 William Rossetti was sitting to Brown when Gabriel, as was now typical, came in to interrupt Brown's work. 'William wishing to go early Gabriel proposed that he should wait five minutes & he would go too. When William being got to sleep on the sofa, Gabriel commenced telling me how he intended to get married at once to Guggum & then off to Algeria!!!! & so poor Williams 5 minutes lasted till ½ past 2 am.'[16]

This was Barbara Leigh Smith's doing. She was nursing her sister in Algiers, which was enjoying a reputation as a health resort. Bessie Parkes forwarded some information about Algiers to Gabriel. Gabriel's decision to combine marriage plans and a health trip seems to be inspired totally by these women's latest enthusiasm. Lizzie was unimpressed. She had not particularly enjoyed Nice. Instead, she went to Bath to lick her wounds, and with her declining of the overseas trip Rossetti's offer of marriage seemed to evaporate too.

Christina Rossetti could see all too clearly what was going on. Although with Lizzie back in his orbit, his painting of her tempor-arily refreshed by his fascination with her beauty, Rossetti was increasingly aware that the real woman beyond his canvas and the one he lovingly painted were no longer one and the same:

> One face looks out from all his canvases,
> One selfsame figure sits or walks or leans:
> We found her hidden just behind those screens,
> That mirror gave back all her loveliness.
> A queen in opal or in ruby dress,
> A nameless girl in freshest summer-greens,

> A saint, an angel – every canvas means
> The same one meaning, neither more nor less.
>
> He feeds upon her face by day and night,
> And she with true, kind eyes looks back on him,
> Fair as the moon and joyful as the light;
> Not wan with waiting; nor with sorrow dim;
> Not as she is, but was when hope shone bright;
> Not as she is, but as she fills his dream.[17]

By March 1857 the relationship was in its death throes. 'Miss Siddall has been here for 3 days & is I fear dying', Brown wrote.

> She seems now to hate Gabriel in toto. Gabriel had settled to marry at the time I put down in this book & she says told her he was waiting for the money of a picture to do so, when lo, the money being paid, Gabriel brought it & told her all he was going to pay with it & do with it, but never a word more about marriage. After that she seemed determined to have no more to do with him. However he followed her to Bath & again some little while ago promised to marry immediately, since when he has again postponed all thoughts of it till about a fortnight ago, having found Miss Sid more than usually incensed against him, he came to me & talked seriously about it & settled all he was to do. Again the next morning he called & said the only thing that prevented his buying the licence was a want of tin, upon which I said if it was this that prevented it I would lend him some. He agreed to this & a few days after borrowed £10 but spent it all somehow & last night came for one more. This makes with 6 to Miss Sid £42.10. Of course I am very glad to lend it him but he has quite lost her affection through his extraordinary proceedings. He does not know his own mind for one day.[18]

Rossetti's latest inability to fulfil a promise had come hot on the heels of yet another sorry dispute between him and Lizzie, involving none other than Hunt and Annie Miller. Hunt and Ford Madox Brown had proposed the idea of founding an artists' colony, one in which the brothers – such as they were – could live together with their wives.

Apparently Brown had proposed the idea one night to Rossetti, who, according to a subsequent letter full of fancy footwork, had said he and Lizzie would be up for the scheme once married. For some reason Brown seems to have gone to Lizzie separately to discuss the scheme, at which point Lizzie clearly claimed ignorance of the project, and interpreted this as further evidence of Rossetti's duplicity and lack of matrimonial intention. To add insult to injury, on hearing that Hunt and Annie Miller were proposed as co-habitants, Lizzie descended into hysterics. Her dislike of Hunt and hatred of the woman with whom her 'fiancé' had been unfaithful placed Rossetti in a trap from which there was now no escape. He was damned as duplicitous if he had concealed the proposal from her, but insensitive beyond belief if he had intended to participate in the scheme with Hunt and Annie Miller.

It seemed as though there would be no way out. 'My dear Brown', Gabriel wrote on 26 February 1857,

Last night a misunderstanding occurred between Lizzy and me about what passed when you were there concerning the scheme of a college . . . I had spoken of the scheme to her some days ago, but she seemed to take little interest in it and I did not say much. She now says that she understood only a range of studios, & would strongly object to the idea of living where Hunt was, of which objection of hers I had no idea to any such extent. I have myself wished to keep him & her apart hitherto, as I do not think he has acted lately as a friend towards me in her regard, but that feeling would have left me when once we were married. However my wishes as to this scheme would entirely depend on hers, supposing that it would really affect her happiness; in which case I should cease to care for it or think of it. As it is, she seemed last night quite embittered and estranged from me on this account, whether for the moment or permanently I cannot yet tell, and it has made me most unhappy ever since, more so than anything else could make me. I am going there to-day now, & shall probably be there in the evening. After to-day she talks of going to stay for a week at her sister's.[19]

The next day Rossetti wrote to Brown and told him that Lizzie was not eating. 'What to do I know not . . . Kind and patient she has been with me many and many times more than I have deserved; and I trust this trouble is over. It is but too natural that her mind should be anxious and disturbed.'[20]

II

New Knights of the Round Table

WHILE HIS RELATIONSHIP with Lizzie was crumbling fast, as a painter Rossetti's reputation was soaring. His friends were somewhat bemused by the fact that this man, who had still not exhibited at the RA or completed a major work in oil, was now being courted for juicy business. Thanks to Ruskin, significant commissions had come his way. There was an assignment worth £400 to produce a triptych in oil for the cathedral at Llandaff, which was being renovated, despite lack of evidence of success in the medium in question. While Rossetti's profile was running ahead of his ability and experience, he was also commissioned to decorate the Oxford University debating chamber with a series of murals, a task for which he would have to recruit a team of artists.

Rossetti was thriving on all the attention. The old energy and enthusiasm were back. And his desire to create, inspire and lead was emergent once more. But to lead one must have followers. He needed to re-create something akin to those magic, charged days of the early Brotherhood.

Hunt and Millais were no longer candidates, of course. The idea of reviving the Pre-Raphaelite Brotherhood as such was inconceivable. Personal matters aside, Mad and Johnnie were way beyond Rossetti now and needed nothing further from him. Millais's pictures sold for sums so bedazzling that the papers dutifully reported them. In 1856 *The Times* had made a special point of alerting its readers that 'we are given to understand that Mr Millais's pictures now exhibiting at The Royal Academy are all sold and that he has realised £2000'.[1] His work was everywhere.

Reproduced in papers and magazines, sold in special editions by fashionable dealers and printmakers such as Ernest Gambart, he was now the most famous painter of the day.

But it was Hunt who would go down in history as the first living artist to secure more than £5,000 for a single work. In 1860 he finished a picture he had been slaving over for six years: *The Finding of the Saviour in the Temple*. Begun in the Holy Land, the picture showed Christ discovered by his family debating with the elders at the temple. It was another strike in the name of sacred realism. The figures had been drawn meticulously from models in Palestine, and each one represented a minute character study.

On the advice of his former adversary Charles Dickens, who after the Calmuck incident was apparently prepared to make some amends for the discomfort he had caused Hunt, Mad asked Gambart for 5,500 guineas for full rights to the work. This unprecedented sum was not regretted by Gambart. The picture went on private exhibition in his gallery in Bond Street, where people wanting to view this extraordinarily opulent and exotic painting would have to pay a shilling entrance fee. Soon between eight hundred and a thousand people a day were cramming in to have a peek, and Bond Street became choked with the carriages of those visiting the exhibition. There was such a scrum that the Prince Consort found himself unable to view the work – which in the end was sent to Buckingham Palace for him and the Queen to view privately. Moreover, Gambart, having secured copyright, would now exploit the picture by publishing prints. He even commissioned Fred Stephens to write a substantial pamphlet about Hunt's life and works to accompany the reproductions.

But as luck would have it, Rossetti no longer needed Hunt and Millais, because two new affiliates presented themselves. Six years or so younger than him and fresh from Oxford University, two former theological students turned aspirant artists, Edward Burne-Jones and William Morris, had attached themselves to the artist poet, whose star was finally rising.

*

An admissions error had thrown Burne-Jones and Morris together. Both had entered Exeter College, Oxford, in 1853, only to find that it was oversubscribed. They were allocated daytime rooms in town and were forced to camp in other students' rooms at night. These unfortunate circumstances forged an immediate friendship, enhanced by their mutual aversion to what they considered the rather dull teaching the university was offering them.

The affinity between the two men went beyond their shared bad luck. Burne-Jones attributed their closeness to the fact that they were both 'Goths' – with a similar sense of morality, creative energy and a love of the medieval Gothic. They both had a strong sense of colour and a sense of fun. When they decided Oxford was particularly dull in their first term, they both wore purple trousers for a while.

Morris was born out of the industrial revolution. Hailing from a huge family mansion in Walthamstow, he had come to Oxford from the privileged fields of Malborough College and with a considerable private income built on his family's interests in Cornish tin-mining. He cut an intriguing and rather comical figure: short, a little dumpy and called 'Topsy', in reference to a mound of unkempt curls that bobbed on his head, he marched around with a peculiar drunken gait. Already a defined eccentric, with little tics and twitches, sudden outbursts of rage and little care for hygiene or manners, he was a man who could not be ignored.

Ned Burne-Jones shared none of Morris's financial privilege, coming from a respected but modest family of Birmingham picture framers who had sufficient foresight to send him to the more accessible King Edward's School for Boys. He could not have cut a more different figure from Morris. Where Morris was stout, Ned was wafer-thin. Where Morris was loud, Ned was quiet.

Aware of the differences in their circumstances, Morris touchingly offered to share half his money with Ned – who refused on principle. Only a little later, when Ned visited the mansion in Walthamstow and realized just how wealthy Morris was, did Ned

William Morris and Ned Burne-Jones, caricature by Burne-Jones, *c.* 1871.
Ned always enjoyed the discrepancy in size between himself and his
best friend

wonder whether he might after all have accepted the token of
friendship.

By Christmas 1853 Morris and Ned were finally roomed in college. Delighted by his medieval surroundings, Morris set about
filling his rooms with brass rubbings he felt compelled to make of
various medieval gems he found in his new environs. The two men
began to escape the drudgery of their studies by immersing themselves in poetry and literature. Morris's energy and general noisi-
ness attracted a wider group of students to what became a reading
group that devoted itself to Tennyson, Shakespeare and Ruskin.
Before long Morris began to write poetry himself and to everyone's complete amazement discovered that he had a huge talent.

The reading group had also heard, through reading Ruskin's
Edinburgh lectures, delivered after that holiday in the Trossachs,
of the Pre-Raphaelites and immediately recognized a shared

intellectual position. And enthusiasm for the group was fired by a nice coincidence. On display in a local Oxford art gallery was one of the pictures that Mr Combe, that loyal PRB patron, had bought. It was Millais's *Return of the Dove to the Ark*, the very picture that Ruskin himself had tried to buy. When Morris and Ned saw this, they must have felt their fate was sealed.

Ned, emboldened by the same youthful intellectual zeal that once characterized Rossetti himself, decided to go to London for the day to try and see one of these PRBs they had heard so much about. He was aware that Rossetti worked at the Working Men's College. 'I had no dream', he wrote later, 'of ever knowing Rossetti, but I wanted to look at him and as I had heard that he taught in the Working Men's College in Great Ormond Street, a little University . . . where men skilled in science or history gave lectures and their services of evenings, I went to the college one day to find out how it would be possible that I should set eyes upon him.'[2]

There was a monthly faculty meeting at the Working Men's College, which, for a small fee to cover the bread, butter and tea provided, anyone could attend. Ned duly did so, but as he sat at his trestle munching bread and butter he became fearful that his trip was a waste, that Rossetti might not show and that anyway he had no idea what Rossetti looked like. But Fate played him a kind hand. Sitting next to Ned was Vernon Lushington, a legal man by profession but one passionate about education and culture, and Lushington knew Rossetti. Lushington reassured Ned that, even if he did not get to meet Rossetti that night, he could do so at a party in Lushington's rooms a couple of days later.

But then Rossetti entered the room, and Lushington nudged Ned, who was instantly star-struck. 'And so I saw him for the first time,' he later wrote, 'his face satisfying all my worship, and I listened to the addresses no more but had my fill of looking, only I would not be introduced to him.'[3]

A few days later in Lushington's rooms the introduction was made as promised, and something of the glowing brilliance that people later claimed shone from Sir Edward Coley Burne-Jones RA must have already been nascent in the then simple Ned. Rossetti invited the youngster to his studio, and the friendship was practically made.

Almost immediately the intertwining vines of coincidence began to cement the new friendship. Rossetti has read and admired some of Morris's poems in the *Oxford and Cambridge Magazine*, which had been published by Morris and his associates in the spirit of *The Germ*.

Although Morris was enjoying successes in some departments – specifically his poetry – in other areas he was suffering. He was having problems with his temper, which could easily rage out of control: the tiniest frustration would send him into a fury that then turned into a seizure in which Morris became frozen and 'strangely absent'. His friends coped as best they could with these fits, with schoolboy humour. After one 'storm' their chum Charley Faulkner stuck a label saying 'HE IS MAD' on Morris's hat before they went out.

It is remarkable that Fate, which had already contrived to throw such extraordinary men as Millais, Hunt and Ruskin into Rossetti's path, would now give him two more collaborators of equal, if not greater, gifts. Although the potential of these two new disciples had yet to be proven, Rossetti, with his impetuous generosity and strange prescience, embraced them enthusiastically. They were just the blank sheets of paper that he needed.

William Michael recalled, 'There is no exaggeration in affirming that the feeling with which Burne-Jones regarded Rossetti, at that time and for years ensuing, was one of passionate homage, stopping a little on the hither side of worship.'[4] Their geniuses still in embryo, both Burne-Jones and Morris were more than happy to play squire to Rossetti's knight and to follow wherever he led.

Despite his willingness to assume the role of mentor, Rossetti was as enraptured by his new-found friends as they were by him. Morris and Burne-Jones were both 'wonders after their kind', Rossetti waxed lyrical to Allingham.

Jones is doing designs . . . which put one to shame, so full are they of everything . . . He will take the lead in no time. Morris, besides writing those capital tales, writes poems that are much much better than the tales . . . Morris' facility at poetising puts one in a rage. He has been writing at all for little more than a year I believe, and has already poetry enough for a big book. You know he is a millionaire and buys pictures. He bought Hughes' *April Love* & lately several watercolours of mine and a landscape by Brown . . . You would think him one of the finest little fellows alive – with a touch of the incoherent but a real man.[5]

By 1856 the influence of Rossetti had had its effect. Morris and Ned had put their university theological studies behind them and determined to devote their lives to art. Morris eventually arrived at fine art via architecture: he initially enlisted with the architect George Edward Street in Oxford before moving to the London offices. Ned took up paintbrushes straight away under the tutelage of Rossetti.

Rossetti discovered that the sorry lodgings he and the unfortunate Deverell used to share in Red Lion Square were empty, and so Morris and Ned moved in, following in their master's footsteps. On the day of Morris Ned's installation, Rossetti discovered a sorry reminder of his original flatmate in the form of an address that he and Walter had scribbled on the bedroom wall.

It was only natural that a year later Morris and Ned would be core members of the group Rossetti would assemble to paint the Oxford murals, along with Rossetti's other painter friends Arthur Hughes, Val Prinsep, J. R. Spencer Stanhope and J. Hungerford Pollen. This band of happy brothers went and, as Rossetti described to Barbara Leigh Smith, painted pictures 'nine feet high with life-sized figures on the walls of the Union Society's new room . . . our pictures are from the *Morte D'Arthur*'.[6]

The new acolytes presented a further threat to Lizzie. With Morris and Burne-Jones, Rossetti was able to recapture something of the excitement of the early days of the Brotherhood. The intense fraternal bonds were renewed. The japes that he once enjoyed with Millais and Hunt were now re-enacted. In the mornings Rossetti and Pollen would burst into Ned and Topsy's rooms and pull off the bedclothes; Morris had suits of armour specially made for the painters to copy but was so pleased with one of them that he wore it to dinner; there was endless teasing and much camaraderie. Lizzie ploughed on with her own artistic ambitions as best she could. Brown organized a Pre-Raphaelite exhibition – the first that would draw together the work of the founding PRBs and their widening circle of associates – and she contributed. Ruskin helped her hang her watercolours *Clerk Saunders*, *Haunted Tree* and *We Are Seven*. She also submitted sketches based on Browning's 'Pippa Passes' and Tennyson's 'Lady of Shalott'.

Lizzie's works drew some critical attention, although it is hard to gauge whether it was entirely positive. *The Spectator* described her work as 'quite unlike the usual productions of lady artists', which barely qualifies as damning with faint praise.

Rossetti was touchy during Lizzie's public début. Perhaps he felt that his own reputation was bound up with his pupil's. Hunt recalled a frosty exchange:

Rooms were secured in Charlotte St off Fitzroy Square; and when all was arranged I went to a private view. Rossetti was there, and immediately on my arrival called me to come and see 'the stunning drawings' that the Sid . . . had sent. I complimented them fully, and said that had I come upon them without explanation I should have assumed they were happy designs by Walter Deverell. 'Deverell!' he exclaimed 'they are a thousand times better than anything he ever did'. I had thought that to compare the attempts of Miss Siddall, who had only exercised herself in design for two years, and had no fundamental training, to those of Gabriel's dear deceased friend, who had satisfactorily gone through the drilling of the Academy schools, would be taken as a compliment, but Rossetti received it as an affront, and his querulous attitude confirmed me in the awkward painful suspicion that he was seeking ground of complaint against his former colleagues.[7]

Despite Rossetti's defence of Lizzie's art, his personal relationship with her did nothing but deteriorate. Perhaps Lizzie could have put up with the fact that Rossetti had shifted his patronage to Burne-Jones and Morris if he had put the other women behind him and allowed her at least full reign over his domestic life. But it seems that he did not. With Annie gone, others took her place.

The infatuation with Jane Burden, another slum girl plucked from the streets – this time of Oxford – was brief though profound. Rossetti met Jane in Oxford while working on the Union murals. She was 'spotted' in much the same way as Lizzie and Fanny, and for that matter Annie and Emma. One October evening during a trip to the theatre in Oxford with Ned, Rossetti saw this strange-looking teenager in the cheap seats. She was extremely tall and very pale, with long, extended limbs and neck, flat grey eyes and black, frizzy hair. Many people who met her described Jane Burden as foreign-looking, almost gypsy-like.

Little is known of Jane Burden's early life, not least because she later refrained from discussing her background. But that her life scraped along the bottom rung of the social scale is certain. Born in 1839, the daughter of a stable hand and a peasant, she had spent her youth living in a tiny cottage in Oxford's St Helen's Passage, just off Holywell. Without running water or sanitation, the Burden family lived in what would have been cramped, smelly conditions. Nevertheless Jane and her sister Bessy were sent to a parish school and were probably anticipating life as domestic servants, although there is no indication that either had reached this status by 1857. In fact, the only description offered by Jane of her working life as a young adult was that she sometimes picked violets on the Iffley Road to sell on in the evening.

By the time Rossetti had returned to his Oxford digs that night, he was already clasping a rough sketch of this girl, who for him had the most mesmerizing beauty. He wanted her to pose for Guinevere, and before long she was in Rossetti's George Street lodgings doing just that. The temptation of a pretty wage and some admiration was too much to resist.

Much as Lizzie had been adopted as the mascot of the young PRBs, so now Jane was embraced by the Oxford muralists. She was swept off her feet. 'I never saw such men,' she remembered later, 'it was being in a new world to be with them. I sat to them and was there with them, and they were different to everyone else I ever saw. And I was a holy thing to them – I was a holy thing to them.'[8]

That Jane fell in love with Rossetti seems almost certain. He must have seemed magnificent to this girl from such a limited and sheltered background. That he had some form of feelings for her also seems likely. At the very end of his life Rossetti explained to his friend Hall Caine that he had loved her in Oxford but felt unable to pursue his feeling properly because of his continuing engagement to Lizzie.

But it was not just Jane that was diffusing the appeal of Lizzie at this time. While working on the Oxford murals and the Llandaff triptych, Rossetti seems to have been torn between his infatuations for this uneducated and illiterate street girl and the glamorous and well-known actress Ruth Herbert (Mrs Edward Crabbe). Despite her marriage to a wealthy stockbroker, Louisa Ruth Herbert by her very choice of career elected herself a member of the *demi-monde*. Acting, like modelling, was not respectable. Although it provided her with fame and adoration, her profession also branded her a form of upper-class whore in the eyes of the pious set.

She was undoubtedly beautiful. Her neck was unusually long, her hair was golden, she had large, almond-shaped eyes and a long, rather over-extended nose that gave her a striking, idiosyncratic profile. In October 1855, after years of acting obscurity in the home counties, Herbert had come to London and relaunched herself and her career, pretending that she was in fact making a dazzling début in *Time Tries All* at the Strand Theatre. By May 1856 'the beautiful Miss Herbert', as she was invariably now known, had moved to the Olympic Theatre, where her celebrity grew. The Olympic, on Wych Street, off Drury Lane, was the most fashionable theatre in town, run by the actor–manager Alfred Wigan. And here her own growing fame and the increasingly fashionable celebrity of the PRBs were associated when the popular press grasped that she was every inch the ideal of Pre-Raphaelite beauty. The *Illustrated Times* wrote: 'I have fallen in love with Mr Wigan's débutante who needs only a little less action with her neck and shoulders to be completely graceful . . . Ah! If I were Millais I would paint her in my next picture in her pure white silk dress, if I were Munro I could carve a lovely medallion from her profile.'[9]

Rossetti finally secured a sitting with Herbert in June 1858. Writing to William Bell Scott, he proudly informed his friend that 'I am in the stunning position this morning of expecting the actual visit, at ½ past 11, of a model whom I have been longing to paint for years – Miss Herbert of the Olympic theatre – who has the most varied & highest expression I ever saw in a woman's face, beside abundant beauty, golden hair &c. Did you ever see her? O my eye!'[10]

Once she had sat to him, Rossetti was under Herbert's spell. Within days of writing to Bell Scott, Rossetti encountered Ruth again at Little Holland House, the home of his friend and fellow Oxford muralist Val Prinsep. This beautiful, comfortable house off Holland Park was the domain of Val's mother, Sarah Prinsep – a socialite with the highest cultural credentials, whose salons and social gatherings enjoyed almost legendary status. Everyone who was anyone would attend. In the summer people would lounge in the building's sumptuous garden, canopies were erected and tables and chairs taken outside. Politicians, novelists, poets and, of course, artists would eat alfresco together in a relaxed, informal, slightly Bohemian ambience.

Little Holland House was also the home of the painter George Frederic Watts, who lodged in an annexe. Ruth also sat to Watts and often graced the corridors of this elegant villa, whether it was a salon day or not. After seeing her again at Little Holland House, Rossetti rushed home and sketched an image of her that had gripped his imagination. Her face is pressed close to a birdcage as she plays with the little bullfinch held within the tiny bars. The crispness of the ink sketch and its indulgence in detail bring to life how he must have seen her that day. Her pretty lace sleeves and ribboned bonnet, her charming demeanour as she leaned forward and blew a kiss to the little pet bird before her, clearly captivated him.

At around the same time Rossetti wrote a poem called 'Bella's Bullfinch'. Alongside the manuscript version of the poem, dated 1858, William Michael made a note that this poem must have been about Lizzie, who also kept a pet bullfinch.[11] He suggests the poem must have been written earlier than indicated on the manuscript, given Lizzie's extended absence from Rossetti's company in 1858. But when the poem is placed against Rossetti's sketch of Ruth Herbert, it is hard not to think that it is about her. Its deeply sexual imagery speaks for itself, and it is tempting to think that the bullfinch is Rossetti himself, trapped within the confines of his promises to Lizzie.

> She fluted with her mouth as when one sips,
> And waved her golden head, brave head & kind,
> Outside his cage close to the window-blind;
> Till her sweet bird, with little turns and dips,
> Piped low to her of sweet companionships.
> And when he stopped, she took some seed, I vow,
> And fed him from her rosy tongue, which now
> Peeped as a piercing bud between her lips.[12]

It was only a matter of days after meeting Ruth that Rossetti felt compelled, with his typical unbounded enthusiasm, to dedicate himself to her cause. In the first instance this was to promote a theatrical fundraiser that had been arranged for the benefit of the actress. His letters in July are dominated by notes to friends and contacts encouraging them to attend 'her benefit . . . on 12th. Now do go & get everyone to go – Monday next. Do really try for she needs it.'[13]

Herbert's descendant Virginia Surtees argues that Herbert and Rossetti were never fully fledged lovers, not least because Herbert was pregnant with her second child at this time. There is no way of knowing how far their relationship went, although if 'Bella's Bullfinch' is about Herbert, it indicates that at the very least Rossetti was fantasizing about all sorts of sexual activities with her.

Lizzie must have felt beleagured on all sides. It is little wonder she finally lost her appetite for the battle.

12

Since love is seldom true

IN JUNE 1857 Lizzie snapped. She gave up Ruskin's pension and left London for Sheffield. Here she contacted a relative, William Ibbitt, who helped secure her lodgings, apparently a house in Eccleshall Road, and became her friend.

It was an act of defiance. No longer able to rely on Rossetti, Lizzie determined to stand on her own two feet or perish. Her relationship with Ruskin was so very bound up in her association with Rossetti that his financial support had to go too. Whether this bold step was inspired by a genuine self-confidence or by a self-destructive tendency is impossible to know, but that Lizzie was bitter and hurt is without question.

Her poetry, full of anger and hatred, could have been pointed at no one else but the man who had at least twice offered marriage and failed to deliver it.

> Oh never weep for love that's dead
> Since love is seldom true
> But changes his fashion from blue to red,
> From brightest red to blue,
> And love was born to an early death
> And is so seldom true.
>
> Then harbour no smile on your bonny face
> To win the deepest sigh.
> The fairest words on truest lips
> Pass on and surely die,
> And you will stand alone, my dear,
> When wintry winds draw nigh.

> Sweet, never weep for what cannot be,
> For this God has not given.
> If the merest dream of love were true
> Then, sweet, we should be in heaven,
> And this is only earth, my dear,
> Where true love is not given.[1]

In Sheffield she cut an unusual figure. She began attending the local art school and as late as 1911 other pupils of that establishment could remember her brief but impressive visit. Some of the students later remembered Lizzie joining them on a trip to the great exhibition in Manchester, where her friendships with and knowledge of the exhibiting Pre-Raphaelite artists must have contributed to her singularity amid her fellow art students.

Lizzie had become a Bohemian without even noticing it. The influence of her modelling days, her relationship with Rossetti and Ruskin, and the bold, free-thinking female intellectuals who befriended her had confirmed those nascent values in her that made her so different. It was not just her red hair that made her stand out in a crowd now. By the autumn Lizzie had left Sheffield and headed to Matlock, 'illness' once again plaguing her.

While Lizzie had been in Sheffield, Rossetti had been happily carrying on with the murals in Oxford. Lizzie was nothing but a name to his new friends and companions, most of whom had never met this woman who belonged now to a different era in his life.

Georgiana 'Georgie' Macdonald, who would soon marry Ned Burne-Jones, kept account of the goings-on through letters to girlfriends. Ruskin had been down to see the work and 'pronounced Rossetti's picture to be "the finest piece of colour in the world"', she wrote to one.[2] But then Georgie recalled that 'about ten days later another letter breathes in awe-stricken distress the fact that Miss Siddall is "ill again". The news had reached me through Edward, who had never even seen her, but so lived in Gabriel's life at that time as not only to share any trouble that Gabriel had, but also to impress real sadness for it upon another.'

Lizzie, although in so many respects broken by Rossetti, still had some residual power over him. 'In Mr Price's diary of November 14th, there is the following entry', Georgie revealed in her memoirs. ' "Rossetti unhappily called away through Miss Siddall's illness at Matlock", and that was the end of the Oxford companionship, for he did not return.'

Rossetti left the finishing of the murals to his disciples. The result was utter disaster, although this was as much the fault of the knight as the squires. No one in the group had any experience in this kind of painting onto plaster. The walls were not properly prepared, the materials used were inadequate for the task in hand and the work was carried out too fast. Within just a few years the beautiful images of the Arthurian myth were fading and peeling away. It was as though the whole escapade had been nothing more than a dream.

Rossetti did not wrest himself from Matlock until January 1858, when he was once again in London. Lizzie stayed put. He headed to Matlock once more in April and then again in July. This toing and froing represented the almost interminably extended termination of a relationship that had in fact been over for years.

Rossetti's sudden departure from Oxford would have left Jane Burden somewhat high and dry, were it not for another member of the group who was more than happy to adopt her as his model. This was William Morris. Morris was not apparently successful with women. In fact, during the Oxford campaign he had found himself the butt of jokes associated with his evident lack of charm. He had been painting a panel depicting Tristram and Iseult, two tragic lovers locked in an adulterous relationship. But unlike Burne-Jones, who was showing genuine flair as a painter, Morris was struggling and the figure of Iseult was severely wanting. Rossetti had told him to go and find a decent model and suggested a specific girl he had seen – the daughter of a local innkeeper. Dutifully Morris set out but, unlike his persuasive silver-tongued colleagues, he failed to get the girl to agree to sit.

Jane Burden, on the other hand, was already in the habit of sitting for Rossetti. Morris must have felt the task of asking her to continue to sit for him in Rossetti's absence much easier than cold-calling on other potential models. And in so doing he was also fulfilling perhaps a different kind of fantasy, one in which the dumpy, awkward Morris might be able to imagine himself something more like his dashing, compelling hero.

And so the sessions began. Before long Morris believed he was utterly smitten. His display of his new feelings was as exceptional as ever. One evening when his chums were talking, apparently disparagingly, about Jane, he managed to bite a fork so hard it bent. He found it difficult to express his feelings to Jane, though. There are accounts of him reading to her in the George Street lodgings. Finally he completed an oil study of her as Iseult and simply wrote on the back of it, 'I cannot paint you but I love you.' Jane may well have carried a torch for Rossetti, but, like all women of her class, she would have been aware of her options. There is some speculation that she contacted Rossetti and that he encouraged her to look favourably on Morris's suit. This solution would at least keep Jane within circulation. And Morris was, after all, a rich man. By April 1858 Morris and Jane were engaged. Many in his circle were utterly flabbergasted by this bold, unconventional and socially outrageous match.

A couple of months later Morris left his new fiancée while he holidayed in France, and while he was away Rossetti returned to Oxford and drew Jane again. George Price Boyce remembered Rossetti being so obsessed with the women in his immediate orbit that he would draw them from memory. But an image of Jane that Rossetti found himself outlining that June was consigned to the grate: 'He made one or two rough pen and ink sketches whilst talking, one of a "Stunner" at Oxford, which he tore in fragments, but which I recovered from the fire grate.'[3]

Rossetti, at this point still in the final throes of his relationship with Lizzie, was also torn. He was a man tortured by his dwindling sense of responsibility to Lizzie, whom he no longer really loved, by his attraction to Ruth Herbert, who was married, and by his infatuation with Jane, whom he had allowed all too easily to slip through his fingers. He continued to draw Ruth and Jane throughout the year, with Boyce making another note that December that he had seen a fine sketch of 'Topsy's stunner' in Rossetti's apartments.

Nevertheless, the following April, a year after their initial engagement, Jane Burden and William Morris walked down the aisle of St Michael's Church in Oxford. Ned Burne-Jones and Charley Faulkner were in attendance, but Rossetti was absent.

Once Lizzie and Rossetti finally confronted the fact that their relationship was built on empty promises, as they doubtless did during these weeks in Matlock, Rossetti's reaction was one of extreme indulgence. All his pent-up desires for other women, all those infatuations and sensations that the relatively brief liaisons with Annie Miller, Fanny Cornforth and the lady in lilac had awakened in him now overflowed. He could not get enough of other girls, and he wanted them all simultaneously. The garden was overflowing with flowers, and he wanted to pick huge bunches and bury himself in their loveliness.

By the close of 1858 – perhaps when Ruth was occupied with her new baby, and Jane Burden was preparing for her marriage to Morris – it was Fanny Cornforth who once again came to Rossetti's attention. This is nowhere made clearer than in the painter George Price Boyce's diary. Boyce was a handsome, warm man, who adored pretty women and made no attempt to conceal this. Photographs of him reveal an open, youthfully soft face framed by dark hair and a neatly clipped beard. His diaries reveal a fun-loving soul who easily wooed women and was an appealing companion to men. He would pursue the opposite sex relentlessly and humorously, once damaging his hip quite seriously when he climbed over a wall in pursuit of some girls who had been flirting with him while he sketched and then ran off. Boyce was also Fanny's lover.

Rossetti's relationship with Boyce was an intense one in the late 1850s and 1860s. They were constant companions. When Rossetti left his rooms in Chatham Place after Lizzie's death, Boyce moved in. He later built a house in Chelsea close to Rossetti's own. The pair had a constant trade in one another's works. Boyce would buy Rossetti's drawings, and Rossetti would take Boyce's. They would swap depictions of the models who sat to both of them. It was as though Boyce and Rossetti shared a delicious secret together. Their open sharing of Miss Cornforth's affections seemed of little consequence to either friend; if anything, it seemed delightfully natural.[4]

On 15 December 1858 Boyce called at Rossetti's studio and admired the studies of Ruth Herbert and Jane, but while these two lovelies were immortalized on canvas, Fanny was available in the flesh at 24 Dean Street, Soho. And so as night fell, Boyce and Rossetti trotted off together for dinner at The Cock before heading into the West End to see their girl.

The next day Boyce collected Fanny from Spencer Stanhope's studio, where she was appropriately typecast as 'a gay woman in her room by side of Thames at her toilet'.[5] From Spencer Stanhope's rooms Boyce recalled that Fanny 'went to Rossetti and I followed'.

A month later what seems like a playful rivalry for Fanny had grown up between Boyce and Rossetti. Boyce noted that he 'Went to the Argyll Rooms. There met Fanny and took her to supper at Quinn's. She was in considerable trepidation lest Rossetti should come in – and lo! He did so.'[6] The indiscretion was clearly forgiven. While Boyce cemented his affection for Fanny with a range of gifts including a sovereign ('to help her in the furnishing of her new house'), a silver thimble, a little oil sketch of Hambledon Heath and some apples and walnuts, Rossetti was also enjoying Fanny's company in the most intimate circumstances. He was often in her new rooms at Tennyson Street (decoratively enhanced by Boyce's financial and pictorial contributions), and from the fact that Fanny could describe Rossetti's habit of reading

Balzac late at night one infers that he was also in the habit of spending the night there.

Boyce's diary gives the impression that the triangular relationship that embraced these three people was nothing but relaxed and happy. There was no overt sense of jealousy, just accounts of trips to the zoo and taking tea together. Perhaps this is why Rossetti persuaded Boyce to let him paint Fanny's portrait for him. The commission would somehow seal their pact of open, liberal love.

The portrait in question was *Bocca Bacciata*, and is extraordinary not only for its origin but also because it heralded a new direction for Rossetti's work. Apart from the fact that it marked his return to oil painting, it is the first of his pictures of women to celebrate beauty and womanhood for beauty and womanhood's sake. Ruskin was appalled by this new focus in his work, as was Hunt, who saw nothing but indulgent sensuality. But it was a direction that Rossetti would now pursue until the end of his life.

In this new deeply sensual vein Rossetti, who often placed symbolic imagery in his work, painted Fanny against a backdrop of marigolds. She clasps one of these flowers, a white rose is in her hair and an apple is by her left elbow. The marigold was an intriguing choice since it had a range of meanings to a Victorian audience far better versed in the significance of flowers than we are today. It could symbolize sacred love, but also pain and jealousy. The apple must surely relate to the story of Eve and indicate the sitter's worldly status. The white rose would indicate innocence and love. While the white rose and apple balance one another out, arguing that although the girl has tasted the pleasure of life she has done so in the spirit that sex is innocent and natural, the marigolds remain perplexing. If there was ever any jealousy between Boyce and Rossetti, perhaps this is the sole playful expression of it. Or perhaps their presence, in full glory, one even pressed between Fanny's fingers, indicates that jealousy – even at its most playful – is resolved.

If there was a degree of sexual competition, suppressed beneath Boyce and Rossetti's pleasantries, Boyce's diaries reveal that towards the end of 1859 he and Rossetti had another girl to vie over. It was as though Rossetti was insatiable during this period. Not content with one, two or even three women on the go in some form or another, there was room for yet one more as his capacity to adore the female form seemed to be capable of expansion without boundary. This fourth entrant was none other than Annie Miller, suddenly back in the modelling game. But this time her return into the bossom of her artist friends was motivated not so much by opportunity as by dire need.

On 5 October 1859 Boyce took Fanny out for a treat and settled down for a long chat with her. As they caught up on gossip, Fanny revealed that Annie Miller had called on Rossetti but, finding him out, had left her card.

Annie's visit to her former beau had been motivated by two events: Hunt had given Annie up for good, but to Annie's horror so had Lord Ranelagh. Quite suddenly the two avenues she had been exploring with regard to her future had closed. She found herself without income and without prospects.

It was not long before Boyce too received a visit. He was in and discovered Annie to be 'in an excited state'. She was keen for Boyce 'to recommend her someone to sit to. She was determined on sitting again in preference to doing anything else. All was broken off between Hunt and her. I pitied the poor girl very much, by reason of the distraction of her mind and heart.'[7]

A return to modelling was an obvious and pragmatic solution to the situation. Both Rossetti and Boyce were completely chuffed to have her back in their studios. Just after Christmas that year Boyce noted: 'Annie Miller came and sat to me. Rossetti came in and made a pencil study of her. She looked more beautiful than ever.'

Rossetti was hooked again. It seems as though almost every time Boyce and Annie got together, Rossetti turned up like a bad penny. Boyce recalled that on 11 February 1860 she was sitting to him but then 'Rossetti came in towards dusk and touched on my oil portrait of her begun, and went away with her'[8]. A fortnight later Annie returned, but 'Rossetti coming in soon after, I scarely did any work'. Rossetti then managed to intervene and prevent Annie from sitting to Boyce at all. 'Blow you', he wrote tauntingly to Boyce. 'Annie is coming to me tomorrow . . . I'm sure you won't mind, like a good chap. Will you write to her for another day. She would hardly consent to ill-using you in this style, but I bored her till she did.'[9]

But this return to her former profession, and the hilarious rivalry it prompted between Rossetti and Boyce, clearly failed to provide the kind of income that Hunt had formerly provided. It was not long before Annie resorted to more desperate means. Practical and hard-headed, she realized the few assets she had. She had letters from Hunt, love letters of the most personal and revelatory kind. How would these sit in the lap of a journalist after the Calmuck scandal? Hunt was caught. Quietly a sum of money was handed over to Annie, and the letters retrieved. And thus Annie Miller walked out of the Pre-Raphaelite story . . . as a blackmailer.

She did so not before Rossetti, now refining his new-found skills as an oil painter, had made the most ravishing portrait of her. He had her as Helen of Troy. Inscribed on the back of the picture Rossetti wrote: 'Helen of Troy ελεναυσ, ελανδροσ, λεεπτολισ – destroyer of ships, destroyer of men, destroyer of cities. Painted by D. G. Rossetti.' The central claim in this statement was certainly true. And Helen/Annie's placid, daydreaming expression in a painting that sees the towers of Ilium ablaze behind her was not without significance.

Rossetti's life changed irrevocably one day in April 1860. Less than a month earlier he had been taunting Boyce by stealing his sittings with Annie and had been going on happily in his warm and increasingly loving relationship with Fanny, when Lizzie quite suddenly and entirely unexpectedly reappeared.

Lizzie's family had written to Ruskin begging for his help. She was in a terrible state, impoverished and ill. She was in Hastings, where in another life Bessie Parks and Barbara Leigh Smith had tended her in her infirmity. Now she was apparently alone and allegedly close to death.

Rossetti was alerted, and in early April, some eighteen months or more since he had last been with her, he travelled down to see her. On 14 April a letter reached his mother in London, written from 12 East Parade, Hastings. Its contents took the family entirely by surprise.

My dear Mother,

I write to you this word to say that Lizzy and I are going to be married at last, in as few days as possible. I may be in town again first, but am not certain. If so I shall be sure to see you, but write this as I should be sorry that the news should reach you first from any other quarter.

Like all the important things I ever meant to do, to fulfil duty or secure happiness, this one has been deferred almost beyond possibility. I have hardly deserved that Lizzy should still consent to it, but she has done so, and I trust I may still have time to prove my thankfulness to her. The constantly failing state of her health is a terrible anxiety indeed, but I must still hope for the best, and am at any rate at this moment in a better position to take the step, as regards money prospects, than I have ever been before.[10]

That Lizzie was very ill is without doubt. Rossetti wrote to his brother describing her being in such a state that she was vomiting constantly, keeping no food down at all. There are also suggestions in his choice of phrase to suggest that she suffered some form of intermittent violent 'episodes', perhaps similar to seizures or fits: 'The spectacle of her fits of illness when they come on would be heartrending to a stranger even.'

Whether she was actually on death's door will never be known, but that Rossetti thought she was on the point of expiration is clear. The horror that this woman's blood would be on his hands spurred him on to grasp what remnants of romantic chivalry were left in him, and he promised to marry her and make good the wrongs he had visited on her. That he thought that this marriage might be inevitably short-lived with his prospective spouse facing her mortal end is unpalatable but entirely possible.

'The ordinary license we already have,' he wrote to William Michael on 17 April, '& I still trust to God we may be enabled to use it. If not, I should have so much to grieve for, and what is worse so much to reproach myself with, that I do not know how it might end for me.'[11]

It took Lizzie a month to regain sufficient strength to walk down the aisle. One attempt on Rossetti's birthday, 12 May, failed, but on the 23rd of that month the couple entered St Clement's Church in Hastings and tied the knot. Immediately they headed for Folkestone and crossed for Paris. They had known each other for a decade, and yet it felt as though they had married on a whim. William Bell Scott saw this only too clearly, and wrote years later: 'The auguries of happiness were frightfully dispelled. Marriage by the colour of the hair is rather a precarious mode of dealing with the most momentous action of life. For myself, knowing Gabriel better than his brother did though from the outside, I knew marriage was not a tie he had become able to bear.'[12]

By doing the right thing by one woman, Rossetti betrayed another. The attachment between him and Fanny had become profound. In fact, as their later history revealed, in her Rossetti had found a form of true love. Happy in one another's company, and tolerant of each other's weakness, the artist and the whore were ideal companions. Fanny's low-life background and earthy manner appealed to the Rossetti who saw richness and a kind of honesty in the vitality of street life. In Rossetti, Fanny found someone to organize and to mother, a needy soul who appealed to her ability to make things better. And of course there was an honest exchange: for her companionship and sex he could provide financial stability.

Rossetti's sudden and unexpected marriage to Lizzie was for Fanny, like everyone else, a complete shock. Her reaction was to take to her bed. Boyce heard about her misery and recounts it in his diary: 'Called on Fanny Cornforth, who I heard . . . was ill. Found her so in bed. It appears she frets constantly about R, who is with his wife in Paris, the latter very ill and in a deep decline. Altogether a most melancholy state of things. F was seeing a doctor and in a very nervous, critical state.'[13]

Fanny's fretting about Rossetti was not misplaced. In marrying Lizzie, not only was he removed from Fanny, but he was locked in the tyrannical grasp of his needy, invalid spouse. From the outset Lizzie's illness dominated his personal and professional life. And from the outset he knew that this pattern would become the norm of life. Depressed and resigned, he wrote to his brother while honeymooning in Paris, noting 'I need not say what an anxious and disturbed life mine is while she remains in this state. And this is increased by the absolute necessity of setting soon to work again while in fact her health demands my constant care.'[14] Rossetti, the vivacious rascal, was imprisoned.

Once Fanny was over the shock of losing her lover, she rushed into a marriage of her own. Within three months of losing Rossetti she married one Timothy Hughes on 11 August at St John's Church, Waterloo. Hughes was not a good catch: a porter who sold drawing materials to Academy students, he was a drunk. But he was apparently beautiful to look at, and allegedly the model for David in Rossetti's Llandaff triptych. He obviously was able to offer Fanny comfort of sorts.

After her marriage, even more than before it, Lizzie was defined by illness. Almost every single extant letter that Rossetti wrote after his marriage to Lizzie included a reference to her poor health. It makes claustrophobic reading. One assumes that her reliance on laudanum became established during this time.

For Rossetti it seems this was a time of peculiar self-awareness. He was more workmanlike and serious. There is a sense of him, aware of his new responsibilities, trying to turn over a new leaf. And yet there is also a sense that he knew he was in a hopeless situation. Georgiana Macdonald, who married Ned Burne-Jones in June 1860, just weeks after Lizzie and Gabriel tied their knot, picked up on this:

> Rossetti and his wife, after their return from Paris, took a lodging at Hampstead, but she was so ill at first that we never saw her till near the end of July, when to our great delight a day was fixed for our deferred meeting, and Gabriel suggested that it should take place at the zoological gardens . . . Lizzie's slender elegant figure – tall for those days, but I never knew her actual height – comes back to me, in a graceful and simple dress, the incarnate opposite of the 'tailor-made' young lady. We went home with them to their rooms at Hampstead, and I know that I then received the impression which never wore away, of romance and tragedy, between her and her husband.[15]

Rossetti too understood this aspect of their relationship. He began work on a picture of a theme that had haunted him since childhood. This was the myth of the *doppelgänger*, the existence of a double, which, if one ever happens to meet it face to face, presages tragedy.

Rossetti chose to portray not one *doppelgänger* but two. In *How They Met Themselves* a pair of lovers stroll in a dark wood and bump into themselves. It is hard not to read the lovers as Lizzie and Rossetti, who, lost in their own strange landscape, suddenly see their own doom.

In October Boyce called. It remains strange that even now Lizzie is not mentioned by name in his diaries. For Boyce she is written up as a distant character – the 'wife' – with none of the immediate human characteristics that Fanny is given. It is as though she belongs to a part of Rossetti's world that Boyce cannot reconcile. Nevertheless Rossetti is at some level as proud of Lizzie as he had always been, showing his friend 'exquisite drawings from his wife . . . his wife was in his studio, but he said she had been sleeping and was not in a state to see any visitors'.[16]

Lizzie must have been aware of the infatuations her new husband had enjoyed during her absence. Perhaps this is why the head of Ruth Herbert was removed from the Llandaff triptych that Rossetti was painting and replaced with that of Jane Morris, whom Lizzie had befriended. How could she not? Their backgrounds were so similar, and they had much in common. Perhaps she did not realize that Jane too had at one point been a brief fascination of her husband's.

But if Rossetti was able to move on from his former obsessions with the beautiful Miss Herbert and with Jane Morris, *née* Burden, he found it harder to cast off Fanny. At some point after his marriage the liaisons with Fanny began again. She began modelling for him, sitting in his studio while Lizzie lay ill next door. That he may have begun 'keeping' her as his mistress in accommodation paid for by him is entirely possible.

Lizzie meanwhile tried to pick up where she had left off with her career as an artist. She and Georgie Burne-Jones, who also shared ambitions to become an illustrator, began a project together to write and illustrate a book of fairy-tales, but it never materialized. 'It is pathetic to think how we women longed to keep pace with the men, and how gladly they kept us by them until their pace quickened and we had to fall behind', Georgie remembered.[17] 'Mrs Rossetti . . . had original power, but with her . . . art was a plant that grew in the garden of love, and strong personal feeling was at the root of it; one sees in her little black and white designs and beautiful little water-colours Gabriel always looking over her shoulder, and sometimes taking a pencil or brush from her hand to complete the thing she had begun.'

There was much to do, once married, that got in the way of work. Soon the Rossettis moved out of their lodgings in Hampstead and moved back into an expanded Chatham Place: Rossetti had negotiated with the landlord to have his old flat enlarged by knocking through into the neighbouring apartment. Now there were rooms to decorate and furniture to buy.

Rossetti's letters reveal a genuine delight in decorating this new marital home. 'We are hanging our new rooms here with pictures in oriental profusion – one room is hung all round with my wife's drawings', he wrote to William Bell Scott. 'I should like you to see how snug we are making ourselves for the winter. We have now an uninterrupted suite of 6 rooms including a spare bedroom for a friend.'[18]

But the upheaval at home could not have helped Lizzie, whose 'illness' continued. Her whole manner was now fraught with anxiety. Georgie was quite sure this 'illness' was a purely mental one. Her thinness indicates an eating disorder. Accounts of her also point to a woman deeply depressed. 'The question of her long years of ill health has often puzzled me; as has how it was possible for her to suffer so much without developing a specific disease', Georgie tactfully remarked, remembering how 'Lizzie did not talk happily when we were alone, but was excited and melancholy, though with much humour and tenderness as well; and Gabriel's presence seemed needed to set her jarring nerves straight, for her whole manner changed when he came in the room. I see them now as he took his place by her on the sofa and her excitement sank back into peace.'[19]

In February 1861 it seems that the Rossettis' flat was becoming properly habitable. The project had fed Rossetti with a new enthusiasm for interior design – one that he would soon pursue commercially with William Morris in the formation in April 1861 of Morris, Marshall, Faulkner & Co., the great design firm that would ultimately become known as Morris & Co. and dominate the aesthetics of the late nineteenth century.

'We have our rooms quite jolly now', he wrote to Allingham in February. 'Our drawing room is a beauty I assure you already, and on the first country trip we make we shall have it newly papered from a design of mine which I have an opportunity of getting made by a paper manufacturer.'[20]

In the same letter Rossetti revealed to Allingham that 'Lizzie is pretty well for her, and we are in expectation (but this is quite in confidence as such things are better waited for quietly) of a little accident which has just befallen Topsy & Mrs T. who have become parents. Ours however will not be (if at all) for 2 or 3 months yet.'

So Jane Morris had had a baby girl called Jenny, and Lizzie was pregnant. Rossetti seems nothing but jolly in delivering this news, except for the odd bracketed qualification. Although his 'if at all' seems an entirely throwaway aside, it was horribly prescient. On 2 May 1861 Lizzie also gave birth to a daughter, but she was still-born. Rossetti dealt with the incident with strange, business-like efficiency. 'Lizzie has just been delivered of a dead child. She is doing pretty well I trust', he wrote to his mother on 2 May.[21] The letter is almost identical for Brown and for Ned Burne-Jones.

Rossetti's prediction that Lizzie was doing well was misplaced. Once again Georgie Burne-Jones's recollection of the affair reveals how pathetic Lizzie became after this awful event, half mad with grief. 'When we went to see Lizzie for the first time after her recovery, we found her sitting in a low chair with the childless cradle on the floor beside her, and she looked like Gabriel's "Ophelia" when she cried with a kind of soft wildness as we came in, "Hush, Ned, you'll waken it! . . . Lizzie's nurse was a delightful old country woman, whose words and ways we quoted for years afterwards; her native wit and simple wisdom endeared her to both Gabriel and Lizzie, and were the best possible medicine for overstrained feelings'.[22]

The Rossettis' debt to this old nurse, who somehow got an already depressed woman through the loss of her child, was marked by Rossetti in a small, highly personal gift to her. While he sat at Lizzie's bedside, he began to apply a wash of watercolour to one of Lizzie's cartes-de-visite, and gave it as a gift to the old lady. By fate this rare photographic record of Lizzie still exists.

These calling cards, which Victorians would leave at one another's homes when they called unsuccessfully, were normally quite formal portraits of the bearer. Rossetti's own from around this time is exactly that, showing incidentally how he had 'expanded' from slender youthdom into portly middle age. But Lizzie's is something altogether different. She sits in a pose that is beyond formal. It is mannered. It is as though she is adopting for the photographer the character of one of those heroines that she was so accustomed to portraying for those who painted her. Her head is angled, her eyes downcast, her hands clasped. That air of inward suffering and resignation, mixed with gentleness, is there. And suddenly in looking at this picture one wonders if this represents the strange place that she occupied in real life: always playing out a 'role' into which she had willingly been cast.

Just two months after Lizzie delivered her dead baby, on 6 July 1861, the sensational tale of *Lady Audley's Secret* began its first serialization in the weekly *Robin Goodfellow* magazine. Lizzie had a very specific connection with the story's heroine: they had both been painted by members of the Pre-Raphaelite Brotherhood.

The author of *Lady Audley* was shy initially and published anonymously. This was because she was not only female but was from a background that was considered deeply dubious. For at the same time that Ruth Herbert was treading the boards, the woman who would go on to write one of the most popular stories of her day was also making her way in the *demi-monde* of theatre and entertainment. She was called Mary Seyton. Like Ruth, her career was paced out on the stages of provincial theatres before London eventually allowed her into its embrace and she finally got a season at the Surrey Theatre. But unlike Ruth Herbert, it would not be for her skills as an actress or her beauty that Mary Seyton acquired her fame: it would be for her writing.

Mary Seyton's real name was Mary Elizabeth Braddon. Her experience in the theatre taught her about narrative and storytelling, but more than anything it must have taught her about the popular appetite for a good story. She could read what it was that an audience craved and what chimed with the times.

It is testimony to the fame the Brotherhood had achieved a decade after its incarnation that Braddon chose to define her heroine's beauty within the terms of their work. It is also testimony to Lizzie and the others, such as Annie and Fanny, who so influenced the PRB aesthetic. In this regard Lady Audley's very existence – in terms of her bewitching physical beauty – and the space she quickly occupied in the public imagination owed much to these girls.

Lady Audley's Secret was a story of bigamy, deceit and murder. Lady Audley is the young, beautiful second wife of the septuagenarian Michael Audley. But as the tale unwinds it becomes apparent that this charming beauty is in fact a fraudulent con woman who has faked her own death and deserted her child and former husband, only to re-emerge married to the ancient wealthy gentleman. The undoing of her deceit is the coincidental arrival of her former husband, George Talboys, at the Audley homestead with Michael Audley's nephew Robert. Although Lady Audley is away when the young men arrive, George Talboys and the reader simultaneously encounter the mistress of the household via her portrait.

> Yes, the painter must have been a pre Raphaelite. No one but a pre Raphaelite would have painted hair by hair those feathery masses of ringlets, with every glimmer of gold, and every shadow of pale brown. No one but a pre Raphaelite would have so exaggerated every attribute of that delicate face as to give a lurid brightness to the blonde complexion, and a strange sinister light to the deep blue eyes. No one but a pre Raphaelite could have given to that pretty pouting mouth the hard and almost wicked look it had in the portrait.[23]

Braddon chose to make her mesmerizing heroine a Pre-Raphaelite subject not least because the real Pre-Raphaelite models had cast a spell on those who painted them. The tales of tangled love affairs and men swept off their feet by their ravishing muses were common currency. Braddon instinctively tapped into this and was rewarded when her fictional siren, with her masses of golden ringlets and crimson robe, captivated the Victorian public.

By 1862 *Lady Audley's Secret* had become available in novel form, and was a best-seller. A year later stage adaptations were launched to equal acclaim in London. That produced at the St

James's Theatre added further to the complex web of ironies attached to the private lives of the Pre-Raphaelite Brotherhood and the public manifestations of their influence. Because it was this production that sealed the reputation of Ruth Herbert as one of London's most celebrated actresses. She was, everyone agreed, the very incarnation of Lady Audley. The role could have been written for her.

Somewhere at the very root of the Lady Audley phenomenon lay the influence of Lizzie Siddall, that most self-conscious of models, who had after all been the very first Pre-Raphaelite muse. Her dramatic poise and brilliance at informing a pose with the very characterization that her painters sought gave the depictions of her that extraordinary potency. But the sad truth is that *Ophelia* was always her greatest role, not least because that disturbed and distraught girl most approximated her own tortured personality. It was only a matter of time before Ophelia's fate and Lizzie's own would properly converge. On a night in February in 1862 that tragic moment came.

By 1862 Lizzie was a drug addict. Whether it had been in the year she spent away from Gabriel that the opiate laudanum got its grip on her, or whether the pain of her lost baby instigated its use, by the time that she and her husband were setting off to see their friend Swinburne for an informal dinner, she was hooked and had been for some time. As Rossetti and Swinburne both described, the drug had altered her already highly nervous behaviour. She could be flighty or drowsy or move between the two states. That she displayed both these characteristics on the night in question was not unusual any more.

But according to some, when the couple returned home, there was a row. Rossetti stormed out, claiming that he had duties at the Working Men's College to attend to. But many believe that it was to the warm compassionate arms of Fanny Cornforth that he fled, a habit not unknown to his wife. On his return, to his horror, he discovered a suicide note pinned to Lizzie's nightdress. In an ultimate act of self-indulgent misery that at once meted swift punishment for the wrongs that continued to be visited on her, Lizzie made it clear that death was preferable to a tortured life. And to this refuge she fled.

The fact that a suicide note had been discovered was withheld from the twelve jurors at Lizzie's inquest, who finally ruled death by misadventure. But the story of its existence came to light later. Ford Madox Brown finally confided its existence to his daughter. Rossetti himself also confessed this sorry detail when he was close to his own death, to his friend and assistant Hall Caine. And William Bell Scott was also well rehearsed in the details of the deadly night: 'What was said or done at the inquest I know not, but the impatient creature's wildly expressed notions had borne fruit, she had pinned a written statement on the breast of her night shirt and put an end to her troubles, real or imaginary.'[24]

On seeing his wife unconscious, Rossetti pocketed the note, raised the housekeeper and summoned doctors. Frantic, he then headed off to Hampstead to find Madox Brown, who returned with him and, on learning of the note, burned it.

In the very early hours of the next morning, Georgie Burne-Jones remembered, she and Ned were already up when the housekeeper arrived with the news.

I will simply transcribe something I wrote about it in the next day to one of my sisters: 'I scarcely believe the words as I write them, but yesterday I saw her dead . . . four physicians and a surgeon did everything human skill could devise, but in spite of them she died, poor darling, after seven in the morning . . . I went down directly I heard it and saw her poor body laid in the very bed where I have seen her lie and laugh in the midst of illness, but even though I did this I keep thinking it is all a dreadful dream. Brown was with Gabriel and is exactly the man to see to all the sad business arrangements, for under such circumstances an inquest has to be held. Of course I did not see Gabriel . . . I leave you to imagine the aweful feeling there is upon us all. Pray God to comfort Gabriel.'

The Chatham Place days were ended now, and Rossetti in his sorrow turned to his mother . . . and went for a time to live in Albany Street with her and his sisters and brother. Poor Lizzie's bullfinch went there too, and sang as sweetly and looked as sleek and cheerful as ever.[25]

13

Irish roses

THERE IS NO mention of Lizzie's death in John Ruskin's diary. In fact, there is little mention of Rossetti. Ruskin did call on the Rossettis on hearing the terrible news, however, and was received by William Michael, who found Ruskin much altered. The 'whole tone of his thought on religious subjects [had] changed, and the ardent devout Protestant figured as a total disbeliever in any form of Christian or other defined faith', William Michael remembered.[1]

Lizzie's peculiar, untimely death did no more than add to Ruskin's general despair. Things were not as they had seemed for Ruskin. God's treatment of Lizzie could have made little sense to him. But God's failings were only the latest to be observed. Before Ruskin cast doubt upon the immortal creator, there were mere mortals whom he had found lacking. Rossetti's own personal transformation was an example in point. From around the time that Rossetti began to change from someone driven by principle to someone governed by fascination, Ruskin began to withdraw his friendship and support.

It was not just his growing distaste for what he considered the increasing vulgarity of Rossetti's pursuit of 'women and flowers' that was moving Ruskin away from his former protégé. Ruskin's attentions were being drawn elsewhere. He was developing his own interest in flora. Her name was Rose La Touche, and from almost the moment he met Rose in 1858 through the 1860s and even into the 1870s she was the rock to which he clung as he was tossed amid a sea of doubts.

'1862 begins. Spring in London, seeing R[ose] as usual. The tea when they all three sat on the floor by me – her mother, Emily and she', Ruskin notes in his diary for that year.[2] The image is simple. Mrs La Touche and her two daughters sitting at the feet of the great cultural icon Ruskin, being entertained and humoured by the man. One might imagine that Mrs La Touche might have been visiting with her daughters in recognition of the fact that one in particular had caught the eye of the middle-aged, wealthy, singleton. But the image is harder to reconcile when one knows that in the spring of 1862 Rose La Touche had barely turned fourteen.

The meeting between Rose La Touche and John Ruskin had been engineered by her mother some four years previously. Maria La Touche was a cultured wealthy Irish woman who, often in London for the season, wanted her daughter to benefit from art lessons from the greatest authority on art in the nineteenth century. With the brazen confidence of the privileged upper class she wrote to Ruskin, who obligingly called at the family's London home in Great Cumberland Street.

There has been much speculation that Maria La Touche's precocious approach to Ruskin was in fact driven more by her own desire to have the famous man counted among her circle than a real concern for her daughters' education. Rose was, perhaps, used merely as an excuse. Some have also suggested that as the acquaintance developed, Maria La Touche herself fell in love with Ruskin. But what Maria could scarcely have banked on was the immediate impression that her ten-year-old child had on the 39-year-old Ruskin. If she had hoped Rose was sufficient bait for Ruskin's attentions, she was far from disappointed. Ruskin's memory of his very first meeting with Maria's younger daughter was still crystal clear at the end of his life:

Presently the drawing room door opened and Rosie came in (from the nursery), quietly taking stock of me with her blue eyes as she walked across the room; gave me her hand as a good dog gives its paw, and then stood a little back. Nine years old on 3rd January 1858 thus now rising towards ten ... The eyes rather deep blue at that time, and fuller and softer than afterwards. Lips perfect and lovely in profile.[3]

After the first meeting in town at the La Touches' address, it was determined that lessons for the three La Touche children, Emily, Percy and Rose, should be held in the rural setting of Denmark Hill, which as Ruskin noted, was even in the late 1850s, still 'quite in the country as soon as one got past the triangular field at Champion Hill'.

It was not long before Ruskin and his star pupil Rosie devised pet names for one another. She called him Crumpet, then St Crumpet and St C. When Ruskin introduced her to geology, which was a growing fascination for him, she named him 'Archigosaurus'. Rose meanwhile became Rosie-Posie or Irish roses. The two conspirators named Rose's mother Lacerta, or Lizard.

The charming sessions Ruskin spent tutoring the La Touche children stood in strange contrast to his other worrisome task that year. He was sorting through the enormous bequest that Turner had left to the National Gallery after his death in 1851. To Ruskin's horror he found, while looking through the artist's numerous sketchbooks, hundreds of erotic images that Ruskin believed were pornographic.

Ruskin, unable perhaps to reconcile Turner's interest in sex with his own lack of sexual appetite, could only make sense of his discovery by concluding that Turner must have been mad or at least suffered episodes of insanity. This was the same accusation that he had once levelled at his wife. Terrified that both his hero and the august institution to which his hero's work had been left would be tainted by accusations of pornography, Ruskin later claimed that he burned the offending work.

Whether he did burn some of Turner's precious work or not – and today some folders of erotica do most certainly remain, although marked as having been kept 'as evidence of a failure of mind only' – this discovery came at a significant moment for Ruskin. His faith in his great hero was shaken at a time when Ruskin found not just humankind but God himself wanting. As his own religious faith unravelled, Ruskin started to become increasingly solitary and depressed as the foundations of the old world cracked beneath his feet.

Amid this personal chaos Rose awakened something new in Ruskin. Initially it seems it was no more than a new-found fondness for children. The childish talk that he indulged in with the La Touche children and the warmth with which they embraced him fuelled a new avuncular sympathy for youth from a man increasingly appalled with adults. But soon it grew into a genuine appetite that prompted him to seek out encounters with juvenile girls.[4]

Once she had left London, Ruskin continued to correspond with Rose. Her family home was in Harristown in Ireland, and when the London season was over the La Touches retreated there, unless they were on a continental trip. On such excursions Rose would write with childish glee about the countryside she travelled through, and how much she was missing 'Dearest St Crumpet'.

'I can tell you how the fields were white with Narcissi, how the roads were edged with mauve-coloured anemones & how the scarlet anemones stood up in the meadows tantalizing me in the carriage so much because I wanted to feel them', Rose wrote to Ruskin from Nice on 18 March, ending her letter 'I wish so very much that you were happy – God can make you so – We will try not to forget all you taught us – It was so nice of you . . . I like Nice but I don't much like being transplanted except going home. I am ever your rose. Postscript. Yes, write packets – trunks, & we shall like them so much . . . you must see how we think of you and talk of you – rosie posie.'[5]

As Rose's note indicates, in contrast to her doubting drawing master, she had a strong sense of God. Her Christian fidelity was rigorously cultivated by her Baptist father, who encouraged her intense Bible study, which would often take preference over playtime. Her letters also reveal a very intelligent child, with a bold, confident and playfully self-aware manner.

Two years after meeting Rose, and in spite of the fact that she embodied the beliefs he himself was now doubting, Ruskin realized that his feelings for this child went beyond simple affection. In the year in which Ruskin's feelings for his twelve-year-old sweetheart emerged, so too returned the depressive illnesses that he had suffered on and off since his childhood. Just as he had once sought out Effie Gray as a means of dispersing his black mood, now once again and after a seven week rest-cure in Boulogne, he sought solace in his new love. After taking a steamer from Holyhead to Dublin, which offended him with its two stinking smoke-spouting funnels, he soon found himself in the palatial settings of Harristown House, the huge Palladian villa, set in its extensive grounds, inhabited by the Irish banker John La Touche and his family.

The holiday was a happy one. Ruskin's letters home to his father talk of walks along the banks of rivers, of the children jumping streams and paddling, of building bridges, of boating and riding, and trips to local sights. So happy, in fact, was the stay that the La Touches encouraged Ruskin to extend it. On his last night at Harristown House they asked him to join them at a stately dinner at a neighbouring pile. But Ruskin made his excuses and instead dined alone with the children.

After leaving Rose, Ruskin went abroad again, to Switzerland. His diaries make bleak reading. They are nothing more than the accounts of the solitary walks and ascents of a lonely man. Hardly anyone else features in the pages of his diary, except for Rose. The sense of Ruskin's anticipation as he awaits news from her pervades his journal, with only the receipt of correspondence and the momentary ecstasy this brings puncturing the gloom.

The regular correspondence between Ruskin and Rose La Touche continued into 1861. At some point Ruskin began to carry Rose's letters on his person in a little case, lined with sheets of gold. Increasingly he projected his own feelings onto her letters, such as this one from the thirteen-year-old Rose:

I got your letter St C on Saturday morning after I had written the first part of this, just as I was going out riding. So I cd only give it one peep, and then tucked it into my riding-habit pocket and pinned it down, so that it could be talking to me whilst I was riding. I had to shut up my mouth, so tight, when I met Mamma, for she would have taken it and read it if I told her and it wd'nt have gone on riding with me. As it was, we ran rather a chance of me, and pocket, and letter, and all, for Swallow (that's Emily's animal that I always ride now) was in tremendous spirits about having yr handwriting on his back, that she took to kicking and jumping in such a way, till I felt like a Stormy Petrel riding a great wave – so you may imagine I could not spare a hand to unpin my dear pocket, and I had to wait in patience . . . and we were safe at home again.[6]

It is easy to imagine the kind of interpretation Freud would have made of this passage so charged with sexual imagery. If the unfortunate combination of pockets, pinned pockets, riding-habits and frolicking horses were lost on the sexually naïve Rose, at some level they became powerfully charged for Ruskin. By July he was referring to them as 'Rosie's love letters'.[7]

If Rossetti's love for Lizzie had been uneven, so too was his grief for her. In the days and weeks after her death he swung between moments of abject misery and mourning and periods of abandon in the company of some his wilder bachelor friends.

As Lizzie lay in her coffin ahead of her burial in Highgate Cemetery, Rossetti, caught up in grief and remorse, slipped his poetry notebook alongside her body. It was a genuine gesture. He had always been as much a poet as a painter and had been working towards the publication of a volume of his work – which had already been announced. In the notebook that Rossetti now placed next to his dead wife were the workings and reworkings of poems he had been writing and rewriting since the late 1840s. The book contained love poetry that would now die with Lizzie. Its entombment with her was a self-inflicted punishment, for once the lid was bolted down he would never again be able to retrieve work he had toiled over, and the proposed publication could never happen.

But aside from moments of grand gesture such as this, and other episodes of more intimate private grief, by and large Rossetti regained his self-composure fairly rapidly. Soon, some might say too soon, he began to enjoy his new-found bachelor status in the company of other single men. One of these was the extraordinary young poet Algernon Charles Swinburne, whose presence populated the days post-11 February, not least, perhaps, because of the inextricable link there now was between Swinburne and that dreadful date.

'At the beginning of the year 1862 I had been for little more than four years acquainted with Mr Dante Gabriel Rossetti', Swinburne later recalled.

> During this year, also, I had come to know, and to regard with little less than a brother's affection, the noble lady whom he had recently married. On the evening of her terrible death we have dined all three together at a 'restaurant' which Rossetti had been accustomed to frequent. Next morning on coming by appointment to sit for my portrait, I heard that she had died in the night. ... The anguish of the widower, when next we met, under the roof of the mother with whom he had sought refuge, I cannot remember, at more than twenty years' distance, without some recrudescence of emotion. With sobs and broken speech he protested that he had never really loved or cared for any woman but the wife he had lost: with bitter self-reproach he referred to former professions not ostensibly consistent with this assertion: he appealed to my friendship, in the name of her regard for me, as she had felt for no other of this friends – to cleave to him in this time of sorrow.[8]

It was certainly true that Lizzie and Swinburne had had a deep bond. Some went as far as to suggest that Swinburne – although apparently homosexual – had fallen profoundly in love with Lizzie, and that she had returned his infatuation. He certainly eulogized her after her death, claiming he had never known 'so brilliant and appreciative a woman – so quick to see and so keen to enjoy that rare and delightful fusion of wit, humour, character-painting, and dramatic poetry – poetry subdued to dramatic effect – which is only less wonderful and delightful than the highest works of genius. She was a wonderful as well as a most lovable creature.'[9]

But if Lizzie had fallen for Swinburne, the choice would have been as fateful as that she had already made with her love of Rossetti. Swinburne was notoriously wild, with a reputation for vice and excess that matched his long, flaming red hair. And now Rossetti, whose intensified friendship with Swinburne was couched in terms of guilt and grief, would soon find in his company not so much quiet solace as wild escape and bad behaviour – characteristics to which Rossetti had, after all, become inclined before his doomed marriage.

Just days after Lizzie's funeral Rossetti, his brother William and Boyce took an excursion to Greenwich, where, strolling in the park, 'Gabriel catching sight of a girl with a paintable face, made up to her and got her address'. That same day Rossetti and Boyce 'Dined at the Trafalgar. Afterwards returned to the Park – kiss in the ring and out of the ring and larking generally going on. Tea at my place. The brothers left between 2 and 3 in the morning.'[10]

There are hints in Boyce's diary of strange debaucheries seeping into Rossetti's and his companions' behaviour around this time. Boyce recalls Rossetti visiting 'Judge and Jury', a particularly obscene entertainment show that dwelt on the adulteries and sexual perversions of public figures and celebrities.[11] He also recounts catching up with Rossetti 'at Swinburne's rooms where they were looking over *Justine*, by the Marquis de Sade, recent acquisition of the latter'.[12]

Soon the appeal of lodging wore off, and Rossetti began hunting for new accommodation. But it was not for a bachelor pad that the recently bereaved widower looked: rather, Rossetti began to seek out a home that better embodied his own developing eccentricities – a large, rambling house to match the different rooms of his mind, a house with a character of its own that could accommodate the huge personality and foibles of its tenant.

Rossetti wanted companionship too. Inspired by the friendships and shared enthusiasms of those he was cavorting with, he once again returned to the notion of sharing accommodation with a group of like-minded artists and writers. The PRBs had more than once considered communal life, and now Rossetti looked at a large house in Chelsea for this very purpose.

Tudor House in Cheyne Walk, Chelsea, was available. It was a huge abode with plenty of medieval history behind it. Space and heritage aside, it offered Rossetti a view of the Thames but also a large garden. Cheyne Walk was a vibrant and lively place in the days before it became cut off from the river by the Embankment. Giving directly onto the river and its boats, it was bustling with taverns and coffee houses. In October 1862 Rossetti secured the lease.

Rossetti asked the wild, unpredictable Swinburne to become his co-tenant. In addition he made arrangements to share the rent further with part-time lodgers, who would use rooms in the house three days a week. These were the ever amenable William Michael Rossetti and the writer George Meredith. And so the tone of Tudor House was set.

It would be a place where Rossetti would begin as he meant to go on. The house became an embodiment of the eccentricities, fetishisms and infatuations that would define Rossetti until his dying day. If a simple domestic life had in some degree been attempted with Lizzie, now simplicity was cast away in favour of the theatrical. He began to furnish his new abode with various collections, where a liking for a particular style or item was repeated again and again. First there was a collection of old Renaissance furniture, bought from a man in Buckingham Street,[13] then a collection of blue and white china and also an assembly of mirrors.

Animals became his other fascination. The zoological gardens – open in London since 1828 – had always been a favoured day

trip for Rossetti and his friends. But now Rossetti saw the opportunity to create his own zoo in the ample gardens at Cheyne Walk.
He had a menagerie in his grounds that included fawns and deer
along with more exotic birds and even at one stage a kangaroo.
These poor animals invariably died through neglect. There were
armadillos that would burrow out of their confines and appear in
neighbouring homes and gardens, and peacocks that kept the
entire neighbourhood awake with their piercing squawks.

His co-habitants proved as badly behaved as the menagerie.
Swinburne was known for drinking and tantrums. He would run
around naked and slide down the banisters in this newborn state.
Often suffering violent fits of instability, he would dance around
Gabriel's studio like a wild cat, making work impossible. There
were food fights and pranks, one of which involved Meredith's
shoes disappearing. But there were also bitter arguments. One
morning tempers became so heated that a cup of tea was thrown
in Meredith's face. He left. Swinburne's stay lasted hardly longer.
His wild drunkenness and complex personality brought on a
nervous breakdown, and within a year he too had departed.
Rossetti was left with his brother, and just one other co-habitant
– Fanny Cornforth.

Whether or not Fanny had taken up residence in Cheyne Walk
the day the lease was signed, she was certainly part of the furniture
by November – a mere nine months since Lizzie's demise. Boyce's
diary notes that on 29 October 'R . . . is in the process of moving
into Tudor House 16 Cheyne Walk Chelsea.'[14] Just a fortnight
later he called at the new house and 'Found Fanny there'. By early
December he was referring to Rossetti and his old flame as a
couple, writing that 'he went up to Chelsea to see Rossetti. Found
him and Fanny at home. Stayed and dined. He gave me a pencil
sketch of her as she lay on a couch, hair outspread.'[15]

Ruskin saw Rossetti just a little after Lizzie's death. Ruskin's great
friend and Rossetti admirer Charles Eliot Norton commissioned
a portrait of the former from the latter. The talk during the sitting

was apparently gloomy, with Ruskin stating his lack of faith in established religion more and more fervently.

Despite the portrait, Ruskin's gradual alienation from Rossetti left him in need of a new candidate for his patronage. It seems that he always needed a protégé. In this respect he was much like Rossetti. And there is some irony in the fact that, as Ruskin fell out of love with Rossetti, it was the latter's own protégé that superseded his master in the critic's affections.

With the encouragement of his idol Rossetti, Ned Burne-Jones was by the early 1860s an up-and-coming painter of some note. It was not long before Ruskin's beady eye fell on the young man and his work. If Ruskin's reputation and patronage had become sullied for some, such as Millais and Madox Brown, Ned Burne-Jones had been protected from the effects of the Effie scandal by the simple fact of his age. A few years younger than the PRBs, he was still at Oxford when Millais and Ruskin were holed up together in the Trossachs. And although it is impossible that he did not know of the *brouhaha*, it had in no way tainted his view of the great critic. For Ned, Ruskin, whom he had encountered at university through his writing, remained as much a hero as Rossetti.

Back in 1856 Rossetti had introduced Ned to Ruskin, and the former had been star-struck. 'Just come back from being with our hero for four hours – so happy we've been', he had written in a letter.

> He is so kind to us, calls us his dear boys and makes us feel like such old friends. To-night he comes down to our rooms to carry off my drawing and shew it to lots of people; tomorrow night he comes again, and every Thursday night the same – isn't that like a dream? Think of knowing Ruskin like an equal ... Oh ! He is so good and kind – better than his books, which are the best in the world.[16]

The paternal aspect that Ruskin adopted towards Ned was enhanced by the fact that many actually interpreted them as father and son. Ned shared the same fair complexion as Ruskin and had a similar very slender build. Ned was positively thrilled when, living in Rossetti and Deverell's old lodgings in Red Lion Square, Ruskin was shown in by the housekeeper and introduced without thought as 'your father, sir'. Ruskin's delight in this relationship was reciprocated.

'Our friendship with Mr Ruskin was one of the happiest things of these early days, for we loved him profoundly and he drew us very near to him', Georgie wrote in her memoirs.[17] 'When he was in England we saw him often, and when abroad he wrote to us, at first as "My dear Edward and Georgie" and afterwards as "My dearest children", which name was never quite dropped.'

In May 1862 Ruskin took the Burne-Joneses to Italy with him. But during this trip Ruskin received some disturbing news. His relations with the La Touches had been intensely friendly up to this point. He had left England with an offer from them of the use of a little cottage on their Harristown estate. But once Ruskin had set off on his latest continental jaunt, the La Touches suddenly withdrew their offer, saying their Irish neighbours could never understand it.[18] It was as though the scales had fallen from their eyes and they could now see the inappropriateness of the relationship between John Ruskin and their pubescent daughter. And so rather than heading to Harristown, Ruskin fled to Mornex, near Geneva. Here, seeking solace from his Alpine surroundings, and with both his career and his close relationships foundering in Britain, he began to plan to make Switzerland his home.

But Ruskin's search for freedom from his troubles in the Alps was misguided. The effect of the grand landscape on him was double-edged. Although the beauty of the mountainscape could lift his spirits, he could also become lost in it. For as many days as there is a note of sublime appreciation in his surroundings, his diary also records days utterly lost in the hills, dates simply accompanied by the words 'don't know' or 'forget'.

As Ruskin sank into a deeply reclusive Alpine life, his temperament and feelings seemed to merge with those of the Alps. He became as changeable as the weather, and if the latter was gloomy, his depression would return. Only letters from Rose La

Touche seemed to puncture the strange state of mind into which Ruskin was falling. Amid his accounts of ill-health in the form of a recurring sore throat, and of repeated 'languidness', the only rays of light are offered by news of this young girl. The joy that words from her brought to Ruskin could apparently colour both him and the landscape around him, as he related on 25 August 1862 in his diary: 'To Geneva. Got nice letter . . . Read letter on rock at foot of Saleve. Glorious afternoon and sunset.'[19]

Despite her apparently remedial effect on him, Ruskin's influence on Rose was proving far from healthy. Rose was finding the adult world she was entering hard to reconcile. Fervently religious, she was becoming troubled by the adult debates she heard hammered out at home between her parents and their friends, which seemed to throw doubt on the clear-cut vision of religion she had been invited to swallow and digest. Whether one of those voices was Ruskin's is not made clear in Rose's own account of events, although Ruskin had revealed his religious doubts to Maria La Touche in the period before their apparent estrangement.

> It was a most terrible time for I got utterly puzzled and the terrible feeling of wickedness haunted me like a nightmare. I could not say my prayers, for the doubts and arguments I had listened to quietly in the daytime would come thronging into my head till they were but crys of despair or, worse than all, blank hopelessness of doubt . . .
>
> And by degrees things did get better – I do not know how, exactly, but I got happier, and the black despair did not come over me at the creeds in Church, and certainly my trust in God remained firm . . . The letters Mr Ruskin wrote to me at this time only helped me and did me no harm – whatever others may say. Well I got better anyhow of my doubts and troubles though health, spirits and temper had suffered.[20]

Ruskin was at once part of the cause and the cure for Rose's distress. This strange mixture would from now on define this unconventional relationship between the middle-aged man and the young girl, trapping them in an impossible situation.

The growing tensions in Harristown were magnified when, in October 1863, although just fifteen, Rose suffered a nervous breakdown. It came as her parents – who now took different positions on Christian practice – were rowing over whether or not she should be confirmed. He father, now a Baptist, wanted her to take communion. Her mother wanted her to be confirmed first, as per the Anglican tradition. Her father objected to confirmation, believing it to be unnecessary. Rose was tossed to and fro. In the end, on Sunday 11 October, she took her father's side and went to church and took communion, without having been confirmed. But the act that defied her mother's will had grave consequences, as Rose later recounted:

> I suppose all the trouble of body, soul and spirit had been too much for me, for on Monday morning I had a terrible headache and before evening was very ill. It was a strange illness – I can't tell about it gradually but looking back upon it – I know I suffered terribly. (I was in bed for about four weeks.) Everything hurt me. People coming in and talking ... Light hurt me. Food hurt me ... I got very weak and thin and the Doctors were frightened.[21]

And so Rose sank into a period of mental fragility that coloured her daily life for the next few years. She slipped away from society into a twilight of doctors and recuperation, while Ruskin continued in his solitary doubts and torments.

It was not until December 1865 that Rose and Ruskin saw one another again, when, shortly before her eighteenth birthday, the La Touches were once again in London. They could not avoid seeing Ruskin. Perhaps Maria La Touche felt that such a long separation between Rose and her erstwhile admirer would have dampened any inappropriate feelings that Ruskin might have harboured. But if this was her opinion, it was ill judged.

The moment Rose and Ruskin were reunited, the fire that had burned so bright in them was reignited. Ruskin was smitten once more. He began to see Rose as often as he could. On 16 December, his diary notes, he took Rose to the British Museum.

Five days later they were walking around the garden at Denmark Hill.

On Rose's eighteenth birthday, 3 January 1866, Ruskin took Rose out to dinner along with Maria La Touche and his cousin Joan Agnew, who was living with him and his family at Denmark Hill as his ward. He spoke to barely anyone but the birthday girl during the entire meal, with Mrs La Touche raising her eyebrows to Joan every now and then in recognition of the attention her daughter was being given. According to Ruskin, Rose clung tightly to his arm and hung on his every word. To him it seemed quite clear what her body was conveying. Released from the loneliness and uncertainty of his last few years, he felt that his future was now clear. And so either that very night, or shortly afterwards, he asked the frail, devout Rose La Touche to become his wife.

14

The towers of Topsy

SINCE THEIR MARRIAGE in 1859 William Morris and his wife, the former Jane Burden, had been enjoying a wonderful adventure. After their low-key wedding Morris had dug into his pockets and decided to spend some of his not inconsiderable wealth on a new family home, the Red House. It still stands today in Bexleyheath – a bizarrely out-of-place monument to medievalism in what is now an unremarkable suburban road. Surrounded by the commuter homes that have engulfed the countryside it once dominated, it is a veritable castle.

'The Towers of Topsy', as Rossetti called it, was designed for Morris by the young architect Philip Webb, whom Morris befriended while exploring his own architectural potential in the offices of George Edward Street. In the Red House Morris and Webb created something quite unlike anything that any other Victorian would have encountered. It was their vision of what good architecture could be. The house was conceived on a grand scale by today's standards. Harking back to medieval great halls, its ceilings are high and beamed, but its lines are clean, and the oak and red brick from which it is made are laid bare. But more than that, it became their Camelot: a manifesto for good taste and a wholesome approach to life and work that consciously stepped away from established Victorian models.

Morris, remembering the happy days of the jovial campaign in Oxford, invited his friends to help furnish and decorate the Red House. In exchange for companionship and good fun Rossetti, Ford Madox Brown and Morris's college chum Charley Faulkner all joined in. Ned and Georgie Burne-Jones and their baby Phil moved into the house for a six-month working holiday.

The Red House was a place for pranks. Brown sewed up the back of Morris's waistcoat one night so that in the morning everyone could enjoy Morris's fury and consternation at his apparent doubling in size overnight. Charley Faulkner managed to fall out of the minstrels' gallery. There were great games of hide-and-seek, which Jane (who had perhaps never had sufficient fortune or privilege to enjoy such things during her own slum childhood) particularly adored. And the apple orchard became the arena for huge windfall fights.

Inspired by the large medieval pieces Morris himself had created for Red Lion Square, Webb designed a new kind of furniture on a huge architectural scale for the Red House: tall-backed sofas, great chests and cabinets, monumental sideboards. In the drawing-room Rossetti worked on a pair of doors painting the tale that he so loved and had already expressed in watercolour: the story of Dante and Beatrice. Jane and William painted the ceilings together before working on the textile designs for the house.

Morris also painted an elaborate *trompe-l'oeil* tapestry in the drawing-room, with the intention of including in it his motto, 'If I can'. While the work was in a half-complete state, Rossetti preempted Morris and completed the work for him with the words 'If I can't'. It was a joke of course, but one that highlights Rossetti's tendency to reserve his undermining sarcasm for Morris in particular. Although the two were ostensibly the best of friends, Rossetti was always quicker than the rest to exploit Morris's blatant behavioural peculiarities and his willingness to play the group buffoon.

Rossetti had always been supremely competitive with his friends: this had been evident particularly in his relationship with Hunt. But with Morris a sharper jealousy was forming. Since Morris and Ned had sought out their hero in the mid-1850s, Rossetti had been more than content to see himself as the senior partner in the triumvirate. But with the construction of the Red

House Morris, funny though he was, had displayed a number of qualities that, if anything, placed Rossetti in his shade. Beneath his dumpy, jovial exterior lurked a fierce intelligence and a powerful ambition, and the fruits of this combination were beginning to show themselves. This, as well as Morris's personal circumstances, were beginning to increase his status in the group. On several counts Rossetti was clearly feeling a little challenged by his former squire.

First was Morris's considerable personal wealth (which paid not only for the Red House fantasy but also for the accompanying details of affluence, such as its specially designed carriage with leather curtains). Second was Morris's boldness of vision and driving enthusiasm. Then there was the issue of poetry. Rossetti had always swung between his ambitions to be a painter and a poet. Morris too was an evident polymath and had established himself as something of a bard while at university. But unlike Rossetti, he had managed to cement this reputation with the extremely successful publication of a major narrative poem, 'The Defence of Guenevere', in 1858. It had been well received. Rossetti meanwhile, had done no more than announce his intention to publish a major poetry collection before denying himself the opportunity by burying his manuscripts with his dead wife.

Then, of course, there was Morris's unlikely marriage to the beautiful and increasingly confident Jane. No matter how much Rossetti enjoyed the visual incongruity of this couple – she so tall and slender, her spouse so rotund and short – his amusing caricatures of the Morrises can have done little to dampen the memory of his own infatuation with Jane Burden, as she had been.

Jane Morris came into her own during the decoration of the Red House. The strange girl from the Oxford slums began to buy the fabric for the house and quietly but firmly to make her own contribution to Morris's grand project. Topsy was particularly delighted with a piece of blue worsted that Jane bought, and embroidered a clump of daisies on it. He then repeated the design. This was the very first of his daisy patterns – a design that would become a classic of Morris & Co. and was soon also transferred to wallpapers.

She became a mother during this period too, giving birth to Jenny first, in 1861, and then, just four weeks after Lizzie's awful death, delivering Mary into the world, who became known as May. And Jane also became established as something of a social phenomenon. Married to one of the growing stars of the London scene, who had been readily adopted by Mrs Prinsep and the Little Holland House set, she quickly became a much talked-about addition to the social circuit. Statuesque, silent and still, often reclining slightly aloof and removed from the focus of events, she was like a mysterious angel looking down on life around her and immediately acquired a status somewhere between icon and curio.

It seems that, as with Lizzie, Jane's appeal to Rossetti and Morris was not entirely a case of these men projecting their fantasies onto a blank canvas. Although there may have been a significant element of that, like Lizzie, Jane was inherently 'different'. She had an intrinsic 'artistic' aura. Just as Lizzie had been marked out by her unusual dress, so Jane's outfits were apparently unusual by the standards of the day. She had nothing to do with the lace, hoops, collars and corsetry that other Victorian middle- or upper-class women were proudly sporting. Rather, she chose to wear plain but voluminous dresses in dark rich silks – purple, green and blue. Even in the very early days of her marriage she wore heavy, 'outlandish' beads around her slender neck, which, when on her honeymoon in Normandy, made the locals giggle out loud and point at her in the street, just as the Sheffield girls had pointed at Lizzie.

The outcome of the Red House decorations was 'The Firm' – the interior decoration business that would bind Rossetti, Brown, Burne-Jones and Morris together beyond friendship. The venture, incorporated initially as Morris, Marshall, Faulkner & Co., intended to produce items that would make the everyday world more beautiful for all, and was formalized in 1861. Each partner held a £20 share and was expected to make at least one or two items of stock. They set up a workshop and showroom near Ned and Morris's old studio garret in Red Lion Square.[1]

In the spirit of the original PRB, 'The Firm' was conceived as an enterprise of opposition: anti-pomposity, anti-inane luxury. The establishment – this time in the form of J. G. Crace, who was the leading decorator of the day to the great and the good – was once again a focus of antipathy. 'We are not intending to compete with Crace's costly rubbish or anything of that sort, but to give real good taste at the price if possible of ordinary furniture, and we expect to start in some shape about May or June', Rossetti informed Allingham in a letter.[2]

In 1862 the firm took a stall at the South Kensington Exhibition – the follow-up to the Great Exhibition. It was the first public unveiling of their work. In an act of massive over-ambition they booked 900 square feet and displayed stained glass and painted furniture, along with a motley collection of furnishing accessories, embroideries, painted tiles and some of Webb's jewellery. But the bold move proved fruitful, and in addition to receiving two medals of commendation £150 worth of goods were sold.

Interestingly the press's response to these new artistic products was as reactionary as that given to the juvenile PRB a decade earlier. Just as the Pre-Raphaelites had been ridiculed and berated for what appeared to be artless paintings, now the firm was criticized for medievalism, for being out of tune with the machine age.

But whereas the PRB had faced a genuine initial uproar, the firm was in the slipstream of the now established success of Millais and Hunt, and of Rossetti's emerging popularity. It was not long before orders began to flood in for this new kind of medieval furniture, and Morris, at the hub of the firm, found himself becoming an increasingly busy shopkeeper.

By 1864 the firm was expanding so rapidly that the rooms in Red Lion Square were proving insufficient. In addition to the cramped conditions, the growing demands of the business meant

Morris was commuting almost daily between Bexleyheath and central London and becoming tired and grumpy. His typical outbursts of anger were getting worse.

Recognizing that something must be done, Morris decided to extend the Red House. Once again the idea of an artistic colony, a genuine brotherhood, was revisited. This time the plan was for a new wing to be added to the house for the Burne-Joneses, as well as extensions for The Firm's workshops. Topsy and Ned would create a new kind of living/work space, allowing thriving industry in the heart of the inspirational countryside.

In September 1864 Georgie Burne-Jones was well into the third term of her second pregnancy, and the new plans for the extended Red House were well under way. But then tragedy struck. The Burne-Joneses' young son Phil went down with scarlet fever. The robust little boy weathered the disease, but Georgie caught it and went into premature labour. Her new baby lived just three weeks, and she herself sank into deeper illness. Their friends rallied round as best they could, but Morris himself was ill with rheumatic fever, and Rossetti was in Paris on holiday with Fanny. And so it was Ruskin who stepped in. In an extraordinarily tender gesture he paid for the entire street outside the Burne-Joneses' London home to be strewn with tan bark 'as deep as a riding school'[3] so that the din of the horses' hoofs was sufficiently dulled to let Georgie sleep.

Although Georgie recovered, the episode had a more profound effect on the Burne-Joneses. Once Ned was assured that his wife would survive, he wrote to Morris and explained that he had decided against moving to the Red House. It was as though the proposed adventure now felt too much for them in the delicate emotional state in which they found themselves.

The whole sorry episode of this infant death and the subsequent scuppering of plans had yet further ramifications. As 1865 approached, Ned found himself a less happy man and one who would soon seek the arms of someone other than the devoted Georgie to ease his sorrows. Morris, meanwhile, made a decision that he would rue for the rest of his life. Unable to bring his collaborators to him, he must go to them; and unable to bring The Firm to the Red House, the latter must be given up for the former. He and his family would leave the Red House for good and return to the smoke and bustle of London. The move would place him closer to his work and ease the strain of commuting, which was beginning to affect his marriage. But unfortunately a return to London also put Jane back within Rossetti's easy grasp, something that would ultimately prove far more damaging.

When Ruskin proposed to Rose La Touche in January 1866, on or just after her eighteenth birthday, she did not reject him. She thought about it a while and talked to Ruskin's ward and cousin Joan. Then on 2 February she gave her response. She could not commit to Ruskin, but she suggested that he should ask her again in three years, when she was twenty-one. He would then be fifty.

Ruskin was crestfallen. He was deeply aware of his age and mortality and felt that marriage in three years was simply too late, but he had little choice but to accept Rose's terms. Under the circumstances, all he could do was continue to contrive to see his sweetheart as often as possible. Since December he had been trying to introduce Rose and her mother to his friend Georgiana Cowper, Lady Mount Temple. Ruskin had known Mrs Cowper since the mid-1850s but had become particularly close to her from around 1863, when, with his religious faith crumbling and finding himself searching for answers to fundamental questions, he had begun to explore spiritualism with her.

Spiritualism was in vogue. Seances were a relatively regular occurrence in society, and it is clear from Ruskin's letters that Mrs Cowper took him to some.[4] However, it was no seance that Ruskin wanted Mrs Cowper to arrange this time, but simply a dinner party to which the La Touches could be invited. Typical of the extremely pedantic and anxious Ruskin, however, the arrangements for even the simplest soirée soon became the subject of minute examination on his part, proposing guests of just the right size to allow the perfectly matched, slender Ruskin to accompany his sylph-like Rose down to dinner.

A few days later Ruskin briefed Mrs Cowper yet further, revealing the deep complexities of his relationship with Rose. His anxiety was now such that he wanted to make sure that his hostess did not exacerbate anything with any misplaced remarks:

> Now observe – in any word you speak to the mother – you must remember that she knows perfectly how I feel: but there is no confidence between Rosie and her; and she knows nothing of the child's depth of feeling – . . . Rosie's just like Cordelia – so you had better not in any way speak otherwise of Rosie to her – it would only make things a little more difficult for me, if she thought more of her daughter – and they cannot at least at present – be brought into any quite true or happy relations. Now with the Father, it is nearly the reverse. Rosie is infinitely precious to him, and there is great and true sympathy between them; – except about me; – for he cannot understand me at all, nor has he any idea of caring for her otherwise than as a goodnatured and – to him – inconvenient friend. – But he knows that neither Rosie nor I would ever do anything in the least betraying his trust in us: and in now checking our intercourse, I think he is really acting more in fear for me than for her – and dreads, for my sake, that my feelings may become now – what they have been for these seven years.[5]

But the dinner party, so meticulously planned to be cosy and intimate, did not go according to plan. Afterwards Ruskin wrote to Ned and revealed that Rose had suffered a headache throughout the entire evening and in the end had left early.

Despite his obvious distress at the turn-out of events, Ruskin, dogged as ever, refused to believe that Rose's headache could have been in any way manufactured as a way of excusing herself from engaging more fully with Ruskin that night. When she then stood him up at a concert of Mendelssohn's *Elijah* that had been arranged for some time, he also sought to cast the most optimistic complexion on her absence.

'The black fates have surely had their will enough by this time', he explained to Mrs Cowper, who was now his chief confidante in the La Touche issue.

> For you know it *was* fate – the child was really ill, and tried hard to keep up for me; and even her mother, cruel as she is, wouldn't have played me a trick like that; – wantonly: – It was worse still at that horrible Elijah – for that was Rosie's own plan, and she had wanted to hear it, & make me attend to it – ever so long; and I had got leave to have her beside me; – and she had a violent cold & cough, & couldn't come, and tried to keep it off to the last moment and had to send me word when I was just waiting for her – & I couldn't get away till the first act.[6]

The image of Ruskin sitting alone, despairing and tortured, an empty seat next to him, is easy to conjure. From his diaries and letters of this period one can see that he was a man falling apart at the seams. Reading his note to Mrs Cowper, and his reference to Rose as a 'child', one cannot also help but recognize the paedophiliac nature of his fascination with Rose. If his treatment of Effie had been bizarre and unsavoury, his obsession with Rose was yet more so.

Given the detrimental effect Ruskin's attentions were having on Rose's health, the La Touches must have been relieved when they left London and returned to Harristown. They had concluded that Ruskin should never marry their daughter, and they forbade Rose from communicating with him further. But in light of this, their behaviour was particularly provoking. They taunted him with Rose like a kitten with a cork on a string, for though Rose could no longer write to 'St C', they nevertheless invited Ruskin's cousin Joan to stay with them in April. After a month's sojourn in Ireland, Joan returned to London in time to travel to the continent for a short vacation with Ruskin.

With direct contact with Rose now withdrawn, Ruskin quickly sought vicarious contact with her. As the summer of 1866 moved on, it was Rose's letters to Joan that he now craved. Even this second-hand contact with Rose could perk Ruskin up temporarily and raise him from the depressive stupor into which he had sunk after their enforced separation.

But then, as if to dangle the dancing cork yet more tantalizingly, the La Touches invited Joan to return to Harristown again, for August. As his cousin made her way to Ireland, Ruskin was left on tenterhooks. On 31 July his diary noted that a 'Letter from Joanna in the morning strikes me with deadly cold about R'. A couple of days later Ruskin was full of anticipation, trying to work 'at minerals'. He noted in his diary that he 'Expected letter from Joanna saying she was to be at H[arris]town, and got none, Patience.'[7]

When the letters did come, they apparently offered little hope. He describes 6 August simply as a 'Dark day'. From this point on words began to fail Ruskin, who resorted to drawing little squares in his diaries. The square indicated that either he had received no correspondence concerning Rose or that what had arrived was negative.

Bursting with frustration, Ruskin turned to Mrs Cowper. His misery was total, her preparedness to listen and soothe him forthcoming. 'Just glance at these letters,' he pleaded, enclosing a selection of Rose's letters, 'that you may see a little what the child has been to me for so long, and how cruel it is of them to take her from me now so utterly in an instant – how cruel, and vain, because what human thing – that was human – could be made to feel less, merely by silence – after years of love.'[8]

Joan returned to London with news that must have been met with some ambivalence by Ruskin. During her second stay at the Harristown estate Rose's brother Percy had fallen in love with Joan and proposed to her. The two were informally engaged. Joan's apparent success with the La Touches must have been a bitter pill to Ruskin, whose own suit had been so brutally rejected. But this new twist in the tale cemented the relationship between the two families in a new way, and Ruskin may have hoped that it would extend the opportunity of contact with Rose.

More good news was that the Cowpers were to visit Ireland,

and intended to be in Harristown by mid-September. A flurry of correspondence ensued. 'I don't want to know a single word of what passes in Harristown', Ruskin wrote disingenuously. 'I want . . . you to go there – in kindness & truth to all of us . . . to act – according to your power for – or against me as you see good . . . It is just because there is more clandestine character in the matter at present than I like, that I want you so much to go.'[9]

In this last note to Mrs Cowper, Ruskin enclosed a portion of a letter sent by Joan while at the La Touche estate in Harristown, which apparently conveyed confirmation from Rose that Ruskin's affections were returned. Mrs Cowper wrote back and conceded that indeed Joan's communication seemed to indicate mutual feelings, and she must have expressed some surprise because Ruskin replied in fine form, teasing his correspondent: 'I felt always convinced that you did not know how much ground for hope I had – but you seemed to think it so fearfully impossible that she could care for me that I couldn't tell you . . . Rosie is a real Irish child . . . fancy her telling Joan that "now I had waited so long, it couldn't be much matter to wait that little bit longer!" a fine reason truly. It's just eight hundred and twenty eight days – twenty four hours long each – to her 21st birthday. And its eight hundred and fifty eight to the day when she told me I might "ask the same".'[10]

But if Ruskin's spirits were raised by the potential of Joan and Percy's engagement, and Mrs Cowper's new-found optimism, the Cowpers' visit did nothing but dash Ruskin's hope once more. The news, when Mrs Cowper was able to write fully, was that it 'could never be'.[11] Ruskin broke down. Unable to meet his friend to discuss her mission more fully, he excused himself on grounds of ill heath.

And then a letter from Rose's father dealt what felt like a death blow. On 23 October Ruskin's diary notes that he received a 'Bad letter (Mr La Touche's)' and consequently 'Lay awake long at night'. He wrote to Mrs Cowper shortly afterwards and revealed that 'the father's letter was insolent in the last degree'. He also learned that Maria La Touche had burned all the letters he had ever sent Rose: 'there were years of my life in every sentence of them. She destroyed them all – slowly murdered me, day by day, and now she calls it treason, because I cannot lay my whole heart bare to the woman I love, without also telling her what it was that so long kept me from esteeming or understanding the deep grace she did me.'[12]

Ruskin was broken. He was left simply counting the days to Rose's twenty-first birthday, but with little real hope. Three days before London erupted into the usual Christmas cheer, Ruskin saw nothing to feel merry about. 'Such a black day of hopeless fog as I have seldom known', he wrote on 22 December 1866. Incapacitated, he did little but 'write letters' and 'dream of R'. There was nothing he could do but dream of his true love. She was apparently beyond his reach.

The 1860s were defined by growing social permissiveness and experimentation. These traits of an emergent modern world were played out against religious doubts that were not confined just to the troubled mind of John Ruskin. And then with the expansion of the workforce and the industrialization of the land, there came the new politics of socialism.

Despite his early pretensions to religious painting, Rossetti was part of the growing secular population. He also showed a nodding sympathy for socialism with his association with the Working Men's College. But with his long hair, complex relationships, nocturnal habits and louche lifestyle few could doubt that above all he rode at the crest of the wave of another 'ism' – bohemianism.

The very notion of Bohemia – a place, intellectual as much as geographical, where like-minded artists lived and behaved unconventionally, forging new approaches to domestic arrangements and relationships – first came into being around the middle of the nineteenth century. William Makepeace Thackeray, an associate of the PRB circle, made reference to bohemianism in his novel *Vanity Fair*, published in 1848. Perplexed members of the public who found themselves unable properly to understand the increasingly bandied term were enlightened in 1862 by the *Westminster Review*, which explained to its readership that 'A Bohemian is simply an artist or *littérateur* who, consciously or unconsciously, secedes from conventionality in life and in art.'[13]

As the 1860s progressed, Rossetti would become the grand prince of bohemianism as his deviations from normal standards became more audacious. And as he became this epitome of the unconventional, his egocentric demands necessarily required his close friends to remodel their own lives around him. His bohemianism was like a web in which others became trapped – none more so than William and Jane Morris.

In their rural retreat the Morrises had been nicely protected from the evils of the big city. But this happy sojourn proved all too momentary, and the day came far too soon when they found themselves heading back into the teeming metropolis and all its madness.

Topsy and Jane packed up and left the Red House in November 1865. For Jane, the fairy-tale of living in the countryside in such a beautiful home was all too sharply over. Putting apple fights in the orchard and hide-and-seek behind them, Morris moved her and the two 'littles' back to central London – Queen Square, where there were premises sufficient to house the family and firm together.

The square, in Bloomsbury, was on its way down. Once fashionable, it paled next to the more recently constructed and grander Russell Square, just the other side of its border with Southampton Row. The long, narrow garden at the centre of Queen Square could not match the grand gardens at the heart of its new neighbour in either scale or landscaping. And so the residents had migrated, leaving the rambling Georgian houses of Queen Square to a mixture of residential and industrial usages. Here, where Jane Morris had once looked out on orchards and countryside, she now saw a backyard and outbuildings full of bustle and work. Where once she had walked through her own front door into her own perfect Camelot, now she walked off the street into a shopfront and offices.

During the Red House years and after Lizzie's death Rossetti's attentions, both professional and personal, had been largely been tied up in the increasingly voluptuous form of Fanny Cornforth. Rossetti's overtness about the place Fanny now held in his life appalled Ruskin, with whom by 1865 relations were becoming strained. The two had been bickering. Rossetti had grumpily accused Ruskin of selling some of his pictures. Ruskin was criticizing Rossetti for a coarseness in his painting technique and for being 'sensational' in his treatment of his subjects.[14] Despite the idiosyncracies of his own life, Ruskin also took it upon himself at this time to reprimand Rossetti for the bad company he was keeping. 'In your interests only – and judging from no other person's sayings, but from my own sight – I tell you the people you associate with are ruining you', Ruskin grumbled.[15]

But Rossetti was not interested in or influenced by Ruskin's opinions on his personal life. He had leased Fanny an apartment in Royal Avenue close to Tudor House, and she split her time between this *pied-à-terre* and Tudor House itself, very much in charge of Rossetti's domestic affairs and without doubt his lover and companion. Quite what had become of Fanny's apparently reprobate husband, Mr Hughes, is shrouded in mystery. Fanny, who shared with William Michael the tendency to tidy up truth into a more palatable and respectable version of events, later claimed that 'her husband died within a year or two after their marriage', and thus she was quite free to live in the neighbourhood around Cheyne Walk and take 'charge of his [Rossetti's] housekeeping arrangements' while also sitting to him for 'a great number of pictures'.[16]

But the truth was indeed more morally complex. Fanny's husband did not, in fact, shuffle off his mortal coil until 1872. Rossetti mentions the death in a letter in which he also refers to Mr Hughes as Fanny's 'incubus', suggesting that some marital demands were still being made on Fanny by her legal spouse throughout her time as Rossetti's mistress.

Rossetti's testimony to his affection for his model-cum-lover and housekeeper are his pictures of her at that time. Fanny sat for the compelling *Fazio's Mistress*, which Rossetti painted in 1863. The picture makes no attempt to conceal the artist's infatuation with his sitter. In fact, the very subject of the painting was infatuation, drawing on a poem by the medieval Italian poet Fazio degli Uberti, which described the poet conjuring his lover's assets to mind. Just like the poet, Rossetti unashamedly shares his fascination with his lover's 'crisp golden-threaded hair', 'beautiful amorous mouth' and 'white easy neck'.

And two years later Fanny's appeal was still holding fast, when Rossetti depicted her in *The Blue Bower*, and immortalized both her name and his passion for her by painting a little bunch of blue cornflowers in the foreground, complemented by passion flowers in the background.

Fanny, whom as she grew plumper Rossetti nicknamed Elephant, was capacious in more ways than one. She was the first to understand that, when it came to women, no one would ever have the exclusive attentions of Rossetti. For Fanny was having to share Rossetti with models both new and old, whose images she found sitting alongside hers in the studio in Cheyne Walk.

For a start there was the spectral image of Lizzie, which Rossetti in his moments of guilt continued to resurrect, particularly in studies for an oil painting that he finally completed only in 1870: *Beata Beatrix*. Although ostensibly a picture of Dante's Beatrice at the moment of her death, the picture is a meditation on Rossetti's dead wife, drawn from memory and old sketches.

Then there was Alexa Wilding, a fabulous auburn-haired woman whom Rossetti saw walking along the street out of his studio window and bolted after. His charms as persuasive as ever, Rossetti persuaded Miss Wilding not only to pose for the audacious nude *Venus Verticordia*, but also to continue as a regular sitter for some years.

But in spite of these intrusions into their life, Rossetti had at least found some equilibrium and happiness with Fanny. Living unconventionally as a marked Bohemian, he was now defined. As such, he could have just got on with his life. His intrinsic flair for chaos would, however, preclude Rossetti from ever just getting on with life. It would be only a matter of time before even the easy, amoral life with Fanny was challenged.

15

Obsession

As 1866 PASSED and 1867 began, the desperation that had ruined Ruskin's Christmas was alleviated by a turn of events. Just seven days into the new year the enforced silence from Ireland was broken. Ruskin received a 'lovely letter'[1] from Rose herself, and the very next day to his complete joy he received another, 'with flowers on the envelope'.[2] Just over a week later came a third.

Quite how Rose had managed to write in light of her parents' views is shrouded in mystery, but Ruskin certainly saw in her words confirmation that, despite the prevailing wishes of her parents, what he had always believed to be true remained so: Rose loved him.

His hopes rose further on 19 January, when yet another 'Divine letter from Rose' arrived at Denmark Hill. A fortnight later a further 'divine letter from Rose'[3] came with the morning's post. And one of these must have contained news that the La Touches were packing up in Harristown and preparing for one of their stays in London, for on 5 February at half-past ten in the evening Ruskin sat in his study in Denmark Hill and noted in his journals that Rose was 'perhaps within four miles of me'.

If Rose's clandestine missives offered hope, her mother soon dashed it. Maria La Touche understood the danger London held for her daughter. For this town, although home to many of Ruskin's critics, was equally where his supporters would be encountered – and, of course, the man himself. And so as soon as the La Touches' cases and trunks had crossed the threshold of their

Above: Lizzie Drawing Gabriel,
by Dante Gabriel Rossetti, 1853.
Rossetti is often credited with
being the Svengali figure who
turned Lizzie into an artist, but
it is possible that she had always
harboured this ambition

Above: Self-Portrait, by Lizzie
Siddall, 1853. Rossetti left Lizzie
in sweltering London to produce
her first oil painting. Her mood
is perhaps reflected in the
resigned expression on her face

Above: Fanny Cornforth, by Dante Gabriel Rossetti,
1859. There are several accounts of the fateful meeting
between Fanny and Rossetti. According to one, Fanny
passed Rossetti in the Strand and spat out at him a
nutshell that she had cracked provocatively between
her teeth

Lizzie Letting Down her Hair,
by Dante Gabriel Rossetti, *c.* 1860

Annie Miller Letting Down her Hair,
by Dante Gabriel Rossetti, *c.* 1860

The same infatuations that Rossetti expressed in his drawings of Lizzie were repeated in his sketches of Annie

Jane Morris, by Dante Gabriel Rossetti, 1857. Jane Burden (as she was born) was spotted in the cheap seats of an Oxford theatre by Rossetti and Ned Burne-Jones and was quickly swept up by the group of artists that Rossetti had assembled in the town

Ruth Herbert, by Dante Gabriel Rossetti, 1876. While working on the Oxford murals and the Llandaff triptych, Rossetti seems to have been torn between his infatuations for the uneducated and illiterate Jane Burden and for the glamorous Ruth Herbert

Fanny with George Price Boyce, by Dante Gabriel Rossetti, 1858. Rossetti's relationship with Boyce was an intense one in the late 1850s and 1860s. The pair had a constant trade in one another's works and would swap depictions of the models who sat for both of them

Bocca Bacciata, by Dante Gabriel Rossetti, 1859. Rossetti persuaded Boyce to let him paint Fanny's portrait for him. The result was extraordinary not only for its origin but also because it heralded a new direction for Rossetti's work: a celebration of women for the sake of beauty and womanhood

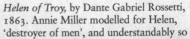

Helen of Troy, by Dante Gabriel Rossetti, 1863. Annie Miller modelled for Helen, 'destroyer of men', and understandably so

Above: Elizabeth Siddal – carte de visite, coloured by Rossetti, 1861. Lizzie's air of inward suffering and resignation, mixed with gentleness, comes across in this strange photograph, which suggests that even in 'real life' she played out a 'role' into which she had willingly been cast

Above left: Beata Beatrix, by Dante Gabriel Rossetti, 1864. Although ostensibly a picture of Dante's Beatrice at the moment of her death, the picture is a meditation on Rossetti's late wife, drawn from memory and old sketches

Left: William Morris, by Dante Gabriel Rossetti, *c.* 1856. This was a study of Morris as David which Rossetti made for the Llandaff triptych

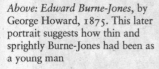

Above: Edward Burne-Jones, by George Howard, 1875. This later portrait suggests how thin and sprightly Burne-Jones had been as a young man

Above right: Georgiana Burne-Jones, by Edward Poynter, 1870. Although Georgie did not have the arresting looks of other PRB wives, she and her sisters all had extraordinary fates: one married the artist Sir Edward Poynter; another was the mother of prime minister Stanley Baldwin; and a third was the mother of the writer Rudyard Kipling

Right: Jane Morris, by John Parsons, taken in the garden at Tudor House, 1865. Jane was posed to emphasize those elements that Rossetti loved in his women: their profile, necks, their bodies twisted or bent in a way that at once suggests the informal and intimate

Above left: The Artist and Mary Zambaco, by Edward Burne-Jones, 1866–72. In this sketch Burne-Jones shows he is all too aware of his own physical inadequacies compared with his statuesque model and lover

Above right: Phyllis and Demophoon, by Edward Burne-Jones, 1870. According to Ovid's tale, Demophoon prises himself away from his admirer Phyllis, promising to return after six months. When he does not do so, Phyllis hangs herself and is turned into an almond tree. On embracing the tree, Demophoon transforms her back to human form. Mary Zambaco was the model for both figures, and she herself had attempted suicide over Edward Burne-Jones

Right: The Beloved, by Dante Gabriel Rossetti, 1865–6. Commissioned by George Rae, who allegedly knelt before it nightly with his wife, this overtly sexual picture has an underlying religious source in the Song of Solomon, from which Rossetti included the lines 'My beloved is mine and I am his' and 'Let him kiss me with the kisses of his mouth: for thy love is better than wine' on the frame

Left: The Beguiling of Merlin, by Edward Burne-Jones, 1874. Commissioned by Frederick Leyland in the late 1860s, the picture became a visual realization of Burne-Jones's own sense of utter submission to the powers of his mistress Mary Zambaco

Proserpine, by Dante Gabriel Rossetti, 1874. Based on the tale of Proserpine, who is held in Hades for six months of each year, this picture hints at the reality beneath the 'ideal' triangular arrangement between Rossetti, Morris and Jane

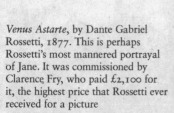

Venus Astarte, by Dante Gabriel Rossetti, 1877. This is perhaps Rossetti's most mannered portrayal of Jane. It was commissioned by Clarence Fry, who paid £2,100 for it, the highest price that Rossetti ever received for a picture

London residence, a note from Mrs La Touche was sent out to Denmark Hill restating the terms on which her daughter was in town. There was to be no further communication and certainly no meeting.

Ruskin immediately sought solace with his housemate Joan. But to his dismay and horror for once Joan, no doubt exhausted by this seemingly unending romantic saga, offered little sympathy. This girl, who like Mrs Cowper had borne the burden of his incessant whining and endless self-examination *vis à vis* Rose, must have snapped. A huge row ensued. For three days Joan and Ruskin did not speak to one another. Ruskin took his pen and marked his diary with three crosses, and then simply wrote, 'the aweful day when I learnt what Lacerta was – and Joan forgot me. And Rose suffered it.'[4]

More was to come. The La Touches were extraordinary in their ability to compartmentalize their affairs with Ruskin. The day after Mrs La Touche's letter, another letter came bearing the La Touche crest, this time from Percy. As Joan Agnew's legal guardian, Ruskin was *in loco parentis*. If Percy wanted to marry Joan, tradition said that Ruskin must give his permission, and so Percy now sought that permission.

The bitter confusion and sense of injustice at what Ruskin must have considered the La Touches' double standards ignited his anger yet further. More oil was thrown onto the fire when, just two days later, Joan left Denmark Hill at the La Touches' invitation to visit the Crystal Palace with Rose.

The great glass construction that had once housed the 1851 exhibition had moved to Sydenham in 1854 and been reinvented as a kind of theme park for Londoners. Here they could enjoy magnificent tropical gardens, fantastic fountains and regular concerts. While themed courts displaying treasures from around the world, on the model of the original 1851 exhibition, were an element of the attraction, the Crystal Palace was much more in the vein of the pleasure gardens that Londoners so loved. As such, it offered a range of extraordinary sights, spectacles and activities.

In the ample parkland surrounding the Palace itself life-size concrete dinosaurs had been created by the sculptor Benjamin Waterhouse Hawkins, and on a daily basis the events bill could range from firework displays to rocket launches, circus tricks and even the latest in 'electric magic'.

One can only imagine Joan, Rose and Maria enjoying these fantastic sights while Ruskin, who to make matters worse had been publicly critical of the Crystal Palace when it opened, was left alone to stew in his study. The days that followed took on farcical qualities. Ruskin's torment now pushed him to extremes that some might well have interpreted as the behaviour of someone quite depraved. The 48-year-old man was no longer able to control himself. Unable to cope with the knowledge that the object of his affection was so geographically close to him, he began to wander the streets of London in the hope of seeing her.

During days of 'terrible suspense'[5] Ruskin roamed haunts that he thought Rose might visit. Like a mad stalker, he hung around theatres, wandered the fashionable Mayfair streets around her family home and even chased a carriage in which he glimpsed a blonde girl who momentarily looked like Rose. After running after the carriage for a quarter of mile until it was slowed enough by traffic for him to catch it, he peered into the coach and, not surprisingly, frightened the female passengers.

Amid his desperation and confusion Ruskin decided it was time to publish his views on religion. He began to pen a series of 'letters' to a Sunderland workman under the title *Time and Tide*. Here he outlined what he saw as four prevailing views on scripture. The first, held by the 'illiterate', was that every word in the Bible was dictated directly by God. The second was that everything in the Bible is 'absolutely true'. The third was that the Bible is a collection of 'false statements mixed with true . . . but that nevertheless they relate, on the whole, faithfully the dealings of the one God with the first races of man'. Finally there was what Ruskin clearly believed himself: 'that the mass of religious Scripture contains merely the best efforts which we hitherto know to have been made by any races of men towards the discovery of some relations with the spiritual world; that they are only trustworthy as expressions of enthusiastic visions or beliefs of earnest men oppressed by the world's darkness, and have no more authoritative claim on our faith than the religious speculations and histories of the Egyptians, Greeks, Persians and Indians.'[6]

As Ruskin penned his bleak views, his own dark world took on an even deeper hue. For now matters simply got worse. His published views on religion would doubtless have offended Mr La Touche. But perhaps the La Touches had also heard about Ruskin's London prowling. Perhaps they had speculated that he was no longer mentally stable. Perhaps someone had whispered in their ears the story of his insane grandfather who had slit his own throat, and perhaps they determined that the Ruskin gene was one they wanted to protect not only their daughter from, but also their son. Or perhaps it was just simply that Percy changed his mind. Whatever it was, on 23 February Percy broke off his engagement with Joan. Two days later Ruskin wrote a 'prayerful' letter to Maria La Touche, perhaps about Joan, perhaps about his own interest, or perhaps about both. Maria answered by return, and Ruskin simply indicated her response with another black cross in his diary.

Four days after this event, which had made Ruskin feel physically ill, his feelings exploded again and in the small hours of the morning, 'not being able to eat – nor sleep – and moaning about my room'[7] he once more picked up his pen and wrote to Mrs Cowper. Ruskin was now clutching at straws, lost and broken. All he could do now was go back over past events to try and make some sense of it all, to try and understand where Rose herself really stood in the matter. 'Neither you nor she, poor thing, can help me now', he explained. 'If she could understand the suffering and the deadliness of it & how it kills the body and does not purge the soul, she might help me – not thus – not by grave words one day – & going to Crystal Palace within two miles of me to amuse herself the next.'[8] Perhaps Mrs Cowper delivered a dose of reality by return. Two days later Ruskin wrote again, acknowledging that she could not give him any cause for comfort.

The bizarre story continued to play out across the year. In a repeat of previous events Ruskin would suffer months of utter despair and dejection and then enjoy momentary relief when suddenly, unexpectedly and apparently in contradiction of her parents' wishes, a tender letter from Rose would find its way to Denmark Hill. Ruskin would reply and receive furious missives back from either or both parents. Rose would continue to write lovingly despite all this, until she too would turn and send something venomous. The behaviour of everyone concerned was extraordinarily mercurial. Rose, whether being tossed this way and that by her parents or whether genuinely so flighty that she could not alight on a consistent position herself with regard her suitor, could be 'for' or 'agin', dependent on the direction of the wind. The parents, with regard to correspondence between the parties, could be at once censoring and then temporarily lenient. Ruskin was driven mad, and consequently his diary began to fill with strange images that now came to him in sleep.

In April he had 'A singular night,' his diary records, 'dreaming of a haunted castle, and of a bright apartment in it, looking out on a lovely view, with two skeletons standing, one at the window, one at the side of the room – very ghastly.'[9] Over the summer these remembered dreams become more frequent. And now not only did vivid dreams haunt Ruskin, but so too did the words of the Scripture that he had learned to query. During a visit to the Lake District in the summer, his diary took on a weird, chanting aspect, where at the beginning of each day he cited a religious passage in his journal before noting the strenuous outdoor activities and increasingly eccentric behaviour of the day, finishing with a dream to round it all off.

In this vein his entry for 14 August, written in Langdale, takes on a maniacal quality:

Thou has loved righteousness, and hated iniquity, wherefore God, thy God, hath anointed thee with the oil of gladness . . . Intending to read the parallel rendering of this verse in Bible psalms, I opened at Isaiah XXXIII, 17. My old bible often does open there, but it was a happy first reading.

By Grasmere and St John's vale to Keswick.

a) Met poor woman at Wythburn and helped her.
b) Crossed my forehead three times with water of the spring at St John's Chapel.
c) Conquered petty anxiety. Forded brook and found good of it.
d) Drank healths after dinner – seven; my mother, Mr and Mrs L, Joan, Percy, Rose and me.

But no noble dreams yet. Base and paltry. Must see to reason of this, and conquer it. Much too hot all day. Out on lake in evening. Fell asleep in boat near St Herbert's isle. Glorious sky of broken white, silvery jagged-edged clouds.[10]

All the time the intensely peculiar entries are also accompanied by figures – the number of days that Ruskin was counting down to Rose's twenty-first birthday. He was a man obsessed, and yet his obsession was unlikely to be rewarded, as his own subconscious often reminded him. On 12 August he noted that he had dreamed of 'Rose being in a boat, and looking pained when she saw me on the shore, and rowing away from me'.[11]

Given Ruskin's sexual history, it is hardly surprising that many of his dreams seemed to be working through his own issues in this department. Snakes began to slither into his dreaming subconscious. In March 1868 one dream, so explicitly Freudian to twenty-first-century eyes, seemed to be working out his doubts about his own ability to perform sexually. In a later letter to Mr Cowper he admitted his virginity, and here he seems to be at once admitting his desire to have sex and recognizing an inherent, fearful repugnance: 'Dreamed of . . . showing Joanna a beautiful snake, which I told her was an innocent one; it had a slender neck and a green ring round it and I made her feel its scales. Then she made me feel it and it became a fat thing, like a leech, and adhered to my hand, so that I could hardly pull it off – so I woke.'[12]

But the extraordinary thing is that, despite all the determination of her parents otherwise, the enforced separations, her own obvious doubts and the particularly unusual nature of the prospect of marrying a now deeply neurotic and eccentric man, by May 1868 Rose La Touche seemed to be close to agreeing to marry John Ruskin. And on 6 May Ruskin received a letter that seemed to offer this conclusion to their bizarre courtship. She was just seven months away from her twenty-first birthday, after all. Ruskin could not have been happier. It was a bright, sunny day and as the sun sank he walked down to his village post office 'with an answer'.[13]

Jane Morris had featured in Rossetti's work only very occasionally since her marriage. The Llandaff triptych, which Rossetti finished only in 1864, bore her dark features in place of Ruth Herbert's fair ones. But outside this her change in circumstances had confined Rossetti's capture of Jane to little more than a few drawings. It was not just the fact that Jane was living outside London that may have affected her willingness to model. It was also that Jane was married. Married, respectable women did not model. Effie had scandalized many people by posing for Millais, and the ensuing débâcle would have confirmed in the mind of many that modelling represented a genuine risk to one's reputation.

Morris had made a huge investment in converting Jane from a slum girl to a social sensation. And Jane may well have felt a certain relief that she could move away from the associations that modelling work had once conferred on her. But Rossetti was a friend, and during the decoration of the Red House the sense of painting within a framework of companionship and co-operative working prevailed. So the odd session sitting for Rossetti continued. He managed to steal a few sketches, and those he did make he was evidently pleased with.

'This morning the book remains open at Mrs Topsy', Rossetti wrote to Boyce in May 1865, referring to his sketchbook.

Knowing Boyce's taste in women he added: 'Certainly £10 would be preferable. So if you like to make the cheque . . . I'll send her on Monday with the rest.'[14]

There is something about this friendly exchange that is both reminiscent and prophetic. Boyce and Rossetti had always enjoyed a shared appreciation of models. Annie and Fanny had both been the subject of similar exchanges of admiration, and their images had prompted similar business transactions. But in the case of the latter two Rossetti had allowed his admiration to be converted into a sexual relationship. The mutual appreciation of Boyce and Rossetti was a heavy indicator of those models that either one or the other or both of these friends would end up sleeping with. Their appreciation of the image on the page all too often mirrored real-life attraction.

In June 1865, before the thought of moving from Red House had been crystallized, Rossetti decided he must find a way of accessing his occasional model *in absentia*. And so exceptionally he had hired the photographer John Robert Parsons and asked Janey over to Cheyne Walk for an extended modelling session.

Photography, in its infancy, was something Rossetti was beginning to exploit more generally at this time. He had Lizzie's sketches photographed and mounted into commemorative portfolios which he gave to friends. But the photographing of a model was something new and experimental.

As Jane struck a range of poses both inside Tudor House and in its garden on that warm June day, she and Rossetti once again found themselves engaged in intense collaboration. The resulting images are an extraordinary record of this young woman, not least because her persona somehow comes through despite the arduous technical requirements of the process.

In what must have been a long and exhausting session Rossetti and Parsons produced several different shots of her, arranged, as always, to emphasize those elements that Rossetti loved best: the profile, neck, the body twisted or bent in a way that suggests the informal and intimate.

Even today Janey's brooding, sorrowful presence reaches out through the black-and-white images. She is seated in profile in a spoon-backed chair similar to the one in which Lizzie and Annie had also posed, her sharp jawline and long nose picked out by the light. Her eyes, when downcast, convey deep inner contemplation. When gazing direct at the camera they penetrate the lens darkly, but even so she remains withdrawn, profound and mysterious.

It is not clear just when Rossetti realized that he was falling in love with Jane again, but it is tempting to speculate that this photo session was the catalyst. Afterwards, plans for a portrait of Jane were made, but although Rossetti wrote to Brown a year later and mentioned Jane was going to sit to him for it, the actual picture took another two years to emerge.

Perhaps Jane – in a new home, with all the attendant upheaval – could not come to the sittings, or perhaps sketches were begun but not completed. Rossetti too was a busy man now, much in demand and with dealers such as Gambart – who a decade earlier had made Hunt's fortune so spectacularly – now part of his commercial universe. Gone were the days of indolence and paralysis, unfinished pictures and frustration. He could paint in oils now, he had a market and he was in demand. People liked his women and flowers.

But Rossetti's commercial universe was different from that of his former brothers-in-arms Hunt and Millais. While they both continued to exhibit with increasing celebrity, Rossetti had retreated into a closed world. He did not exhibit. He worked on private commissions. The women he now specialized in were for the personal consumption of the rich industrialists who could display and worship his luxurious goddesses within the quiet confines of their own homes. These men would acquire his *femmes fatales* in the original, and Rossetti would photograph them and produce reproductions for a wider, but still relatively discrete, market.

Rossetti's reluctance to show his work in front of a wider public can be attributed to the emotional scars he still bore from the swingeing remarks made about the PRB in the early 1850s. But it was more than just the memory of unkind criticism that had encouraged his retreat into this different universe of commission and clientele. His pictures had always flown in the face of convention: his early religious art, like that of Millais and Hunt, had had a whiff of the sacrilegious for some critics because of its insistence on treating even holy subjects with sometimes brutal realism. But such work could always be defended from its critics with the argument that at its core it was art that was morally motivated, and as such of a serious nature.

But Rossetti's pictures were different now. As though flattened out, they lacked the narrative depth and didactic content of his earlier work. They were consciously more decorative. Beauty was his subject-matter: beauty for beauty's sake, art for art's sake. Today these works are recognized as the beginning of what became known as the Aesthetic Movement, which reached its culmination in the writing of Oscar Wilde. But in the 1860s Rossetti, in the vanguard of this movement, simply risked offending the public further. Overtly sexual, worshipping women for the sake of their beauty and sex appeal above all else, these highly erotic pictures not only transgressed the boundaries of social acceptability; they were less easily morally defensible.

In March 1868 Rossetti decided to paint *La Pia de' Tolomei*, and three years after their photography session in the garden he asked Jane if she would be the model for the picture. The subject was one drawn from Rossetti's beloved Dante. The story was of an abused wife, La Pia, who, imprisoned by her jealous husband in a castle, finally dies in misery.

Rossetti's decision to approach Jane Morris may well have been a loaded one. Were there signs that Jane, now in those Queen Square apartments that she had never wanted to take, was feeling deserted by her husband? Certainly Morris was exceptionally busy at this time. The other partners in the firm – Brown, Rossetti and Ned – were still first and foremost painters, with their contributions to the decorative arts business a second string to their bow.

Morris, on the other hand, had made the firm his mainstay. There are accounts of him being on the shop floor in his dark blue linen blouse, showing wallpaper patterns to prospective clients and writing out the bills himself when he made a successful sale. Or, if not selling, he could be found at this desk designing wallpaper patterns. It was not quite a one-man show, but it was not far off.[15]

But it was not just the firm that was on Morris's agenda. He was also writing. The extra hours that had been lost in commuting to the Red House could now be redirected elsewhere, and he dedicated this spare time to poetry. Perhaps this too riled Jane. Although her husband had more time to spend with her, he chose not to do so. Morris now began a great epic poem, *The Earthly Paradise*. Its theme was the quest for true love. The irony of its creation is that it was written at a time when the author's own quest for true love was clearly foundering.

And so the painting began. The letters Rossetti wrote to Jane in his fluent, loopy writing reveal how charming this man could be, how he was careful to show his concern and care for his sitter. 'All is ready for the picture,' he wrote soothingly to Jane on 6 March 1868, 'as I have already made some studies and know exactly what I have to do as to the action of the figure, which, my dear Janey, is a very easy one, so you shall be punished as little as possible for your kindness.'[16]

One can imagine how Rossetti bolstered Jane, his attentions and courtesies making her feel special. One can imagine her revealing her sorrow at how little interest her own husband showed in her compared to Rossetti. One can imagine Rossetti sympathizing and pitying, and then feeling the injustice of the situation: this beautiful creature trapped in an unloving marriage. Perhaps he mused on the irony that he had let this creature slip through his fingers once before, blaming himself for sending her into the marriage she now so resented.

As had been proved before, there was nothing so compelling as a tragic woman. A month after the sittings for *La Pia* began, Rossetti took the tiny stamp-sized notebook in which he scribbled anything from shopping lists to recipes to medicinal recommendations and jotted a tiny design for a bracelet. Next to it he noted 'sept 57 ⊕ April 14 1868'.[17] What was this cryptic note, presumably intended as an inscription? Were these the dates of stolen kisses – the first during that jovial campaign when the then Jane Burden had modelled for him before her engagement to Morris and briefly succumbed to his spell. And the second during this current modelling session?

Rossetti was now quick to secure a further opportunity for Jane's modelling services. The portrait of Jane for William Morris that had stalled in 1866 was quickly resurrected and begun instantly. And with every sitting the relationship between the artist and his model was cemented further. Rossetti was masterful in his ability to bolster self-esteem. If Jane was feeling neglected at home, by contrast Rossetti's letters during this period reveal how crucial he wanted her to feel to him in his work. In his discussions with her he treated her not just as a model but as a creative collaborator. Thus a dialogue developed about her costume for her portrait. Jane set to work on the blue silk dress she was to wear, and Rossetti would offer her designs for the embroidery to be done on it, carefully pointing out that his own suggestions were only offered unless 'as is very possible a better idea strike you'.

And then there is the playful, tender side of Rossetti that he chose to reveal to Jane in letters at this time. He sent dormice to her two daughters, Jenny and May. He then wrote and recounted how one of the intended dormice had got lost in Cheyne Walk and how he has only just found it in a trap, going on to describe how thin and boney it had become, but also how he had happily managed to revive it. Scholars of Freud may well be tempted to interpret these letters in a different vein and suggest that the small, vulnerable mouse to which Rossetti is paying such attention is, at a subliminal level, Jane's own neglected sex.

As part of his wooing of Jane, Rossetti was quick to undermine her husband. The neglectful Morris began to become a butt of jokes between them. His new long narrative poem *The Earthly*

The Bard and Petty Tradesman, by Dante Gabriel Rossetti, 1868.
Rossetti designs a banner for an imagined newspaper that Morris
might launch. The caption pokes fun at Morris's foul language, since
Campbell's parliamentary act was designed to repress obscene
publications

Paradise was being celebrated by his friends in the form of a dinner
party, and Rossetti was quick to use this to ridicule those personal
habits of Morris that Janey had obviously revealed her distaste for.
His appetite was clearly a problem for her.

'I shall keep Wedy 27th sacred to the Earthly Paradise', he wrote
to Janey on 22 May 1868, 'I was touchingly reminded of his Eden
today by the advent of asparagus at dinner. How each fresh article
of food as it appears recalls the progress of the Poet's year!' In his
stride now, Rossetti went further in his cruel taunting of Morris.
It was not just that he was an over-eating poet: he was also a shopkeeper poet! And so Rossetti sent the shopkeeper's wife a caricature of her husband entitled 'The Bard and Petty Tradesman'.[18]

Quite soon Jane and Rossetti's time together was extending
beyond their professional sittings. Just as Mrs Cowper had drawn
Ruskin into the world of spiritualism, so now Rossetti began to
take Jane to seances. At first Morris was there too, to witness the

notorious Mrs Guppy at work. Jane apparently saw an other-worldly light. But soon Rossetti and Jane were exploring this dark work together without Morris in tow.

In the summer Jane and Morris left town for a holiday in Suffolk, and Rossetti headed north for a break at Speke Hall, near Liverpool. And it was here, separated from Jane, that the depth of his dependency on his latest lover seemed to become apparent. He had persuaded his friend Charles Augustus Howell to go with him to Speke, but Howell, no doubt anticipating an enjoyable sojourn with his friend, reported home that Rossetti was miserable the entire stay. He was lost without Jane. So desperate was his desire for contact with her that Rossetti began using Howell as a go-between during this period, the latter's letters to Jane containing clandestine ones from Rossetti that were to be concealed from Morris.

Charles Howell – or Owl, as he was affectionately known to Rossetti and Ned – was an important yet murky and somewhat insalubrious intimate of the Pre-Raphaelite circle. Anglo-Portugese, brought up in Portugal but returned to England with his family at sixteen, he was a charismatic character who had inveigled himself into the very heart of the PRB circle and was for a good while utterly adored by Rossetti and Burne-Jones in particular.

When not entertaining his chums with wild tales and providing the moral support and companionship that they clearly sought from him, Howell was an entrepreneur and arts wheeler-dealer. He was something of an expert in beautiful things both ancient and modern, and would acquire anything for anyone. From the late 1850s he had been a kind of gofer and Mr Fixit for the PRB, acting informally of behalf of almost everyone in the circle at one time or another, but specifically hired by Ruskin as his secretary in the mid-1860s. He later became Rossetti's semi-formal agent.

Howell could not stop himself from lying. He lived a shadowy existence of half-truths and fantasy but did so with a panache and theatricality that many found entrancing. He wore a red ribbon on his waistcoat which he claimed was a symbol of his mother's noble Portuguese lineage, a heritage that most of his friends ended up with the impression was pure fantasy. He also adored intrigue. He loved manipulation and enjoyed the lethal combination of being both a confidant and a terrible gossip. His untrustworthiness was not purely social. Acting as agent not only for Ruskin and Rossetti but also at different times in his colourful career for Morris and Whistler, Howell managed to fall out with every single client over financial irregularities. But his temptations towards opportunism and petty fraud were at this time still largely concealed by what Rossetti, Ned and others saw as genuine close friendship. His relationship with Rossetti, in particular, seems to have stretched back to the times of the latter's engagement with Lizzie, which Howell had discouraged. And so perhaps it was no surprise that now Rossetti once again chose to involve him in his affairs of the heart.

Rossetti's revived interest in Jane did not go unnoticed, nor did his increased attentions to her in public. Gossip began to spread. At one dinner party held by William Bell Scott guests witnessed Gabriel and Jane quite openly flirting with one another, with Gabriel spending the entire evening doting on Jane and Jane alone, so that it was quite clear to everyone that he was besotted with her. Morris was observed watching every detail of the unfurling scandal. At other parties Rossetti spoon-fed Jane strawberries and cream. At another she is described sitting on a 'throne' in an 'unfashionable' cream velvet gown, with Rossetti perched on a hassock at her feet for the entire duration of the soirée. Fanny was, needless to say, enraged.

But even if Rossetti had somehow managed to persuade himself that for the liberal-minded marriage should not prevent 'love' between like-minded souls, his treatment of Morris at this stage implies a deep-seated sense of guilt and jealousy. Rossetti continued to ridicule his friend with increasing venom. In doing so, he was perhaps trying to persuade himself and his friends that his betrayal of Morris could be justified. Morris was an oaf: he did not deserve Jane and she certainly did not deserve Morris.

But Rossetti had another preoccupation at this time. For the past year or so he had been complaining about his eyesight and was concerned that he might be facing blindness. This may well explain his sudden neediness when Jane once again became available to him. He was suffering from a mist across his eyes, which he feared might spell his ruin as a painter. His father had become blind before he died, and Rossetti was terrified that the same thing might be happening to him. Sinking into more reclusive behaviour, he began to shun some of his former pastimes. Miserable, he wrote to Howell, pointing out that he no could no longer enjoy the theatre and that he was afraid of the effect the gaslight would have on his vision.

Despite Rossetti's growing concern for his eyesight, the doctors he visited seemed unaminous in their opinion that there was little more than tiredness and overstrain at the heart of the condition. Rossetti slept badly and worried too much. He began to self-medicate and take chloral.

Chloral, or chloral hydrate, which first became available over the counters of Victorian apothecaries in the 1830s, was offered specifically as a soporific. By the 1860s its users had discovered that its efficacy was enhanced by mixing it with alcohol. Tradition has it that Fanny was responsible for encouraging Rossetti's use of choral. One can easily imagine her in her role as mistress and housekeeper preparing the anxious Rossetti his 'knock-out drops' or his 'Mickey Finn', as the chloral and alcohol cocktail became known to its admiring dependants. Rossetti's own preference was for neat chloral followed by whisky chasers.

Although this terrible mixture would finally get him to sleep, it had side-effects. First Rossetti developed a dependency on both its elements. The man who had once been teetotal quickly became began to develop strong addictions. Second, it did nothing but strengthen a nascent hypochondria. No wonder that he perceived little improvement with his eyes.

It is also tempting to see the mist across his vision at this time as in part a psychosomatic response to his own deceitful behaviour, since the condition did not develop into the blindness he dreaded. If so, the deep irony is that his continued pursuit of Jane to soothe himself would have done nothing but exacerbate the condition itself. If Gabriel was tying himself in a knot, it would not have been the first time.

Nevertheless he was clearly hurt at Morris's apparent lack of concern for his own troubles. But then who could blame Morris for some distance, given Rossetti's overtures to his wife? The schism was set. All it could now do was widen.

One January day in 1869 somewhere on the towpath where the Grand Union and Regent's canals meet, in the area described by the locally resident Robert Browning as Little Venice, a slight, fraught-looking man could be seen wrestling a beautiful, hysterical woman to the ground. The woman in question was Mary Zambaco, a Greek painter and socialite. The man who wrestled her to the ground that freezing winter day was her lover, Edward Burne-Jones.

Ned Burne-Jones had always been the good boy in the Pre-Raphaelite pack. From his middle-class Birmingham background he had always followed conventional Victorian behaviour – at least when compared with his friends and associates. He had married conventionally. His courtship with Georgie Macdonald – a minister's daughter – had been properly conducted, and to all intents and purposes his behaviour ever since had been that of a charming, well-behaved husband.

But beneath his somewhat slender and boyish demeanour, his gaiety and love of jokes, and his delightful charming manner, which saw him sketching childish caricatures of himself and his friends in his correspondence, there was a darker side to Burne-Jones. Georgie once noted that she believed Rossetti wore a 'surcoat of jesting' to disguise his deep, complex inner turmoil.[19] She could also have written those lines about her own spouse.

Its first hint came with the birth of his first child, Phil. Georgie noted that 'I do not think that Edward was a man with whom parental feeling was very great in the abstract, but from the moment he had a child of his own, strong natural love for it awoke in his heart. This new love was accompanied, however by a fearful capacity for anxiety which was a fresh drain upon his strength. "A painter ought not to be married", he once said: "children and pictures are too important to be produced by one man".'[20] And in the case of Ned the pictures in many ways came first.

Georgie described how motherhood banished her and her children from Ned's professional life – a life she had hitherto shared: 'The difference in our life made by the presence of a child was very great, for I had been used to be much with Edward – reading aloud to him when he worked, and in many ways sharing he life of the studio – and I remember the feeling of exile with which I now heard through its closed door the well known voices of friends together with Edward's familiar laugh, while I sat with my little son on my knee and dropped selfish tears upon him as "the separator of companions and the terminator of delights".'[21]

After the death of their second child and the decision to pull out of the Red House extension Ned and Georgie moved to a new home in Kensington Square. As she stepped into this new residence and shut the door behind her, Georgie knew that 'something was gone, something had been left behind – and it was our first youth'.[22]

By 1866 Georgie was pregnant again. Ned, racked with anxiety, looked on at the private lives of his increasingly Bohemian friends and, it seems, simply took a leaf out of everyone else's book. A new model was in town, and this time it was he who would become hooked.

Mary Zambaco (née Cassavetti) was a wealthy heiress from a very successful clan of Greek immigrant businessmen. She had the reputation of being independent, assertive and impetuous. She had an enormous private income and, liberated by this, enjoyed unusual personal freedom compared with most women of her time. Mary would not think twice about pursuing single men, whether chaperoned or not. Equally she would not think twice about ignoring people who bored her. She was utterly driven by her own momentary desires and could make someone feel the centre of her universe should she choose, while making another person feel utterly worthless.

In 1864 Mary had taken herself off to Paris and married a Greek doctor there, Demetrius Zambaco. But by 1866 she had returned to London with two children in tow, claiming that life in Paris had been dull and her marriage a failure. This incident was a scandal in itself, but Mary seemed to brush off opinions that would have sunk other women and simply began to seek out her next prey.

Mary's wealthy mother, known as 'The Duchess', commissioned her portrait from Ned. Impulsive and unstable, it was easy for Mary to be charmed by him with his gentle ways and precocious sense of humour. She fell madly in love with Ned, and he, it seems, fell madly in love with this woman, who was in every way the opposite of his quietly intelligent, loyal, unostentatious and frankly rather plain wife.

'I believe one thing that drew men and women to him was that he never suspected them beforehand', Georgie later wrote. 'To him each acquaintance was new-born. Never in any sense did he become a man of the world, and up to a certain point it was always easy to take advantage of him. . . . Two things had tremendous power over him – beauty and misfortune – and far would he go to serve either; indeed his impulse to comfort those in trouble was so strong that while the trouble lasted the sufferer took precedence over everyone else.'[23]

The combined appeal of beauty and tragedy in a woman seemed irresistible to the men who form the focus of this narrative. In succumbing to it, Ned now entered a period of personal turmoil that mirrored Rossetti's suffering at the hands of the statuesque Jane Morris. Looking back, all the women who had ensnared or been caught up with this band of brothers fitted in their different ways the profile of the tragic heroine: Lizzie, Annie, Fanny, Effie and even Rose La Touche. Somehow the second phase of the Pre-Raphaelite Brotherhood, such as it was, was regurgitating different versions of stories that had already been played out once before.

Burne-Jones's pictures of Mary make the extent to which he had fallen under her spell quite clear. Some six years after he first met this woman he painted her as the witch Nimue in *The Beguiling of Merlin*. Commissioned by Frederick Leyland in the late 1860s, the picture became a visual realization of his own sense of utter submission to the powers of this woman. Just like Merlin in the picture, Ned had been caught off-guard, enraptured by the beauty of a woman and consequently paralysed.

There is another little sketch Ned made during his time with Mary that is also telling. In it the beautiful, statuesque Mary sits like a Greek goddess before a thin, haunted and utterly unworthy artist. His humility and shabbiness compared with the deity before him are comical. How could he ever have resisted her advances? He was bedazzled by her from the start.

Mary's love for Ned fast turned to obsession. She sunk her claws deep. She was intense and demanding. Ned's work suffered terribly. His obsession with Mary, balanced against his responsibility to his family, ate into him.

Caught in a situation from which he felt he could no longer extricate himself, Ned did what so many cheating husbands do: he allowed himself, probably unconsciously, to get found out. He left a letter in a pocket that Georgie, going through his clothes, found.

The effect of the discovery was devastating. Once Georgie knew, Mary saw her opportunity to force Ned into some form of action. She became terribly clinging, holding sway over him more than his wife. Georgie sank into quiet misery and stayed at home. Mary, by contrast, continued to socialize, confident that with Georgie desperate to avoid her at social events, she could now have the run of them with Ned to herself.

Ned's strained loyalties became tested by Mary to the extreme. When his young son Phil needed to return from a sojourn with family in Bewdley in the west Midlands, Mary prevented him from leaving town to fetch him. In the end Georgie cracked. She left the family home with her children and went to Clevedon for a long holiday. Perhaps it was while she was there that Mary and Ned began to plan their elopement. They were to leave the country together.

But Ned was not as strong as Mary had hoped. Instead of running away with her, he met her at their intended rendezvous by the canal in London's Little Venice and told her that he could not leave his family in this way. Mary had come prepared for this eventuality.

On 23 January 1869 Rossetti wrote to Brown describing what happened next. It was clear that he was not alone in being apprised of the details. The whole affair was now rather grimly the talk of the town. 'Poor old Ned's affairs have come to a smash altogether', he explained.

> He and Topsy, after the most dreadful to-do, started for Rome suddenly, leaving the Greek damsel beating up the quarters of all his friends for him and howling like Cassandra. Georgie has stayed behind. I hear today however that Top and Ned got no further than Dover, Ned being now so dreadfully ill that they will probably have to return to London. Of course the dodge will be not to let a single hint of their movements become known to anybody, or the Greek (who I believe is really bent on cutting) will catch him again. She provided herself with Laudanum for two at least, and insisted on them winding up matters in Lord Holland's Lane. Ned didn't see it, when she tried to drown herself in the water in front of Browning's house &c. – bobbies collaring Ned who was rolling with her on the stones to prevent it, and God knows what else.[24]

Morris stepped in. He could talk no sense into his old friend while he was still within temptation's reach. He had to remove Ned overseas for a while. Just before he left town with Ned, Morris instructed Jane that she was not to see Rossetti in his absence. This may well have been the first open recognition on her husband's part that he knew what was going on. Interestingly, though, she obeyed him. Perhaps the terrible scandal now focused on Ned, Mary and, of course, Georgie, had proved a timely warning to Jane.

Georgie, meanwhile, was locked up in the home the Burne-Joneses had moved to in 1867, The Grange in North End Road, West Kensington. Although blameless in the eyes of a harsh and judgemental society, she was also helpless. Married women had few rights, and Georgie, from her humble background, did not enjoy the freedom or fortune of her rival in love. With her husband swept away and subsequently incapacitated by his own anxieties, no one was sure what kind of provision had been made for her and the children. Her friend Rosalind Howard drove round to The Grange and left Georgie £50.

Georgie's stance was one of silence. Apart from the pain that discussing Ned's infidelity must have caused her, there was an old-fashioned streak in Georgie that detested disloyalty. She had married for better or worse and was apparently abiding by this pledge. When Ned returned from his failed flight to the continent, the couple began to go through the grim remnants of their marriage. Letters between Georgie's friends at the time indicate that initially Ned stayed away from the marital bed, and possibly the marital home entirely, in the evenings. But his studio was at The Grange, and so during the day the couple would have been forced to go through some form of domestic routine.

Georgie eventually packed her bags, and those of her children, and moved into lodgings in Oxford. She gave Ned a month to decide what he wanted to do. Apparently he wanted to stay with her, since by March she was back at home. But the marriage operated on different terms from this moment onwards. Those terms were a continuation of the affair with Mary.

Ned's relationship with Mary now proceeded with an openness that could have been nothing but terribly painful for Georgie and still hugely emotionally problematic for Ned. It was an openness that did not fail to disgust those on whom the benefits of bohemianism were lost. Mary became a social pariah.

Amid this climate of public outrage and personal pain, Charles Howell did a very peculiar thing. Howell had been a confidant from the start, and Ned's affection towards him is clearly expressed in the heaps of extant letters between the two, always bedecked by Ned with fond, twirling sketches of owls.[25] It is unclear whether Howell's next actions were prompted by Mary or whether he was acting on an impulse of his own, but he decided that the best thing for everyone was to bring Georgie and Mary face to face. Howell orchestrated the meeting at The Grange. Whether he had contrived for Ned to join the party or whether Ned had arrived unexpectedly, arrive he did. Such was Ned's distress and incapacity to deal with the situation that he fainted and hit his head on the mantelpiece. Howell was from that moment cast out. Ned never forgave him what he must have considered an enormous breech of trust.

But for all his squeamishness over bringing his wife and lover face to face, Ned did not shy away from continuing to exhibit his lover to his public. In 1870, a year after Mary's attempted suicide and the pursuant hullabaloo, Ned's continuing fascination with his model scandalized society yet again when he cast her as Phyllis, Queen of Thrace, in his picture *Phyllis and Demophoon*.

The story comes from Ovid. Phyllis falls in love with Demophoon, son of Theseus. Demophoon prises himself away from his passionate admirer but promises that he will return to her in six months' time. But he does not keep his promise, and Phyllis hangs herself. The gods then turn her into an almond tree. When Demophoon eventually returns, guilt-ridden, he embraces the tree, which, bursting into blossom, is transformed back into Phyllis, who subsequently forgives her faithless lover.

Pinned to the back of the picture, and annotated in the catalogue, Burne-Jones added a quotation from Ovid, which did nothing but cement the autobiographical significance of the picture further: 'Dic mihi quid feci? Nisi non sapienter amavi', he scribbled: 'Tell me what I have done? I loved unwisely.'

It is an extraordinary picture. Reminiscent of Botticelli, in true

Pre-Raphaelite tradition, Burne-Jones's figures of Phyllis and Demophoon are painted as mirror images of Botticelli's Zephyrus and Chloris, who occupy the right-hand side of his *Primavera*. Botticelli's story there is one of violent rape. Zephyrus, the god of wind, pursues Chloris and then also marries her against her will. Later, full of remorse, he turns his prey into Flora, the goddess of the spring.

In making this mirror reference, and in identifying the figure of Mary with Zephyrus, Burne-Jones makes it clear that this work is as much about a woman's violent entrapment of a man as about a man's desertion of a woman. At some level Ned was suggesting that Mary had forced herself on him. But the picture also admits his regret for his subsequent abandonment of her. All these emotions are held within the complex mutual gaze of Phyllis and Demophoon, which is full of longing and regret. The eyes of the two lovers are locked in a triangle of emotion. It is a hugely moving, complex, confessional picture that digs deep into the very fundaments of human relationships.

The obvious allusion to Burne-Jones's own private life, coupled with the fact that he chose to display Demophoon in full frontal nudity, caused a complete stir when the picture was unveiled at the Old Watercolour Society's summer show. Sexually provocative and socially unpalatable, the picture was pelted with complaints and, humiliated, Burne-Jones withdrew both the picture and from membership of the institution. To those looking on from afar it must have seemed almost impossible that the ingenuous young man from the provinces, so physically meagre and of such apparently naïve charm, could have become the centre of such sexual turmoil and produce such blatantly sexually charged work.

That Morris was struggling with this transformation in his friend is hinted at too. Apart from the physical tussle that must have gone on at Dover, where Ned collapsed rather than be taken abroad by his friend, the two were quarrelling more often. But the quarrels were born not just from Ned's situation –

Morris was caught up in his own version of events with Jane and Rossetti.

'My dearest Ned,' Morris wrote to Ned in May 1869, 'I'm afraid I was crabby last night, but I didn't mean to be, so pray forgive me — we seem to quarrel in speech now sometimes, and sometimes I think it hard for you to stand me, and no great wonder for I am like a hedgehog with nastiness — but again forgive me for I can't on any terms do without you.'[26] On the same day he also apologized to the artist and collector Charles Fairfax Murray, who had obviously been simultaneously subjected to Morris's bad temper at The Grange. 'I could explain all to you in a word of two if an explanation were necessary to you, which I doubt', Morris wrote. What was the point of going further? Evidently everyone knew about his wife and his friend.

Georgie, as ever, held her tongue about everything. But she was not suffering in utter silence. Through the troubled times of marital betrayal Georgie had sought solace among her close friends. And now there was one in particular to whom she was becoming more drawn, and on whom much of her happiness now rested. And this was someone who, like her, had been betrayed by their spouse: William Morris.

As Rossetti's longing for Jane Morris became deeper, his health worsened. In addition to his eyes, he was now suffering from headaches and insomnia. His doctors suggested he took more fresh air and exercise: he had always been hopeless in this respect. Even in the early days, when Millais and Hunt would play cricket or box, Rossetti would never join in. His concession to this advice was to take long walks in the depths of night. This merely added to his increasingly spectral demeanour.

In September 1868 he left town again in search of a rest cure. He headed to Penkill Castle in Scotland, the home of Alice Boyd, a close friend and almost certainly lover of William Bell Scott. Scott had never been very happily married, and now he and his wife, Letitia, had apparently come to an arrangement that allowed him and Alice to be left to their own devices. Scott would stay at Penkill, and Letitia would visit for the sake of adding some veneer of respectability now and then. Equally Alice would visit the Scotts in London.

The trip was successful in that Rossetti began to sleep better. But death and the dead were hovering over him. In his memoirs Scott recalled Rossetti reciting a lot of his old love poetry from memory during the trip, and getting very worked up. This poetry was, after all, that which now lay with Lizzie Siddall in her coffin. He also mentioned that Rossetti was feeling suicidal. During all this the clandestine letters to Jane also continued, fusing in his mind perhaps the association of Lizzie with Jane.

By June 1869 Rossetti was back at Penkill again and 'more hypochondriacal than ever'.[27] He began to suffer from hallucinations. In this first manifestation he thought he heard Lizzie. 'Mounting the ascending road towards Barr, we observed a small bird, a chaffinch, exactly in our path', Scott recalled. 'We advanced: it did not fly but remained quite still, continuing so till he stooped down and lifted it. He held it in his hand: it manifested no alarm. "What is the meaning of this?" I heard him say to himself, and I observed his hand was shaking with emotion . . . "I can tell you what it is, this is the soul of my wife, the soul of her has taken shape; something is going to happen to me." '[28]

When Scott and Rossetti returned to the house, they were met with a story that while they were out the house bell had mysteriously rung, but no one was there. If Rossetti's visits with Jane to seances had been a bit of fun, now the world of the afterlife began to take on an all too real aspect.

Terrified by the apparently supernatural phenomena around him, Rossetti sank further into some form of paranoid despair. Scott described how he went out into the Scottish countryside and, discovering a little cave, cowered there writing the poem 'The Stream's Secret'. A contemplation on love and death, its reference to Lizzie is clear. It begins:

What thing unto mine ear
Wouldst thou convey, — what secret thing,
O wandering water ever whispering?
Surely thy speech shall be of her.
Thou water, O thou whispering wanderer,
What message dost thou bring?

and ends:

O water whispering
Still through the dark into mine ears, —
As with mine eyes, is it not now with hers? —
Mine eyes that add to thy cold spring,
Wan water, wandering water weltering,
This hidden tide of tears.[29]

In the evenings at Penkill, Rossetti was in the habit of leaving the dinner table and going upstairs to read aloud to himself, Scott recalled. After Rossetti had left the party and returned home to London, the strange phenomena that characterized the sojourn continued. Both Scott and Alice Boyd were quite certain they could hear Rossetti reading upstairs in the evenings, even though he had been gone some time. In so many ways he was already a ghost.

On his return to London the one person who might have helped Rossetti had gone. Jane too was ill, suffering the strain of her situation. And now, just as Morris had sought to help Ned by removing him from Mary's influence, he decided it was time to take Jane away from Rossetti. The Morrises were heading for Bad Ems, a fashionable health spa on the Rhine. Rossetti could hardly bear the separation, and the minute the couple were gone, he was avidly seeking news of his lover. In fact, he was in such a rush to reply to a note he had received from Jane that he failed to attach the correct postage stamp, an error that had significant consequences.

This first letter to Jane at Bad Ems still conforms to some pretence regarding their relationship. In it Rossetti says how glad he is that her journey went well, and was pleased that some cloaks he

The M's at Ems, by Dante Gabriel Rossetti, 1869. Ridiculing Morris, Rossetti features him reading aloud from his own poetry while Janey enjoys the shower bath at Ems

had given her proved 'of service'. He talks about going to Little Holland House and meeting Mrs Prinsep and dining outside. And then, in a kind of coded reference to their own affair, he expresses a desire to paint another picture of her soon. 'I want beyond everything to paint another portrait picture of you – a little more severe in arrangement than the last – as I am sure I can do something more worthy of you.'[30]

But when Jane failed to respond to this letter, the paranoia that had been eating away at Rossetti began to show itself. Writing a few days later, on 27 July, he could barely conceal a genuine need for some communication from Jane: 'As I have no letter from you I fear it is possible mine may have miscarried. I find on enquiring that the stupid people at the post office here never weighed it and only stuck on a four penny stamp . . . If you have not got it, you must indeed have thought me a beast for not answering your kind good letter written when you hardly write . . . It enrages me beyond measure to think that through a detestable blunder, days may yet pass leaving you under the impression that I did not answer your letter.'

When Jane responded and told Gabriel that, in spite of the blundering post office, she had finally received his letters, his anxieties felt such release that he no longer attempted to disguise his feelings. In an explosion of love for her his writing flowed from his pen. He admitted that his drawing of her was now the unique expression of his love, and as such very much for his own private consumption.

> All that concerns you is the all absorbing question with me, as dear Top will not mind my telling you at this anxious time the more he loves you, the more he knows that you are too lovely and noble not to be loved: and, dear Janey, there are too few things that seem worth experiencing as life goes on for one friend to deny another the poor expression of what is most at his heart. But he is before me in granting this, and there is no need for me to say it. I can never tell you how much I am with you at all times. Absence from your sight is what I have long been used to, and no absence can ever make me so far from you again as your presence did for years. For this long inconceivable change, you know now what my thanks must be . . . I have done the drapery of that drawing of you with the head resting on the hands, and think it certainly the best I have done, I shall not let Norton have it of course but keep it and make him a copy, I must paint for myself.[31]

If Morris saw the letter, it would only have confirmed what he already knew – what everyone knew. Taking Jane away from Rossetti would do little good. When they returned, he was going to have to find a way of dealing with the situation.

16

Resurrection

IN THE VAULTS of the University of Princeton Library is a piece of pale blue paper. It is an invoice for an exhumation, made out by The Funeral Company on 5 October 1869 to Charles Augustus Howell. This extraordinarily macabre document records the fact that for the sum of £2 2s. Howell had secured 'two men attending at Highgate Cemetery to open & close coffin'. His payment had also guaranteed 'conveyance & driver, conveying men and tools to the cemetery' as well as 'men's expenses for refreshments' and 'tools to complete'.[1] The invoice was paid on 29 December 1869.

Howell, along with William Bell Scott, had placed the grotesque idea of exhuming Lizzie's body into Gabriel's troubled mind.[2] Whether they actually crafted the notion that Rossetti should retrieve his buried manuscripts or whether they simply helped Gabriel undertake a course of action he had been mulling for some time, Howell ended up as the facilitator in this grizzly business.

Rossetti's preoccupation with the love poetry he had written at the height of his infatuation with Lizzie had been resurrected by Jane. His obsession with his latest conquest was returning his thoughts to his long-lost verse. What is more, Jane was encouraging him to publish his work.

Throughout the summer of 1869 he became preoccupied with reviving these old poems and getting them typeset and revised. Many he remembered, and for those that had become dimmed by time he sought out old copies. He wrote to his friend the lawyer

Vernon Lushington asking him if he had 'a M.S. copy of a poem of mine called "Jenny"? I want a copy, not having one in a perfect state.'[3] William Michael was drawn in to edit and assist. While Jane was languishing at Bad Ems, Rossetti wrote to her and declared: 'You see your idea has not been sown in barren soil but has immediately borne fruit.'[4] But although Rossetti began his project with a flurry of enthusiasm, he was quickly frustrated. 'I have got very imperfect copies of some other longer poems in M.S. but I cannot remember many important alterations which I had once made in other copies now lost', he wrote to Janey a few weeks later.[5]

And so on 16 August Rossetti wrote to Howell and confirmed that he felt 'disposed, if practicable by your friendly aid, to go in for the recovery of my poems if possible, as you proposed some time ago. Only I should have to beg absolute secrecy to every one, as the matter ought really not be talked about . . . It is a matter on which – having been lately taking up my old M.S.S – I begin to feel real anxiety.'[6]

Anxious, haunted by love and, by death, and yet feeling ambitious and industrious, Rossetti was a strange mix of despair and optimism, of light and dark. In spite of the seriousness of the matter on which he was about to embark, his sense of commercial opportunism remained acute, as did his ability to appear casual in the face of momentous things. As ever disorganized when it came to 'tin', Rossetti suggested that he could reward Howell for his gruesome task with 'the swellest drawing conceivable'. Howell cheekily responded by asking for a particularly beautiful picture of Jane. If the demand was in some way a test of Rossetti's gratitude, then Howell may have felt a little affronted since with an arrogant panache typical of Rossetti he was granted his desire on condition that Howell would exercise self-denial and let Rossetti 'have it again at any time that I wanted it for myself, by giving you something instead'.[7]

Neither were Rossetti's amusing eccentricities diminished by the dark matters at hand. His predilection for exotic beasts did not wane. In fact the menagerie at Cheyne Walk enjoyed at this time

Rossetti's Wombat Seated on his Master's Lap, by William Bell Scott, 1871. Wombats had long been admired by Rossetti and his friends, but Rossetti's attempts to keep them as pets were not successful

the addition of a wombat.[8] In an image that bizarrely encapsulates the peculiar worlds of Rossetti and Ruskin as they were that summer, Rossetti described an encounter between the critic and his latest pet. 'Ruskin called the other day, & seemed to tend towards a grand proposal of banding together for the regeneration of the world. I told him at once that any individual I came near was sure to be the worse for it. You should have seen him waving his hand and soul towards his forlorn species, while the Wombat burrowed between his coat and waistcoat.'[9]

It is quite likely that this was the last time Rossetti and Ruskin saw one another, the critic's distressed state of mind so clear, his former protégé's lack of interest and lightly worn self-loathing also apparent. Perhaps its not surprising that the wombat did not last long in the Rossetti household. Anecdotally, its demise was the result of its eating a box of cigars.

But while Rossetti and his friends were enjoying the novelty of the wombat, behind the scenes Howell was proceeding with arrangements for Lizzie's exhumation. It was proving doubly tricky, since Rossetti's desire for secrecy extended to his own family. He did not want them to know his macabre intentions lest they should try to stop him. In this instance not even the aid of the endlessly compliant and obliging William Michael was sought.

But keeping the news from his mother was going to be hard. Frances Rossetti owned the burial plot in which Lizzie was buried, and since she had died an aunt had been buried in close proximity. It was highly likely that Mrs Rossetti would object on grounds of impropriety if her permission were sought, not least because her aunt's remains might also be disturbed.

And then Rossetti, with again a sense of casualness that seems inappropriate to the delicacy of the situation, remembered something that he thought might be useful. A Home Office licence would have to be sought as part of the legal process of exhumation. How handy, then, that he had a rather good contact in that place. He did not hesitate to jot a line to Howell: 'It has suddenly flashed upon me that I believe a man I know pretty well is now Home Secretary. Is it not Henry A. Bruce? Will you look in some list and see. I cannot find any here. If this is so, I had better write him direct as enclosed, and tell him that (his sanction obtained) an intimate friend has undertaken to manage the matter for me.'[10]

It is a mark of Rossetti's self-absorption and of the very reclusive lifestyle that he now led, that he did not know who was Home Secretary. This, however, did not prevent him from using his famous skills of persuasion on the man. A fortnight later he had corresponded with Bruce and was able to write to Howell: 'I send you Bruce's answer just received, and also a note of introduction to him, in case you think it well to see him, which I should think might facilitate his movements. I write to him with this to say I am sending you such a note. He is an old friend & will I know receive you cordially . . . PS . . . The book in question is bound in rough grey calf and has I am almost sure red edges to the leaves. This will distinguish it from the Bible also there as I told you.'[11]

The combined charm of Rossetti and his henchman was enough for Bruce. He approved the exhumation in spite of the irregularity that the actual owner of the grave was ignorant of the proceedings. And so on 28 September Rossetti was able to write to The Funeral Company of London and assert that 'In accordance with the order granted by the Right Honourable Henry Austin Bruce, Her Majesty's Secretary for the Home Department, for the exhumation of the body of my late wife Elizabeth Eleanor Rossetti, buried at Highgate Cemetery: I hereby authorise my friend Charles Augustus Howell of Northend Grove, Northend, Fulham, to act in all matters as he may think fit, for the purpose of opening the coffin and taking charge of MS volume desposited therein.'[12]

On 5 October Rossetti went to Howell's home in West Kensington and sat with his wife while Howell and another friend and legal adviser, Henry Virtue Tebbs, presided over Lizzie's temporary reprieve from her subterranean resting place. The grim task was carried out, as was customary, at dead of night. A bonfire was lit to illuminate the area where the workmen had to dig. Although legal, the scene must have sent a shudder down the spine of anyone who might have chanced upon it.

Howell returned home that night and told Rossetti that his mission had been accomplished. Lizzie's body was still perfect, her long red hair even more voluptuous than it had been before, continuing to grow after death and filling the coffin. And he had the manuscript.

It is hard to believe Howell's account of the state of Lizzie's corpse. Although indeed he had the manuscript, it was utterly sodden and rotten, there were great holes in it, it stank terribly and had been handed over to a certain Dr Llewellyn Williams from Kennington for drying and disinfecting. If the manuscript was so damaged by the damp conditions of its subterranean resting place, how could Lizzie's body have failed to suffer some decomposition?

Howell's lie was born from the Pre-Raphaelite tradition that linked suffering with beauty and tragedy with appeal. Howell instinctively understood this. He understood the iconic status Lizzie occupied in her husband's mind and did not want to disappoint. It seems that for a while at least Howell did his best to conceal the state of the manuscript from Rossetti. Four days after the exhumation Rossetti told Bell Scott that 'I have not the thing yet, as it is in someone's hands for necessary arrangements. It, and all with it, was found quite perfect.'[13]

A week after the exhumation Rossetti confessed what had taken place to William Michael. He revealed that Janey, Scott and Rossetti's assistant Henry Treffry Dunn knew about everything, as did for that matter Morris and Burne-Jones. He was going to write to Brown and Swinburne. Rossetti still wanted the matter kept as quiet as possible, and told his brother he would 'say at present that I have made the rough copies more available than I hoped'. He added with a rather telling but unfortunate choice of phrase that 'I suppose the truth must ooze out in time'.

The truth did indeed 'ooze out' – certainly the truth about the condition of the manuscript. Ten days after it had been retrieved, Rossetti finally saw his old notebook himself at the doctor's house. 'It will take some days yet to dry, and is in a disappointing but not hopeless state', he confessed to William. 'The poem of "Jenny" which is the one I most wanted, has got this great worm-hole right through the very page of it . . . it has a dreadful smell – partly no doubt the disinfectants – but the doctor says there is nothing dangerous.'[14] Perhaps Howell's attempt to preserve the memory of Lizzie had been unnecessary after all. Rossetti reacted to the obvious signs of corruption with simple, cool, matter-of-factness.

In the same letter that Rossetti tells his brother about the all too mundane worm-hole he also adds a cryptic postscript. 'You know I always meant to dedicate the book to you', he writes. 'This I shall of course still do, failing only one possibility which I suppose must be considered out of the question.' The possibility so out of the question was not a dedication to his deceased wife, which by contrast would have felt entirely appropriate. Rather, Rossetti wanted to dedicate his old love poetry to his new lover, Jane. And that was out of the question since she was another man's wife. As he had shown before, Rossetti could be blinded by infatuation at the expense of propriety. He felt no qualms about trampling over the memory of Lizzie, just as he had managed to abuse her during her lifetime.

On 18 May 1868 Effie Millais sat down at her desk to write what she must have felt was a deeply unsavoury yet necessary letter. It was nearly thirteen years since she had married John Millais and just over fourteen years since she had walked out of Denmark Hill and her relationship with John Ruskin.

She was a very different creature now from the beautiful, flirtatious but essentially tragic girl whom John Millais had drawn adorned with foxgloves in the Scottish hills. She had risked much to escape a deeply unhappy marriage, and by and large her bold steps had paid off. She was now the mother of eight children and the wife of a very successful and famous painter living comfortably between London and Scotland.

But Effie and John had paid the price for their unconventional courtship. Ruskin, although initially offering some form of professional amnesty to Millais, soon stopped his favourable reviews of the latter's work. And Effie, in spite of the best efforts of friends such as Lady Eastlake, had been punished too. Although there were many in the Eastlake circle who continued to include Effie in their social gatherings, many did not. The Victorian reverence for the institution of marriage offered little room for those who were seen to have deviated from a straight path. The whiff of adultery coupled with what was widely seen as Effie's divorced status made her unpalatable social fare for many. [15] Her days of unlimited parties and 'at homes', balls and dinners were long gone. Receptions at Court were quite out of the question: the Queen, the epitome of the loyal wife, made it clear that there would never be room for a divorced woman at court or in her presence.

It is small wonder then that Effie, capable and intelligent, had retreated into preoccupations that allowed her some sense of worth. She was a matriarchal figure now, taking a firm guiding hand over a huge family. And it is hardly surprising that Effie would not allow John Ruskin, the architect of her situation, any quarter. So when Maria La Touche wrote to Effie begging her to help her persuade her daughter not to marry Effie's former spouse, Effie was quite clear what she would do. 'If the Banns of marriage are proclaimed I shall feel obliged in justice to my own character to give it [the decree] publicity', she warned. [16]

This was just the kind of threat Maria La Touche had hoped for. With this letter, in which it seems that Effie may well have included a copy of the decree in question, the La Touches were armed not only with the means by which to embarrass Ruskin publicly again, but also with words of warning to pass on to Rose. They wasted no time. Rose was shown Effie's letter.

Rose, confused and distraught, once against turned against the man to whom she had begun to offer some hope. As her twenty-first birthday approached, she retreated from Ruskin once more. Just days after Effie entered into the business, Ruskin wrote to Mrs Cowper in the bleakest terms:

You know, without doubt by this time it is all over: – and perhaps you will not even read this note.

It is only to say that now, the only thing possible to me is to persevere in all that I have been endeavouring to do. I cannot measure what I may have to endure, nor what those who have loved me (– they are many –) may suffer for me. But I know now that this thing, whatever it is, has been openly against me from the year 1854 till now; and as I had partly lived it down – I believe in the end – that through all this evil – what I know there is of good in me will yet have some office upon the earth. [17]

Despite further attempts by Ruskin to persuade Mrs Cowper to plead on his behalf, 1869 came and Rose's twenty-first birthday went without any communication on the subject of marriage. Instead, Rose once again suffered some form of breakdown and was confined once more to bed. Her doctors and parents were well aware that her illness had to be linked to the extraordinary stress from her situation. All correspondence relating to Ruskin was once again firmly banned – letters not just from Ruskin himself but from anyone who might be offering an opinion about him. The Cowpers were a strong influence on Rose on Ruskin's part, and now Maria determined to stem their power too.

Effie was good ammunition indeed, but the La Touches were determined to be as well fortified as possible against Ruskin. So they also dug into their pockets and sought legal advice as to whether Ruskin actually could ever marry again. After all, if, as the decree implied, he was incurably impotent, then how could any marriage be consummated? Their legal advice indicated that indeed it could not. Regardless of Ruskin's desire for their daughter, in the eyes of the law he could not have her. This opinion Maria La Touche sent defiantly on to Mrs Cowper. She knew that if this news had gone to the Cowpers, it would be in Ruskin's hands in no time.

Although Ruskin mustered some practical response to this latest parry – he managed to find counsel that offered an opposing legal position in his favour – the general effect of the war that the La Touches now waged was to unhinge further a man only just holding on to sanity. His depression deepened, his reclusive tendencies intensified and Rose haunted his mind. Everything in the world around him began to offer a parallel meaning; reminders of Rose lay everywhere. Writing to what one imagines was a rather weary Mrs Cowper, Ruskin revealed that, unable to do much, he was 'working chiefly at my botany for I have much material that it would be wrong to waste – (only it is so very strange to work at it now – when one always shudders if one comes across a particular family of flowers – that one had meant to trace all down from)'.[18]

His dreams, meanwhile, became yet more menacing. In his mind the society that once celebrated him was now rejecting him, and the horror of his outlaw status vented itself at night. In his sleep he found himself often at court, but invariably as an impotent buffoon. In one dream he crushed the Empress's dress with his feet but found himself unable to move off the hem; in another he discovered himself on the way to court but could not find his entrance ticket.

And still the dreams of snakes kept coming: 'Got restless – taste in mouth – and had the most horrible serpent dream I ever had yet in my life. The deadliest came out into the room under a door. It rose up like a Cobra – with horrible round eyes and had woman's, or at least Medusa's breasts. It was coming after me, out of one room, like our back drawing room at Herne Hill, into another; but I got some pieces of marble off a table and threw at it, and that cowed it and it went back; but another small one fastened on my neck like a leech, and nothing would pull it off.'[19]

There is something in this description of the sexualized snake, moving towards Ruskin, that recalls Rossetti's picture *The Beloved*, painted in 1865. In this picture a woman with hypnotic eyes seems to be moving forward as though about to step out of the canvas. Pressed on by her exotic female companions, it feels as though she is about to overpower the viewer with a sexuality one can almost smell. No wonder Ruskin was horrified by Rossetti's luscious pictures of women, tempting their onlookers as they stared out of the canvas. Everything predatory and erotic in womankind that Rossetti sought to idolize was the stuff now of his former patron's nightmares.

Haunted in sleep, somnambulant in the daytime, Ruskin was living a nightmare that reached its climax in January 1870, when, just days after her twenty-second birthday, he quite unexpectedly met Rose La Touche face to face. Ruskin bumped into her at the Royal Academy, at the top of the stairs in the Academy's first gallery. In confusion Rose walked past Ruskin without saying anything. Ruskin caught her. She broke away and continued looking at paintings. Ruskin took the little case in which he kept Rose's letter pressed between two gold sheets from his breast pocket. He held it out to her, suggesting she had dropped her pocket book. She denied it was hers. He asked her once more. And again she shook her head, at which point Ruskin returned the letter to his breast pocket and left.

The incident had a therapeutic effect on Ruskin. His pain turned to indignation. A series of angry letters now flew between the two, Ruskin accusing Rose and her religion of treating him cruelly. But as ever the mercurial Rose did not fail to turn events once more. Extraordinarily and unexpectedly she wrote to say that she did love him after all.

Ruskin's friends were amazed by his preparedness still to imagine a happy conclusion to this now farcical affair. Ruskin once more believed that he had grasped victory from the jaws of defeat. Writing to Mrs Cowper in newly joyous and defiant tones, he declared that his love had 'come back' to him. And then in March he shared more with his confidante and correspondent. He transcribed one of the latest letters to him that Rose has apparently smuggled out of the house:

> I do love you. I have loved you though the shadows that have come between us could not make me but fear you and turn from you – I love you, & shall love you always, always – & you can make this mean what you will.
>
> I have doubted your love. I have wished not to love you. I have thought you unworthy, yet – as surely as I believe God loved you, as surely as my trust is in His Love.
>
> I love you – still, and always.
>
> Do not doubt this any more.
>
> I believe God meant us to love each other, yet life – and it seems God's will has divided us.
>
> My father and mother forbid my writing to you, and I cannot continue to do so in secret. It seems to be God's will that we should be separated, and yet – 'thou art ever with me'. If my love can be any sunshine to you – take – and keep it. And now – may I say God bless you? God, who is Love – lead-guide, & bless us both.[20]

Although Rose's letter is ambiguous in some respects – it is as much a resignation to separation as it is a declaration of love – she must have expressed something of her renewed feelings for Ruskin to her parents. For they now became fearful that their influence over their single-minded daughter was once again slipping. Rose was of age now. She could, technically, elope. And so in the autumn of 1870 the La Touches once again sought the help of Ruskin's most ardent enemy. That, of course, was Effie. And this time her husband also got involved.

In June 1872 William Morris took a bundle of blue-lined foolscap pages, put it in an envelope and posted it to his friend Louisa Macdonald Baldwin, Georgie Burne-Jones's sister.

> Herewith I send my abortive novel: it is just a specimen of how not to do it, and there is no more to be said thereof: 'tis nothing but landscape and sentiment: which thing won't do ... the separate parcel 1 to 6 was a desperate dash at the middle of the story to try and give it life when I felt it failing: it begins with the letter of the elder brother to the younger on getting his letter telling how he was going to bid for the girl in marriage. I found it in the envelope in which I sent it to Georgie to see if she could give me any hope: she gave me none, and I have never looked at it since – so there's an end of my novel writing I fancy unless the world turns top-sides some day.'[21]

The 'Novel on Blue Paper', as it has subsequently been described, was never finished, as Morris's rather plaintive letter suggests. As he also suggests, writing it was a complete departure for him. All his work to date had been poetic and set most firmly in a deeply mythological past. This, by contrast, was not just a foray into prose but was also set in the contemporary world.

Morris's decision to drop the project was not entirely to do with his self-deprecating claim that he lacked the talent for prose. His friends could see clearly that this work drew on painful personal circumstances that were best left to their private circle. There had been enough scandal in the group, and its damaging consequences were easy to see.

For this very reason what remains of this aborted project makes fascinating reading. While the story does not mirror any particular one of the various Pre-Raphaelite love triangles, it seems to offer an amalgam of them all. Passionately and forcefully written, in an utterly modern voice, it gives us a vivid and immediate impression of the emotional pain Morris himself was suffering when he put pen to paper, as well as a glimpse of the personalities and the private tortures of those around him. Suffused with tragedy from the very first page, the novel is a terrific summary of the terrible waste, the hopeless misjudgements, the messy, unhappy domestic situations that a once happy and idealistic band of brothers were now facing in the 1870s. The consequences of their social audacity in the 1850s and of their wanton behaviour in the '60s were becoming clear. A group of middle-aged people found themselves a long way away from the youthful walks on Hampstead Heath, the brotherhood soirées, the jovial campaign in Oxford and the warm orchard times at the Red House.

Morris's story begins in the imaginary village of Ormslade, where a widowed rector lives with his two sons. The rector is a man trapped by circumstance. Parson James Risley standing in his garden in Chapter 2 and 'remembered what he might have been, rather than what he was. Old aspirations and old enthusiasms, the kindling of what he thought true love – and the slaking of it – was too bitter to let him muse long.'[22]

The regretful Risley, at this initial moment, seems clearly based on Morris himself, a man also trapped by wrong choices. But then we discover a darker past to Risley that has more than a shade of Rossetti. The rector once had a wife, we are informed, 'a pale, thin, querulous, flaxen haired women with blue eyes'.[23] This wife discovers that her husband has married her for money and left behind a mistress called Eleanor. There is some suggestion that Eleanor may have left her husband and thus forsaken her reputation for Risley. In the story the deserted Eleanor has subsequently written to Risley and Mrs Risley had intercepted the letters. On her deathbed Risley is left to discover the letters, which so clearly reveal her husband's betrayal of her, under his dead wife's pillow.

And here the references jump again, becoming a jigsaw of different elements drawn from the different tragedies by which Morris felt surrounded. The discovery of Eleanor's letters mirrors the discovery that Georgie made of Mary Zambaco's correspondence with Ned. The leaving of the letters for the husband to find post-mortem feels like the cruel punishment that Lizzie dealt out to Rossetti in his suicide note, in return for his continuing deception with Fanny.

In Chapter 4 Eleanor comes to Ormslade to confront and reclaim her former lover in the wake of his wife's death. When this woman enters the rectory sitting-room, it is as though the fiery Mary Zambaco had come into the room. Risley is now Ned more than anyone else. He admits his fear of his mistress, referring to her as intelligent but furious. 'Even when we were getting on best I was afraid of you. I wondered whether you wouldn't cut my throat', he pleads.[24]

Morris does not finish the story of Risley and Eleanor. It is left hanging, hauntingly unresolved, as indeed was everyone's fate at the time of writing: Rossetti's and Jane's, Ned's and Mary's, Georgie's and Morris's own.

Perhaps this is why Morris strove so hard to work out his own feelings and situation more pertinently in the story of Risley's two sons, Arthur and John. The two teenagers are close friends with Clara, the daughter of a rich farming widow, Mrs Mason. At the beginning of their story Arthur is ill in bed, and John visits Clara alone. During this visit he realizes he is attracted to her, but while there Clara gives him a letter for his brother Arthur. On receipt of this correspondence Arthur hides it under his pillow rather than share it with his sibling, reading it greedily later and falling asleep with it in his arms. In the letter to Arthur, Clara reveals:

I was thinking of you and your brother, and wishing that I could see you and hoping so much that you were better: then I began to wonder how our three lives would run on together, and then, all of a sudden, I felt so strange! As if I understood all about it – why we were alive and liked each other so, and it felt so sweet and delightful that I think I never felt so happy in all my life; and yet I was longing for something, but the longing didn't seem any pain to me; I can't tell you now what I thought of in that minute – though if you had been by, I think I could have then – but it slipped away very fast and left me wondering what it was that had made me so happy.[25]

As Arthur sleeps with the letter in his hands, he has a foreboding dream:

Clara was clad in light fluttering raiment, like what he had seen on angels in old pictures, instead of her usual dress, and she spoke to him in verse, in the rhythm of some fragment of old poetry that he had forgotten when awake. And so they passed on till, as it happens in dreams, the landscape changed. . . . There were big blue mountains all about the mead and a rushing stream through it, and suddenly his heart seemed to stop beating for fear; and she stopped him and faced him, with fear in her eyes too. And as she tried to speak, and could not, she had turned into his brother, and he thought that they had lost themselves, and were to die.[26]

The reference is so raw. Two brothers in love with the same woman, the same woman with feelings for both. The consequences of this triangle would be terrible, as Morris himself knew. It is impossible to read the story without thinking of Morris, Janey and Rossetti. But which brother is Morris and which is Rossetti?

As the story goes on, it is clear that John has much of Rossetti and Arthur is very like Morris. John goes to work for a Russian merchant, leaving Arthur and Clara to explore their love and marry, after seeking John's blessing. John encourages the union, concealing his true feelings and acting nobly. Clara is desperate for John to step in and save her, and regrets that she did not broach John's feelings. Clara and Arthur are committed to a less than ideal marriage.

These actions chime with those accounts that claim Jane and Rossetti were deeply in love back in the 1850s during the jovial campaign in Oxford, but that Rossetti, out of loyalty to Morris and because of his entanglement with Lizzie, encouraged his friend's pursuit of the young violet-seller rather than pursue her properly himself. Jane had hoped Rossetti would step forward and prevent the engagement because of his feelings for her, but when he failed to act, she continued with the marriage since Morris had wealth and prospects beyond anything she could otherwise have hoped for.

In the novel Morris writes a letter from John to Arthur, in which John encourages his brother to marry in spite of his own competing feelings for Clara. Did Rossetti ever write something similar to Morris in connection with Jane?

> When I was down there with you the whole air seemed full of this [love]. It lurked in dark corners in the twilight, and the dark throbbed with it as I lay alone on my bed, till I felt as if it would burst into a cry; and as I went up in the train the noise of the wheels and engine seemed to be telling the world of it . . .
> . . . And now I will talk sense and give you advice – and believe me, for whatever reason, I am inspired tonight, and if you follow my advice all will be well with you. If otherwise, if you let any half heartedness deceive you, it will be better for you to grow miserable and die, than to be contented and live . . . if you are sure as you say you are that Clara loves you and that you love her, heed nothing, heed nobody, but live your life through with her, crushing everything that comes in your way – everything – unless, perhaps, there was somebody who loved her better than yourself. Yet you will not be able to imagine that, if you truly love her . . . all is either love or not love. There is nothing between. Everything else – friendship, kindness, goodness is a shadow and a lie.[27]

Dreams play an important role in the 'Novel on Blue Paper', synthesizing all the liaisons and scandals, turmoils and emotions within Morris's life and the lives of his wider group. Not just Jane and Rossetti but several of his close friends could have picked it up and felt buttonholed by the story.

But these are words that could also come from Morris's mouth. If Jane and Rossetti loved one another so passionately, then how could Rossetti's friendship with Morris, let alone Jane's foundering marriage to him, stand in the way of their relationship? In these words Morris is conceding his wife to his friend and admitting to his powerlessness in the situation. It is an extraordinarily sad testimony to Morris's own view of love and to his capitulation to the desires of two people he held dear.

The fact is that Morris had realized that the best way forward was to endorse the relationship between his friend and his wife. In an act of moral generosity that is quite extraordinary, when their affair was at its very height, Morris agreed to lease a house with Rossetti out of London. Here Jane and Rossetti could live together, away from the society gossips that could otherwise damage reputations and businesses.

'I have been looking about for a house for the wife and kids,' Morris revealed to his business partner and chum Charley Faulkner in May 1871, 'and whither do you guess my eye is turned now? Kelmscott, a little village about two miles above Radcott Bridge – a heaven on earth; an old stone Elizabethan house like Water Eaton, and such a garden! Close down on the river, a boat house and all things handy. I am going there again on Saturday with Rossetti and my wife because he thinks of sharing it with us if the thing looks likely.'[28]

The 'old stone Elizabethan house' was Kelmscott Manor. It is still standing today, little changed from Morris's day. With willow trees that trail in a lazy slow river running at its side, it is easy to understand how Morris fell in love with it. It embodies Morris's medieval aesthetic.

The plan to find such a house with Rossetti had in fact been agreed for a good month before the scouting visit to Kelmscott, during which time the latter had been particularly keen to conceal the proposed arrangement from Fanny. Rossetti knew what ructions his latest adventure was going to cause with his long-suffering mistress/housekeeper. But leaving Fanny in the dark was already creating chaos.

In April he had to write to Howell about a chest of drawers that the latter had secured for Rossetti and now wished to buy back. Rossetti initially agreed to the transaction but then changed his mind because he realized the drawers could be useful in the furnishing of his country retreat. He failed, however, to inform Fanny of this. Confusion consequently reigned.

Nor, it seems, was Fanny any better informed when a month later Rossetti actually went to visit Kelmscott with Morris and Janey. He simply wrote a note to his 'Dear Fan' which said: 'I will not expect you today. The fact is I feel so unwell that I am going to take a train to some country neighbourhood and have a walk there.'[29]

It is possible that the relatively uncomplicated triangular relationship Rossetti had once enjoyed with Fanny and Boyce had established a blueprint in the former's mind of the kind of consensual relationship he could have with the Morrises. The arrangement that William Bell Scott had negotiated with his wife, allowing him to stay for extended periods with Alice Boyd in Penkill, also served as a model.

Morris had shown himself to be willingly complicit in some form of arrangement as early as 1870, when, on the publication of Rossetti's book of love poetry, revived from Lizzie's coffin with Jane in mind, Rossetti asked him to write a complimentary review. This act was typically selfish and insensitive on the part of the self-obsessed Rossetti. Morris's condescension to oblige showed less his desire to kowtow to his friend than a desire to protect his wife from gossip. If there was scandal brewing about just who was the subject of Rossetti's poetry, at least positive praise from Morris might deflect it for a while.

But unlike Boyce, who had always been an equal and eager partner with Rossetti in a *ménage à trois*, Morris resented the steps he was being forced to take for the sake of his wife's reputation. After he had written the review, he dropped a line to his friend and confidante the socialite Aglaia Coronio and revealed his genuine feelings: 'I have done my review, just this moment – ugh!'[30]

In this vein it is hardly surprising that, although the co-tenant of Kelmscott Manor, Morris did not move in there with his wife and her lover. Instead, he headed off for Iceland on an adventure with his friend Charley Faulkner. He would be gone most of the summer.

Despite his distaste for the situation in which he found himself, Morris coped with it with resigned bravery. He was becoming increasingly political in his thinking and, a natural socialist, he began to see his current domestic arrangement in political terms. Years later he wrote to Charley Faulkner and outlined how he believed couples should be 'free', how they should never conceal from one another any 'distaste' that arose, and that 'friendship should go along with desire, and would outlive it, and the couple would remain together, but always as free people'. Morris must have come to this view of his marriage at the point he leased Kelmscott. He loved Janey and he loved Rossetti, for all his faults. He formulated an intellectual proposition that could accommodate his feelings for them and their feelings for one another.

Jane and Rossetti installed themselves in their country retreat in July, and one senses from Rossetti's letters the fun he had home-making. Not since he first moved into Chatham Place with Lizzie had his correspondence been so filled up with talk of carpenters and curtain makers.

By 16 July he was writing to his old friend Ford Madox Brown to tell him that Kelmscott was 'simply the loveliest place in the world – I mean the house and garden & immediate belongings ... we have got the house well fitted with furniture ... but (the place is) just such a "haunt of ancient peace" ... that one can hardly believe one has not always lived here ... Janey is perfectly well ever since she came here, and takes walks with [me] of 5 or 6 miles at [a stretch] just as easily as I do. Her babes are dear little things and amuse themselves all day long, & are never tiresome in the least.'[31]

His enchantment with his new life and new surroundings prompted a positive flurry of happy letter-writing to all and sundry. After writing to Brown he put pen to paper to William Michael and told him how 'wonderfully beautiful' the house and surroundings were. Scott received an epistle describing the house and garden 'with all their riverside fields and sleepy farmbuildings' making up a 'delicious picture to the eye and mind'.

And yet even this early on something at Kelmscott unsettled Rossetti. In just about every letter he also talked about the dullness of the flat landscape beyond the village and the isolation of the place. It was a long way from the life he had been living in Chelsea, with its friendly taverns and chop houses.

By the time Rossetti was writing this flurry of letters to his friends, Morris was already in Reykjavik, writing to Janey and the girls. His first letter is a long description of the journey to Iceland and feels like a jolly, meandering attempt to avoid the subject. There is no reference to Rossetti; the casual fond greetings that Rossetti used to offer to 'Top' in his letters to Bad Ems are not copied here. He signs off quite simply with the request: 'Please dear Janey be happy ... The boat starts back for England September 1st so I hope to be at home about the 8th (in London I mean) if you are still at Kelmscott I will come at once to see you.'[32]

In spite of its shortcomings, Kelmscott did seem to give Rossetti a creative fillip. His proximity to Jane inspired more new poetry, and he painted her under a willow tree, Kelmscott in the background, in a picture that speaks of the lovers' contentment together.

Rossetti's satirical snipes at Morris diminished and were restricted to brief mentions in letters to mutual friends. One to Philip Webb, presumably referring to the famous temper and bad language, noted that Iceland had recently become 'as hot as hell'. But if Rossetti, Jane and Morris had managed to find some happy solution to their personal affairs over the course of that summer, Fanny was by contrast in a terrible state.

Forbidden to visit Rossetti at Kelmscott, Fanny was confined to hot, smelly London to look after Tudor House while alterations were being made to Rossetti's studio. She did what she could to remain in his affections and in his mind. Knowing Rossetti's propensity for animals, she bought a fawn with the idea of sending it on to Kelmscott. But her plan went horribly wrong when Rossetti's assistant decided it would not survive the journey and so killed it and buried it in the garden. When she found out the fate of her gesture, she was distraught. Alienated and alone, Fanny was reliving the suffering she had felt once before at the hands of Rossetti – when he had married Lizzie at her expense.

'My dear Fanny,' Rossetti wrote in a conciliatory tone, 'Your poor letter has almost made me cry. It comes at a moment when I happen to feel in very low spirits, and I cannot tell you how grieved I feel to think that your affectionate remembrance of me in sending the poor fawn should only have brought you disappointment and vexation. I wish I was with you at this moment poor kind Fan, to kiss you and tell you how much I feel about it.'[33]

By October the first summer at Kelmscott was over. Morris, returned from Iceland, visited the house briefly and Rossetti caricatured him, as was *de rigueur*: this time it was Morris fishing and all the fish fleeing. But it was a gentle satire. Rossetti returned in high spirits to the awaiting Fanny, and Morris and Jane resumed their distant but cordial and understanding marriage.

The previous October Mrs La Touche had once again written to Effie Millais:

What we now want is contradiction of the statement Mr Ruskin is now making to Mr Cowper Temple who with his wife has real influence over my daughter – and is using that influence eagerly to justify Ruskin in all things & persuade my unhappy child that she is bound to reward his love and constancy by . . . allowing him to renew his addresses . . . he wholly denies the impotence stated in the decree & he accounts for the word being there by the fact which he fully admits that he lived with you as with a sister for six years . . . he states that no love on either side preceded or accompanied the marriage which was arranged for quite other reasons

between his family and yours . . . that he never loved you, nor you
him and that therefore he respected you too much to be anything
but a protector & companion to you – that he made every possible
effort to make you happy & that failing to do so & finding you
desired your liberty he resolved to retire altogether . . . this story
appears to W Cowper Temple as not only creditable but extremely
credible . . . the Cowper Temples press upon her that his past
history is all perfectly beautiful pure & heroic.[34]

Both Effie and her husband responded in furious vein. The
once light-hearted, rather flighty Millais, now with the tone of the
eminent painter and middle-aged public figure he had become,
wrote to Mr La Touche:

Dear Sir

I am disturbed to hear from you that you are again troubled concerning your daughter. My wife was six years beside Mr Ruskin
and he never so much as made an attempt to make her his wife,
professing at the same time the greatest devotion. She was examined by two London doctors Sir Charles Locock on the part of the
Court and Dr Lee of Saville Row and their doctor all of whom at
once testified to her being a Virgin. When called upon to defend
the charge he decamped to Switzerland . . .[35]

While Effie replied to Mrs La Touche and pulled no punches:

Mr Millais is extremely averse to my being brought into contact
even by correspondence with your daughter who, if she is still
under the mischievous influence of Mr Ruskin, will not think
differently whatever I say. If your daughter can for a moment
believe such a statement as his that he should marry a girl of 19
without professions of the most devoted kind, how can any words
of mine undeceive her.

He pursued exactly the same course with me as with her; he
always took the tone of his love and adoration being higher and
above that of ordinary mortals, and immediately after the ceremony he proceeded to inform me that he did not intend to marry

me. He afterwards excused himself from doing so by saying that I had an internal disease . . . Our marriage was never arranged by anybody. There was no inducement but the utmost determination on his part to marry me . . .

Now that I am a married woman and happy with a family I think his conduct can only be excused on the score of madness as his wickedness in trying his dreadful influence over your daughter is terrible to think of. I can easily understand the hold he has acquired, as it was exactly the same over myself. His conduct to me was impure in the highest degree, discreditable and so dishonourable that I submitted to it for years not knowing what else to do, although I would have often been thankful to have run away, and envied the people sweeping the crossings. His mind is most inhuman; all that sympathy which he expects and gets from the female mind it is utterly impossible for him to return excepting on artistic subjects which have nothing to do with domestic life . . .

From his peculiar nature he is utterly incapable of making a woman happy. He is quite unnatural and in that one thing all the rest is embraced.

He always pretended to me to the last that he was the purest and holiest of men and had a peculiar influence over a young mind in making himself believed . . .

I think if your daughter went through the ceremony with him that her health would give way after time and she would be submitted to the same kind of treatment as I was.

It is very painful for me to write all this and be again obliged to recall all those years of distress and suffering, of which I nearly died. But I hope your daughter may be saved and come to see things in a different light.[36]

Effie's letter was an unequivocal character assassination. Not surprisingly, it hit its mark. On seeing the missive Rose turned against Ruskin yet again. Effie's letter, or accounts of it, must have enjoyed some circulation in society. Ruskin found friendships suddenly dissolved and appointments inexplicably not kept. Lady Desart, a long-standing friend of Ruskin and a relation of the La Touches, who until now had apparently prevailed from taking sides in the Rose affair, abruptly stopped her correspondence with Ruskin. The Bishop of Limerick also stood Ruskin up, leaving him sitting for two hours at the Athenaeum.

Ruskin felt his energy flowing away. He likened himself to the great Samson, brought down by his foolish, careless love of the betraying Delilah, although his Delilah was not the black-haired amazon of biblical tales but was 'very narrow waisted – & very shy, and had the trimmest little sweet knot of golden hair at the back of her head. And she had grey eyes – and was so good – so very good – and always did as people bid her.'[37]

Ruskin was now dividing his time between Denmark Hill and Oxford University, where since 1869 he had been the Slade professor of art. And now Ruskin, his indignation sharpened by the wrongs he saw visited upon him, and with an acute sense of his own purity in an otherwise corrupt world, chose to share his inherent prurience with the world. He began to work on a lecture on Michelangelo.

Intriguingly Ruskin chose to read his lecture to Ned Burne-Jones before delivering it. Ned had continued as a loyal friend to Ruskin, although the two of them were bickering with one another more and more. Ned sat in the study and listened to Ruskin's assault on an artist whom Ned held up as not only the pinnacle of artistic achievement but as a hero on whose work he drew quite freely. His Demophoon, which he had had to withdraw from the walls of the Old Watercolour Society just months earlier, was a very direct reference to some of Michelangelo's great nudes. He may well have been in a pose reminiscent of Botticelli, but Demophoon's musculature, so detailed and indulged, was from Michelangelo's Adam. And the sensuous embrace of Phyllis's robes wrapped around Demophoon's thigh was a homage to the highly sexual bondage that encircled Michelangelo's dying slave, whose expiration is nothing if not orgasmic. Ned's bondage to Mary was at once a torment and a pleasure.

Now Ruskin laid out his cards. Michelangelo's art chose 'instead of joy or virtue, at the best, sadness, probably pride, often sensuality, and always by preference vice or agony as the subject of thought'.[38] The great artist was ultimately flawed for his 'love of sensation' and his tendency to indulge in 'shadowing, storming and coiling', when in fact 'Light is, in reality more aweful than darkness – modesty more majestic than strength; and there is truer sublimity in the sweet joy of a child or the sweet virtue of a maiden that in the strength of Antaeus.'[39]

In making these statements Ruskin was outlining his own moral compass. Painters who dramatized carnal pain and pleasure on canvas were not only egotistical but ultimately failing in their moral responsibility to their public. They represented the decadent failings of civilized society whose 'conscience is entirely formed' but which 'finding it painful to live in obedience to the precepts it has discovered looks about to discover, also, a compromise for obedience to them'.[40]

That night Ned went home and despaired. He felt like throwing himself in the canal. How could he and the man who had been such a friend and inspiration to him have drifted so far apart? How could Ruskin not understand the profound human truths embodied in Michelangelo's nudes?

But more than this Ned suspected that, in choosing to read this lecture to him, Ruskin was pointing his disapproval at the bohemian choices and practices of his former protégé. Art was, after all, the mark of the man himself. The incident became a significant moment in their relationship, from which their friendship would never quite recover.

That summer Ruskin took a holiday in Matlock. He wrote a calm, business-like letter to Rose, setting out the legal advice he had gathered and asking her to correspond with him and make her own choice regarding marriage. While he waited for her response, Ruskin pathetically played out the remnants of his obsession with her by sketching wild roses. But the kind of dreams that had been visiting Ruskin in his sleep now came to him in a waking hallucinatory state. Joan, who was with him, was so worried that she sent an emergency telegram to Ruskin's old Oxford chum Dr Acland. The latter jumped on the next available express train, pulling the train's emergency cord to expedite an otherwise unscheduled stop at Matlock.

Ruskin was bedridden for three weeks. Physically and mentally he was broken. When Rose's reply to his letter finally arrived, it was

> an answer which for folly, insolence and selfishness beat everything I yet have known produced by the accursed sect of religion she has been brought up in. I made Joanna re-enclose the letter, writing only on a scrap of paper with it – 'my cousin and I have read the enclosed – You shall have the rest of your letters as soon as he returns home – and your mother shall have hers' – so the letter went back, and the young lady shall never read written, nor hear spoken, word of mine more. I am entirely satisfied in being quit of her.[41]

17

Torments of the flesh

O N 2 JUNE 1872 any admirers of the reclusive poet and painter Dante Gabriel Rossetti hoping to get a glimpse of their hero by loitering outside his notorious abode in Cheyne Walk would not have been disappointed. But they might have been surprised. Instead of the charismatic man in his plum-coloured painter's frock coat strolling from his grand mansion with the latest model on his arm, they would have seen a dishevelled, disorientated, ranting, overweight man being manhandled by three other gentlemen into an awaiting cab.

The tragic demise of Rossetti had perhaps begun the moment he met Lizzie Siddall, but it began to reach its conclusion after his first summer at Kelmscott. On 23 October 1871 William Bell Scott, despite his own unconventional domestic arrangement, nevertheless found himself shocked by new goings-on. 'I went to Morris to dinner at 6', Scott explained to Alice Boyd. 'I asked Gabriel the evening before if he was to be there, and on his answering no, I said "Why, then?" His reply was "Oh I have another engagement". This engagement was actually Janey at his own house for the night! At Top's there were Jones, Poynter, Brown, Huffer, Ellis and Green. Of course no Janey. Is it not too daring, and altogether inexplicable?'[1]

The habit of togetherness that Jane and Rossetti had shared at Kelmscott was, it seems, now being carried on in London, in spite of earlier sensitivities about reputation. This was a new blatant step, born from the liberties Morris has bestowed on his wife and friend. But it was an experiment in living that did not last long.

In the very month that Rossetti and Jane began this bolder phase of their relationship the *Contemporary Review* published a piece written by a man called Maitland, entitled 'The Fleshly School of Poetry: Mr D G Rossetti'. News of the piece, an attack on the moral vacuity and overt eroticism of what Maitland considered Rossetti's over-rated poetry, soon reached Rossetti's attention. The article was particularly close to the bone, taunting him for his reluctance to exhibit his art in public and picking on his obsession with all things sensual.

Gabriel's friends rallied around him, not least because Morris and Swinburne were also the object of swingeing criticism in the article. The general tenor of advice given to him seemed to be to let the thing go, but Gabriel, perhaps precisely because the article was so close to the bone, would not let it lie. He began his own personal investigation into the true identity of 'Maitland' and soon discovered it was a poet, writer and critic called Robert Buchanan, with whom William Michael had a long-standing literary feud.

This information was too much for Rossetti to resist and, now goaded on by Swinburne, who loathed Buchanan, he wrote a response to the article, entitled the 'Stealthy School of Criticism'. It was typeset in pamphlet form, but Rossetti held back from this full-blown attack while an abridged version appeared in *The Athanaeum* in December 1871, vilifying Buchanan for not having the courage of his convictions and choosing to write under a pseudonym.

This retaliation backfired. Rather than quieten Buchanan, it simply encouraged him to plan a pamphlet version himself, this time with his name attached. And while he was preparing this, other critics joined in the public kicking of Rossetti, Swinburne and Morris, quoting Buchanan to bolster their own negative criticisms.

In mid-May 1872 Buchanan's pamphlet found its way into Rossetti's hands. He was immediately distraught and fled to his faithful friend Brown, unburdening his anxieties on him until the small hours. On 15 May, still in a state, Rossetti tried to rouse Swinburne to discuss the matter, but the poet, now a confirmed alcoholic, was in bed with delirium tremens and in no state to talk about anything. So from Swinburne's place Rossetti headed off to find William Michael. Rossetti's brother tried to calm him down, and with some success since Gabriel jotted a note to Brown from his brother's home, apologizing for keeping him up previously and conceding that 'I probably may have been making too much of this matter'.

Whatever William Michael said to his brother at the time, years later he admitted that 'the charges brought forward and reinforced by Mr. Buchanan were by no manner or means light ones. They were sufficient – if believed, which I suppose they very scantily were – to exclude Rossetti from the companionship of virtuous and even of decent people; and it was no fault of this "accuser of sins" (to use Blake's expression) if such a result did not ensue.'[2]

To twenty-first-century readers Rossetti's alleged sin seems negligible. But outside the closed Bohemian circuit in which Rossetti and his friends operated, Victorian society in the 1870s remained particularly prudish – or at least chose to consider itself so. Fleshliness or sensuality in art was a scourge that many saw the need quickly to stamp out. And Buchanan knew he had a ready audience for his puritanical position.

It was not just the criticisms of himself that were gnawing at Rossetti; so too were calls in the press for him to respond to the accusations properly, his reticence at best a sign of cowardice and at worst one of guilt. As William Michael recalled, there was

a leading article in the *Echo*, one word in which, 'coward' or 'cowards,' disturbed my brother unduly. This article – possibly without the least reason – has been ascribed to Mr. Buchanan himself. So overstrained was the balance of his mind at the time that my brother seriously consulted me as to whether it might not be his duty to challenge the writer or the editor to a duel. I need hardly record my reply – that duels in this common-sensible country are equally illegal and risible.[3]

Although the idea of the unfit and portly Rossetti with either a sword or pistol in hand is laughable, its earnest proposal marks the extent to which he had become obsessed by the pamphlet. Although he had promised Brown he would take no heed of it, it had taken a hold of Rossetti's paranoid mind, which began to interpret what was essentially negative literary criticism as a specific personal attack on not just his work but also his morally wanton lifestyle. He saw it as a public exposé. He also began to suspect that this moral outing had been deliberately organized by a group of conspirators.

Of course, the key conspirator was Buchanan himself. Reading the pamphlet, Rossetti would have noticed that certain passages from the original article had now been embellished in the much meatier publication. These passages, to Rossetti's corroding sanity at least, held a double meaning. Just as Hunt, at the height of his paranoia about Annie Miller, felt sure *The Times*'s classified section was publishing details of his own embarrassment, so now Rossetti saw this pamphlet as being a public treatise on his own recent behaviour, on the still secret disinterment of Lizzie, on his adultery with his best friend's wife and on his continuing relationship with Fanny.

Finally Rossetti snapped. On 2 June William came to Tudor House, only to discover his brother in an utterly terrible state of mind. He was ranting about the supposed conspiracy against him and had even added his friend the poet Robert Browning to the group of betrayers.

'On that fatal 2 June, and for many days and months ensuing, I was compelled to regard my brother as partially insane, in the ordinary sense of that term', William Michael later recalled. 'It was only after an interval of time, and as I had opportunity to compare and consider the opinions expressed by medical men and others well qualified to judge, that I came to the conclusion that he never had been and never became thus insane at all, but was on the contrary the victim of chloral, acting upon strained nerves, mental disquiet, and a highly excitable imagination – all these coupled with a grievous and fully justified sense of wrong.'[4]

William sought immediate help in the form of William Bell Scott, who now lived a few doors away in Cheyne Walk. But Scott and William Michael soon realized that they were ill equipped to deal with Rossetti's ravings, and professional help was sought in the form of a friend, Dr Hake. At this point the enormously eminent psychiatrist Dr Henry Maudsley was also called in.

However much William Michael later chose to protect his brother from the detrimental slur of insanity, the symptoms Rossetti showed indicated something Maudsley would have almost certainly diagnosed as 'melancholy madness', which psychiatrists today would call severe depression with psychotic features or mood-congruent delusions.[5] Rossetti was deteriorating fast, accusing Maudsley of being a wolf in sheep's clothing, intent on poisoning him. It was decided that Rossetti should be removed to Hake's home in Roehampton. Brown had now also been summoned, as Rossetti was becoming increasingly aggravated. Hake, Brown and William Michael bundled a babbling Rossetti into a cab. During the trip across London, Rossetti persisted with the accusation that someone was ringing a bell to annoy him.

The next day things were, if anything, worse. Hake took Gabriel for a walk, but Rossetti was now inhabiting an entirely parallel world. The entourage of a funfair became interpreted as a public demonstration against Rossetti himself. He became violent and was removed back to Hake's house, where William and the doctor managed to calm him again. William sat up with Rossetti until late into the night, but once left alone, Rossetti found himself haunted by voices and visions, all apparently accusatory. Many who have gone through the accounts of the evening have speculated that it was his memories of Lizzie, and accusations of his responsibility for her death, that plagued and tormented him that night. In the end Rossetti could bear it no more and took a bottle of laudanum that he had somehow hidden in his belongings and drank the lot.

In a strange, horrid imitation of his own wife's suicide Rossetti sank into what Hake and William Michael initially thought a deep slumber. But when by the following afternoon Rossetti had not stirred, Hake began to suspect a more worrying conclusion. Another doctor was sent for and concluded that Rossetti had suffered some terrible affliction. He was dying. William Michael hailed another cab and flew to his aged mother's house to bring her to her son's bedside.

Once he had picked up their mother, William Michael called at Brown's house:

> I got out, and announced the crushing calamity. Brown, the warmest and most helpful of friends, refused to regard the case as absolutely desperate, and ran off at once for Mr Marshall, in Savile Row. And so – after nightfall in early June, or towards nine in the evening – we started again, and rolled onward to Roehampton. Arriving, we learned that Dante was still alive. Dr Hake had stationed himself at his bed-head, and held to his nostrils a large bottle of strong ammonia, which staved off his sinking into total lethargy; and I have little doubt that this wise precaution was the first and indispensable stage in the process which saved my brother's life. Very soon the Doctor took me quietly aside, and produced an empty bottle which he had found in a drawer. It was labelled 'Laudanum – Poison'. We exchanged few words, but were quite at one as to the meaning of this bottle.[6]

Hake filled Gabriel with black coffee. It was some three days before he came around. Between them William, Brown and Scott watched a slow recovery over the next few days and weeks. These three true friends, at this time of utter calamity, stood by Rossetti. Indeed, it is hard not to see William particularly as someone who had in so many ways been the ultimate undemanding carer of his needy brother for his entire life.

Rossetti cheated death, but it left its mark on him. He awoke from his stupor in many ways an emasculated man. His time frozen motionless in the laudanum-induced coma caused a paralysis of his hip, and from this point on he found walking without a stick difficult. His precarious financial affairs went into meltdown. Brown and William Michael took them over, transferring all his business through Brown's own personal accounts with William Michael as a co-signatory. Rossetti's beloved collection of blue china had to be sold to stave off angry creditors. What is more, Gabriel developed a hydrocele – a collection of fluid on the scrotum that caused a swelling or cyst – that needed surgical removal. The punishments were all too biblical for anyone with the inclination to read them as such.

When he came out of his darkness, although alive, Gabriel's mind was still misted over, a glaze of paranoia and suspicion lay over everyday events. As William Michael remembered, 'Browning had just published his singular poem "Fifine at the Fair", and he sent (as in previous instances) a presentation-copy to my brother.'

'Fifine at the Fair' is the story of a gypsy girl circus performer, a product of hardship and circumstance who is exploited by a Don Juan figure who becomes obsessed with his lust for her. Gabriel

> looked into the book; and, to the astonishment of bystanders, he at once fastened upon some lines at its close as being intended as an attack upon him, or as a spiteful reference to something which had occurred, or might be alleged to have occurred, at his house. In a moment he relented, with an effusion of tenderness to this old, attached, and illustrious friend; but in another moment the scarcely credible delusion returned. Browning was regarded as a leading member of the 'conspiracy'; and, from first to last, I was never able to discern that this miserable bugbear had ever been expelled from the purlieus of my brother's mind.[7]

Browning may well have been less a fan of Rossetti's poetry than Rossetti was of his, but he had not been a conspirator. The conspiracy was forged in Rossetti's mind by his very own guilt. For Rossetti it must have been all too easy to find a parallel between Browing's fiction and his own genuine personal history.

'Fifine' is essentially written as an address from a husband to his wife. The Don attempts to excuse and justify his desires for Fifine to his wife, Elvire. Elvire, the Don explains, is like a Raphael who when first acquired is a trophy 'evermore to glorify my wall', and in front of which for 'a fortnight more, I spend in Paradise'. But eventually familiarity breeds contempt and the Don realizes that 'one chamber must not coop my life in'. And so the focus of the Don's obsessions shifts: he indulges himself in cheaper fashionable acquisitions, such as the mass-produced picture books by the painter Gustave Doré. But, the Don argues, his indulgences do not obscure his appreciation of Raphael's value. If there were a fire, he would still save the Raphael before anything else.

The Don's arguments do little to sustain Elvire. She becomes phantom-like, fading away in person as she dwindles in his affections, until one day when he returns from seeing Fifine he finds his home empty.

The Epilogue, which sees the Don alone in his rambling home, haunted by his dead wife, could be a portrait of Rossetti. And this is no doubt what Rossetti himself saw only too clearly. Miserable, lonely and pained by the world around him, the Don now courts death, which, his ghost of his wife tells him, fails to offer solutions.

> 'Ah, but if you knew how time has dragged, days, nights!
> All the neighbour-talk with man and maid – such men!
> All the fuss and trouble of street-sounds, window-sights:
> All the worry of flapping door and echoing roof; and then,
> All the fancies . . . who were they had leave, dared try
> Darker arts that almost struck despair in me?
> If you knew but how I dwelt down here!' quoth I:
> 'And was I so better off up there?' quoth She.[8]

Jane had been intending to spend the summer of 1872 with Rossetti at Kelmscott and was already waiting for him in the warm June sunshine there when news of his attempted suicide reached her. She returned to London instantly.

Morris was, as ever, generous in this moment of crisis. One letter to Brown seems to imply that he offered not only his own services as a nurse but also, by association, Jane's. 'Come by all means and talk to Janey,' he told Brown, 'she will be glad to hear anything you have to say about Gabriel. For my part I am quite ready to do anything to help you in your work there: I mean to say for instance if staying there for a few days seemed desirable or in any place Gabriel goes to hereafter.'[9]

But those who had heard Rossetti's ramblings felt it was better for Jane to stay away. One can only speculate what she had come to represent in his tortured mind. When Jane was finally allowed to visit, Morris accompanied her. While there must have been an element of Morris wanting to maintain the façade of respectability during the crisis, his letters also indicate that he was genuinely upset and worried about Rossetti. Something of the friendship still lingered.

Rossetti did not return to Tudor House over the summer. Brown went and removed his work from the studio for safe keeping while Rossetti began a number of different recuperations with willing friends and clients, all as far away from the gossiping, watchful streets of the capital as possible. It was not just caution against gossip. Rossetti's removal from society was also part of a wider scheme to prevent him having to go into an asylum, a course that his family feared would have led to utter social ostracism and professional downfall.

While Rossetti was away, Fanny was still at home in London. Although Rossetti's health was improving, the financial mess that had accompanied his breakdown had not. Fanny, Rossetti's dependant, was in a hysterical state. Although her legal spouse was still alive, it seems that either no support was sought or none was available from that quarter, and so it was William and Brown, still managing Rossetti's affairs for him, that had to find ways of keeping Fanny afloat. They moved her into Tudor House on a full-time basis and sub-let the apartments in Royal Avenue that Rossetti paid for.

'What you tell me about Brown and William telling you that you ought to let your rooms was, I think, on the whole, the best step to take at present, particularly as you seem to have a quiet lodger', Rossetti assured her. 'You must not suppose that either

William or Brown are anything but true friends to you; and as for myself, you are the only person to whom it is my duty to provide for, and you may be sure I should do my utmost as long as there was a breath in my body or a penny in my purse.'[10] But Rossetti was aware that the future was looking precarious.

After three months of recuperation in Perthshire, Rossetti finally returned to Kelmscott towards the end of September. Jane and Morris had been back and forth between the manor and their London home over the summer, and now Jane stayed there to be with Rossetti once more. But as Morris pointed out to his confidante Aglaia Coronio, he would not 'go there so often now as Gabriel is come there, and talks of staying there permanently: of course he won't do that, but I suppose he will stay some time.'[11]

Dr Hake's son George was also a house guest at Kelmscott. Rossetti was not out of the woods and needed a watchful eye. The arrangements stood in sharp contrast to the golden summer of the previous year, when Jane and Rossetti had taken long five- or six-miles walks together while the children played happily in apparently safe seclusion.

Once installed at Kelmscott, Rossetti began to paint again. He was now fixated with the idea of Jane cast in one specific role, that of Proserpine. He began the first of eight pictures on the same subject that he painted obsessively over the next six years – each depicting Jane as the mythical goddess. One version hangs in Tate Britain. Jane is clad in the rich blue silk that Rossetti often chose for her. Her hair is pushed over one shoulder to expose her kissable back and long, sensuous neck. But she stands in gloom, only her face lit by a small window. Her gaze is downcast and withdrawn. The pomegranate in her hand reminds us why.

Proserpine is captured and married against her will and dragged down into Pluto's domain, the subterranean hell or Hades. Here she unwittingly confirms her fate by eating from Pluto's table six pomegranate seeds. As a result she must be held prisoner in Hades during the six winter months, one month for each seed consumed. Only in the summer months is she released from this torture.

This terrible picture hints at the reality beneath the ideal of the triangular arrangement that Rossetti, Morris and Jane had come to. As far as the former was concerned, in the summer he and Jane enjoyed the fruits of idyllic Kelmscott, but in the winter Jane returned to the personal hell of life with Morris in London.

Despite his intellectual altruism, Morris was not emotionally immune to the situation. He too was beginning to sink into depression. Finding himself isolated from his wife and friend, his only companion at home was, ironically enough, Jane's sister Bessy, who lived up to her surname, Burden. It was as though he found himself in an arranged marriage with this woman, whom he clearly barely tolerated. The epitome of the dependent woman who, without prospects of marriage is thrown on the mercy and charity of relatives, Bessy was everything Morris had saved Jane from becoming. 'I am going to stay for a day or two with Ned next week I fancy', he wrote to Aglaia in October 1872. 'I have had a hardish time of it here all alone with Bessy with whom I seldom exchange any word that is not necessary. What a wearing business it is to live with a person with whom you have nothing whatever to do!'[12]

A month later Morris wrote again to Aglaia. This time not only was his misery spelt out even more clearly, but one gets a sense of the issues engulfing the whole group of once carefree friends. Morris paints the picture of Jane living her quite separate life now, of Rossetti banished to Kelmscott, of Mary Zambaco and Ned continuing their hopeless, damaging relationship, of Georgie stoically standing by her often absent husband:

> I suppose you will have heard before this reaches you all about Mary's illness and how very ill she has been; though I hope it will all come right now. I did not see Ned for a fortnight, and Georgie scarcely more; it was a dismal time for all of us ... I must confess this Autumn has been a dismal time with me: I have been a pretty good deal in the house here – not alone, that would have been

pretty well, – but alone with poor Bessy . . . I am so glad to have Janey back again: her company is always pleasant and she is very kind & good to me – furthermore my intercourse with G[eorgie] has been a good deal interrupted not from any coldness of hers . . . but from so many untoward nothings: then you have been away so that I have had nobody to talk to about things that bothered me: which I repeat I have felt more than I, in my ingratitude, expected to: another quite selfish thing is that Rossetti has set himself down at Kelmscott as if he never meant to go away; and not only does that keep me away from that harbour of refuge, (because it is really a farce our meeting when we can help it) but also he has all sorts of ways so unsympathetic with the sweet simple old place that I feel his presence there is a kind of slur on it.[13]

Morris's openness with Aglaia indicates the intimacy of their relationship and Morris's obvious need for close female companionship. But there is little evidence that this closeness developed into anything more profound or sexual. But there was another woman with whom he did develop a relationship that went further: Georgie Burne-Jones.

From the very first moment she met Morris, Georgie had considered him attractive. They encountered one another at the Royal Academy, in front of Millais's picture *The Rescue*: 'He was very handsome of an unusual type – the statues of medieval kings often remind me of him – and at that time he wore no moustache, so that the drawing of his mouth, which was his most expressive feature, could be clearly seen.'[14]

As Morris got to know Georgie through Ned, despite his apparent lack of initial interest, his affection for her grew and grew. By the time their respective marriages were in tatters their affections for one another were well established, and the fact that they were in such similar positions much have invited them to console one another.

In light of this, it is tempting to speculate that the 'Novel on Blue Paper' that Morris wrote and sent to Georgie was a comment not just on his situation with Rossetti but also on his situation with Ned. Was, in fact, the brothers' love of the same girl a reflection of his feeling for Georgie? There is some sense that Morris was only able to tolerate his wife's affair with Rossetti because his initial love of Jane had waned. If so, the passionate writing about love in Morris's unfinished novel was perhaps inspired specifically by his very strong and current feelings for Georgie.

But Georgie and Morris were not cut of the same cloth as their spouses. Georgie had a strong sense of the marriage vows she had taken, and Morris was loyal to his friends. They did not, it seems, extend this brief indiscretion into a fully flung affair. Instead they became companions.

Morris would visit The Grange regularly. Most weekends he would be at the Burne-Joneses' Sunday breakfast table, as much to see Georgie as to see Ned. He would write to Georgie in a vein that Jane Morris was never privileged to enjoy, and give her gifts and tokens of affection that held more heart-felt significance than anything offered to other friends. When Morris went to Iceland that first Kelmscott summer, it was Georgie who received a copy of the journal he had written while there.

Ruskin really did put Rose out of his life. His decision to give up his pursuit of her came not long before his mother let go of her great love for him, although it was only death that finally loosened her grip. With both parents dead, the house that had once held such comfort for Ruskin lost its appeal. Denmark Hill was sold.

After the disappointment with Percy, Joan finally married, and now the house Ruskin had once shared with Effie in Herne Hill was given over to his loyal cousin and her new spouse, the water-colour painter Arthur Severn. Meanwhile Ruskin had acquired a new property away from the scrutiny of London society: Brantwood in the Lake District, on the shores of Coniston Water.

And yet, although Ruskin had in every sense moved on from Rose, their story was not yet ended. In 1872 Ruskin made one of his habitual trips to the continent, but while away the extraordinarily unpredictable Rose La Touche took the melodrama of their on-off relationship to a new height. Beyond expectation, she decided that she wanted to see Ruskin again and approached his friends to this end.

Quite what kind of figure Rose must have cut at this stage in her life is not hard to imagine. Years of stress and mental illness had left her weak and nervous. Many have suggested that she was anorexic and had been for years; her extremely slight physique had certainly always appealed to Ruskin, and it is tempting to hypothesize that this particular disorder, which so often suppresses the development of fuller womanly attributes such as breasts and hips, may well have heightened Rose's appeal to the sexually averse Ruskin.

Rose, now often in England on long sojourns for the sake of her health, wrote to George and Louisa Macdonald, mutual friends of Ruskin and her parents. Sensing Rose's renewed interest in Ruskin, the Macdonalds wrote to him, and in the summer of 1872 Ruskin came flying back across Europe to spend three whole days with the young woman whom he had not seen in six years.

It was an utterly blissful reunion. The two, inseparable, walked in gardens together, boated and picnicked. Locked in each other's company, Ruskin and Rose seemed to slip back into their former relationship. After this reunion they met again for the day at the Cowper Temples, and here Ruskin even managed to steal a kiss.

But Rose's years of illness and anxiety had exaggerated her neuroses. And just as the strange tug-of-war between Ruskin and her parents had served to unhinge Ruskin, so they had also unhinged her. For Rose the proximity and affection of Ruskin were a comfort as long as they did not engage with actual desires for the future. While they remained dreamy, she found solace in them; once Ruskin pressed the practical application of a domestic life together, of marriage and sex, then the real implications of the relationship became unbearable for her. Once she addressed the harsh realities of real life, then all became troublesome once more.

After spending time together, Ruskin and Rose separated. She travelled to relatives in Toft in Cheshire, and Ruskin, miserable, returned to Herne Hill. But his torpor was broken when two letters, both from Rose, arrived begging him to join her in Toft. He ran to the train at Euston and was with her again that night.

The couple now spent a further weekend together at Toft. Ruskin read nothing but mutual feeling into Rose's needy request for him to join her, and so on the Sunday, as they attended the village church together, Ruskin slipped a letter into Rose's hand. In it he once again asked her if she would marry him. He felt that every indication had been given to him that this request would come as no surprise.

He could not have been more wrong. The couple left Toft together and took a train to Crewe, where they were due to separate. During the whole journey Ruskin was subjected to Rose screaming at him in a bitter and furious attack. Hysterical, she left him no opportunity to speak, but her horror of his past spouted from her as though she was possessed. In no uncertain terms she rejected his latest proposal, and then at Crewe she simply left him.

Ruskin, stunned, carried on to London but, weak and distraught, was unable to return home and checked into the Euston Hotel. He stayed there nearly a week in a state of total collapse, his world once again having imploded around him. He wrote to Rose asking her to explain herself. Finally a packet arrived from Ireland – she simply returned his letters unopened.

Ruskin could only conclude that Rose was mad. The separation at last seemed final. Ruskin went abroad once more, to Italy, and concentrated on Botticelli and other painters. Although Rose constantly crept back into his thoughts, he fought against her intrusion into his mind.

And then in 1874 came the final twist in the tale. Since her mad outburst on the train to Crewe, her life has been defined by solitary stays in hotels and sanatoriums in the name of improving her health – which had done nothing but deteriorate. At their wits' end, her parents had finally given up any resistance to Ruskin. Exhausted by everything, they simply wanted their daughter to find some happiness amid the pain and illness that now defined her. Rose had proved herself nothing but a wilful handful: defiant, inappropriate and now a burden in her sickness, they realized that keeping Ruskin at bay could have little effect. Rose was beyond marriage. She was beyond hope. In 1874 Rose wrote to Ruskin and asked him to marry her.

Ruskin met Rose in the London Hotel, where she was staying. For six months Ruskin visited her there daily and played out a quiet domestic fantasy of tea and chats. Whereas before there had been real purpose in Ruskin's pursuit of Rose, he now instinctively understood that it was impossible. And so he played along with Rose's pretended wishes, complicit in making plans for a marriage that although now finally agreed, everyone understood would never be. In February 1875 Rose's illness worsened. Self-starved, she was no longer lucid. Ruskin kept a bedside vigil:

> Of course she was out of her mind in the end. One evening she was raving violently into the night; they could not quiet her. At last they let me into her room. She was sitting up in bed. I got her to lie back and lay her head in my arms as I knelt . . . they left us and she asked me if she should say a hymn, and she said 'Jesus lover of my soul' to the end. And then fell asleep. And I left her.[15]

He did not see Rose again. Somehow her family took her back to Ireland, and she died in May 1875. She was just twenty-seven years old. The week of her death is ripped from Ruskin's diary. On the day of her death Ruskin simply drew two hawthorn leaves in his journal. Hawthorn had long been the emblem of hope, its branches carried in the wedding processions of the ancient Greeks. The Celts were supposed to have used hawthorn to heal broken hearts.

*

In the summer of 1873 Morris set sail once more for Iceland. Jane returned to Kelmscott, where Rossetti had spent the winter. The tone of their stay together was quite different. Kelmscott had become to all intents and purposes Rossetti's residence and in doing so had acquired some of the attributes of chaos that were part and parcel of his life. A dog was now in residence, and a string of models – both local and from London – began to disturb the medieval manor's former seclusion. Rossetti's few remaining close friends were also around: the Browns came to stay, his mother and sister, and Howell came down with Alexa Wilding, the ravishing auburn-haired model who had posed for Rossetti's nude *Venus Verticordia*.

Alexa sat for *La Ghirlandata* (or *The Garlanded Lady*), a painting intended for Rossetti's client Mr Graham, with whom he had stayed in Perthshire during the darkest days of his breakdown a year earlier, and a work supposed to show the hypnotic power of women. Rossetti intended to paint deep blue monkshood in the foreground of the picture. This symbolic reference was perhaps intended as a warning against infatuation. Love could be a fatal drug, as Rossetti well knew. But Rossetti's focus was a little frayed around the edges. He painted larkspur instead.

His conversations with Alexa were clearly intimate and personal during the days she sat for the painting. Much of them concerned the fate of Fanny Cornforth. Recently widowed, Fanny was still holed up in Tudor House. She had not seen Rossetti for months and feared the worst in terms of her own fate at his hands. Either out of some form of spite or out of genuine friendly concern, the minute that Alexa got back from Kelmscott she tracked down Fanny and told her in no uncertain terms that her fears were well founded. Rossetti was not coming back to Fanny, and his support for her would end.

Fanny had anticipated this and had begun to remove valuable items from Tudor House: vases and sketches were secreted away, and she even buried more robust items in the garden. Rossetti knew what was going on, probably because his assistant Dunn, who did not get on with Fanny, was providing intelligence. Rossetti looked on at Fanny's antics with benign amusement and spent many a long hour over this summer attempting to calm her.

Over the course of the summer Fanny became increasingly frustrated. At one point she attempted to come to Kelmscott to see him, but Rossetti, unable to face the encounter between her and Jane, refused to allow it. It is hard to know what place Fanny held in Rossetti's heart any more. Over this summer another of his clients, Mr Rae, had returned a picture of Fanny – *Fazio's Mistress* – to be glazed. Rossetti found himself thrown back in time by the picture, back to the era when Fanny had reigned supreme in Tudor House and in his affections. 'I have got an old picture of you here which I painted many years ago', he wrote to her. 'It is the one where you are seated doing your hair before a glass ... but I am not working at all on the head, which is exactly like the funny old elephant, as like as any I ever did.'[16] But although this image of an earlier version of Fanny clearly encouraged tenderness towards her, she was also obviously becoming a burden on a man barely able to cope. Much altered from the dashing, confident cove so full of panache and devil-may-care ways, Rossetti now stayed away from London as much to avoid confronting Fanny as to avoid critics or gossips.

Morris returned from Iceland in September. He too came back a much-changed man. He was no longer the innocent, funny Pooh Bear who could be the butt of jokes and pushed around. Somehow in the period between his return from Iceland and the spring of 1874 Morris decided he had had enough.

He said little, but he acted. First he dissolved the firm as it was constituted, as Morris, Marshall, Faulkner & Co. and reconstituted it under his sole ownership. In doing so he broke the formal business ties he held with Rossetti, as well as with Brown and, of course, Ned. Although the split with Brown was hugely acrimonious and ended their friendship, it nevertheless achieved exactly what Morris wanted. The firm was his and his alone.

Then, in April 1874, Morris wrote a terse note to Rossetti. He must have known that, despite its brevity, it would at once explode his world. In it was included a cheque for his share of the Kelmscott rent.

My dear Gabriel,

I send herewith the £17.10 to you ... As to the future though I will ask you to look upon me as off my share & not to look upon me as shabby for that, since you (may) have fairly taken to living at Kelmscott, which I suppose neither of us thought the other would do when we first began the joint possession of the house; for the rest I am both too poor &, by compulsion of poverty, too busy to be able to use it much in any case and I am very glad if you find it useful & pleasant to you.[17]

Morris was pulling out of the Kelmscott arrangement. In doing so, he was also withdrawing Rossetti's unfettered access to Jane. With her husband no longer a co-tenant, the pretence under which Jane had been able to live at Kelmscott was removed. As though to ram the point home, he even took Jane away himself, on a trip to Bruges that retraced the journey they had made on their honeymoon.

Morris must also have known that Rossetti was struggling financially and could not possibly cope with taking on the full rent. But in some ways the blow dealt by him could not have been more timely. Rossetti's days at Kelmscott were numbered anyway. The old troubles were coming back.

It may well be that Rossetti's paranoid delusions had never entirely left him. He had remained very concerned about conspiracies. An opened letter from Jane arrived at Kelmscott one day, and Rossetti was quick to see this not as an accident of the postal service but as evidence that he remained at the centre of some planned personal persecution.

These paranoid concerns had severe consequences. Although Brown and Howell visited, and Scott was still part of the circle of concerned comrades, other friends were dismissed from Rossetti's orbit. Cruelly, both Swinburne and Ned suffered the fate of Robert Browning and were edited out. 'A sad inertia slowly changed him,' Georgie recalled in her memoirs, 'and soon Edward had to realize that all the joy in their intercourse belonged to the past.'

Most indicative, though, of the continuation of some form of madness was that Rossetti continued to hear voices. In the spring of 1874 he and Hake were walking in Kelmscott when he thought he heard a group of fishermen talking about his private affairs. He confronted them, and some form of ugly tussle ensued. If there had been no gossip in the village before, there certainly was now.

Other personal tics were all too predictable. Rossetti's addiction to chloral and whisky continued. So too did his odd timekeeping. Rossetti was inhabiting the shadowlands once more: often up until daybreak, then asleep until the afternoon. He had become grossly fat too.

In July Rossetti gave up his lease of Kelmscott and left its mellow stone walls for the last time. In a marvellous piece of uncharacteristic sleight of hand, Morris, obviously not as impoverished as he had claimed, retrieved the lease once more. The whole business was over, but so too were the lingering threads of friendship between these two men who had once believed they were destined for everlasting mutual admiration.

Rossetti returned to London, but only briefly. His affairs were still in chaos. Howell had taken advantage of the situation: on the promise of raising funds for Fanny he had removed paintings and drawings, which had then simply evaporated. Fanny had suspected Howell of double-dealing for some time and had been nagging Rossetti about it. Rossetti had brushed her away. Now, however, the fact that he had been taken for some kind of a ride was obvious. Ruskin, Morris and Ned had all fallen out with Howell by now and were all persuaded that he was a charlatan. Rossetti, strangely, forgave him. 'I have only to say that I consider you, after some 9 or 10 years' intercourse a very good-natured fellow and a d–d bad man of business', he wearily wrote.[18] Perhaps he saw too much of himself in this man.

The relationship with Jane continued for a while, but it was never the same again. A year after he left Kelmscott, Rossetti leased a house by the seaside in Bognor – Aldwick Lodge. Here he envisaged that Janey and he might continue something akin to the freedoms that they had enjoyed at Kelmscott. Here he would paint a great picture of her as the goddess of love Venus Astarte.

Jane had seen Rossetti changing. She knew of his addictions and deficiencies now. She was more cautious. Although she did come for extended visits and sit for the picture, she did so with less abandon than before. Gradually her feelings for him were cooling. As Jane moved slowly away, Rossetti sank further into addiction and neediness. He saw fewer and fewer people. His letters in the late 1870s are an anxious deluge of notes to Jane seeking news of her and expressing concern for her health. His need for her is clear. Her reticence is also evident. Finally Jane ended the affair in 1876. She and Rossetti agreed to burn their letters.

Venus Astarte is perhaps Rossetti's most mannered portrayal of Jane. In it she is raised to a new dimension, more greatly idealized and idolized. Her figure is large and muscular. She is a goddess, after all, and the embodiment of sex or love. Yet the artist's sensual engagement with the image is complex. Venus stares out of the picture with a blank, cool expression. There is a callousness in her lack of sympathy for the onlooker. This is a Venus without pity, who could emasculate the men who dared approach her if she so chose.

And certainly it must have reflected the emasculation Gabriel now felt. Although he longed for Jane and female companionship, he had become an enfeebled invalid who could no longer play the lover properly. One of the very last times the former lovers were together Rossetti was unable even to see Jane out of the carriage and through her garden gate. Although Rossetti was barely fifty, he was like an old man.

Without Jane, Rossetti descended into a hell from which he

never returned. His illness and drug-dependency, played out in various retreats, by the sea and with kind patrons, worsened. He tried unsuccessfully to shake the addiction to chloral, always returning to his nightly doses, which left him stumbling drunk and disoriented until sleep finally fell upon him.

Whether he was alone in Tudor House with only the disgruntled Fanny to care for him or hidden away by the sea, many of Rossetti's friends had ceased to call on a man whose nocturnal habits and daytime slumber were out of step with normal life. He became to all intents and purposes a recluse.

With the end of the last great love affair between Rossetti and Jane the wider story that had begun in the year of revolution found its end. The final twist in the intertwining fates of a group of young people who had found and inspired one another had finally come undone. Freed from the knot of intense interwoven relationships, the Pre-Raphaelites had run their course, and their ways were now once again separate.

In an era before Freud and Jung the potency of the Pre-Raphaelites' work had been its ability to grip and fascinate its audience at an almost instinctive level. Their dreamlike pictures and poems, in retelling ancient myths and legends, interrogated concerns that were shared at a deeply profound level. The simple, mundane frailty of the protagonists in this saga aligned them with the myths they themselves felt compelled to retell. Within the narrative of their own personal biographies were versions of Launcelot and Guinevere's betrayal of Arthur, of Dante's infatuation with Beatrice, of the tragedy of Phyllis and Demophoon, or Pluto and Proserpine. The men and women in this story were all extraordinary. But their combined tale tells us that, in spite of their greatness, they were all only too human. Human weakness is at the heart of their tale.

In spite of his terrible state, in the very last years of what turned out to be his short life Rossetti found himself once again pouring out poetry. He had done this during the height of his love affair with Lizzie and during his illicit affair with Jane and their first year at Kelmscott together. Now, though, as he wrote for an envisaged new collection, he found himself in a different mood. There was no muse to hand any longer, no Jane nor Lizzie. As he knew only too well, now all he had were his memories.

Epilogue

IN 1888 THE Royal Academy held an Old Masters exhibition. The attendant great and good were captured by the painter Henry Jamyn Brooks. In his depiction of the event Brooks painted, to the left of the picture, a senior-looking bald man. Clean-shaven, oval-faced but stocky, the man appears in rude health. His dress is sharp but unostentatious. He might be an eminent banker. In fact this was John Everett Millais – at fifty-nine the epitome of the establishment.

After his marriage to Effie, Millais's success did nothing but escalate. Paintings such as *Ophelia* and *The Order of Release* secured him a huge following. He continued to dazzle his public with other imagined moments caught in time: *The Blind Girl*, resting by a road side, unable to see the rainbows of hope behind her; a group of young girls burning fallen foliage, silhouetted by a sunset that made *Autumn Leaves* a haunting, melancholic contemplation of mortality. These were two of many memorable pictures.

Millais's work, with its sharp sense of the narrative moment and its strong characterization, made him the artist of choice to illustrate the many magazines and journals that were being launched for a rapidly expanding, highly literate middle class. The combination of his mass-market work and his commissioned pictures meant that in his late middle age Millais was commanding a huge income – around £30,000 a year – and living in a handsome home in Kensington. He had become a brand of considerable potency. His celebrity was enormous.

Millias's reputation had also spread beyond British shores. As early as the 1850s he had been showing in Paris, but in 1878 he sealed his international reputation when he won the gold Médaille d'Honneur at the Exposition Universelle in Paris and was consequently given the Légion d'Honneur. In 1885 the Prime Minister, William Gladstone, made him a baronet.

A year after receiving this hereditary honour Millais painted the picture that subsequently accounted for the downfall of his reputation. This was *Bubbles* – a portrait of his grandson staring up at a large soap bubble he has just blown through a clay pipe. A sentimental picture, it stands in stark contrast to much of his other work, but its inherent popular appeal was not missed by the publication that had always lauded Millais. The *Illustrated London News* snapped it and its copyright up and published it in its Christmas edition of 1887. The Pears Soap company then bought the picture from the *Illustrated London News* and exploited the power of the Millais brand to their own ends. It was their own way of claiming a celebrity endorsement for their product and has remained one of the most famous advertising campaigns of all time. But the use of the picture served to categorize Millais among subsequent generations, wrongly, as primarily a commercial illustrator.

Whatever effect *Bubbles* had on Millais's subsequent reputation, it did not interfere with his continued elevation in his own time. In February 1896 he was given the ultimate accolade that the art establishment could bestow when he was made the President of the Royal Academy – a position held for life.

It was a position he barely enjoyed. Years of pipe-smoking had encouraged throat cancer. Just three months after taking on the role Millais was given an emergency tracheotomy by the celebrated surgeon Frederick Treves. By August he was dead.

He was buried in St Paul's Cathedral. One of the pall-bearers was his lifelong friend William Holman Hunt. On 22 August, *Punch* printed its own homage to Millais:

At last Death brings his Order of Release,
And our great English painter lies at peace ...

Men love the man, and Art the artist crowned.
The brush that pictured poor Ophelia drowned.

Although Effie naturally enjoyed the same material comforts as her husband, her own place in the public imagination was somewhat differently construed. She remained tainted by the Ruskin scandal for the rest of her life. The story of her flight had acquired mythical status. Long after the event the facts of the incident has been forgotten, but versions of the story continued to circulate at home and abroad.

In 1889, for example, a pamphlet reprinted from a New England newspaper began circulating in the USA. Entitled *Ruskin's Romance*, with a fabulous degree of misinformation the pamphlet cast Ruskin as a benign and honourable fool who had allowed Effie and Millais to fall in love, had sanctioned their marriage and had 'stood beside the couple in one of London's quiet churches and saw them made man and wife'. Then, the pamphlet alleged, he became a 'welcome guest and almost daily visitor to the man and woman whose lives he so unselfishly crowned with happiness'.[1]

The lingering appeal of the tale prevented Effie from enjoying the social success she had briefly achieved in her first marriage. This was exemplified most cruelly by Queen Victoria's persistent refusal to receive her, despite the royal family's genuine affection for her husband. This particular slight was something that Millais attempted to repair, begging the Queen to receive his wife, which she did only when it became his dying wish.

Effie's brother Sir Albert Gray took it upon himself to attempt to restore Effie's reputation. In 1898 he began to a campaign to correct what he felt were libellous and incorrect statements made about Effie in W.G. Collingwood's biography of Ruskin. After Gray it was Effie's son John Guille Millais who, a decade later, took over as guardian of her reputation. In his biography of his father he felt compelled to note that 'on behalf of those who loved their mother well, it may surely be said that during the course of judicial proceedings instituted by her, and throughout the period of the void marriage and the whole of her after years, not one word could be, or ever was, uttered impugning the correctness and purity of her life.'[2]

Effie outlived her husband by just a year. On 24 December 1897 the *Daily News* brought its readers news of Lady Millais's demise, recounting that she had been 'in her time one of the most brilliant and most hospitable among London hostesses' and that before her marriage to John Ruskin a friend had described her as 'then fresher and brighter than Millais shows her as the wife in *Order of Release*'.

William Holman Hunt never became a member of the establishment in the same way as Millais. He had been refused membership of the RA in 1856, and from this point he determinedly ploughed his own furrow. His experiences in the Holy Land had had a profound effect on him, and as he cemented his reputation as the leading religious painter of his generation, his need to be repeatedly exposed to the real landscapes and peoples of the biblical lands became paramount, alongside an instinct to imbue his work with the essence of the exotic East.

Hunt eventually got over his penchant for slutty girls and finally married one of the respectable kind that the Combes had tried to persuade him towards all that time ago. On 28 December 1865 he married Fanny Waugh at Paddington. It was his old PRB colleague Thomas Woolner who had introduced them. The daughter of an eminent and wealthy chemist, George Waugh, who was druggist to the Queen, Fanny was a well-noted beauty whom Woolner had himself been courting. But when Fanny refused him, Hunt made his move. Woolner ended up marrying Fanny's sister Alice.

The Waugh family were unsure about Hunt's pedigree. The whiff of scandal clung to him. The tale of Annie Miller and his astonishing extended relationship with her was still in circulation. When Hunt was confronted and had to confess all to Mrs Waugh, she was utterly horrified. But Fanny was getting on in Victorian terms – her thirtieth birthday was behind her – and so eventually and extremely reluctantly the Waughs gave their approval for the marriage.

Their concerns over the unsuitability of the union were confirmed when, just weeks after the wedding, *Punch* featured Hunt's work in an extended satire called 'The Legend of Camelot'. This high-profile and long-running jab at Hunt and the women who sat for him took the form of a ballad extending across six volumes and running from the issues of 3 March through to that of 31 March. The central reference of the ballad was to Hunt's famous portrayal of Annie Miller as the Lady of Shalott with her long wild hair wrapped around her.

The Waughs were not amused. Amid the family's disappointment, Fanny and Hunt decided to head off east. Fanny was in fact heavily pregnant by the time they left, however, and the pair got no further than Florence. Here, after a difficult and long labour, their baby was delivered by some form of rudimentary procedure. Fanny did not last long. A few days after her son Cyril was born, she was dead and Hunt was already a widower.

Cyril was taken in by the Waughs, but their already heavily strained relationship with Hunt hit rock bottom a few years later, when Hunt and Fanny's younger sister Edith – who bore a strong resemblance to the deceased – announced their love for one another and intention to marry. Marriage between brothers- and sisters-in-law was illegal, and had been since 1835. Although there was no genetic relationship, the prevailing view of the day was that those connected by marriage were related to each other, and that any relationship between them would be incestuous.

Both Edith's and Hunt's families disowned them, and Woolner never spoke to Hunt again. But despite this, the lovers circumvented the legal barrier to their union and married in Switzerland in 1875. In spite of his irregular second marriage, Hunt went on to be the defining religious painter of his generation. *The Shadow of Death,* his image of a young Christ in a pose prescient of the Crucifixion, became the stable print in schools and churches.

In 1892, in his mid-sixties, Hunt made his final trip to Palestine. He died in Kensington in 1910 at the age of eighty-three, but not before writing a long and detailed account of the Pre-Raphaelite movement. This he dedicated to Edith, as 'one of my insufficient tributes to her whose constant virtues ever exalt my understanding of the nature and influence of womanhood'. In its lengthy obituary *The Times* noted that Hunt had contributed to the campaign to overturn the law forbidding a widower marrying his deceased wife's sister. This was done in 1907, to his approval.

Ned Burne-Jones did not exhibit any work at all between 1870 and 1877. After his resignation from the Old Watercolour Society over his Demophoon picture, Ned knew he was a mere hair's breadth away from seeing his own work and private life being subjected to a thorough public raking-over. So he took a leaf out of Rossetti's book and worked on quietly and steadily for the liberal-minded private clients who continued to admire his work.

It was only the establishment of the Grosvenor Gallery in Bond Street in 1877 that encouraged him finally to submit his work once again for wider scrutiny. The gallery, established by a rich enthusiast, Sir Coutts Lindsay, was set up with the overt intention of showing more progressive, challenging work than the RA. And so within this benign environment Burne-Jones revealed his hand. Eight pictures were hung together, including some that were to become signature pieces: *The Beguiling of Merlin* and *The Mirror of Venus.* The public and critics were taken quite by surprise. No one had any idea that his work had progressed so. They suddenly all recognized him as a genius.

The heralding of Ned as the new bright light of English art had an almost instant effect. The area in which he lived and worked became the centre of the new Bohemia. The PRBs were now gone, and in their place emerged PBs – so called for living and working in what was termed 'Passionate Brompton'. In 1885 the RA made an important gesture to Ned and elected him an Associate, but it was an honour that he neither sought nor set much store by. Having exhibited at the Academy just once, he finally resigned from it in 1893.

One accolade that Ned did accept, however, was a baronetcy in 1894. As a Bohemian and an anti-establishment figure, his acceptance of the honour caused embarrassment among his friends. He took the title, he told everyone, for the sake of his son Phil, but he still could not bring himself to tell Morris about it face to face. Morris, by now a staunch socialist, read the news in his morning paper with utter incredulity, such was the growing distance between him and his lifelong friend – despite their continued habit of spending Sundays together.

It was not just Morris from whom Ned grew more distant in his old age. The wounds of the Mary Zambaco affair never properly healed, and Georgie and Ned, although continuing to live together, did so unhappily. Ned briefly sought reprieve from his defunct marriage with a return to Mary in 1888, when she took a studio next to his own at The Grange. But by the early 1890s Mary was replaced in Ned's affection by May Gaskell. He fell madly in love with this socialite in her late thirties, who was married with children, and wrote to her daily, often more than once; his passion for her only highlighted his lack of rapture with his own plain wife.

The utter tragedy of the Burne-Jones relationship was spelt out most forcefully when Ned revealed to May that he had had only eleven years of true happiness in his life, and those were from the late 1850s: 'years of the beginning of art in me and Gabriel every day, and Ruskin in his splendid days and Morris every day and Swinburne every day, and a thousand visions in me always more real than the outer world.'[3]

Under these circumstances Georgie could do little but throw herself into other things, and she did so with formidable energy.

She embraced socialism and local politics, spurred on by the man who had become to all intents and purposes her second husband: William Morris. Ned and Georgie bought a country home in 1880 in Rottingdean, on the south coast. Here in the mid-1890s Georgie was elected a parish councillor. She also joined the council of management of the South London Fine Art Gallery, a community-based project that under Georgie's stewardship set up a library for the locals.

Like Morris, Georgie was vociferous in her views, which became particularly radical. She also shared Morris's readiness to make her opinions quite public, whatever the consequences. When the Boer War broke out, Georgie outraged her patriotic neighbours by hanging a banner outside the house in Rottingdean that read, 'We have killed and also taken possession'. Her nephew Rudyard Kipling, who lived in the same village, had to quell a potential riot.[4]

Ned died quite suddenly in 1898. In the middle of the night of 16 June he called out, and when Georgie came to him he passed away quickly in her arms. They were quite alone.

Once Ned was dead, Georgie set about writing his biography. The work remains a brilliant, vivid and generous account of their life together. Mary Zambaco is never mentioned. Georgie lived well into the next century and died in February 1920.

In the same way that Georgie and Ned ploughed on together, so Jane and William Morris also remained married, but after the Rossetti saga it was clear that they too could only do so on the understanding that they should live as separate lives as possible. For Morris the tragedy of his relationship was not just his wife's betrayal of him with such a close friend, but ultimately his realization that he himself had never truly loved her.

Jane and Morris were struck by tragedy in 1876, when their eldest daughter, Jenny, suffered an epileptic fit, the start of what would prove to be an utterly debilitating affliction. Jane, who had played nurse for Rossetti at Kelmscott, was now forever cast in this role. The burden of her disabled daughter became something that sank her into periodic illnesses.

While Jane would spend much time away from London and Morris, holidaying with friends or at Kelmscott with the girls, Morris threw his energy into work. Morris & Co. was a success, and its repertoire expanded to include wallpaper design, dyeing and weaving. The influence of Morris's own designs is almost impossible to quantify. They have become part of the fabric of English life. Morris's career as a poet also continued, and his recognition and fame within his own day made him the natural successor to Tennyson as poet laureate. Although this accolade was offered to Morris in 1892, he declined it.

From the late 1870s the focus of Morris's energies began to turn towards politics. One of the earliest expressions of this was his foundation of the Society for the Protection of Ancient Buildings in 1877. A man who always claimed he was 'born out of his time' could no longer bear to stand by and watch the old world demolished in the name of progress, and so he began a campaign to save and protect buildings that were part of the English heritage.

Morris's natural inclination towards campaigning, and his deep involvement with the role of the working men in his firm, led him towards socialism. He and his daughter May became founder members of the British socialist movement. In 1883 he joined the Social Democratic Federation, and a year later founded his own breakaway party, the Socialist League, which published its own magazine, *Commonweal,* and would often hold open-air gatherings where Morris became known as an ardent and persuasive public speaker.

In 1887 Morris was arrested after a demonstration in London. In the same year he also participated in what became known as Bloody Sunday, a huge socialist demonstration in Trafalgar Square in which three people were killed. Morris spoke at the funeral procession of one of the victims, Alfred Linnell.

It was his engagement with politics that returned Morris to

prose writing. In 1889 he wrote a Utopian novel, *News from Nowhere*, that featured the story of a Victorian socialist who falls asleep by the grimy banks of the Thames in industrial London only to awake in a dreamlike, verdant future where men and women are free and equal.

In January 1891 Morris's enthusiasm found yet another outlet when he founded the Kelmscott Press, with the ambition of raising printing and book design to a new level of artistic recognition. Seeking to create a holistic product in which the methods of printing, the type of illustration, the choice of typeface, paper and ink all contributed to a highly crafted product, the Kelmscott Press became the most famous of the private presses of the Arts and Crafts Movement, a movement of which Morris was the undisputed heart. It operated until 1898 and produced fifty-three works, among which were exquisite editions of *The Nature of Gothic*, by John Ruskin, and *The Works of Geoffrey Chaucer*, illustrated by Burne-Jones.

By 1896 Morris had developed kidney disease, and his health was failing. As his condition declined, Ned and Georgie were with him almost daily, as was Philip Webb, who had built him his Red House so many years earlier. On the morning of 3 October Morris died at his London home.

Ned was distraught. They had grown into old men who held different views, but their utter devotion to one another had never faltered. 'What should I do, or how should I get on without him?' Ned wondered. 'I should be like a man who has lost his back.'[5]

Morris's body was not placed in St Paul's Cathedral, like Millais's. It was laid to rest in the little graveyard in Kelmscott's country church, but not before it had travelled from London, where crowds had come out to say farewell, most notably workers from Morris's own concerns and deputations from various socialist societies. Once the body arrived at Kelmscott, it was carried to Morris's resting place on a simple farm wagon, which had been carpeted with moss and garlanded with vines and willow boughs.

Ned commissioned Morris's biography, although he did not live to see it published in 1899. He was never the same after Morris's demise.

Jane Morris did not suffer the same agony over the loss of her husband as Ned. In the days after his death she lay on her sofa in the same repose that had defined her still, silent character throughout their married life. And this was how the wealthy poet and adventurer Wilfrid Scawen Blunt found her when he came to offer his condolences. 'I am not unhappy,' she told him, 'though it is a terrible thing, for I have been with him since I first knew anything.'[6]

Jane had had an affair with Blunt some thirteen years earlier. She met him in 1883 at the home of the socialite Rosalind Howard, and Jane soon introduced him to Morris. Whether she was aware of his reputation as a Casanova or not, she soon became another of his many conquests. Like Rossetti, Blunt was obsessively fascinated by women. But unlike Rossetti, whose passion for Jane never diminished, Blunt tired of her. When staying with the Morrises at Kelmscott, Jane would signal her desire for Blunt by leaving a pansy for him. But one night Jane left her hopeful pansy only to discover that Blunt did not creep into her bed. Despite the cruelty of her second betrayal of Morris, one senses the inherent sadness that motivated Jane's willingness to sleep with Blunt.

Jane continued to spend much of her time at Kelmscott after her husband's death, and she eventually bought the manor house and grounds in 1913. Here she would preside over her memories of the past, still wearing her long Pre-Raphaelite robes, her once black hair turned a bright snow white.

The writer Richard Le Gallienne took tea with the aged Jane at Kelmscott. She gave him some quince jam. He said it was like receiving it from Helen of Troy. By January 1914 Jane was dead.

After Jane ended her affair with Rossetti in 1876, his life became plagued with legal and financial complications that his poor health and increased dependence on chloral meant he had little resilience to deal with.

After his extended stay in Bognor he returned to Tudor House, but there was much to worry him in the capital. To his horror the Buchanan affair rumbled on. Swinburne had written a riposte to Buchanan's enlarged pamphlet on the 'fleshly' school, called *Under the Microscope*, which had been published by *The Examiner*. Buchanan launched a libel case against the publishers of *The Examiner* from which Rossetti barely escaped subpoena. To everyone's dismay Buchanan won the case, to the tune of £150.

In addition to this blow, Rossetti was also facing more problems in connection with Howell. Another legal storm was brewing against Howell, who owed £40 for costumes that he ordered on Rossetti's behalf. And then in a separate incident Rossetti was presented with some drawings, apparently by him, to authenticate. They were not his work and, to his dismay, seemed to be by Howell's mistress the painter Rosa Corder. In the end Rossetti, like everyone else, severed relations with this strange man.

In 1877 Rossetti's mental health deteriorated further, and the voices and paranoid delusions he had suffered so terribly in the early 1870s returned. As before, his mental illness was accompanied by the growth of a hydrocele, and Rossetti underwent another operation, which left him bedridden for weeks. His family moved him to a new seaside retreat at Herne Bay.

Fanny had remained loyal all these years and nursed Rossetti during his latest relapse while he was in London, but the Rossetti family's hostility to her was increasing. While in Herne Bay, Rossetti wrote a letter to Fanny that caused a major rift in their twenty-year relationship. He indicated that such were his health and incapacity, he could no longer guarantee his financial support of her, and he certainly could not pay the rent of her official home in Royal Avenue in the short term.

Fanny saw the writing on the wall and was immediately resourceful. She returned her house keys to Rossetti and left without leaving a forwarding address. Rossetti was devastated. His mother and sister were threatening to move into Tudor House on Rossetti's return to London to care for him. But now, with Fanny gone, he realized that his 'ways' were not compatible with those of his family. Only in his desertion and solitude did he finally realize that the only companion he really sought was Fanny. He sent his assistant to track her down.

Fanny had found another man, a Mr Schott, whom she may well have met through Rossetti. Correspondence between Rossetti and Schott that pre-dates the rift suggests Schott was acting as a business agent for Rossetti in a role similar to that formerly performed by Howell. Schott and Fanny took over a public house, the Rose Tavern, in Jermyn Street.

After great efforts Rossetti managed to resume his relationship with Fanny, in spite of the fact that she became Mrs Schott in 1879. It is unlikely, given the state of his health, that the resumption of their relationship was in any way sexual. But Fanny's desertion had proved to Rossetti that, in spite of all her faults, he needed her companionship, for otherwise he was entombed in Tudor House as a solitary recluse.

At the same time they had courted Ned, the Grosvenor Gallery had also tried to persuade Rossetti to exhibit his pictures in public. But although they were successful with Ned, Rossetti remained steadfast in his refusal to show his work in public at this time. He did, however, continue to paint and in his final years completed, alongside the *Venus Astarte,* another large canvas, *The Blessed Damozel.* Although unseen, his work did not go unrecorded. The former PRB Fred Stephens continued to write up Rossetti's pictures for a public who remained eager to hear about this man who had become a mysterious myth in his own lifetime.

By 1879 Rossetti had become obese. Apart from the effects of his addictions and his chronic lack of exercise, the second operation on his hydrocele may well have involved the removal of either one or both his testicles, which would have also contributed to his increased corpulence.

Despite his declining physical condition, Rossetti managed to issue two new publications of his poetry in 1881. One was an edition of his poems that had been the centre of the 'fleshly' debate a decade earlier. Another was a collection of ballads and sonnets. Jane Morris was terrified that these publications might kickstart the 'fleshly' débâcle once more. But it seems that its time had passed. The only apparent negative response to the publication was the Gilbert and Sullivan opera *Patience*, which featured a satirical but relatively innocuous parody of Rossetti in the form of the central character, Bunthorne, a 'fleshly poet'.

In fact, Buchanan sorely regretted the awful consequences of his earlier campaign. In his own book *God and the Man*, published in the same year as Rossetti's new edition, Buchanan included the following dedication:

> TO AN OLD ENEMY.
>
> I would have snatch'd a bay leaf from thy brow,
> Wronging the chaplet on an honoured head;
> In peace and tenderness I bring thee now
> A lily-flower instead.
>
> Pure as thy purpose, blameless as thy song,
> Sweet as thy spirit, may this offering be:
> Forget the bitter blame that did thee wrong,
> And take the gift from me!

In 1881 Rossetti also finally sold a picture for public consumption. The huge work, *Dante's Dream*, was acquired by the municipal gallery in Liverpool, where it still hangs today. It is tempting to see the picture, painted around the time of Lizzie's exhumation, as a reflection of Rossetti's obsessions at this time: his memories of Lizzie and his infatuation with Jane. The painting shows the poet Dante gazing at his dead lover, Beatrice, who has long red hair like Lizzie. The floor is strewn with poppies, perhaps in a reference to the opiate that took Lizzie into the underworld. But on closer examination, Beatrice's face is undoubtedly that of Jane.

On 11 December 1881 Rossetti suffered a stroke. His family moved him to a bungalow at Birchington, on the north Kent coast. William Michael later recalled how his bedridden brother was wrapped in hot towels, with a mustard and linseed poultice on his 'loins'. The heat was an attempt to draw out the poisons circulating around in his body, the poultice presumably intended either to soothe yet another hydrocele or to deal with post-operative complications from the one he had had removed previously. His brother and a nurse rubbed his back frequently, and when Gabriel suggested he was going to die, William persuaded him he still had plenty of good work left to achieve. But for Rossetti, for whom love and companionship had been at the heart of his early creative drive, a life of lonely illness would never bear creative fruit. His little notebooks full of doodles and scrawls continued, but in this year, which proved his last, he penned the two words 'sorrowful solitude' with terrible foreboding.[7]

In early April 1882 Gabriel drew up a new will, in which he made his brother William and his mother the main beneficiaries of his estate. Ford Madox Brown, William Bell Scott, Ned Burne-Jones and Swinburne were named among nine friends to receive a drawing or memento of their choice. In addition, Jane Morris was left the largest and best chalk drawings of her in his possession, and a profile head of her hanging in his studio.

On Easter Sunday, 9 April 1882, at around nine in the evening Dante Gabriel Rossetti cried out twice, suffered some form of seizure, slumped into unconsciouness and died. He was just fifty-three years old. On 14 April the funeral was held in the parish church at Birchington. Rossetti's family were joined by George Price Boyce and Fred Stephens, among others. Burne-Jones attempted to attend, but in the end turned back at the station, apparently unwell. The Morrises were not present. Brown, who was in Manchester, could not attend but went on to design Rossetti's tombstone, in the form of an Irish cross.

Fanny, who had not been mentioned in Rossetti's will, read about his demise in the papers. She wrote to William and asked if she could say her goodbyes to Rossetti at his open coffin, but she had not been one of those notified of the funeral arrangements, and it was too late. 'Dear Madam,' William Michael wrote, 'Your letter of the 12th only reached me this morning about 9. The coffin had been closed last evening, & the funeral takes place early this afternoon – there is nothing further to be done.'[8]

On 17 April William Bell Scott received a letter from Hunt. The former PRB was bereft. 'Rossetti's death is much in my mind at present mixed up with all my thoughts. I had long ago forgiven him, and almost forgotten his offence to me, and I have long intended to call upon him . . . Illness of him and of myself hindered still more and thus our talk over the past is deferred to our meeting in the Elysian fields.'[9]

After Rose died in 1875, Ruskin fulfilled Rose's wishes and returned to Christianity. On 20 December he had attended a seance at Mrs Cowper's house, and Rose had appeared as an apparition from the other world. It was the straw he needed to grasp in his grieving.

Like Morris, Ruskin turned to politics in his third age, both in his thoughts and in his actions. When his father died, Ruskin realized that there was an inherent conflict in being rich and holding socialist views, and so he gave away much of his inheritance. Many of his drawings, including those by Burne-Jones and Rossetti, were donated to Oxford University. Part of the redistribution of his own wealth was in the form of the foundation of a charitable institution, the Guild of St George.

The guild was intended to be a band of philanthropists who, by giving up a tenth of their income, would join together to build a new kind of Utopian Britain. The guild eschewed the trappings of modern progress, such as railways and steam engines, in favour of rural cultivation and new, honest standards in living. At around the time he set up the guild, Ruskin dabbled in experiments in trade that renounced the modern commercialism he saw around him. One of the more eccentric ventures in this respect was his establishment of a teashop in Marylebone, its sign over the door painted by Arthur Severn.

In addition to his work with the guild and his teashop, through the 1870s and into the 1880s Ruskin disseminated his views through a series of letters to the workmen of Britain, under the title *Fors Clavigera*. If the guild and *Fors Clavigera* were attempts to rebuild, and do good in, a world that held little sense for the disillusioned and mentally frail Ruskin, unfortunately the latter led him into a new scandal. In 1878 Ruskin found himself embroiled in an ugly libel case that stemmed from a review he had written in *Fors Clavigera* of work shown at the new Grosvenor Gallery. Ruskin had accused James McNeill Whistler, who showed his painting *Nocturne in Black and Gold: The Falling Rocket*, of 'ask[ing] two hundred guineas for throwing a pot of paint in the public's face'. Whistler sued and won, although the court awarded him only a farthing's damages.

Although Ruskin continued lecturing, from the mid-1870s he was prone to increasingly frequent and ferocious bouts of insanity. In periods when he became delusional he would be tormented by Satan and monsters from Hell. And even when apparently lucid, his behaviour became more and more eccentric. In his later letters to the ever tolerant Mrs Cowper, he wrote in a strange, childish manner, casting himself as a naughty little boy.

Although the press began to relate news of Ruskin's mental failure, his considerable influence on the cultural thinking of his day was recognized. As his biographer and friend W.G. Collingwood noted, he was 'the first writer whose contemporaries, during his lifetime, formed societies to study his work. The first Ruskin Society was founded in 1879 at Manchester, and was followed by the Societies of London, Glasgow and Liverpool. In 1887 the Ruskin Reading Guild was formed in Scotland, with many local branches in England and Ireland, and a journal to promote study of literary and social subjects in Ruskin.'[10]

In 1884 Ruskin resigned his professorship at Oxford in protest at the university's intention to practise vivisection, which he felt was an affront to natural history and cruel to animals. His later life was played out at Brantwood, where he worked slowly on his autobiography, *Praeterita*. Ruskin continued to rail against what he saw as the damaging influences of progress, writing among other things an article that decried the intrusion of the railways into the Lake District. His cousin Joan and her husband cared for him there until, on 20 January 1900, he died of heart failure. By the time of his death Ruskin had spent the entire inheritance of £200,000 that his father had left him.

Ruskin was offered a tomb in Westminster Abbey, but he was to the end unconventional. 'If I die here,' Collingwood recalled his saying, 'bury me at Coniston. I should have liked, if it happened at Herne Hill, to lie with my father and mother in Shirley churchyard, as I should have wished, if I died among the Alps, to be buried in the snow.' And so, according to his wishes, his friends and family

> carried him on Monday night down from his bed-chamber and laid him in the study. There was a pane of glass let into the coffin-lid, so that the face might be kept in sight; and there it lay, among lilies of the valley, and framed in the wreath sent by Mr Watts, the great painter, a wreath of the true Greek laurel, the victor's crown, from the tree growing in his garden, cut only thrice before, for Tennyson and Leighton and Burne-Jones. It would be too long to tell of all such tokens of affection and respect that were heaped upon the coffin, – from the wreath of the Princess Louise down to the tributes of humble dependants, – above a hundred and twenty-five, we counted; some of them the costliest money could buy, some valued no less for the feeling they expressed. I am not sure that the most striking was not the village tailor's, with this on its label – 'There was a man sent from God, and his name was John.'[11]

Annie Miller left Mrs Stratford's establishment and moved in with her new lover in Mayfair, Captain Thomas Ranelagh Thomson, a relative of Lord Ranelagh. On 23 July 1863 they married at St Pancras Church, and Hunt's investment in her education had proved such that Anne was able to write her own name in the register. They moved into Thomson's deceased mother's house in

Richmond and by accounts lived comfortably. Both Millais and Rossetti saw her about town in her later life, and even Hunt encountered her riding in a carriage with several children on Richmond Hill.

Later Annie and her captain moved to Shoreham in Sussex. Thompson died in 1916, but Annie carried on to the grand old age of ninety and saw out the first quarter of the new century.

Ford Madox Brown finally achieved financial stability as he grew older, but never attained the heights of wealth that Millais or Hunt enjoyed. Today his best-known pictures are perhaps those with a strong dose of social realism. *The Last of England*, which he painted after seeing Thomas Woolner depart for Australia the early 1850s, is now a much loved image of Victorian emigration. And his great canvas *Work*, based on the writings of Thomas Carlyle, remains a great depiction of the Victorian social divide.

Brown's personal life was never entirely happy. His relationship with his wife, Emma, could be rather tempestuous, as his diary reveals, and this was aggravated by her reliance on alcohol as she became older. Also Brown lost his much loved and very talented son Nolly.

In the late 1870s he was commissioned by Manchester Town Hall to paint twelve murals, and this work took up much of his late career. He died on 6 October 1893 in London at the age of seventy-one and is buried in St Pancras Cemetery. His grandson was the acclaimed novelist Ford Madox Ford.

William Michael Rossetti married Brown's daughter Lucy in 1874. It was something of a surprise move for the man that many had seen as a confirmed bachelor. The rock of the Rossetti clan, he continued to work at the Inland Revenue, but although his extracurricular literary activities were often associated with the work of his eminent brother and poetess sister Christina, it would be unfair to cast him as solely dependent on his family's genius for his own literary profile. He became a well-known and well-respected critic and biographer and wrote for *The Spectator*, *Fraser's Magazine* and *The Academy*. He was a contributor to the *Encyclopaedia Britannica* and wrote biographies of Swinburne, Whistler, Walt Whitman and Shelley. He also appeared in Whistler's defence in the notorious legal case against Ruskin.

William Michael outlived his brother by some thirty-seven years, dying in February 1919. His accounts and records of the Brotherhood and its members remain an invaluable source.

After Rossetti's death Fanny Cornforth lost little time in capitalizing on the rather extensive remnants of her relationship with the painter. Although she had not been included in his will, Fanny and her new husband, Mr Schott, pursued Rossetti's estate for what they believed was Fanny's due. A year after Rossetti's demise the Schotts sent William Michael an IOU for £300, which Rossetti had offered Fanny in 1875. William Michael was nonplussed. He added up all the cheques for which he could find a record, and concluded that Fanny had received over £1,000 after 1875, as well as a considerable number of works of art. Particularly galling to William Michael was the fact that a portrait of Rossetti by George Frederic Watts, which Rossetti had not much cared for, had ended up in Fanny's hands. Apart from its considerable value, Fanny was enjoying the benefits of copyright payments from engravings made of the work.

The Schotts were nothing if not entrepreneurs, and if their claim for £300 fell on deaf ears, the Rossetti family could do little to prevent them benefiting in other ways. Soon after Rossetti's death they opened the Rossetti Gallery at 1a Old Bond Street to exhibit the extensive works Fanny had managed to acquire from her former lover. Calling cards and stationery from the gallery, preserved in the archives of Princeton University Library, indicate that by 5 May 1883 the gallery was on its third exhibition.[12]

But Fanny's days as a gallerist did far from secure her riches. Even though there is evidence that her stepson Fred Schott still had work to sell as late as 1895, she ended her life a woman of modest means. When her husband died, she became the dependant of her sister-in-law Mrs Villiers, who took care of her board and lodging in Hammersmith. In 1905 Mrs Villiers sold anything of remaining value belonging to Fanny and moved her to Brighton, where she died.

Notes

Prologue

1. W. E. Fredeman (ed.), *The Correspondence of Dante Gabriel Rossetti* (Woodbridge, 2002–6), vol.1, p. 61. Rossetti wrote to his aunt and complained that 'for the whole of the past week I have been afflicted with a return of my old atrocious boils, which has effectually precluded the possibility of my stirring out'.
2. As indicated by *Kelly's Postal Directory*, 1851
3. *The Times* (11 April 1848)
4. *Ibid.*
5. William Holman Hunt, *Pre-Raphaelitism and the Pre-Raphaelite Brotherhood*, 2nd edn, 2 vols. (Chapman and Hall, London, 1913), p. 69
6. A. H. Hamilton, *The Summer Guide to the Amusements of London; and Provincial Excursionist for 1848* (Kent and Richard, London, 1848)

Chapter 1: The dark secret

1. John Ruskin, *Praeterita and Dilecta* (Everyman's Library, New York and London, 2005), pp. 40–42
2. *Ibid.*, pp. 177–8
3. *Ibid.*, p. 40
4. *Ibid.*, p. 158
5. 'I am ... a violent Tory of the old school; – Walter Scott's school, that is to say, and Homer's. I name these two out of the numberless great Tory writers because they were my own two masters. I had Walter Scott's novels, and the Iliad ..., for constant reading when I was a child.' *Ibid.*, p. 13

6. In 1967 a debate arose in the letters pages of the *Times Literary Supplement* regarding Effie's status at the time she met Ruskin again in 1847. Malcolm D. Kennedy wrote: 'My mother told me . . . that her father, the late Lieutenant-General William Kelty Macleod, had become unofficially engaged to Effie Gray when he was a young subaltern in the 74th Highlanders, somewhere around 1845 or 1846.' *Times Literary Supplement* (30 March 1967)

7. Sir W. James (ed.), *The Order of Release: The Story of John Ruskin, Effie Gray and John Everett Millais Told for the First Time in their Unpublished Letters* (John Murray, London, 1948), p. 28

8. *Ibid.*, p. 21

9. 'The bonnets this season are quite round in front and not at all large at the ears. I see a great many cloaks of pale glacé silk with ruished [*sic*] frills round them.' *Ibid.*, p. 31

10. *Ibid.*, p. 32

11. *Ibid.*, p. 33

12. Effie's sensitivity to home comforts is apparent when she left the Ruskins in June and went to visit some other family friends, the Gardners in Sussex Gardens. She wrote, 'The Gardners I think are very kind . . . but not of so refined a class as the Ruskins', and then two days later, 'I like the family here on the whole very well but after being with the Ruskins it makes one rather particular.' Mary Lutyens, *The Ruskins and the Grays* (John Murray, London, 1972), p. 39

13. Ruskin, *Praeterita*, p. 379

14. James, *The Order of Release*, p. 38

15. Joan Evans and John Howard Whitehouse (ed.), *The Diaries of John Ruskin* (Clarendon Press, Oxford, 1956), vol. 1, p. 364

16. James, *The Order of Release*, p. 46

17. *Ibid.*, p. 48

18. *Ibid.*, p. 50

19. Lutyens, *The Ruskins and the Grays*, p. 106

Chapter 2: Long live the revolution

1. A story mentioned by both Ruskin and Millais's family is that, when stationed in Dinan in France, some soldiers were so amazed by the

sophistication of the seven–year–old Millais's work that they took some drawings into the mess to show their colleagues. The incredulous colleagues bet that no child could do such work, at which Millais was presented and drew 'live' for the assembled crowd. The doubters naturally lost the wager.

2. William Holman Hunt, *Pre-Raphaelitism and the Pre-Raphaelite Brotherhood*, p. 55

3. This is recounted by Holman Hunt's granddaughter Diana Holman Hunt in her *My Grandfather, His Wives and Loves* (Hamish Hamilton, London, 1969), p. 101

4. John Guille Millais, *The Life and Letters of Sir John Everett Millais* (Methuen & Co., London, 1890), vol. 1, p. 12

5. William Holman Hunt, *Pre-Raphaelitism and the Pre-Raphaelite Brotherhood*, p. 23

6. Ironically, the publisher John Murray turned down the opportunity to publish the first volume of *Modern Painters*; he wanted something on the Nazarenes in preference to Ruskin's tome.

7. Hamilton, *Summer Guide*. According to the Royal Academy archive, 96,944 people attended in 1850 and 136,820 in 1851. By 1869, 314,780 people where cramming in to see the show.

8. William Holman Hunt, *Pre-Raphaelitism and the Pre-Raphaelite Brotherhood*, p. 70

9. F. G. Stephens, *Dante Gabriel Rossetti*, Portfolio Artistic Monographs (Seeley & Co., London, 1894), p. 10

10. Dante Gabriel Rossetti, *The Works of Dante Gabriel Rossetti*, ed. W. M. Rossetti (Ellis, London, 1911), p. 261

11. Fredeman, *Correspondence of Dante Gabriel Rossetti*, vol. 1, p. 57

12. Holman Hunt, *Pre-Raphaelitism and the Pre-Raphaelite Brotherhood*, p. 76

13. *Ibid.*

Chapter 3: Muse and amusement

1. Pierpont Morgan Library, Bowerswell Papers, MA 1338, folder T50

2. James, *The Order of Release*, p. 138

3. *Ibid.*, p. 220
4. Pierpont Morgan Library, Bowerswell Papers, MA 1338, folder T50
5. James, *The Order of Release*, pp. 117–8
6. *Ibid.*, p. 123
7. *Ibid.*, p. 129
8. Tim Hilton, *John Ruskin* (Yale University Press, New Haven and London, 2002), p. 127
9. Pierpont Morgan Library, Bowerswell Papers, MA 1338, folder T50
10. James, *The Order of Release*, p. 137
11. Suzanne Fagence Cooper, *The Victorian Woman* (V & A Publications, London, 2001), p. 30
12. William Holman Hunt, *Pre-Raphaelitism and the Pre-Raphaelite Brotherhood*, p. 137
13. *Ibid.*
14. Carol Jacobi, 'Millais, Sex and the Synthetic Subject', *Contents, Discontents, Malcontents*, AAH Conference, Leeds, 2006
15. William Michael Rossetti, *The Pre-Raphaelites & their World* (Folio Society, London, 1995), p. 99
16. 'Art: The National Institution', *The Critic* (1 July 1850), pp. 334–5
17. Gay Daly, *Pre-Raphaelites in Love* (William Collins, Glasgow, 1989)
18. 'They were to love one another all their lives. Neither of them felt in the least self-conscious about the emotion they showed. Years later Woolner was to accuse them of being homosexuals in their youth. When Hunt wrote indignantly to Millais of this, Millais replied "I *can't* think how Woolner can have circulated any story about you and me ... nowadays, no one would have thought anything else." ' Diana Holman Hunt, *My Grandfather*, p. 38
19. Georgiana Burne-Jones, *Memorials of Edward Burne-Jones* (Lund Humphries, London, 1993), vol. 1, p. 139
20. Fagence Cooper, *The Victorian Woman*, p. 30
21. *Ibid.*
22. James, *The Order of Release*, p. 138
23. *Ibid.*, p. 146. Alice was Effie's young sister
24. *Ibid.*, p. 142
25. *Ibid.*, p. 146
26. *Ibid.*, p. 153
27. Mary Lutyens, *Effie in Venice* (John Murray, London, 1965), p. 98

28. Pierpont Morgan Library, Bowerswell Papers, MA 1338, folder K 21–34
29. Pierpont Morgan Library, Bowerswell Papers MA 1338, folder k.09
30. James, *The Order of Release*, p. 156
31. Lutyens, *Effie in Venice*, p. 134

Chapter 4: Town talk and table talk

1. *Chambers Edinburgh Journal* (July 1852)
2. *The Times* (4 May 1850)
3. F. W. Warre-Cornish, 'Dante Gabriel Rossetti – His Family Letters', *Quarterly Review* (July 1896)
4. *Ibid.*
5. *Illustrated London News* (4 May 1850)
6. Joseph Cundall, *A Glance at the Exhibition of the Royal Academy* (London, 1850)
7. *Household Words* (15 June 1850)
8. *The Ladies' Companion* (25 May 1850)
9. 'Fine-Art Gossip', *The Athenaeum* (7 December 1850)
10. *Blackwood's Magazine* (July 1850)
11. James, *The Order of Release*, p. 158
12. *Ibid.*, p. 164
13. William Michael Rossetti, *The Pre-Raphaelites & their World*, p.70
14. Fredeman, *The Correspondence of Dante Gabriel Rossetti*, vol. 1, p. 151
15. Dante Gabriel Rossetti, *The Works of Dante Gabriel Rossetti*, p. 537
16. James, *The Order of Release*, p. 162
17. Victoria and Albert Museum, *The Great Exhibition of 1851 Commemorative Album* (HMSO, London, 1964)
18. Millais, *Life and Letters*, p. 91
19. 'I have abandoned my painting and with it the idea of exhibiting this year. I have done so for various reasons, the main one being that I felt degraded every day by working on such a trifle … please don't blame me.' Fredeman, *The Correspondence of Dante Gabriel Rossetti*, vol. 1, p. 169
20. Fredeman, *The Correspondence of Dante Gabriel Rossetti*, vol. 1, p. 170

21. Colonel Sibthorp in the House of Commons, 29 July 1851. Victoria & Albert Museum, *The Great Exhibition of 1851 Commemorative Album*, p. 28

22. Figures provided by the Royal Academy archive

23. *The Times* (13 May 1851)

24. William Holman Hunt, *Pre-Raphaelitism and the Pre-Raphaelite Brotherhood*, p. 48

Chapter 5: Ophelia

1. *Burlington Magazine* (May 1903)

2. *Illustrated London News* (8 May 1852)

3. 'Our Critic among the Pictures', *Punch* (22 May 1852), pp. 216–7. As popular as *Ophelia* was Millais's *A Huguenot, on St Bartholomew's Day, Refusing to Shield Himself from Danger by Wearing the Roman Catholic Badge*. Millais depicted the tragic scene of a young Catholic woman attempting to persuade her protestant lover to disguise his faith by wearing a white tie around his arm, a Catholic symbol. The St Bartholomew's Day massacre was also the subject of a popular opera by Giacomo Meyerbeer in London at the time.

4. Fredeman, *The Correspondence of Dante Gabriel Rossetti*, vol. 1, p. 176

5. *Ibid.*, p. 181

6. *Ibid.*, p. 186

7. William Michael Rossetti, *The Pre-Raphaelites and their World*, p. 121

8. William Bell Scott, *Autobiographical Notes of the Life of William Bell Scott*, ed. W. Minto (Osgood, McIlvaine & Co, London, 1892), p. 315

9. Lutyens, *Effie in Venice*, p. 225

10. *Ibid.*, p. 319

11. Mary Lutyens, *Millais and the Ruskins* (John Murray, London, 1967), p. 12

12. *Morning Chronicle* (21 July 1852)

13. Lutyens, *Millais and the Ruskins*, p. 12

Chapter 6: The awakening conscience

1. Lutyens, *Effie in Venice*, p. 261
2. Bodleian Library, The Marriage of John Ruskin, MS Eng. Misc. d 653
3. James, *The Order of Release*, p. 197
4. The Hunt–Ruskin letters, at www.Victorianweb.org/painting/whh/HRLet/letters.html
5. Bodleian Library, Ruskin Papers, MS. Eng. Letters C 228
6. Lutyens, *Millais and the Ruskins*, p. 69
7. *Ibid.* p. 89
8. Pierpont Morgan Library, Bowerswell Papers MA 1338, folder 11–S 20 (S. 13)
9. *Ibid.* (S. 15)
10. Hilton, p. 193
11. Princeton University Library, Troxell Collection of Rossetti Manuscripts, C0189, folder 30/1
12. Victoria & Albert Museum, MSL/1998/5/1/14
13. The Hunt–Ruskin letters, www.victorianweb.org/painting/whh/HRLet/letters.html
14. James, *The Order of Release*, p. 207
15. *Ibid.*, p. 219

Chapter 7: Luscious fruit must fall

1. Antony Harrison, *The Letters of Christina Rossetti*, (University Press of Virginia, 1997), Vol. 7, p. 79
2. R. W. Crump, *The Complete Poems of Christina Rossetti*, (Louisiana State University Press, 1990), Vol. 3, p. 223
3. Fredeman, *The Correspondence of Dante Gabriel Rossetti*, vol. 1, p. 294
4. *Ibid.*, p. 207
5. Virginia Surtees, *The Diary of Ford Madox Brown* (Yale University Press, New Haven, 1981), p. 78
6. Fredeman, *The Correspondence of Dante Gabriel Rossetti*, vol. 1, p. 208
7. Once he even wrote to William asking him to return home so that

Gabriel could borrow the trousers he had on for the opera that night.

8. William Michael Rossetti, *The Pre-Raphaelites and their World*, p. 121

9. W. E. Fredeman (ed.), *The P.R.B. Journal: William Michael Rossetti's Diary of the Pre-Raphaelite Brotherhood, 1849–53* (Clarendon Press, Oxford, 1975), p. 80

10. Diana Holman Hunt, *My Grandfather*, p. 115

11. Two pictures by Millais painted in 1854, *Waiting* and *The Violet's Message*, feature Annie Miller.

12. Fredeman, *The Correspondence of Dante Gabriel Rossetti*, vol. 1, p. 335

13. *Ibid.*, p. 336

14. *Ibid.*, p. 339

15. Brown describes going to Rossetti's studios and finding whole drawers full of 'guggums'.

16. *Burlington Magazine* (May 1903)

17. *Ibid.*

18. *Ibid.*

19. *Ibid.*

20. *Ibid.*

Chapter 8: The order of release

1. Fredeman, *The Correspondence of Dante Gabriel Rossetti*, vol. 1, p. 255

2. *Ibid.*, p. 256

3. William Michael Rossetti, *The Pre-Raphaelites and their World*, p. 110. William Rossetti notes this late lunch happened on 25 April, but in a letter to William Allingham on 24 May his brother notes that he has just returned from lunching with Ruskin.

4. Fredeman, *The Correspondence of Dante Gabriel Rossetti*, vol. 1, p. 339

5. Pierpont Morgan Library, Bowerswell Papers, MA 1338 (T. 35)

6. *Ibid.* (T. 40)

7. *Ibid.* (T. 47)

8. *Ibid.* (T. 43)

9. James, *The Order of Release*, p. 228

10. *Ibid.*, p. 239

11. Pierpont Morgan Library, Bowerswell Papers, MA 1338 (UV 02)

12. *Ibid.*, MA 1338 (UV 12)

13. *Ibid.*, MA 1338 (UV 15)

14. Some are in the Pierpont Morgan Library.

15. Princeton University Library, Troxell Collection of Rossetti Manuscripts, Co189, box 30, folder 1

16. Fredeman, *The Correspondence of Dante Gabriel Rossetti*, vol. 1, p. 353

17. Ernest Gambart was a publisher and dealer.

18. Fredeman, *The Correspondence of Dante Gabriel Rossetti*, vol. 1, p. 354

19. *Ibid.*, p. 339

20. Princeton University Library, Troxell Collection of Rossetti Manuscripts, Co189, box 20, folder 10

21. Diana Holman Hunt, *My Grandfather*, p. 286

22. Surtees, *The Diary of Ford Madox Brown*, p. 101

23. Fredeman, *The Correspondence of Dante Gabriel Rossetti*, vol. 1, p. 345

24. *Ibid.*, p. 361

25. Surtees, *The Diary of Ford Madox Brown*, pp. 100–01

26. Scott, *Autobiographical Notes*, vol 1, p. 285

27. James, *The Order of Release*, p. 259

28. Violet Hunt, *The Wife of Rossetti: Her Life and Death* (John Lane and Bodley Head, London, 1932), p. 103

29. In Albert Gray's papers in the Bodleian, next to a copy of the Decree of Annulment, is a handwritten document on blue paper on which this statement appears. It appears to be a *verbatim* account of the various testimonies given during the actual court hearing on 15 June 1854 and is very similar to the handwritten *verbatim* accounts included with other court hearings (such as inquests) at this time. Bodleian Library, Ruskin Papers, MS. Eng. Letters, C 228

30. *Ibid.*

31. This decree is quoted from the Bodleian MS but is also reproduced in James, *The Order of Release*, p. 236

Chapter 9: Dim phantoms of an unknown ill

1. City of London, London Metropolitan Archive, CLA/041/1Q/03/079

2. Surtees, *The Diary of Ford Madox Brown*, p. 126

3. *Ibid.*, p. 133

4. Based on figures provided in Lee Jackson, *A Dictionary of Victorian London* (Anthem Press, London, 2006)

5. Surtees, *The Diary of Ford Madox Brown*, p. 126

6. John Ruskin, *Works*, ed. E. T. Cook and A. Wedderburn (George Allen, London, 1906), vol. 36, p. 198

7. *Ibid.*, p. 200

8. Fredeman, *The Correspondence of Dante Gabriel Rossetti*, vol. 2, p. 48

9. *Ibid.*, p. 45

10. *Ibid.*, vol. 1, p. 358, n.

11. *Ibid.*, vol. 1, p. 357

12. Jan Marsh, *Elizabeth Siddall, 1829–1862: Pre-Raphaelite Artist* (Ruskin Gallery, Sheffield, 1991), p. 31

13. Princeton University Library, Troxell Collection of Rossetti Manuscripts, Co189, folder 30,1

14. Ruskin, *Works*, vol. 36, p. 217

15. Surtees, *The Diary of Ford Madox Brown*, p. 148

16. *Morning Chronicle* (7 July 1855)

17. James, *The Order of Release*, p. 248

18. *Ibid.*

19. *Ibid.*, p. 245

20. *Ibid.*

21. *Ibid.*, p. 246

22. 'Stoneless' is a reference to Ruskin's *The Stones of Venice*, but also a *double entendre*, 'stones' meaning 'testicles' in Victorian slang. Surtees, *The Diary of Ford Madox Brown*, p. 144

23. William Holman Hunt, *Pre-Raphaelitism and the Pre-Raphaelite Brotherhood*, vol. 2, p. 86

24. *Ibid.*, vol. 2, p. 94

25. Surtees, *The Diary of Ford Madox Brown*, p. 130

26. *Ibid.*, p. 169

27. *The Times* (30 May 1856)

28. *The Times* (27 May 1856)

29. Paul Franklin Baum (ed.), *Dante Gabriel Rossetti's Letters to Fanny Cornforth* (Baltimore, 1940), p. 2

30. Scott, *Autobiographical Notes*, vol. 1, p. 314

31. Doughty quotes Rossetti's friend John Henry Middleton, Cambridge

professor and Director of the South Kensington Museum. Oswald Doughty, *A Victorian Romantic* (Frederick Muller Ltd, London, 1949), p. 255

Chapter 10: Not as she is but as she fills his dream

1. William Holman Hunt, *Pre-Raphaelitism and the Pre-Raphaelite Brotherhood*, vol. 2, p. 78
2. *Ibid.*, p. 85
3. Surtees, *The Diary of Ford Madox Brown*, p. 181
4. *Ibid.*
5. *Ibid.*
6. William Michael Rossetti, *Dante Gabriel Rossetti: His Family-Letters with a Memoir* (Ellis & Elvey, London, 1895), p. 201
7. Diana Holman Hunt, *My Grandfather*, p. 168
8. Surtees, *The Diary of Ford Madox Brown*, p. 201
9. Virginia Surtees (ed.), *The Diaries of George Price Boyce* (Real World, Norwich, 1980), p. 20
10. James Coombs (ed.), *A Pre-Raphaelite Friendship: The Correspondence of William Holman Hunt and John Lucas Tupper* (UMI Research Press, Ann Arbor, 1986), p. 52
11. Surtees, *The Diaries of George Price Boyce*, p. 32
12. Diana Holman Hunt, *My Grandfather*, p. 205
13. G.S. Layard, 'Tennyson and his Pre-Raphaelite Illustrators: A Book about a Book', quoted in Diana Holman Hunt, *My Grandfather*, p. 205
14. Diana Holman Hunt, *My Grandfather*, p. 206
15. Millais's original portrayed an old battle-worn knight returning from his quest and greeted by two young children who climb onto his weary steed. The author of this particular humorous take on the picture had Ruskin as the mule bearing Millais, with Rossetti and Hunt clinging on to his coat tails for dear life.
16. Surtees, *The Diary of Ford Madox Brown*, p. 191
17. Christina Rossetti, 'In an Artist's Studio', *The Poetical Works of Christina Rossetti*, ed. W. M. Rossetti (Macmillan, London, 1904), p. 330

18. Surtees, *The Diary of Ford Madox Brown*, pp. 195–6
19. Fredeman, *The Correspondence of Dante Gabriel Rossetti*, vol. 2, p. 172
20. *Ibid.*, p. 173

Chapter 11: New Knights of the Round Table

1. *The Times* (June 27 1856)
2. Burne-Jones, *Memorials*, vol.1, p. 128
3. *Ibid.*, p. 129
4. William Michael Rossetti, *The Pre-Raphaelites & their World*, p. 136
5. Fredeman, *The Correspondence of Dante Gabriel Rossetti*, vol. 2, p. 147
6. *Ibid.*, vol. 2, p. 195
7. William Holman Hunt, *Pre-Raphaelites and the Pre-Raphaelite Brotherhood*, vol. 2, pp. 97–8
8. Burne-Jones, *Memorials*, vol. 1, p. 169
9. *Illustrated Times*, quoted in Virginia Surtees, *The Actress and the Brewer's Wife* (Michael Russell, Norwich, 1997), p. 28
10. Fredeman, *The Correspondence of Dante Gabriel Rossetti*, vol. 2, p. 214
11. www.rossettiarchive.org/docs/msbook/huntms, rad.html#p3
12. *Ibid.*
13. Fredeman, *The Correspondence of Dante Gabriel Rossetti*, vol. 2, p. 219

Chapter 12: Since love is seldom true

1. Quoted in Jan Marsh, *Elizabeth Siddal: Pre-Raphaelite Artist*, p. 31
2. Burne-Jones, *Memorials*, vol. 1, p. 168
3. Surtees, *The Diaries of George Price Boyce*, p. 24
4. Boyce's diaries are frustratingly incomplete since the originals were lost in a fire. An edited version of the diaries, reproduced by the Old Watercolour Society, does exist, however. This still manages to give a vivid picture of the intimate and convivial relationship between Rossetti and Boyce. Given the depth of their friendship, it is a peculiar fact that the version that does exist fails to mention Lizzie Siddall by name or indeed to give any real account of her or of Rossetti's relationship with her.

5. 'Gay' here means a prostitute. Stanhope was one of the artists working with Rossetti on the Oxford murals.

6. Surtees, *The Diaries of George Price Boyce*, p. 26

7. *Ibid.*, p. 28

8. *Ibid.*, p. 28

9. Fredeman, *The Correspondence of Dante Gabriel Rossetti*, vol. 2, p. 289

10. *Ibid.*, vol. 2, p. 292

11. Marriage licence, *Ibid.*, Vol. 2. p. 292

12. Unexpurgated MS of William Bell Scott's autobiography, Pinceton University Library, Troxell Collection of Rossetti Manuscripts

13. Surtees, *Diaries of George Price Boyce*, p. 30

14. Fredeman, *Correspondence of Dante Gabriel Rossetti*, vol. 2, p. 297

15. Burne-Jones, *Memorials*, vol. 1, p. 208

16. Surtees, *The Diaries of George Price Boyce*, p. 30

17. Burne-Jones, *Memorials*, vol. 1, p. 218

18. Fredeman, *The Correspondence of Dante Gabriel Rossetti*, vol. 2, p. 330

19. Burne-Jones, *Memorials*, vol. 1, p. 220

20. Fredeman, *The Correspondence of Dante Gabriel Rossetti*, vol. 2, p. 342

21. *Ibid.*, p. 353

22. Burne-Jones, *Memorials*, vol. 1, p. 223

23. M. A. Braddon, *Lady Audley's Secret* (Tinsley Bros., London, 1862), pp. 140–42

24. Unexpurgated MS of William Bell Scott's autobiography, Princeton University Library, Troxell Collection of Rossetti Manuscripts

25. Burne-Jones, *Memorials*, vol. 1, p. 238

Chapter 13: Irish roses

1. William Michael Rossetti, *Some Reminiscences* (Brown, Langham & Co. London, 1906)

2. Evans and Howard, *Diaries of John Ruskin*, vol. 2, p. 560

3. Ruskin, *Praeterita and Dilecta*, p. 467. It seems that Ruskin, in the confusion of old age, misremembered Rose's age. Her own diary declares her nineteenth birthday on 3 January 1867, so she must have been just ten in 1858, and born in the year of Ruskin's marriage to Effie Gray.

4. In 1859, about a year after meeting Rose, Ruskin began what was to become a regular retreat to Winnington Hall in Cheshire, a girls' boarding-school.

5. Ruskin cites this letter in *Praeterita*, but seems to imply it was written in the first year he knew her. Unless Rose wrote the date wrong, 18 March fell on a Monday in 1861, and according to Rose's diaries she was indeed abroad at this time. *Praeterita and Dilecta*, p. 474

6. Hilton, *John Ruskin*, p. 310

7. Letter to his father, Boulogne, 14 July 1861, Van Akin Burd (ed.), *John Ruskin and Rose La Touche: Her Unpublished Diaries of 1861 and 1867* (Clarendon Press, Oxford, 1979), p. 50

8. A. C. Swinburne, 'A Record of Friendship' (printed for private circulation, London, 1910)

9. William Michael Rossetti quoting Swinburne in his article in the *Burlington Magazine* (May 1903)

10. Surtees, *The Diaries of George Price Boyce*, p. 34

11. Surtees, in her notes on George Price Boyce's diaries (p. 35), says this was an obscene entertainment show which took the form of parodying celebrated cases of the day, invariably those of adultery or seduction of an exceptionally depraved nature.

12. Surtees, *The Diaries of George Price Boyce*, p. 35

13. *Ibid.*, p. 36

14. *Ibid.*

15. *Ibid.*

16. Burne-Jones, *Memorials*, vol. 1, p. 147

17. *Ibid.*, vol. 1, p.232

18. Hilton, *John Ruskin*, p. 324

19. Evans and Whitehouse, *Diaries of John Ruskin*, vol. 2, p. 568

20. Akin Burd, pp. 160–164

21. *Ibid.*, p. 169

Chapter 14: The towers of Topsy

1. There were seven partners in Morris, Marshall, Faulkner & Co.: Ford Madox Brown, Morris, Burne-Jones, Rossetti and Philip Webb were joined by Morris's university friend Charles Faulkner and by Peter

Paul Marshall, a friend of Brown. Faulkner was training to be a civil engineer but worked part-time as the firm's general manager. Marshall was a surveyor, engineer and amateur artist but applied himself to making stained-glass windows for the firm.

2. Fredeman, *The Correspondence of Dante Gabriel Rossetti*, vol. 2, p. 343
3. Burne-Jones, *Memorials*, vol. 1, p. 282
4. Ruskin certainly seemed to see manifestations at some of these seances. In April 1864 he wrote to Mrs Cowper: 'I am too much astonished to be able to think, or speak yet – yet observe, this surprise is a normal state with me; and has been so, this many a day. I am not now more surprised at perceiving spiritual presence, than I have been, since I was a youth, at not perceiving it. The wonder lay always to me, not in a miracle, but in the want of it; and now it is more the manner and triviality of manifestation than the fact that amazes me.' J. L. Bradley (ed.), *The Letters of John Ruskin to Lord and Lady Mount-Temple* (Ohio State University Press, Columbus, 1964), p. 31
5. *Ibid.*, p. 52
6. *Ibid.*, p. 62
7. Evans and Whitehouse, *Diaries of John Ruskin*, vol. 2, p. 595
8. Bradley, *Letters*, p. 81
9. *Ibid.*, p. 84
10. *Ibid.*, p. 87
11. *Ibid.*, p. 97
12. *Ibid.*, pp. 102–3
13. http://www.etymonline.com/index.php?term=bohemian
14. William Rossetti, *Rossetti Papers, 1862–70* (Sands & Co., London, 1903), p. 136
15. *Ibid.*, p. 137
16. These are accounts based on interviews between Fanny and Mr Bancroft, related in Paul Franklin Baum, *Dante Gabriel Rossetti's Letters to Fanny Cornforth* (Johns Hopkins Press, Baltimore, 1940).

Chapter 15: Obsession

1. Evans and Whitehouse, *Diaries of John Ruskin*, p. 608
2. *Ibid.*

3. *Ibid.*
4. *Ibid.*, p. 610
5. *Ibid.*
6. Hilton, *John Ruskin*, p. 399
7. Bradley, *Letters*, p. 109
8. *Ibid.*
9. Evans and Whitehouse, *Diaries of John Ruskin*, p. 615
10. *Ibid.*, p. 629
11. *Ibid.*
12. *Ibid.*, p. 645
13. *Ibid.*, p. 647
14. Fredeman, *The Correspondence of Dante Gabriel Rosetti*, vol. 1, p. 291
15. In fact at this time Morris hired the very efficient George Warrington Taylor to help him manage the business.
16. British Library, Jane Morris Correspondence, ADD 52332
17. British Library, Ashley MS 1410 673 B, book 1
18. Fredeman, *The Correspondence of Dante Gabriel Rossetti*, vol. 4, p. 73
19. Burne-Jones, *Memorials*, vol. 1, p 229
20. *Ibid.*, p. 230
21. *Ibid.*, p. 236
22. *Ibid.*, p. 286
23. *Ibid.*, p. 309
24. Fredeman, *The Correspondence of Dante Gabriel Rossetti*, vol. 4, p. 147
25. Princeton University Library, Troxell Collection
26. Norman Kelvin (ed.), *Collected Letters of William Morris*, vol. 1, *1848–1880* (Princeton University Press, Princeton, 1984), p. 76
27. Scott, *Autobiographical Notes*, p. 111
28. *Ibid.*, p. 113
29. Rossetti, *Works*, p. 114
30. Fredeman, *The Correspondence of Dante Gabriel Rossetti*, vol. 4, pp. 207–8
31. *Ibid.*, p. 217

Chapter 16: Resurrection

1. Princeton University Library, Troxell Collection, C0189, box 11, folder 1
2. Rossetti wrote to Howell on 16 August saying, 'I feel disposed . . . to go in for the recovery of my poems . . . as you proposed some time ago.' Fredeman, *The Correspondence of Dante Gabriel Rossetti* vol. 4, p. 235. In a letter to his brother Gabriel also mentions Scott had also suggested this course of action.
3. *Ibid.*, p. 226
4. *Ibid.*, p. 223
5. *Ibid.*, p. 259
6. *Ibid.*, p. 235
7. *Ibid.*, p. 265
8. The wombat had been espoused by the PRBs as a mascot in the 1850s. It was often referred to in their letters, rendezvous were often convened at the 'wombat's lair' in London Zoo and during the 'jovial campaign' small wombats appeared in the Oxford frescoes.
9. Ruskin established the Guild of St George, an ambitious movement to create a Utopian society.
10. Fredeman, *The Correspondence of Dante Gabriel Rossetti*, vol. 4, p. 264
11. *Ibid.*, p. 280
12. *Ibid.*, p. 285
13. *Ibid.*, p. 299
14. *Ibid.*, p. 305
15. Her supporters were always very rigorous to point out that annulment and divorce were not one and the same, but to little avail.
16. Pierpont Morgan Library, Bowersell Papers, MA 1338, xyz 03
17. Bradley, *Letters*, p. 165
18. *Ibid.*, p. 171
19. Evans and Whitehouse, *Diaries of John Ruskin*, vol. 2, p. 685
20. Bradley, *Letters*, p. 273
21. Kelvin, *Letters of William Morris*, p. 162
22. Penelope Fitzgerald (ed.), *The Novel on Blue Paper, by William Morris* (Journeyman Press, London and West Nyack, 1982), p. 6
23. *Ibid.*, p. 7
24. *Ibid.*, p. 15

25. *Ibid.*, p. 53
26. *Ibid.*, p. 54
27. *Ibid.*, p. 72
28. Kelvin, *Letters of William Morris*, p. 133
29. Fredeman, *The Correspondence of Dante Gabriel Rossetti* vol. 5, p. 57
30. Kelvin, *Letters of William Morris*, p. 116. A member of the high-profile Ionides family, Aglaia's father was the Greek consul-general, a director of the Crystal Palace company and a notable art collector.
31. Fredeman, *The Correspondence of Dante Gabriel Rossetti*, vol. 5, p. 77
32. Kelvin, *Letters of William Morris*, p. 141
33. Fredeman, *The Correspondence of Dante Gabriel Rossetti*, vol. 5, p. 139
34. Pierpont Morgan Library, Bowerswell Papers, MA 1338, xyz 03
35. *Ibid.*, xyz 02
36. *Ibid.*, xyz 04
37. Bradley, *Letters*, p. 296
38. 'The Relation between Michelangelo and Tintoret', Cook and Wedderburn, *Works of John Ruskin*, vol. 22, p. 86
39. *Ibid.*, p. 102
40. *Ibid.*, p. 80
41. Bradley, *Letters*, p. 109

Chapter 17: Torments of the flesh

1. Jan Marsh, *Pre-Raphaelite Sisterhood* (Quartet, London, 1985), p. 298
2. William Michael Rossetti, *Family-Letters*, vol. 1, pp. 305–6
3. *Ibid.*, pp. 305–6
4. *Ibid.*, p. 309
5. This insight thanks to Dr Mike Isaacs, consultant psychiatrist, The South London & Maudsley NHS Trust.
6. William Michael Rossetti, *Family-Letters*, vol. 1, p. 315
7. *Ibid.*, pp. 308–9
8. Robert Browning *Fifine at the Fair* (Smith and Elder, London, 1872)
9. Kelvin, *Letters of William Morris*, vol. 1, p. 59
10. Fredeman, *The Correspondence of Dante Gabriel Rossetti*, vol. 5, p. 264
11. Kelvin, vol. 1, p. 165

12. *Ibid.*, p. 167
13. *Ibid.*, vol. 2, p. 171
14. Burne-Jones, *Memorials*, vol. 1, p. 110
15. Hilton, *John Ruskin*, p. 584
16. Fredeman, *Correspondence of Dante Gabriel Rossetti*, vol. 6, p. 281
17. Kelvin, *Letters of William Morris*, vol, 1 p. 222
18. Fredeman, *Correspondence of Dante Gabriel Rossetti*, vol. 6, p. 579

Epilogue

1. *Ruskin's Romance*, reprinted from a New England newspaper, 1889, British Library shelf mark 1608/1609
2. Millais, *Life and Letters*, p. 287
3. Judith Flanders, *A Circle of Sisters* (Viking, London, 2001), p. 280
4. Georgie's sister Alice had married the artist John Lockwood Kipling in 1865; Rudyard was their son.
5. J. W. Mackail, *The Life of William Morris*, 2 vols. (1899), p. 366
6. Fiona MacCarthy, *William Morris* (Faber & Faber, London, 1994), p. 671
7. British Library, Ashley MS 1410 673 B, book 4
8. Baum, *Rossetti's Letters to Fanny Cornforth*, p. 116
9. Princeton University Library, Troxell Collection of Rossetti Manuscripts, CO 189, box 30, folder 1 (MS version of autobiographical notes and *The Life of William Bell Scott*)
10. http://www.gutenberg.org/etext/13076
11. *Ibid.*
12. Princeton University Library, Troxell Collection of Rossetti Manuscripts, box 11, folder 11

Unpublished sources

Bodleian Library, University of Oxford
    Ruskin Papers, MS. Eng. Letters C 228
    The Marriage of John Ruskin, MS. Eng. Misc. d 653
    The Marriage of John Ruskin, MS. Eng. Misc. d 652

British Library, London
    Jane Morris Correspondence, ADD 52332
    MS 45353
    Ashley MSS, 1363
    Ashley MSS, 1467
    Ashley MSS, 1410 673 B

London Metropolitan Archive, Corporation of London Records
    Coroner's inquest (L) 1862, no 25
    Inquest papers for Elizabeth Rossetti, 12 February 1862

Pierpont Morgan Library, New York
    Bowerswell Papers, MA 1338

Princeton University Library, Princeton, NJ
    Troxell Collection of Rossetti Manuscripts, CO 189
    H.V. Tebbs Collection of Pre-Raphaelite Photographs, 1866–1897

Victoria & Albert Museum, London
    Ref. MSL/1998/5

Select bibliography

Akin Burd, Van (ed.), *John Ruskin and Rose La Touche: Her Unpublished Diaries of 1861 and 1867* (Clarendon Press, Oxford, 1979)

Allingham, William, *William Allingham's Diary, 1847–1889* (Centaur Press, London, 2000)

Baum, Paul Franklin, *Dante Gabriel Rossetti's Letters to Fanny Cornforth* (Johns Hopkins Press, Baltimore, 1940)

Bradley, J. L. (ed.), *The Letters of John Ruskin to Lord and Lady Mount-Temple* (Ohio State University Press, Columbus, 1964)

Buchanan, Robert, *God and the Man: A Romance* (Chatto & Windus, London, 1881)

Burne-Jones, Georgiana, *Memorials of Edward Burne-Jones*, 2 vols. (Lund Humphries, London, 1993)

Chamberlin, E. R., *The Awakening Giant: Britain in the Industrial Revolution* (Batsford, London, 1976)

Champneys, Basil, *Memoirs and Correspondence of Coventry Patmore* (Bell and Sons, London, 1900)

Collingwood, W. G., *The Life of John Ruskin* (Methuen, London, 1900)

Coombs, James (ed.), *A Pre-Raphaelite Friendship: The Correspondence of William Holman Hunt and John Lucas Tupper* (UMI Research Press, Ann Arbor, 1986)

Cundall, Joseph, *A Glance at the Exhibition of the Royal Academy 1850* (London, 1850)

Daly, Gay, *Pre-Raphaelites in Love* (William Collins, Glasgow, 1989)

De Mare, Eric, *London 1851: The Year of the Great Exhibition* (Folio Press, London, 1973)

Dimbleby, Josceline, *A Profound Secret: May Gaskell, Her Daughter Amy, and Edward Burne-Jones* (Doubleday, London, 2004)

Doughty, Oswald, *A Victorian Romantic: Dante Gabriel Rossetti* (Frederick Muller Ltd, London, 1949)

Evans, Joan, and Whitehouse, John Howard (ed.), *The Diaries of John Ruskin,* 2 vols. (Clarendon Press, Oxford, 1956, 1958)

Fagence Cooper, Suzanne, *The Victorian Woman* (V & A Publications, London, 2001)

Faulkner, Peter (ed.), *Jane Morris to Wilfrid Scawen Blunt* (Exeter University Press, Exeter, 1986)

Fitzgerald, Penelope (ed.), *The Novel on Blue Paper, by William Morris* (Journeyman Press, London and West Nyack, 1982)

Flanders, Judith, *A Circle of Sisters* (Viking, London, 2001)

Fredeman, W. E. (ed.), *The Correspondence of Dante Gabriel Rossetti*, 6 vols. (D. S. Brewer, Woodbridge, 2002–6)

Fredeman, William E. (ed.), *The P.R.B. Journal: William Michael Rossetti's Diary of the Pre-Raphaelite Brotherhood, 1849–1853* (Clarendon Press, Oxford, 1975)

Goodway, David, *London Chartism, 1838–1848* (Cambridge University Press, Cambridge, 1982)

Hall Caine, Thomas, *Recollections of Dante Gabriel Rossetti* (Elliot Stock, London, 1882)

Hawksley, Lucinda, *Lizzie Siddal: The Tragedy of a Pre-Raphaelite Supermodel* (Andre Deutsch, London, 2004)

Hellerstein, E. A., Hume, L. P., and Offen, K. M. (ed.), *Victorian Woman: A Documentary Account of Women's Lives in Nineteenth-Century England, France and the United States* (Harvester Press, Brighton 1981)

Hill, George Birkbeck (ed.), *Letters of Dante Gabriel Rossetti to William Allingham, 1854–1870* (Fisher Unwin, London, 1897)

Hilton, Tim, *John Ruskin* (Yale University Press, New Haven and London, 2002)

Hobhouse, Christopher, *1851 and the Crystal Palace* (John Murray, London, 1950)

Holman Hunt, Diana, *My Grandfather, His Wives and Loves* (Hamish Hamilton, London, 1969)

Holman Hunt, William, *Pre-Raphaelitism and the Pre-Raphaelite Brotherhood*, 2nd edn, 2 vols. (Chapman and Hall, London, 1913)

Hunt, Violet, *The Wife of Rossetti: Her Life and Death* (John Lane and Bodley Head, London, 1932)

Jackson, Lee, *A Dictionary of Victorian London* (Anthem Press, London, 2006)

James, Sir William (ed.), *The Order of Release: The Story of John Ruskin, Effie Gray and John Everett Millais Told for the First Time in their Unpublished Letters* (John Murray, London, 1948)

Kelvin, Norman (ed.), *The Collected Letters of William Morris*, vol. 1, *1848–1880* (Princeton University Press, Princeton 1984)

Lutyens, Mary, *Effie in Venice* (John Murray, London, 1965)

Lutyens, Mary, *Millais and the Ruskins* (John Murray, London, 1967)

Lutyens, Mary, *The Ruskins and the Grays* (John Murray, London, 1972)

Lutyens, Mary, and Warner, Malcolm, *Rainy Days at Brig o'Turk: The Highland Sketchbooks of John Everett Millais 1853* (Dalrymple Press, Westerham, 1983)

MacCarthy, Fiona, *William Morris* (Faber & Faber, London, 1994)

Mackail, J. W., *The Life of William Morris*, 2 vols. (1899)

Mancoff, Deborah, *Jane Morris: The Pre Raphaelite Model of Beauty* (Pomegranate, San Francisco, 2000)

Marsh Jan, *Pre-Raphaelite Sisterhood* (Quartet, London, 1985)

Marsh, Jan, *The Legend of Elizabeth Siddal* (Quartet, London, 1989)

Marsh, Jan, *Elizabeth Siddal, 1829–1862: Pre-Raphaelite Artist* (Ruskin Gallery, Sheffield, 1991)

Marsh, Jan, *Dante Gabriel Rossetti: Painter and Poet* (Weidenfeld and Nicolson, London, 1999)

Millais, John Guille, *The Life and Letters of Sir John Everett Millais* (Methuen & Co., London, 1890)

Morris, William, *Poems by the Way and Love is Enough* (London, 1902)

Morris, William, *The Earthly Paradise*, ed., Florence S. Boos (Routledge, New York and London, 2002)

Pennell, Joseph, *The Whistler Journal* (Lippincott, Philadelphia, 1921)

Plant, Margaret, *Venice: Fragile City, 1797–1997* (Yale University Press, London, 2002)

Reynolds, George W. M., *The Mysteries of London*, ed. Trefor Thomas (Keele University Press, 1996)

Rosenfeld, Jason, and Smith, Alison, *Millais* (Tate Publishing, 2007)

Rossetti, Dante Gabriel, *The Works of Dante Gabriel Rossetti*, ed. W. M. Rossetti (Ellis, London, 1911)

Rossetti, William Michael, *Dante Gabriel Rossetti: His Family-Letters with a Memoir* (Ellis & Elvey, London, 1895)

Rossetti, William Michael, *Ruskin: Rossetti: PreRaphaelitism: Papers 1854 to 1862* (Allen, London, 1899)

Rossetti, William Michael, *The Rossetti Papers, 1862–70* (Sands & Co., London, 1903)

Rossetti, William Michael, *Some Reminiscences* (Brown, Langham & Co., London, 1906)

Rossetti, William Michael, *The PreRaphaelites & their World* (Folio Society, London, 1995)

Rossetti Angeli, Helen, *Dante Gabriel Rossetti: His Friends and Enemies* (Hamish Hamilton, London, 1949)

Rossetti Angeli, Helen, *Pre-Raphaelite Twilight: The Story of Charles Augustus Howell* (Richards Press, London, 1954)

Ruskin, John, *The Works of John Ruskin*, ed. E. T. Cook and Alexander Wedderburn (George Allen, London, 1906)

Ruskin, John, *Praeterita and Dilecta* (Everyman's Library, New York and London, 2005)

Scott, William Bell, *Autobiographical Notes of the Life of William Bell Scott*, ed. W. H. Minto (Osgood, McIlvaine & Co., London, 1892)

Stephens, F. G., *Dante Gabriel Rossetti*, Portfolio Artistic Monographs (Seeley & Co., London, 1894)

Surtees, Virginia (ed.), *The Diaries of George Price Boyce* (Real World, Norwich, 1980)

Surtees, Virginia (ed.), *The Diary of Ford Madox Brown* (Yale University Press, New Haven, 1981)

Surtees, Virginia, *The Actress and the Brewer's Wife* (Michael Russell, Norwich, 1997)

Swinburne, Algernon Charles, *A Record of Friendship* (printed for private circulation, London, 1910)

Victoria and Albert Museum, *The Great Exhibition of 1851 Commemorative Album* (HMSO, London, 1964)

Wood, Christopher, *The Pre-Raphaelites* (Weidenfeld and Nicolson, London, 1981)

Illustration acknowledgements

Plates 1, 2, 3, 4, 6, 7, 32 National Portrait Gallery, London. 5 Guildhall Art Gallery/The Bridgeman Art Library. 8 Getty Images. 9 National Museums Liverpool, Walker Art Gallery. 10 Ashmolean Museum, University of Oxford. 11, 13, 14, 17, 18, 21, 22, 30, 38, 39 Tate, London 2008. 12, 19, 23, 31, 37 Birmingham Museums & Art Gallery. 15, 40 Manchester Art Gallery/The Bridgeman Art Library. 16, 36 Peter Nahum at The Leicester Galleries. 24 Kelmscott Manor/The Bridgeman Art Library. 25 Yale Center for British Art, Paul Mellon Collection/The Bridgeman Art Library. 26 Tullie House Museum & Art Gallery, Carlisle. 27 Museum of Fine Arts, Boston. 28 Hamburger Kunsthalle, Hamburg/The Bridgeman Art Library. 29 The Walters Art Museum, Baltimore. 33 The Bridgeman Art Library/Getty Images. 34 V&A Images/Victoria and Albert Museum, London. 35 National Museums Liverpool, Lady Lever Art Gallery.

Integrated illustrations: page 34 Birmingham Museums & Art Gallery. Page 92 www.cartoonstock.com. Page 125 Sir Geoffroy Millais. Page 129 The Pierpont Morgan Library, New York. Page 203 William Morris Gallery, London. Page 212 V&A Images/ Victoria and Albert Museum, London. Pages 286, 301 The Trustees of the British Museum. Page 305 Tate, London 2008.

Every effort has been made to contact the copyright holders of illustrations reproduced in this book. John Murray would be happy to rectify the position in the event of any inadvertent infringement of their rights.

Index

D.G. Rossetti is generally referred to as 'Dante Gabriel'. Euphemia Chalmers Gray (*later* Ruskin; *later still* Millais) is referred to as 'Effie' and Elizabeth Eleanor Siddall as 'Lizzie'.
'PRB' refers to the Pre-Raphaelite Brotherhood.
References in italics indicate illustrations within the text.